Also by **Ashgate**

W.G.L. RANDLES
The Unmaking of the Medieval Christian Cosmos, 1500–1760: From Solid Heavens to Boundless Æther

CONSTANCE BLACKWELL and SACHIKO KUSUKAWA
Philosophy in the Sixteenth and Seventeenth Centuries: Conversations with Aristotle

JOHN CLEARY
Traditions of Platonism: Essays in Honour of John Dillon

ROGER FRENCH and ANDREW CUNNINGHAM
Before Science: The Invention of the Friars' Natural Philosophy

MARK JOYAL
Studies in Plato and the Platonic Tradition: Essays Presented to John Whittaker

and in the Collected Studies Series

F. EDWARD CRANZ
Nicholas of Cusa and the Renaissance

MARJORIE REEVES
The Prophetic Sense of History in Medieval and Renaissance Europe

DOMINIC O'MEARA
The Structure of Being and the Search for the Good: Essays on Ancient and Early Medieval Platonism

CHARLES TRINKAUS
Renaissance Transformations of Late Medieval Thought

JOSEPH S. FREEDMAN
Philosophy and the Arts in Central Europe, 1500–1700: Teaching and Texts at Schools and Universities

C.P. BAMMEL
Tradition and Exegesis in Early Christian Writers

KENT EMERY, Jr
Monastic, Scholastic and Mystical Theologies in the Later Middle Ages and Beyond

VARIORUM COLLECTED STUDIES SERIES

Abelard and his Legacy

Dr Constant J. Mews

Constant J. Mews

Abelard and his Legacy

Ashgate
VARIORUM

Aldershot · Burlington USA · Singapore · Sydney

This edition copyright © 2001 by Constant J. Mews.

Published in the Variorum Collected Studies Series by

Ashgate Publishing Limited
Gower House, Croft Road,
Aldershot, Hampshire GU11 3HR
Great Britain

Ashgate Publishing Company
131 Main Street,
Burlington, Vermont 05401–5600
USA

Ashgate website: http://www.ashgate.com

ISBN 0–86078–861–X

British Library Cataloguing-in-Publication Data
Mews, Constant J.
    Abelard and his Legacy. (Variorum Collected Studies Series: CS704).
    1. Abelard, Peter, 1079–1142 – Criticism and Interpretation. 2. Theology –
    Early Works to 1800. I. Title.
    230'.01'092

US Library of Congress Cataloging-in-Publication Data
Mews, Constant J.
    Abelard and his Legacy / Constant J. Mews.
        p.   cm. – (Variorum Collected Studies Series: CS704).
    Includes bibliographical references and indexes.
    1. Abelard, Peter, 1079–1142. I. Title. Collected Studies: CS704
    BX4705.A2M48   2001
    189'.4–dc21   00–050224

The paper used in this publication meets the minimum requirements of the
    American National Standard for Information Sciences – Permanence of
    Paper for Printed Library Materials, ANSI Z39.48–1984.   ∞   TM

Printed by St Edmundsbury Press, Bury St Edmunds, Suffolk

VARIORUM COLLECTED STUDIES SERIES CS704

CONTENTS

This volume contains xii + 330 pages

PREFACE

The papers collected in this volume, most of which were published in the 1980s, all relate in one way or another to the controversial career and literary output of Peter Abelard (1079–1142). Indirectly, however, they owe their genesis to research undertaken in 1976 for an MA thesis, completed within the Department of History at the University of Auckland, New Zealand: 'Peter Abelard and Monastic Reform in the Twelfth Century'. At Auckland, I had the good fortune to have been introduced to the vibrancy of Late Antiquity by Phillip Rousseau, as well as to the excitement of twelfth-century Europe by Valerie Flint. From both of them I learned how ideas that might seem arcane, if not absurd to a modern reader, come to life when we appreciate the fluidity of the social and cultural milieu in which they emerged. Having become fascinated by the age of Augustine and Jerome, my initial idea was to explore the legacy of patristic tradition on Peter Abelard, a figure conventionally revered as both a schoolman and as a precursor of modernity, but not as someone profoundly shaped by the values of the past. I was particularly struck by the way the *Historia calamitatum* registered Abelard's deep sense of self-identification with St Jerome, with whose writings he was evidently very familiar. Like so many readers, I was also intrigued by Abelard's literary dialogue with Heloise. Yet while I was aware that since the time of Petrarch, scholars had been fascinated by the apparent modernity of Heloise's protestations of love, I could not help but notice that the monastic dimension of their correspondence tended to attract far less attention than the so-called 'personal' letters (to evoke the category popularised by Betty Radice in her 1974 Penguin translation, *The Letters of Abelard and Heloise*). At the time unaware of the passions being provoked in Europe in the 1970s by a fresh round of scholarly debate about the authenticity of these letters, I thought that the writings of Abelard and Heloise deserved to be interpreted in terms of twelfth-century concern for renewal of the religious life rather than as providing a foretaste of the values of modernity. I went to Oxford in 1977 naively determined to re-interpret a figure about whom I knew much had been written, but with little understanding either of the enormous textual problems surrounding Abelard's writings, or of the complexity of his reflection on language (apart from what I had gleaned from Jean Jolivet's magistral *Arts du langage et théologie chez Abélard* (Paris: Vrin, 1969).

It was thus a wise suggestion of Sir Richard Southern that I turn my attention away from Heloise and the foundation of the Paraclete, to look at the evolution of Abelard's writings on theology, of which Fr Eligius-Marie Buytaert ofm (1913–1975) had published two volumes within the series Corpus Christianorum. Continuatio Mediaeualis 11 and 12 (Turnhout: Brepols, 1969). Through the good graces of Professor David Luscombe, of the University of Sheffield, I received from the editors of Corpus Christianorum copies of the typescript editions of the *Theologia 'Summi boni'* and *Theologia 'Scholarium'* that Father Buytaert had left incomplete at the time of his death. The complexity of his arguments about the relationship between different recensions of the *Theologia christiana* and the *Theologia 'Scholarium'* confused me enormously until a solution presented itself with astonishing clarity: the strange abbreviations and cross references copied out by the scribes of two manuscripts of the *Theologia christiana* (Tours, Bibliothèque municipale 85, printed in PL 178, 1123–1330, and Monte Cassino, Archivio della Badia 174) were all part of a heavily annotated exemplar in which Abelard sketched out those sections he wished to preserve and amplify within the *Theologia 'Scholarium'*. Through the medium of two imperfect copies, I could glimpse something of how Abelard struggled to bring always improved ideas into being.

This resolution to what might seem to be a relatively minor textual problem, first presented at a conference in Trier in 1979 (Article I) and developed more fully in 1985 (Article V), turned out to provide a key to unlocking many hitherto intractable problems associated with understanding Peter Abelard. For all the notoriety that Abelard acquired during his lifetime for writing the *Theologia*, prompting him to revise its text constantly during the last twenty years of his life, very few readers had been able to make sense of what Abelard was trying to achieve in this work. Unlike Gilbert of Poitiers or Hugh of St-Victor, Abelard leaves us with no finished product, clearly expressing his final point of view on any question. He was always as quick to put pen to parchment as he was to modify what he had said, in response to some challenge or criticism. Being able to track the evolution of his *Theologia* provided an opportunity to glimpse the inner logic behind the development of his intellectual concerns. It also enabled me to make sense of the close relationship between revisions he made to the *Theologia*, and charges made against him by St Bernard at the council of Sens (Article IV).

Along the way, I was obliged to question the conclusions of a number of outstanding scholars who had tried before me to make sense of Abelard's literary output as a whole. Close comparison between different recensions of the *Theologia 'Scholarium'* and various versions of theological *sententie* on faith, the sacraments and charity, long interpreted as compositions of

Abelard's disciples led me to conclude that they needed to be interpreted as records of a continuously evolving course of lectures given by Abelard on these subjects (Article VI). In many ways, these sentence collections provide a more accessible point of entry into Abelard's teaching than the *Theologia*, in which he goes into more depth on what he has to say about faith in God, the foundation of his theology (Article III). A gloss on Porphyry, attributed to Abelard by Ottaviano in 1933, but conventionally assigned to a disciple, rather than to the master himself, turned out to throw much light on the *Theologia 'Summi boni'* (Article II). The traditional judgement that the sole surviving manuscript of the *Dialectica* reflected opinions of Abelard from very late in his career presented me with a more serious problem, as it was not initially clear how it related to the glosses of the *Logica 'Ingredientibus'*. Again awareness of the evolution of Abelard's *Theologia* provided me with the realisation that these glosses reflected more mature thinking about language than the *Dialectica*. It even allows us to gain insight into his *Grammatica*, a work that tragically has not survived (Article VIII).

One clear illustration of the way Abelard evolves as a thinker can be seen in his continually evolving grasp of the Fathers of the Church. In my study of his familiarity with the letters of St. Jerome (Article IX), I pick up a theme with which I had been concerned in my initial studies of Abelard and monastic tradition. After he entered the monastic life, Abelard became increasingly familiar with the writings of the Fathers. St Jerome provided him with a particularly fascinating role model, because of his close friendship with pious Roman women like Paula and Eustochium. Abelard's ever deepening knowledge of the Fathers did not mature at the expense of his interest in philosophy, however. In an essay in which I revisit my earlier reflections on the dating of Abelard's *Collationes* or *Dialogue of a Philosopher with a Jew and a Christian*, I explore how Abelard used the literary form of dialogue to revisit familiar themes of Christian doctrine from the perspective of a philosophical viewpoint (Article X).

The papers in this volume provide the intellectual foundation for my studies of the *Epistolae duorum amantium*, developed in *The Lost Love Letters of Heloise and Abelard: Perceptions of Dialogue in Twelfth-Century France* (New York: St Martin's Press, 1999). Abelard was a restless spirit, always eager to probe further questions raised both by others and by his own questioning mind. He can never be isolated, however, from the clerical milieu in which he was raised. By being aware of the traditions of which he was part, we can appreciate more fully the journey of inquiry on which he embarked.

CONSTANT J. MEWS

Melbourne,
October 2000

PUBLISHER'S NOTE

The articles in this volume, as in all others in the Collected Studies Series, have not been given a new, continuous pagination. In order to avoid confusion, and to facilitate their use where these same studies have been referred to elsewhere, the original pagination has been maintained wherever possible.

Each article has been given a Roman numeral in order of appearance, as listed in the Contents. This number is repeated on each page and quoted in the index entries.

ACKNOWLEDGEMENTS

Grateful acknowledgement is given to the following for permission to reproduce the articles in this volume: Paulinus Verlag GmbH, Trier (I); *Freiburger Zeitschrift für Philosophie und Theologie*, Freiburg (II); Peeters Publishing, Leuven (III, V, VI); *Revue Bénédictine*, Denée (IV); Archives d'histoire doctrinale et littéraire du moyen âge, Paris (VII); BIBLIOPOLIS, edizioni di filosofia e scienze, Naples (VIII); Études Augustiniennes, Paris (IX); University of Pennsylvania Press, Philadelphia (X).

I

The development of the Theologia of Peter Abelard

Diese Abhandlung richtet den Blick auf einige Probleme, die Abaelards *De trinitate* oder *Theologia „Summi boni"*, *Theologia Christiana* und *Theologia „Scholarium"* betreffen. Abaelards anfängliche Erörterung über die Trinität ist angelegt auf dem Hintergrund seines Interesses an Logik und seiner Schriften über diesen Stoff. Alle diese Schriften scheinen einer früheren Periode anzugehören, einschließlich die *Dialectica*. Es gibt keine positive Offenkundigkeit, es ist darauf hingewiesen, daß die Kritik an der Idee der Weltseele in dem späteren Werk irgendeinen Widerruf aufzeigt, da völlige Vereinbarkeit mit dem besteht, was Abaelard in der *Theologia „Summi boni"* sagt. Fr. E. M. Buytaerts Hypothese betreffend die Beziehung zwischen der *Theologia Christiana* und *Theologia „Scholarium"* und ihre gleichzeitige Entfaltung hat eine kritische Prüfung erfahren. Die geheimnisvollen abgekürzten Passagen, in zwei Handschriften der *Theologia Christiana* (Montecassino, Bib. abbaz. 176 und Tours, Bib. mun. 85) gefunden, deren gleichlautende vollständige Texte in der *Theologia „Scholarium"* können vielmehr nicht als Abbreviaturen jenes Werkes erklärt werden, sondern als Verweisungen, welche Teil von Abaelards persönlichem Entwurf für ein zukünftiges Werk waren. Die Abbreviaturen zeigen an, welche Stücke der *Theologia Christiana* er zu gebrauchen wünschte. Die verschiedenen Versionen der *Theologia* offenbaren, wie Abaelards Denkprozeß sich von einem frühen Interesse an Logik zu einem wohldurchdachten Verständnis des Wesens Gottes und seiner Wirksamkeit in der Welt entfaltete.

Study of the development of the *Theologia* of Peter Abelard owes much to the work of a number of scholars of this century, particularly H. Ostlender, D. Van den Eynde and above all the late E. M. Buytaert[1]. In this paper I would like to outline some of the outstanding problems still posed by the many different versions of the *Theologia*. The major issues that need to be faced concern the establishment of the correct order of the various versions of the *Theologia,* the degree of continuty between these versions, and the extent to which the work developed over the twenty years or so it was written and re-written.

There are three major versions of the *Theologia* of Abelard, the treatise *De Unitate et Trinitate divina* or *Theologia 'Summi boni,'* the *Theologia Christiana* and the *Theologia 'Scholarium'.* Each of these works is extant in a number of MSS., many of which themselves indicate Abelard was continually involved in correcting and expanding what he had said[2]. Because almost every MS. is different from another, it is crucially important that each MS. be correctly placed within the overall development of the *Theologia* if a picture is to be built up of the development of his thought.

De Trinitate (Theologia 'Summi boni')

The first version of the treatise can be dated with reasonable accuracy to the period between Abelard's entry into St. Deniṣ and the council of Soissons, perhaps around 1119–20[3]. The title of *Theologia* is not used in the MSS. of the earliest version of the work, which instead describe the work as *libri de trinitate*, although the word is used as the explicit of the slightly extended Berlin Staatsbibl. MS. Theol. lat. Oct. 95, f. 64[4]. Abelard described the work in his letter to the bishop of Paris against Roscelin as a treatise *De fide sanctae trinitatis,* while in the letter of consolation, written at least some ten years later, he twice emphasised the trinitarian title of the work, *theologiae tractatum De Unitate et Trinitate divina* and *illud opusculum quod de Trinitate composueram*[5]. Heloise described the work condemned at Soissons as *glorioso illo theologiae opere,* perhaps from the phrasing of his description[6]. Abelard seems to have introduced the term *theologia* only in the first major revision of the work, to which he gave the title *Theologia Christiana*[7]. Within the text of this work, he replaced the term *divinus* with *theologus,* a term not found in the earlier treatise[8]. For these reasons, I would prefer to call the work titled by Ostlender *Theologia 'Summi boni,'* by its original title in the MSS. *De Trinitate,* to distinguish it from later versions of the *Theologia.*

The particular concern of this first treatise was to defend the idea of a trinity of persons in one God. The closest parallel to the work, on which Abelard may have based the broad approach of his treatise, was the *De Trinitate* of Boethius, a work he knew, but did not quote directly in the first treatise and which he quoted slightly in the *Theologia Christiana*[9]. Both works were concerned to establish a philosophical resolution of unity and plurality within God. Both writers drew on Aristotle and Porphyry to discuss the possible modes of identity and difference, before going on to discuss whether they could be applied to God[10]. However, although they shared a common interest in logic, they differed profoundly in philosophical approach and consequently in their approach to the Trinity. Boethius had argued that the unity of God consisted in his being pure form while possessing plurality of relations. Abelard by contrast asserted that the trinity of God lay in the divine *proprietates* of *potentia, sapientia* and *benignitas,* which in accordance with his view of universals had no real existence in themselves outside of the subject they predicated, in this case God[11]. The whole treatise was structured around an analysis of the unity and trinity of God and sought a logical solution of the problem. The work was divided into three books, the first setting out authorities, scriptural and philosophical, the second, objections which could be made against orthodox doctrine and preliminary logical discussion on which any argument had to be based, and the third book, his solutions to the questions he had raised. He opened the second book with a long prologue directed against contemporaries who abused logic and reduced the ineffable mystery of God into their own formulae. Their arguments, however, had to be met on their own ground[12]. Abelard wrote the work against the background of the vigorous debate provoked by his logic, of which it was the natural continuation. The work was tightly constructed and dealt with a traditional theological subject, albeit in an original manner.

The works on logic

Some light on the genesis of this *De Trinitate* may be shed by examining the works of logic which led immediately up to it. He had written the *Logica 'Ingredientibus'* some time after he had first begun to study and teach *lectico sacra* if his mention of certain patristic authors and theological issues in the commentary is any firm indication[13]. In this work, Abelard became much more free in his commentary on Boethius than he had been in his earlier literal glosses and took issue with the ideas of Boethius, particularly his 'realist' interpretation of universals[14]. In his subsequent commentary on Porphyry, *Logica 'Nostrorum Petitioni,'* he was even more free in his interpretation of the text, which he used as a base from which he could put forward his own ideas about logic. Not only did he introduce his definition of a universal as *sermo*, rather than *res* or *vox*, but he abandoned the Boethian classification of identity and difference as genus, species and number, and replaced it with a set of six modes. He used exactly the same discussion of identity and difference in his *De Trinitate*[15]. In the *Theologia Christiana* he revised this discussion slightly to incorporate the new mode of identity and difference by property, and so relate it more closely to his argument about the Trinity[16]. This would suggest the *Logica 'Nostrorum Petitioni'* is chronologically closer to the *De Trinitate* than to the *Theologia Christiana*, which modifies its teaching[17].

Abelard made specific mention in his *De Trinitate* of a *Dialectica* he had already written[18]. Much controversy has gone into the correct dating of the work that survives by this title in the Paris BN MS. lat. 14164[19]. Cousin first suggested that the work belonged to a late stage in Abelard's career, on the grounds that in one passage he refuted the Platonist theory of the world soul and its identification with the Holy Spirit, a retraction of his earlier teaching[20]. However, in 1909, G. Robert pointed out that Abelard did not contradict in the *Dialectica* what he had said in any of the versions of his *Theologia* about the world soul, but that he consistently criticised the idea the world soul, the life-giving force of creation should have an eternal existence like the Holy Spirit[21]. T. Gregory has more recently pointed out that Abelard's attitude to Plato in the *Dialectica* and the theological works remained essentially the same and that there is no particular development of thought discernible[22]. In the *Dialectica,* Abelard criticised those who adhered to allegory too closely in attributing faith in the Trinity to Plato, because the world soul was created by and not co-eternal with God: *Sed haec quidem fides Platonica ex eo erronea esse convincitur quod illam quam mundi Animam vocat, non coaeterna Deo, sed a Deo more creaturarum originem habere concedit*[23]. In the *De Trinitate*, Abelard said exactly the same thing: *Illud autem in quo non mediocriter errasse Plato et videtur et dicitur, illud inquam, quod animam mundi factam esse dicit, hoc est initium habuisse cum constet apud omnes vere catholicos tres personas in divinitate per omnia sibi coaequales et coaeternas esse*[24]. He repeated what he said in the *Dialectica* about the absurd implications that would follow if Plato were accepted literally[25]. Plato had to be interpreted *per involucrum* to be understood correctly. He described as *supervacaneum* in the *Dialectica* the idea that the world soul had an eternal existence before birth and after death, not the idea Plato had some insight into the Trinity if understood rightly. Abelard had always been cautious towards Plato in his logic and anxious to interpret figuratively ideas and form which he insisted had no real existence in themselves[26].

Although Robert had made this point in criticism of Cousin, it was ignored by the two subsequent scholars who discussed the date of the *Dialectica*, J. Cottiaux and L. Nicolau d'Olwer[27]. Cottiaux acknowledged the validity of the other point Robert made, that in the prologue of the second and fourth tracts of the *Dialectica* Abelard replied to exactly the same criticisms as he said were made against him after he had entered St. Denis, but before the council of Soissons[28]. In order to reconcile this with the late date of Cousin, he suggested the work was written in parts over a long period.

Nicolau d'Olwer argued against this on the grounds of the internal unity of the work and suggested instead the work was revised a number of times over a long period on the analogy of the *Theologia*[29]. However, if it is acknowledged there is no retraction of position in the *Dialectica*, there seems no reason to apply a late date to the work at all. Buytaert pointed out that Abelard made no such retraction in the last revision of the *Theologia 'Scholarium'* or the *Apologia contra Bernardum* of 1139–40[30]. There seems no need to postulate any further revisions of the *Dialectica* after it was first written, at a date not long after Abelard's entry into St. Denis, but before the writing of the *De Trinitate*. The *Dialectica* was the climax of his achievement in logic, an independent treatise which did not have to follow or amend the Boethian commentary. The *De Trinitate* formed a natural counterpart to the *Dialectica* as an independent treatise, free from reliance on Boethius, on the Trinity.

Theologia Christiana (DR)

While the *De Trinitate* can be dated with reasonable accuracy, there are many more problems associated with the dating of the first major revision of the work, the *Theologia Christiana*. There are four MSS. of this revision, but because the first two, Durham, Cathedral library A. IV. 15 and Vatican, Reg. Lat. 159 (henceforth abbreviated as D and R) are very similar, but quite different from the other two, Montecassino, Bibl. abbaz. 174 and Tours, Bibl. mun. 85 (abbreviated as C and T), I shall discuss them separately. D contains only the first book of the *Theologia Christiana*, but its text is almost the same as that of R, the first complete MS. of the work[31]. The first version of the *Theologia Christiana* has always been dated, with justification, to the period immediately after Soissons, the time of the initial establishment of the oratory of the Paraclete, 1122–26[32]. However, when the Durham fragment came to the notice of Fr. Buytaert, his immediate reaction was to assign it to this period and re-date R to the mid-1130's on the grounds of certain minute textual features which he thought might place it between the first two short versions of a later work, namely the *Theologia 'Scholarium'*[33]. However, Fr. Van den Eynde had demonstrated that R shared with *Sermo* I a less accurate version of an Augustinian text than found in *TChr* CT or *Theologia 'Scholarium'* and that R must have been written before Ep. VII[34]. Buytaert discussed his own dating at length in his edition of the work, but he acknowledged the tenuous nature of the argument[35]. Because the differences between D and R are so minor and date before the correspondence with Heloise, I would suggest they were written fairly close to each other, perhaps between 1122 and 1126, and can be treated as one version.

In this version (DR), Abelard did not adjust the overall structure of the *De Trinitate*, but he expanded the text into twice its length with many new patristic authorities to substantiate his arguments. The criticisms received at Soissons forced Abelard to amplify his more controversial theses, particularly the attribution of power to the Father alone. In the *De Trinitate* he had passed quickly over this, but he defended himself in a new passage inserted into the first book of the *Theologia Christiana*[36]. He also completely rewrote the long and controversial discussion of the generation of the Son from the Father he had used in the third book of the *De Trinitate*[37]. His arguments became much fuller, and he relied much more on his interpretation of patristic authorities, often ones he quoted in the *Sic et Non*, to give weight to his discussion[38]. Not only did Abelard react to doctrinal criticism, but he countered the accusation that he was too involved with pagan philosophy by extending the last part of the first book of the *De Trinitate* into a completely new second book. Abelard used the letters and *Contra Jovinianum* of Jerome along with many passages in Augustine's *City of God* to demonstrate that not only were pagan philosophers worthy of study for their teaching, but also for the example of their lives. He used their example to launch a scathing attack on the worldliness of contemporary monasticism, strikingly similar to his later comments about St. Denis[39]. In the letter of consolation, Abelard drew on many of these passages of the *Theologia Christiana* to describe the early days of the Paraclete[40]. In his long discussion of pagan virtue in this second book, Abelard indirectly developed for the first time many of his ideas about ethics and morality, on which he would expand in his correspondence for Heloise and the Paraclete and develop most fully in the *Scito teipsum*[41].

Abelard used the *Theologia Christiana* to throw back many other charges against those who accused him of heresy. He extended the long prologue which now introduced the third book to attack even further the false logic of his critics[42]. He prefaced his important new discussion of the generation of the Son in the fourth book with a long series of accusations against his contemporaries, the most clearly identifiable of whom is Alberic of Rheims[43]. Some of the charges were distortions of their teaching, but the most important criticism which recurred throughout the *Theologia Christiana* was that certain teachers elevated the divine *proprietates* into things separate from God[44]. The charge was so serious because it directly contradicted Abelard's central point that *proprietates,* like universals, did not have a real existence but were only predicated of God. These digressions, although often fitting awkwardly into the text of the *De Trinitate* provide telling insight into Abelard's personal reaction to Soissons.

One notable feature of the *Theologia Christiana* was the much fuller treatment Abelard gave to the Holy Spirit. This parallels the intensified interest in and devotion to the Paraclete, to whom he re-dedicated his oratory of the Holy Trinity, and which he defended in the letter of consolation[45]. He greatly extended his discussion of the world soul as an image of the vivifying goodness of God working through creation in the first book, while in the fourth book he elevated his discussion of the procession of the Holy Spirit to a position of comparable importance with that of the generation of the Son[46]. He endeavoured to reconcile Greek and Latin tradition about the procession of the Spirit by seeing it as proceeding principally from the Father, but through the Son[47]. In adopting this approach he moved away from the more traditional Augustinian idea of the Holy Spirit as the mutual love of the Father and Son to see the Spirit as the love of God for creation. The Holy Spirit was central to Abelard's theology because it mediated the goodness of God to the world and brought God's revelation to all men.

Abelard made the most significant departure from the structure of the *De Trinitate* in adding to the *Theologia Christiana* a fifth book in which be promised to discuss the nature of God and his mode of operation in the world. The book was short and confused in the presentation of its ideas as well as incomplete, but it marked a significant development in his thought away from a logical analysis of unity and plurality within the Trinity to a study of the rationality of belief in one God and an analysis of what was meant by divine omnipotence. He had been charged at Soissons with undermining divine omnipotence by attributing it to the Father alone. Even before this Roscelin had defended his criticism of Anselm to Abelard on the grounds that Anselm undermined divine omnipotence by speaking of the rational necessity of the incarnation[48]. To Abelard, however, God's omnipotence could never counter his essential goodness. This led to his putting forward the idea that God could never do anything more or better than he did, because he did everything for the good[49]. He acknowledged that there were many authorities and arguments which could be raised against this view, and to which he could not find an easy answer[50]. He did not attempt anything like a complete solution, but put forward the outline of his idea that terms like 'possibility' and 'necessity' could not be used in a literal sense, since they changed their meaning when applied to God[51]. He did not discuss divine wisdom and loving kindness as he had promised at the beginning of the fifth book[52]. The arguments of the fifth book were much less developed than those of the preceeding books and were more like ideas thrown out than fully-fledged solutions. However, they pointed the way forward to ideas with which Abelard would be increasingly concerned.

The *Theologia Christiana* as a work had many limitations. It was too much based on the original text of the *De Trinitate,* while the large amount of new material added to the *Theologia Christiana* only confused its original structure. There were too many idiosyncratic digressions prompted by his immediate reaction to the criticisms of 1121, while the ideas begun in the fifth book demanded development into a major study of the nature of God and divine operation in the world. Abelard had expanded remarkably his interests from those of the *De Trinitate.* His theology of the Holy Spirit as God's goodness working in the world was much more developed, while he had put forward many new ideas about morality and virtue as well as about the incarnation[53]. He promised to deal elsewhere with both the incarnation of the Word and with charity[54]. The whole work would have to be greatly revised if it was to take account of some, if not all, of these new ideas.

Theologia Christiana (CT) and Theologia 'Scholarium'

The major problem Fr. Buytaert had to face in his preliminary studies and in his edition of the *Theologia Christiana* and the shorter versions of the *Theologia 'Scholarium'* was the relationship of the version of the *Theologia Christiana* recorded in the MSS. C and T to the *Theologia 'Scholarium'*. He made a major advance in the study of the problems posed by C and T, when he observed that they were two independent copies of an original exemplar, which he suggested was the personal notebook of Abelard[55]. For the purposes of this discussion, this original will be referred to as (CT). The MSS. of C and T are not identical, but they are very similar in both their text and in frequent annotation. C places these notes in the margin, while T encloses them in boxes within the text, as faithfully reproduced in the Migne copy of the Martène-Durand edition[56]. The central problem posed by the (CT) text is the existence of a number of deliberately abbreviated passages added to the (CT) version of the *Theologia Christiana* within the main body of the text. These abbreviated passages, not found in R, seem to be abbreviations of complete passages found in *Theologia 'Scholarium'*[57]. Fr. Buytaert's solution, on which his entire edition of the *Theologia Christiana* was based, was to claim that these abbreviated passages in (CT) were copied *from* the full text in *Theologia 'Scholarium'*, although many other passages in *TSch* were clearly copied from *TChr*[58]. This hypothesis presupposed a highly complicated process of passages being transferred from *TSch* to *TChr* for no apparent reason and in a completely haphazard order. It implied that Abelard continued to elaborate upon *TChr* after he had begun *TSch*. Buytaert explained this activity of continuing to build up *TChr* by suggesting Abelard was adding new material to defend himself against Bernard, although the bulk of the new material was not in itself controversial[59]. He did not explain why only *TSch* came under criticism and not *TChr* in the years 1139–40.

A curious but crucial point about these abbreviated passages in (CT), which Buytaert himself sometimes noted, but did not explain was that they all correspond to passages quoted in full elsewhere in the text of (CT)[60]. This makes it even more strange that the same passages should be quoted from *TSch* and duplicate so much material. Could these abbreviated passages be deliberate abbreviations of texts elsewhere within *Theologia Chistiana*? The whole pattern behind the apparently complex additions within the text of *TChr* (CT) becomes startlingly simple if it is oberved that these abbreviations occur within a very special order within the text. If the text of (CT) is followed until an abbreviated passage is arrived at, and then the pages are turned to the corresponding full version of the text and its subsequent text followed, the exact text of a large part of *Theologia 'Scholarium,'* particularly the first part of its second book, is reproduced to the letter. A revised concordance of the first part of *TSch* II, 1–35 (PL 178, 1035 A–46 D), showing the order of material taken from *TChr* makes this clear:

TChr II, 1–13 RCT	= *TSch* II, 1–13
II, 13a CT	= II, 13
II, 13b CT – III, 1 RCT	= II, 14–15
III, 2a–b CT – III, 53 RCT	= II, 16–17
III, 54 RCT	= II, 18
III, 55 CT – II, 117 RCT	= II, 19
II, 117a CT	= II, 19
II, 118 T	= II, 20
II, 119 RCT	= II, 21
II, 119a CT	= II, 21
II, 120 RCT	= II, 22
II, 121 CT	= II, 23
II, 122 RCT	= II, 24
II, 123–124a C	= II, 25
II, 124 RCT	= II, 25
II, 125–125a CT – II, 54–55 RCT	= II, 26–27
II, 125b CT	= II, 28
II, 125c CT – III, 6 RCT	= II, 29
III, 7–8 RCT	= II, 30
III, 8a–e CT	= II, 31–35 etc.

At the very beginning of this section, or series of sections in (CT) there is a brief set of notes which describe the themes of *TSch* as a draft outline[61]. Rather than these abbreviated passages being transferred from *TSch*, the text of *TChr* (CT) is being used as a base from which a good part of *Theologia 'Scholarium'* was written. The extensive additions made to the text of *Theologia Christiana* in (CT) from the version in R, become quite comprehensible if (CT) is seen as Abelard's draft copy for a new *Theologia*. Fortunately observable through two independent copies, the draft records how Abelard marked out the existing material he wished to use again in a new *Theologia*, as well as how he wrote in many new ideas he would either incorporate or expand. The draft thus gives us a unique insight into the creation of Abelard's most important work, the *Theologia 'Scholarium'* and enables us to see not only how he worked, but what ideas he wanted to discard and which develop for a major new work.

If (CT) is seen as Abelard's own transcription of the *Theologia Christiana*, extended and annotated for the purpose of making a draft of a quite new revision of the

Theologia, new light is thrown onto the highly abbreviated version of the first part of *Theologia 'Scholarium'* preserved in two MSS., one a copy of the other, Fulda, Seminarbibl., (no pressmark) and Heiligenkreuz, Stiftsbibl. 153. I shall refer to this work as (FH). There has been some controversy over the exact relationship of (FH) to the text of the two shorter versions of *Theologia 'Scholarium'* edited by Buytaert in the same volume as *TChr* found in the MS Zurich, Zentralbibl. C 61 (Z) and the same Tours MS. as contains a copy of *TChr* in its draft form[62]. Not only is (FH) much shorter than the other two MSS in length, but there are considerable textual variations and apparent omissions within (FH) when it is compared with Z and the still longer and revised version of T. There are certain features in the text of (FH) which make it very difficult to claim it is only a very imperfect abbreviation of a much longer text, as has normally been held[63]. It is not a direct abbreviation of *tsch* Z as it preserves the correct incipit: *Scholarium nostrorum petitioni . . .* unlike the incipit of Z: *Discipulorum nostrorum . . .* and also contains the correct order of some patristic material unlike either Z or T. To explain the accuracy of (FH), Buytaert had to postulate a lost proto-redaction behind both (FH) and *tsch* Z[64]. There is one passage in (FH) which is so different from the text of Z or T that it could not have been abbreviated from the extant text, and which Buytaert consequently deemed to be inauthentic[65]. It is striking, however, that this passage, and the passage which replaces it in Z, both lead directly into the first part of *TChr* (CT) that would be used within *TSch*[66]. (FH) does not abbreviate the whole of *tsch* Z, as its text stops short just after the point where the text of *TSch* would be carried on by the draft copy of *TChr* (CT)[67].

The peculiar form of the text of (FH) becomes quite comprehensible as the complementary draft of the first part of the new *Theologia 'Scholarium'*. If the two drafts (FH) and (CT) are put together, the substance of the text of the first part of the new *Theologia* is constructed. Once Abelard had written both draft texts, he proceeded to copy them both out and join them up in one single text. The two MSS. of the shorter version of the new work, *tsch* Z and T, represent this intermediate stage between the writing of the first drafts and the writing of the complete text of *TSch*. *TSch* was not a sudden achievement but the fruit of a long period of patient re-writing of old material and development of new ideas, incorporated into a successive series of drafts, before the final work was ready.

Theologia 'Scholarium'

Because the changes Abelard wished to make to the *Theologia Christiana* were so great, several drafts were necessary to create the new work. The major change in the structure of the work was that the argument of the original *De Trinitate*, particularly óf its second and third books was subordinated into a much wider whole. The over-riding theme of *TSch* was not the logical problem posed by the Trinity, although this was partly its concern, but with the prime object of faith, the divine nature. This too, was set in the wider context of a projected *summa* of sacred learning[68]. The purpose of the draft (FH) was to place the *Theologia* within this much broader perspective, comparable to the overall framework of the *Sic et Non* and of the various sentence collections which record Abelardian teaching[69]. He opened the work after a short prologue with the bold statement: *Tria sunt, ut arbitror, in quibus humana salutis summa consistit, fides videlicet, caritas et sacramenta*, while only gradually did he introduce his older argument about the Trinity[70]. Before doing so, he sketched the outline of his ideas on the sacraments and charity and discussed the nature of the faith necessary for salvation[71].

With great literary skill, Abelard completely rewrote his argument about the three persons of the Trinity as the three *proprietates* in God by starting, not with a bold affirmation of his idea, but with a statement of orthodox doctrine, followed by a discussion of how the three persons did differ from each other[72]. Only once he had established this, did he introduce the ideas of the power, wisdom and loving-kindness of God. He worked the main arguments of the *Theologia Christiana* into his new discussion, but avoided the meandering digressions which had come about by his extensive interpolation into the text of the *De Trinitate*. He gave more attention to his controversial argument about attributing power to the Father alone, while he expanded what he had said about the Son as wisdom by skilfully combining material in the fourth book of *TChr* with what he had already said in the first book. In his draft text (CT), Abelard carefully marked out with abbreviated passages and marginal annotation, how he had to transfer his material[73]. The rest of the first book of *TSch* was copied from the first book of *TChr*, with only a few additions.

The second and middle book of *TSch* abbreviated the argument of the second and third books of the original *De Trinitate* and began with an almost completely rewritten prologue[74]. Abelard marked out most of the material he wished to use in the new prologue in his draft text (CT) by adding into the text as he copied it out, new arguments and authorities and abbreviated references to existing passages within *TChr*.[75] In the *De Trinitate*, Abelard had only been concerned to attack the narrow-mindedness of contemporary teachers of logic. In the *Theologia Christiana* he had had to defend himself on quite a different quarter against the charge of being too involved with pagan philosophy, although he retained what he said about false logicians. However, by the time he was beginning to draft quite a new version of the *Theologia*, he had to draw his attention away from an attack on other logicians to a sustained defence of the use of logic in matters of faith. He picked out passages he had used in the second and third books of *TChr* which might still apply to his situation and added many more passages in defence of reason[76]. This turn-around in emphasis of the prologue reflected the changed circumstances in which Abelard found himself, now much more on the defensive than self-confident as in the *De Trinitate*. A telling illustration of this change was the way he crossed out a reference to Jerome's dream to rewrite it in order to defend himself from the charge that Jerome's dream could be used against his own use of philosophy. This, Abelard insisted, was not the meaning of the dream[77]. In the new prologue of *TSch*, he expressed his idea more clearly than he had ever done before, how essential it was that faith be understood before it was preached to others and how necessary it was that the doubts and questions that people were asking be given a rational solution[78]. He defended his theological writing by claiming that the writings of the Fathers no longer sufficed to answer the questions currently being asked[79]. There was not just the problem of contemporary heresy, but the need to demonstate the validity of the Christian faith to people raised outside a Christian or Jewish tradition, who could not be persuaded by anything except reason[80].

The remainder of the second book of *TSch* was a contraction of the arguments of books three and four of *TChr*. The tedious analysis of individual objections was replaced with the most concise explanation of the generation of the Son and procession of the Holy Spirit Abelard had yet formulated[81]. Instead of giving an account riddled with further questions, he spelled out the essence of his idea that descriptions of the relationship of the three persons were relative terms and could not be forced out of context.

I

The most important new element in *TSch* was the ingenious formulation of an image which synthesised what he had been saying about the relation of the Father to the Son, but encompassed the whole Trinity. He had tried to explain before the idea of the relationship of the Father and Son as genus and species, or wax and a waxen image, but the analogy came to him of a seal which had the property of being able to seal, *sigillabilis* as well as of sealing, *sigillans* [82]. The analogy neatly incorporated, besides the idea of three *proprietates,* his understanding of the Holy Spirit as the 'sealing' power of God on creation, implanting in man the divine image. The Son illustrated the fullest capacity of the seal to make its own image. The analogy of the seal could not be taken too literally, but it did become a favourite image of Abelard and of his followers to express the divine nature [83]. This simply stated analogy was far removed from the involved logical analysis of the *De Trinitate*.

The third book contained a complete exposition of the themes concerning the divine nature which Abelard had only begun to develop in the fifth book of *TChr*. In his draft copy, he added into the text some new arguments, based on further patristic authorities and marked out those parts of the original text he wished to rewrite with marginal annotation [84]. He copied out without change his argument on the rationality of belief in one God from *TChr*, but greatly changed and developed his argument about divine omnipotence [85]. He also then dealt with the other properties of God he had promised to discuss, his wisdom and more briefly, though conclusively, his goodness [86]. Unfortunately, all the extant MSS. of the first full version of *TSch,* as the printed text of the work within the Patrologia, break off within the section on wisdom. However, the complete text is preserved in the Oxford Balliol MS. 296. This was itself a copy of the first full version, but corrected by the scribe having subsequent access to a modified and more complete version [87]. Because Abelard made reference in his *Scito teipsum* to his discussion in this last part of *TSch* of how all things worked together for the good, this closing section must belong to the original text [88].

The argument of the third book of *TSch* appears as the most important development in the whole work, when it is compared to *TChr*, even in the version (CT). Abelard had not devoted his attention in the *De Trinitate* to the nature of God and his operation in the world, but only to the problem of the trinity of persons in God. In *TChr* he had begun to articulate his ideas on the relationship of God to the world, but only in *TSch* did Abelard restructure his study of God to place his trinitarian nature within this broader sphere of interest. The new introduction that began *TSch* and the sophisticated abbreviation of his trinitarian argument in the second book were effected to accommodate the important new ideas developed in the third book. The crux of his argument was the same. Because God's nature was essentially good, he did all things for a reason and he could not do other than he did [89]. He re-arranged the ideas he had thrown out in the fifth book of *TChr* so that he dealt with the question whether God could do other or better than he did under discussion of his omnipotence, but expanded his ideas about whether God was constrained by necessity in the new section on his wisdom [90]. Although this third book was given a loosely trinitarian structure – divine power, wisdom and goodness, each section ran into the other to provide a coherent picture of the nature of God and the working of his goodness in the world.

Abelard based his solution to the objections which could be raised to his apparent limitation of divine omnipotence by subjecting all statements about what God 'could' or 'could not' do to his customary analysis of language. When it was said someone could be saved by God, the possibility applied to man was different from the possibility applied to God[91]. Any statement about God could not be taken literally but had to be related to his fundamental goodness. He used the same approach to discuss providence and freewill, and whether things happened by necessity[92]. He also introduced a quite new section on the incarnation to show how this did not limit God's power[93]. He concluded the third book with a panegyric on the goodness of God. No suffering was without meaning, because all things worked out for the good. Even the death of Christ for our sin was good because it brought about our redemption[94]. Although the last section on the divine goodness was brief, it summarised the whole direction of his theology.

Conclusion

The *Theologia 'Scholarium'* synthesised Abelard's most mature ideas about God. The work was the culmination of a long process of revision and development. The treatise had begun as a study of the trinity of persons in God and had been dominated by his enthusiasm to apply his ideas about language to the problem of unity and plurality within God. In the *Theologia Christiana,* he was forced to react against criticism of his theology, and in so doing developed the implications of his doctrine of God. He threw out suggestive ideas about natural virtue and the incarnation, while he began to apply himself to understanding what was meant by divine power. In the *Theologia 'Scholarium'* he selected the best ideas out of the *Theologia Christiana* and incorporated them into a new work through a skilfull process of successive drafts. A brief paper like this can only hope to outline the broad pattern of development of Abelard's thought from his works of logic, through his study of the Trinity to his most mature thought about God and the world. Much further study needs to be done on the development of Abelard's ideas about the redemption and ethics as far as can be discerned from his other writings and the various sentence collections which survive of his teaching. The fullest record, however, of the gradual development of Abelard's thought is to be found within the successive versions and drafts of the *Theologia..* If their relative chronology is correctly understood, they reveal a process of continuous development and ever maturing reflection on the nature of God.

Notes

    [1] Editions of the various versions of the *Theologia* remain scattered over a number of places, pending the completion of Buytaert's edition: *Theologia 'Summi boni',* ed. H. Ostlender, in: *Beiträge zur Geschichte der Philosophie des Mittelalters* XXXV. 2–3 (1939); *Theologia Christiana* and *Theologia 'Scholarium'* (shorter versions), ed. E. M. Buytaert, in: *Corpus Christianorum Cont. Med.* XII (Turnhoult, 1969); *Theologia 'Scholarium'* (full version, but slightly deficient at end), ed. A. Duchesne and reprinted by Migne, in: PL 178, 979–1114. V. Cousin made a slightly emended edition based on the same Paris, BN MS. lat. 14793, but which included the last pages found only in the Oxford, Balliol College MS. 296, in: *Petri Abaelardi Opera* II (Paris, 1859), 1–149. This did not include modifications within the text of this MS., transcribed in part by Ostlender in his important article 'Die Theologia „Scholarium" des Peter Abaelard,' in: *Aus der Geisteswelt des Mittelalters,* BGPMA Supplementbd. III. 1 (1935), 262–81. Most of the important studies on the *Theologia* by Van den Eynde and Buytaert appeared in *Antonianum* between 1962 and 1969. Buytaert summarised his studies on the *Theologia* in his paper 'Abelard's Trinitarian doctrine,' published in: *Peter Abelard. Proceedings of the*

I

International Conference, Louvain May 10–12, 1971 (Louvain-The Hague, 1974), 127–52. For the sake of consistency reference will be made to Buytaert's division of the text of all the versions, abbreviated as *TSum, TChr, tsch* and *TSch,* with ancillary reference in brackets to the page or column of the older editions of Ostlender and Migne of *TSum* and *TSch* respectively. The author is grateful to the editors of Corpus Christianorum for access to Buytaert's typescript edition of *TSum* and *TSch.*

² There are some eighteen important MSS. of the Theologia:
De Trinitate (Theologia 'Summi boni'). (i) Erlangen, Univ. 128 (Irm. 229), ff. 27–65v (= E); Oxford, Bodl. Lyell 49, ff. 101–28v (= L). (ii) Berlin, Staatsbibl. Theol. lat. Oct. 95, ff. 1–64 (= B).
Theologia Christiana. (i) Durham, Cathed. lib. A. IV. 15, ff. 57–65v (= D). (ii) Vatican Reg. Lat. 159, ff. 1–115 (= R). (iii) Montecassino, Bibl. abbaz. 174, pp. 133–276 (= C); Tours, Bibl. mun. 85, ff. 133–55v (= T).
Theologia 'Scholarium' (shorter versions). (i) Fulda, Seminarbibl. (no pressmark), ff. 94v–98 (= F); Heiligenkreuz, Stiftsbibl. 153, ff. 83–87 (= H). (ii) Zurich, Zentralbibl. C 61 (284), ff. 53v–60v (= Z). (iii) Tours, Bibl. mun. 85, ff. 156–8v (= T).
Theologia 'Scholarium' (full versions). (i) Douai, Bibl. mun. 357 (96), ff. 108–39v (= D); London, B. L. Royal 8. A. I, ff. 3–69 (= B); Magdeburg, Domgymnasium 34 (now in Berlin Staatsbibl.), ff. 193–261v (= M); Koblenz-Ehrenbreitstein, Kapuziner-Archiv (no pressmark), ff. 103–61 (= K). (ii) Paris, BN lat. 14793, ff. 1–69v (= P); Arsenal 265, ff. 65–94v (= A). (iii) Oxford, Balliol College 296 (458), ff. 1–60v (= O).

³ *Historia Calamitatum,* ed. J. M o n f r i n 2e ed. (Paris, 1962), II. 690–701 (henceforth cited as HC).

⁴ Erlangen, Univ. MS. 128, f. 27: *Incipiunt capitula librorum de trinitate magistri petri, clarissimi atque doctissimi viri, cognomento adbaiolardi;* Oxford, Bodl. Lyell MS. 49, f. 101: *Librorum de trinitate capitula.* On this latter MS. not known by Ostlender, but very close to the Erlangen MS., N. Häring, 'A Third MS. of Peter Abelard's Theologia Summi boni (MS. Oxford, Bodleian Lyell 49, ff. 101–28v)' in: *Medieval Studies* XVIII (1956), 215–24. There is no title given in the slight revision of the work in the Berlin MS., while the authenticity of its explicit: *Petri abaelardi palatini perhipatetici telogia* cannot be determined.

⁵ PL 178, 357 A; HC 693, 720.

⁶ Ep. II, ed. M o n f r i n 111, 1. 21.

⁷ This title is used on the Vatican, Tours and Montecassino MSS. of TChr. Abelard quoted this title in the text of his *Dialogus inter philosophum, Judaeum et Christianum,* ed. R. T h o m a s (Stuttgart-Bad Cannstatt, 1970), 98.

⁸ *Theologus* replaces *divinus* in TChr III, 178, cf. *TSum* II, 110, 112 (64), while the rubric opening this chapter changes from *Quot modis persona dicatur* to *Quomodo theologi persona in trinitate accipiunt,* TChr III, 171, cf. *TSum* II, 106 (63). The new term is also used in TChr III, 75, cf. *TSum* II, 34 (39) and TChr IV, 133. In the *Logica 'Ingredientibus'* (henceforth cited as LI), ed. B. G e y e r, in: *BGPMA* XXI. 1–3 (1919–27) 57, the term is used to describe pagan poets. On usage of the term, J. R i v i è r e, 'Theologia,' in: *Revue des sciences religieuses* XVI (1936), 47–57.

⁹ TChr III, 74, 80, 85–86. Abelard invoked the example of Boethius TChr I, 134–5 and III, 52. He had quoted the *De trinitate* in LI 49.

¹⁰ *TSum* II, 82 (54); cf Boethius, *De Trinitate* i, ed. R. P i e p e r, *Boetii philosophiae consolationis libri quinque. Accedunt eiusdem atque incertorum opuscula sacra* (Leipzig, 1871), 151.

¹¹ *TSum* I, 1 (2–3).

¹² *TSum* II, 1–27 (28–36).

¹³ Abelard discussed the question of providence in LI 26–27, 426–31; he cited Augustine *De bono perseverantiae, De praedestinatione sanctorum,* LI 427, *De natura et gratia,* LI 369, *De Civitate Dei,* LI 429, Gregory *Super Ezechielem,* LI 428, Boethius *De Trinitate,* LI 49, Athanasius *Quicumque vult,* LI 49. The reference to Gregory on Ezechiel with another scriptural quotation from Ezechiel in LI 379, may suggest the commentary was written about the same time or after his commentary on Ezechiel.

[14] Abelard had criticised Boethius more or less directly in LI 141, 204, 217, 246, 262–3, 399 and in his *Logica 'Nostrorum Petitioni'* (henceforth cited as *LNP*), ed. G e y e r, in: *BGPMA* XXI. 4 (1938), 544–7.

[15] *TSum* II, 82 (54), *LNP* 558–60; cf. *LI* 66.

[16] *TChr* III, 138; cf. *TSch* II, 95 (1085 A).

[17] Geyer argued *ed. cit.* 601–2 that *LNP* could be dated between *TSum* and *TChr* on a slender piece of evidence, the apparent elimination of the mode of identity by predication in *LNP* and the addition of a line in *TChr* IV, 40 that talked of things as separate by predication. The argument is weak because in Abelard's discussion every mode of identity is also a mode of difference and because predication was not listed in the modes of difference in *TChr*. The change in the list of *TChr* from *LNP* and *TSum* might suggest that *LNP* was written before *TSum*, which, unlike *TChr*, reproduced its text almost exactly.

[18] *TSum* III, 43 (84), cf. *TChr* IV, 59; cf. *Dialectica*, ed L. M. D e R i j k (Wijsgerige Teksten en Studies I, Assen, 1956), 116–7.

[19] The arguments are summarised by De Rijk in the introduction to his edition, p. xxii. Further discussion of its dating is given by M. T. B e o n i o - B r o c c h i e r i F u m a g a l l i in: *The Logic of Abelard* trans. S. Pleasance (Dordrecht, 1969), 4–7.

[20] *Dialectica*, ed. D e R i j k, 588–9; V. C o u s i n, *Ouvrages inédits d'Abélard pour servir à l'histoire de la philosophie scolastique* (Paris, 1836), xxxv.

[21] G. R o b e r t, *Les écoles et l'enseignement de la théologie pendant la première moitié du XIIe siècle* (Paris 1909) 188–90.

[22] T. G r e g o r y, 'Abelard et Platon,' *Peter Abelard. Proceedings . . . Louvain May 10–12, 1971,* 63; this important study was also published in *Studi Medievali* XIII (1972), 539–62.

[23] *Dialectica*, ed. D e R i j k 559.

[24] *TSum* I, 56 (20); cf. *TChr* I, 123, *TSch* I, 186 (1029 CD).

[25] *Dialectica*, ed. D e R i j k 559; cf. *TSum*, I, 44 (16), *TChr* I, 107, *TSch* I, 167 (1023 D–24A).

[26] Cf. *LI* 24, 314.

[27] J. C o t t i a u x, 'La conception de la théologie chez Abélard,' in: *Revue d'histoire ecclésiastique* XXVIII (1932), 263–9; L. N i c o l a u d ' O l w e r, 'Sur la date de la Dialectica d'Abélard', in: *Revue du moyen âge latin* I (1945), 375–90.

[28] C o t t i a u x, *art. cit.* 266. In the prologue of the fourth tract of the *Dialectica*, ed. D e R i j k 470–1, he answered the two charges of teaching pagan learning and without authority he described as made against him, *HC* 683–6. The reference in the prologue to the second tract to obstacles made to his teaching. *Dialectica* 145, need not refer to Soissons, but to the efforts of his enemies, *HC* 686–7.

[29] N i c o l a u d ' O l w e r, *art. cit.* 383. There were certain other small arguments based on subjective interpretation of minor phrases in the text such as about obstruction to his teaching applying to Soissons or about 'a man living in Paris' implying a part was written before 1118. The argument based on whether Abelard knew the *Analytics,* and hence wrote part of it at least after 1132 was cleared up by L. M i n i o P a l u e l l o, 'Note sull'Aristotele Latino Medievale, VII: I "Primi Analitici": la redazione carnutense usata da Abelardo e la "vulgata" con scolii tradotti dal greco,' *Rivista di filosofia neoscolastica* XLVI (1954), 211–34. B e o n i o - B r o c c h i e r i F u m a g a l l i brought up some elements in the *Dialectica* which could indicate stratified composition, but they do not form conclusive evidence, *vid. supra* n. 19).

[30] B u y t a e r t, Corpus Christianorum Cont. Med. XI (henceforth cited as Buytaert XI), xxv n. 45.

[31] The list of additions to R are summarised by Buytaert in the introduction to his edition of *TChr* (henceforth cited as Buytaert XII), 31–32.

[32] R o b e r t, *op. cit.* 198–203 and supported by V a n d e n E y n d e, at the time unaware of the Durham MS., 'Les Redactions de la "Theologia Christiana" de Pierre Abélard', in: *Antonianum* XXXVI (1961), 273–99.

[33] B u y t a e r t, 'An Earlier Redaction of the "Theologia Christiana" of Abelard,' in: *Antonianum* XXXVII (1962), 481–95. He dated D to the same period, 1122–26 as had been assigned to R, Buytaert XII, 44–50. He argued his new date for R on the problematic comparison of *TChr* I, 28 with the first two shorter versions of *tsch* 30, where the text of R and the second

I

shorter version have the correct ascription of a text to Gennadius, *op. cit.*51–52, 387–92. He acknowledged the weakness of the argument from the internal contradictions of the *Sic et Non, op. cit.* 32 n. 17.

[34] Van den Eynde, 'La "Theologia Scholarium" de Pierre Abélard,' in: *Recherches de théologie ancienne et médiévale* XXVIII (1961), 225–41. The crucial textual modification was the correction of the text 'Divina locutio . . .' in *TChr* I, 21 in DR and *Sermo* I, PL 178, 387A (reference misprinted in Buytaert's edition) to 'Dei ante factum suum locutio . . .' in (CT) and *tsch* 70. *TChr* R must have been written before Ep. VII, judging by comparison of the text concerning the Sybilline prophecy in *TChr* I, 128, Ep. VII, ed. J. T. Muckle, in: *MS* XVII (1955), 272 and *TSch* I, 190 (1031 C).

[35] *Vid. supra* n. 33).

[36] *TChr* I, 25–31; cf. the very brief treatment of divine power, *TSum* I, 5 (4). Abelard was condemned after the charge was made he ascribed power to the Father alone, HC 871–7.

[37] *TChr* IV, 82–115; cf. *TSum* III, 52–86 (86–102).

[38] Not all the new material added to *TChr* DR is to be found within the *Sic et Non,* but there are a striking number of similar *catenae* of quotation, as for example *TChr* I, 27–28 = *SN* 17, 1, 3–5, *TChr* II, 78–85 = *SN* 155, 1, 5–7, 10–14, *TChr* II, 114 = *SN* 106, 23–26 etc. The references of Buytaert to the longer version of the *Sic et Non* can be compared with the new critical edition of the text prepared by B. Boyer and R. McKeon (Chicago-London, 1976–78).

[39] Vivid pictures of life at St. Denis are suggested by such lines as *TChr* II, 57: *Erubescant ad haec huius temporis abbates quibus summae religionis monasticae cura commissa est, – erubescant, inquam, et resipiscant, saltem gentilium exemplo commoniti, qui in oculis fratrum vilia pulmentorum pabula ruminantium, exquisita fercula ac multiplicia impudenter devorant.* He attacked intemperate monks in a similar vein, *TChr* II, 71; cf. HC 654–60, 938–40. Van den Eynde suggested this section was based on a lost *Exhortatio ad monachos,* mentioned by Abelard in a *Soliliquium,* PL 178, 1877 D–8 A because of the monastic reference and the address *fratres* in *TChr* II, 46, 'Les écrits perdus d'Abélard' in: *Antonianum* XXXVII (1962), 470–3. However, the term *fratres* is used again in a quite different context in *TChr* (CT) III, 132.

[40] *TChr* II, 61–62; cf. HC 1053–83.

[41] The whole section *TChr* II, 26–108 was taken up just with the question of pagan virtue. He quoted passages from *TChr* II, 104–8 in Ep. VII, ed. Muckle, in: *MS* XVII (1955), 276–7. He stressed the value of intention in *TChr* II, 36 and their virtue as directed to a final end, which was the supreme good or God, in *TChr* II, 28.

[42] *TChr* III, 1–58; cf. *TSum* II, 1–27 (28–36).

[43] *TChr* IV, 72–81.

[44] *TChr* III, 167–70, VI, 77, refuted in IV, 154–8.

[45] The section on the Holy Spirit in the first book covered *TChr* I, 32–37, 68–123; cf. *TSum* I, 17–19, 37–56 (7, 13–20). Abelard justified the rededication of his oratory to the Paraclete with arguments very close to those he had used in *TChr* IV, 65, HC 1120–95.

[46] *TChr* IV, 117–53; cf. *TSum* III, 88–99 (102–7).

[47] *TChr* IV, 132.

[48] *Epistola ad Abaelardum* 5, ed. J. Reiners, in: *BGPMA VIII. 5 (1910),* 67–68, PL 178, 362 A–D.

[49] *TChr* V, 32.

[50] *TChr* V, 41.

[51] *TChr* V, 57–58.

[52] *TChr* V, 17.

[53] *TChr* IV, 62–63.

[54] *TChr* I, 129 on the incarnation, and *TChr* V, 31 on charity.

[55] Buytaert, 'Critical observations on the "Theologia Christiana" of Abelard,' in: *Antonianum* XXXVII (1962), 384–433, and Buytaert XII, 32.

[56] The two MSS. are described by Buytaert XII, 7–13, 16–23. Buytaert's edition, being essentially based on R, did not keep the all-important distinction between additions incorporated within the text of (CT) and its annotations in reproducing the text, although these can be adduced from the apparatus.

[57] *TChr* II, 13b = *TSch* II, 14–15 (1039 C–D), also = *TChr* III, 1–2
TChr III, 2b = *TSch* II, 17 (1040 A–B), also = *TChr* III, 53
TChr II, 125a = *TSch* II, 26–27 (1043 B–44 A), also = *TChr* II, 54–55
TChr III, 8d–c = *TSch* II, 34–35 (1046 C–D), also = *Sic et Non* Prolog.
TChr IV, 66b–c = *TSch* I, 60–63 (996 A–97 A), also = *TChr* I, 16a, 19–21.

[58] Buytaert devoted a long and painstaking analysis to the problem of the additions within the text of (CT), XII, 33–41. The concordance and apparatus throughout the edition follow his interpretation of where each addition came from.

[59] Buytaert XII, 53.

[60] *Vid. supra* n. 57; not all these internal parallels are noted in the edition, notably *TChr* II, 13b–III, 2b.

[61] These notes occur in the text of (CT) after *TChr* II, 13a and are printed in the apparatus, Buytaert XII, 138.

[62] Summarised by Buytaert XII, 384–6.

[63] Ostlender, 'Die Theologia Scholarium des Peter Abaelard' 267; Van den Eynde, 'La "Theologia Scholarium" de Pierre Abélard' 227; Buytaert followed this view, XII, 386.

[64] *tsch* 1, 19; discussed by Buytaert XII, 385.

[65] *tsch* 66; the different text of FH is recorded in the apparatus at this point.

[66] *tsch* 66 (FH) leads straight into *TChr* I, 19, but *tsch* 66–68 in Z leads into *TChr* I, 16a, 19–21. *tsch* 66–68 in Z is the expansion of the heavily abbreviated section in (CT), *TChr* IV, 66a–c. The abbreviations refer to the marginal annotation at I, 16a and the existing passages of I, 19–21. This suggests that (FH) is earlier than (CT) which improved on the transition at this point. In *TChr* (CT) V, 35b, Abelard referred to a quotation of Ps-Jerome *sicut in primo Libro praefati sumus* which had not occurred before in *TChr*, but had been reported in *tsch* 66 in (FH) and expanded in full in *tsch* 66 in Z. This is a further indication *TChr* (CT) was drawn up with *TSch* explicitly in mind.

[67] This can be clearly observed in Buytaert's concordance to *tsch* in XII, 396–7. (FH) concludes with some excerpts from *TChr*, *tsch* 69–74 and then a number of passages (*tsch* 79, 80, 85, 89) which Buytaert assumed to have been accidentally omitted and added on to the end of (FH). If (FH) does not abbreviate Z, but is expanded into Z, these passages make sense as extra ideas put down to be incorporated within the next version.

[68] *tsch* 1, *TSch* Prol. 1 (979 A): *Scholarium nostrorum petitioni prout possumus satisfacientes, aliquam sacrae eruditionis summam, quasi divinae Scripturae introductionem, conscripsimus.*

[69] The most important sentence collections containing Abelardian teaching are: *Sententiae Florianenses*, ed. Ostlender, in: *Florilegium Patristicum* fasc. XIX (Bonn, 1929); *Sententiae Parisienses*, ed. A. Landgraf, in: *Ecrits théologiques de l'école d'Abélard*, Spicilegium Sacrum Lovaniense XIV (Louvain, 1934) 1–60; another collection from the same Paris, BN MS. lat. 18108 has been edited as *Die Sententiae Quoniam misso aus der Abaelardschule*, ed. J. Trimborn (Cologne, 1962) 146–216; the *Epitome Christianae Theologiae*, also known as the *Sententiae Hermanni*, ed. F. H. Rheinwald and printed in Migne PL 178, 1695 A–1758 D. On the difficult question of the relationship of *TSch* to the sentence collections, there have been two major studies, H. Denifle, 'Die Sentenzen Abaelards und die Bearbeitung seiner Theologie vor Mitte des 12. Jahrhunderts,' in: *Archiv für Literatur- und Kirchengeschichte des Mittelalters* I (1885), 402–69, 584–624, and Ostlender, "Die Sentenzenbücher der Schule Abaelards,' in: *Theologische Quartalschrift* CXVII (1936) 208–52.

[70] *tsch* 11, *TSch* I, 1 (981 C); *tsch* 36–39, *TSch* I, 29–32 (989 B–D).

[71] *tsch* 2–25, *TSch* I, 2–18 (981 C–987 A).

[72] *tsch* 26–33, *TSch* I, 19–26 (987 A–988 D).

[73] *Vid supra* n. 67.

[74] The relatively few parts of *TSum* used in *TSch* can be surveyed in the concordance to *TChr*, Buytaert XII, 57–68.

[75] Abbreviated passages listed in n. 57 *supra*. The new prologue became *TSch* II, 1–67 (1035 A–57 B).

I

76 The only part of the original prologue used was *TSum* II, 1–8, 25–26 (28–31, 36). The new tone is evident in the extensions made in *TChr* (CT) III, 8a–e, which became *TSch* II, 31–35 (1045 B–46 D).

77 *TChr* II, 125b in (CT), which becomes *TSch* II, 28 (1044 A–C) is a corrected version of *TChr* II, 123, found only in RT. In T, this would be a meaningless duplication unless the scribe of T was copying material that had been deleted, but still visible in his exemplar. The same phenomenon may be observed in T in the duplication of *TChr* IV, 134a from IV, 115a (CT). This may also have occurred in *TChr* III, 13 and IV, 113, where only T has the text.

78 *TSch* II, 56–58 (1054 A–D).

79 *TSch* II, 61 (1055 C–D).

80 *TChr* (CT) IV, 74d, not copied verbatim, but expanded into *TSch* II, 43–61 (1049 B–55 D).

81 The generation of the Son was discussed *TSch* II, 110–21 (1068 A– 71 D), while the procession of the Holy Spirit was given much more attention *TSch* II, 122–82 (1071 D–85 A). This latter section was extensively revised in the Balliol MS. 296; excerpts of this new revision were transcribed by O s t l e n d e r , 'Die Theologia "Scholarium" des Peter Abaelard' 276–9.

82 *TSch* II, 141–7 (1073 B–75 A).

83 O s t l e n d e r , in 'Die Sentenzenbücher der Schule Abaelards' 213–4, argued that the use of the image *anulum aureum* in the *Epitome* or *Sententiae Hermanni* xii, PL 178, 1714 D–15 A, was occasioned by contemporary criticism of the image of the seal, but the function of the analogy is wholly Abelardian. The seal analogy was a central part of the argument of the work and not introduced 'inadvertently' at 1715 C and further at 1720 BC. *Anulum* was also used in the *Sententiae Parisienses*, ed. L a n d g r a f 9. The *Sententiae Florianenses* 10, ed. O s t l e n d e r 5, use the seal analogy but in a slightly less sophisticated form.

84 *TChr* (CT) V, 30a leads into 35–35 f, copied out as *TSch* III, 30–33, 35–36 (1094 A–96 A). *TChr* V, 25a, 33a, 34a were marginal notes outlining further ideas.

85 *TSch* III, 18–82 (1091 C–1109 A).

86 *TSch* III, 83–116, 117–8 (1109 A–14 B, but broken short; the text is completed by C o u s i n , Opera II, 148–9). Although the last section is short, the phrase *ut ad bonitatem Dei a potentia eius et sapientia transeamus, TSch* III, 117 (Cousin II, 148) is a deliberate introduction, not accidental, as thought by Buytaert XI, 30. He believed the work was incomplete because the commentary on Romans reserved three questions to be dealt with in *TSch,* on idolatry, whether God can justly give someone up to further sin and how God could justly withdraw his grace from someone (*Comm. Romanos,* ed. B u y t a e r t XI, 75–76). The first was not dealt with in *TSch,* but the other two were covered in a general way in *TSch* III, 118–9 (Cousin II, 148–9).

87 Oxford, Balliol Coll. MS. 296, ff. 59r–60v. Examination of the MS. reveals that the scribe deleted the text of the first version and replaced it with a revised version of the text from another exemplar between ff. 35v 1. 37–41r 1. 28, and inserted extra leaves here as at the end to contain the new text. The Balliol MS. originally stopped at the same place as the text in London, B. L. MS. Royal 8. A. I, f. 69r.

88 *Ethics,* ed. D. E. L u s c o m b e (Oxford, 1971), 96.

89 *TSch* III, 32–37 (1094 C–96 B).

90 *TSch* III, 18–56 (1091 C–1101 D); cf. *TSch* III, 97–111, (1112 B–14 B; Cousin II, 142–6).

91 *TSch* III, 49–52 (1099 C–1100 B).

92 *TSch* III, 83–95, 98–113 (1109 A–12 A; Cousin II, 142–7).

93 *TSch* III, 58–64 (1102 A–4 B).

94 *TSch* III, 117–20 (Cousin II, 148–9).

A neglected gloss on the «Isagoge» by Peter Abelard

Within a small article published in 1911 Martin Grabmann drew attention to an anonymous gloss on the *Isagoge*, titled *Glossae super librum Porphyrii secundum vocales*, found in the Milan, Biblioteca Ambrosiana MS. M. 63 sup., ff. 73ra–81vb, alongside glosses of Abelard on the *Isagoge*, the *Categories* and the *De interpretatione* on ff. 1ra–72va of the same manuscript[1]. He showed that these anonymous *Glossae*, as they may be referred to for convenience, contained passages very similar both to parts of Abelard's gloss on the *Isagoge* as found on ff. 1ra–15vb of the same manuscript and to parts of quite different *glossulae* of Abelard, found in the Lunel, Bibliothèque municipale MS. 6, ff. 8r–41r[2]. Because none of these glosses had been edited in full, Grabmann could not undertake a detailed comparison of the three works, but he did point out their close textual interrelationship. He commented that the discussion of universals in the anonymous *Glossae* was of particular interest[3]. Grabmann assumed that the anonymous author of these *Glossae* must have been influenced by the glosses of Abelard on the *Isagoge* of Porphyry as found in both the Ambrosian and Lunel manuscripts, while developing Abelard's ideas further. He justified his claim that the work was written by a disciple of Abelard by quoting the phrase on f. 76ra of the *Glossae*, *Dicebat enim olim magister noster*, which he assumed without explanation was a reference to Abelard himself[4].

---

[1] 'Mitteilungen über scholastische Funde in der Biblioteca Ambrosiana zu Mailand', *Theologische Quartalschrift*, 93 (1911), pp. 538–44.

[2] *Ibid.*, pp. 540–544.

[3] *Ibid.*, p. 540.

[4] *Ibid.*, p. 544.

Grabmann's ideas about the anonymous *Glossae* were developed in more detail by Bernhard Geyer, who, between 1919 and 1933, published critical editions of various glosses of Abelard, as found in the Ambrosian library manuscript under the title of *Logica ‹Ingredientibus›* (hereafter cited as *LI*) and in the Lunel manuscript under the title of *Logica ‹Nostrorum petitioni sociorum›* (hereafter cited as *LNP*)[5]. He promised to edit the anonymous *Glossae* because they were so closely related to the glosses of Abelard on the *Isagoge* in *LI* and *LNP*, but he eventually edited only two small fragments of the work[6]. Because there were many passages in the *Glossae* identical to parts of both *LI* and *LNP*, Geyer used the text of these *Glossae* (A_2 in his terminology) to correct sections of the text of both *LI* and *LNP* (*A* and *L* respectively in his terminology)[7]. Although he acknowledged that the *Glossae* sometimes contained a text superior to that of both *LI* and *LNP*, Geyer followed Grabmann in thinking that they were written by a disciple of Abelard. He postulated that the work was a compilation of various authentic glosses of Abelard, namely *LI*, *LNP* and another intermediary gloss which has not survived[8].

In the same year as Geyer produced his edition of *LNP* and two fragments of the *Glossae*, Carmelo Ottaviano published a complete edition of the latter work and argued that they were written by Abelard himself[9]. Ottaviano based his argument on the close similarity both of the ideas and the text itself of the *Glossae* to those of *LI;* he did not, however, take into account the fact that there were other parallels between the *Glossae* and *LNP*. The intention of this study is to investigate the conflicting claims of Ottaviano and Geyer about the authorship of these *Glossae secundum vocales* and to establish their textual relationship to the known writings of Peter Abelard.

---

[5] *Peter Abaelards Philosophische Schriften, I. Die Logica 'Ingredientibus'*, Beiträge zur Geschichte der Philosophie und Theologie des Mittelalters (hereafter cited as BGPTMA), 21. 1–3, Münster i. W. 1919–27; *II. Die Logica 'Nostrorum petitioni sociorum'*, BPTMA, 21. 4, Münster i. W. 1933 (2nd revised edition 1973).

[6] *Philosophische Schriften*, p. ix: «... die ich ebenfalls edieren werde, weil sie in engster Beziehung zu den Glossen Abaelards stehen und in textkritischer und literaturgeschichtlicher Beziehung für diese von Bedeutung sind.» Geyer edited two fragments alongside *LNP*, pp. 583–8. The manuscript is mistakenly cited as M. 64 sup. instead of as M. 63 sup.

[7] *Philosophische Schriften*, pp. ix–x.

[8] *Ibid.*, pp. 610–612.

[9] 'Un opusculo inedito di Abelardo', *Fontes Ambrosiani*, 3 (Florence 1933), pp. 95–207.

The manuscript

As the manuscript, Biblioteca Ambrosiana M. 63 sup., has been described in some detail by Minio-Paluello, only a few features need be noted here[10]. These glosses on the *Isagoge* (ff. 1ra–15vb), the *Categories* (ff. 16ra–43vb) and the *De interpretatione* (ff. 44ra–71rb) are written in the same hand, while a short text about modal propositions, added in a different hand on ff. 71ra–72va, is not part of Abelard's gloss on the *De interpretatione*, as mistakenly thought by Geyer[11]. Minio-Paluello has shown that the complete text of Abelard's gloss on this work is found only in the Berlin, Deutsche Staatsbibliothek MS. lat. fol. 624, ff. 97r–146r. He has also argued that the short text on modal propositions is not by Abelard, but emanated from the circle of his teaching[12]. The *Glossae secundum vocales*, found on ff. 73ra–81vb, are written on a separate quaternion (with the addition of an extra leaf) from the rest of the manuscript in a hand apparently different from, though very similar to, the hand which wrote the preceeding glosses. The manuscript as a whole seems to date from the late twelfth century, although there is no indication as to where it may have been written[13]. Nothing is known of its whereabouts before it was given to Cardinal Federigo Borromeo, founder of the Ambrosian library, by Camillo Bossi of Modena in 1605[14].

The *Glossae secundum vocales* are incomplete in that they break off in mid-column on f. 81 vb *sed e converso verum omni est...*, presumably due to a deficient exemplar. The final section *de communitatibus* is thus missing as is the last part of the section *de accidente*. Ottaviano thought that the

---

[10] Minio-Paluello, *Twelfth Century Logic. Texts and Studies II. Abaelardiana Inedita* (Rome 1958), pp. xvi–xvii, extending the description of Geyer, *Philosophische Schriften*, pp. viii–x. The manuscript had been noted by B. Montfaucon, *Bibliotheca Bibliothecarum MSS. Nova* (Paris 1739), col. 521D; the editors of *Histoire littéraire de la France*, 12 (Paris 1769), p. 130 (reprinted *PL* 178, 38); A. Rosmini-Serbati, who cited extracts in *Aristotele esposito ed esaminato, 1. Opere edite e inedite*, ed. E. Turolla, vol. 29 (Padua 1963), p. 15n (first published in Turin, 1857).

[11] *Twelfth Century Logic*, p. xvii. The short text which does not belong to Abelard's gloss on the *De interpretatione* is edited by Geyer, *LI*, pp. 497. 20–503. 28.

[12] *Twelfth Century Logic*, pp. xvii–xxi. Minio-Paluello completed and corrected Geyer's edition of Abelard's gloss on the *De interpretatione* on pp. 1–108, 125–8.

[13] *Twelfth Century Logic*, p. xvi.

[14] According to the *Inventario Ceruti: Hic codex fuit ad ill.mum card. Federicum a Camillo Bossio mutina dono missus anno 1605. Olgatius scripsit*, cited by D. E. Luscombe, *The School of Peter Abelard* (Cambridge 1969), p. 89 n. 2.

Glossae also lacked a beginning, although the incipit *Quod antiquitus logicam dicebant, modo logicam sive dialecticam appellant* does serve as an adequate introduction to the work as a whole[15]. The *Glossae* are written in a fine school hand, highly abbreviated and not free from a number of scribal errors. Ottaviano's edition cannot always be trusted to give an accurate rendering of the text and some of his readings have to be treated with caution[16].

The authorship of the Glossae secundum vocales

Ottaviano argued that the *Glossae* were written by Abelard because not only did they express his major ideas, but they contained many passages very similar or sometimes identical to parts of the *Logica ‹Ingredientibus›*[17]. He also argued that criticisms expressed in the *Glossae* corresponded to Abelard's own criticisms of the teaching of William of Champeaux and Roscelin of Compiègne[18]. One particularly important passage which Ottaviano cited deserves to be quoted in full, because it was also used by Grabmann and Geyer as evidence that the work was written by a disciple of Abelard:

> Dicebat enim olim magister noster quod Boethius de rebus agebat per genus et species in illa propositione «Genera et species non sunt», postea in solutione transferre se ad vocabula, quod non multum valet. Potest etiam fortasse intelligi ita illa propositio «Genus et species non sunt», hoc est generalia et specialia vocabula non significant aliquam de rebus existentibus, determinando scilicet eam et discrete agendo de ea, igitur verum est iuxta illud Boethii. Nam cum dico «omnis homo», intellectus audientis quid rationabiliter intelligat non habet. Et secundum hoc etiam non bona prima pars argumentationis, ubi probat genus et speciem non esse, idest non significare aliquid, idest intellectum facere aliquem de rebus concipientem[19].

[15] Ottaviano, 'Un opusculo inedito', p. 97.

[16] Minio-Paluello commented that Ottaviano's edition was 'very unsatisfactory', *Twelfth Century Logic*, p. XVI n. 13. Some idea of its inadequacy can be gained by comparing it with Geyer's edition of two fragments of the *Glossae*. All extracts cited here have been checked against a microfilm of the manuscript provided by the Biblioteca Ambrosiana. The writer is working on a new edition of the *Glossae*.

[17] 'Un opusculo inedito', pp. 102–105.

[18] *Ibid.*, pp. 102–103.

[19] *Glossae* IV. 1, ed. Ottaviano, p. 145.

Grabmann's hypothesis, followed by Geyer, that *magister noster* referred to Abelard makes little sense in the context of the passage, in which the ideas of Abelard, far from being criticised, are reproduced with remarkable fidelity to his thought. The commentary in the *Glossae* on the interpretation of Boethius of the proposition *Genera et species non sunt* immediately preceeding the criticism of the teaching of *magister noster* is in part identical to that given by Abelard in *LNP*[20]. The doctrine imputed to this teacher – that *genera* and *species* did not exist as *res*, but were simply *vocabula* – is much closer to the opinion of Roscelin, whom Abelard criticised in a not dissimilar fashion in the *Dialectica*, than to that of Abelard himself[21]. The much more subtle interpretation advanced in the *Glossae* that general or particular words did not signify anything about existing *res* was precisely that of Abelard, who taught in *LNP* that ‹man› did not signify any particular man:

> Non est itaque necesse, ut si hominem intelligam, ideo hunc vel illum intelligam, cum multi alii innumerabiles conceptus sint, in quibus humana excogitatur natura, sed indifferenter, absque ulla scilicet certitudine personae, sicut haec ipsa conceptio simplex huius hominis «homo» vel huius nominis «album» simpliciter... Sicut est intellectus «omnis» qui ad omnes homines pertinet, quia unumquemque secundum intellectum illius sane possumus deliberare et aliquid esse illius significare[22].

The same idea is repeated in very similar terms later in the *Glossae:*

> Licet omne quod est discretum sit, genera et species non significant aliquid ut discretum, et tamen aliquid significant; ut «homo» haec vox, licet non significet hunc vel hunc, – quia non facit intelligi hanc discrete vel illum, et sic de singulis, – tamen significat hominem, et tamen omnis homo est hic vel ille. Sed non omne significans hominem est significans hunc vel illum, quia non facit intelligi hunc discrete vel illum, et sic de aliis; et modo facit intelligi hominem hunc et talem, acceptum facit quod animal rationale mortale concipio, sed non talem quod hunc vel illum[23].

---

[20] *Dialectica*, ed. L. M. De Rijk (Assen 1956), V. I, pp. 554–555: *Fuit autem, memini, magistri nostri Roscellini tam insana sententia ut nullam rem partibus constare vellet, sed sicut solis vocibus species, ita et partes adscribebat.*

[21] *LNP*, ed. Geyer, p. 531. 14–23.

[22] *Glossae* III. 9, ed. Ottaviano, p. 134.

[23] *Philosophische Schriften*, p. 612.

There is no criticism of Abelard's doctrine implied in the *Glossae* whatsoever. Abelard did not believe that *genera* and *species* were simply *vocabula* in the manner of his former teacher, Roscelin of Compiègne. If this were an inaccurate criticism of Abelard, it would be completely at odds with the whole tenor of the *Glossae*. The reference to *magister noster* makes much more sense as applied to Roscelin by Abelard himself.

Geyer explained the intellectual affinity between the ideas of the *Glossae* with those of Abelard as the result of a disciple drawing on ideas of his master. He based his argument that the work was a compilation of a number of genuine writings of Abelard on a few small irregularities in the text of its opening section [24]. The first was what Geyer believed to be the unnecessary repetition of a reference to the logical writings of Aristotle: the passage of the *Glossae* (ed. Ottaviano, I. 4, p. 112; ed. Geyer, p. 586. 11–27) *Ad naturam itaque simplicium vocum... scripta sunt*, followed by the passage (ed. Ottaviano, I. 5, pp. 113–14; ed. Geyer, p. 587. 10–18) *In scribendo autem logicam hic ordo servatur... Topica et Analetica*. Geyer argued that such a repetition was uncharacteristic of Abelard, but could be explained as the result of a compiler drawing first from *LNP* (ed. Geyer, pp. 508. 32–509. 8) and then from *LI* (ed. Geyer, p. 2. 8–15) [25]. The repetition of ideas is, however, slight as the first passage is about the contents of Aristotle's writings, the second about their logical order. Geyer's claim to detect literary clumsiness, alien to Abelard's literary style, is not backed up by any other examples of awkward repetition of ideas found in both *LI* and *LNP*. It is too subjective an interpretation of one text on which to build a theory of the authorship of the work.

The second example which Geyer cited as evidence that the work was a compilation was the repetition of a passage in the Glossae (ed. Ottaviano, I. 5, p. 114; ed. Geyer, pp. 587. 34 – 588. 5): *Vis argumento- rum... per impossible*, found earlier in the *Glossae* (ed. Ottaviano, I, 4, p. 112; ed. Geyer, p. 586. 6–22). He claimed that the two passages must have been taken from different sources. The repeated version of the passage simply provides, however, a more comprehensible text than occurs in the first version, in which is found the nonsensical syllogism: *hic non est flos, ergo est niger* (ed. Geyer, p. 586. 9). This should read:

---

[24] *Ibid.*, pp. 610–611.
[25] *Ibid.*, p. 611. Geyer's reference in the first paragraph to A_1 (= *LI*) p. 3. 8–15 should read p. 2. 8–15.

... aliquando secundum significationem intellectus, ut: homo non est flos; ergo non est rosa; aliquando ex significatione rerum, ut: hic [MS *add.* homo] est corvus; ergo est niger.

The second version is not without textual error, but it is better than the first[26]. Abelard repeats the same syllogism in *LNP*[27]. Whether the scribe repeated the passage by accident or design, it is clear that the *Glossae* should not be treated as a compilation from different sources, but as a work very similar to the other glosses of Abelard, the single manuscript of which is not always free from fault.

The most important feature of Geyer's analysis was his recognition that some parts of the *Glossae* were based on an authentic gloss of Abelard on the *Isagoge*, different from both *LI* and *LNP*. Part of the repeated passage in the *Glossae* is too different from either known of Abelard to have been copied from one or other. Geyer postulated that this authentic gloss of Abelard on the *Isagoge*, which he presumed to be no longer extant, was the common source behind the striking textual parallels between the section of the *Glossae* on identity and difference and the section of the *Tractatus de Unitate divina* or *Theologia ‹Summi boni›* on this subject[28]. In fact, the manuscript of the *Glossae*, although imperfect, provides a text of these intermediate glosses of Abelard of the same value as do the manuscripts of *LI* and *LNP*.

By careful comparison of the relevant passages on identity and difference with those in the *Theologia Christiana*, Geyer observed that the *Glossae* and *TSum* equated identity of essence with identity of predication, but that Abelard explicitly rejected the idea in *LNP* and omitted any mention of it in *TChr*[29]. This meant that *LNP* had to have been

---

[26] Geyer's reference in the third paragraph to his edition of a fragment of the *Glossae* on p. 587. 34, *vis argumentationum*, should read: *vis argumentorum*. The homoioteleuton begins in fact in the preceeding sentence: *aliarum per alias* ... I am indebted to A. de Libera for suggesting that the repeated passage might be a correction.

[27] *LNP*, p. 508. 15–28 (incorrectly cited by Geyer on p. 611 as p. 4. 15–28).

[28] *Philosophische Schriften*, p. 611–612. Geyer edited this section of the *Glossae*, p. 588. 6–39, equivalent in Ottaviano's edition to VI. 1, pp. 177–179. This parallels the section of the *Theologia 'Summi boni'* II, ed Ostlender, BGPTMA, 35. 2–3, Münster i. W. 1939, pp. 54. 22–61. 13 (hereafter cites as *TSum*).

[29] *Philosophische Schriften*, pp. 600–602. The two modes are identified in the *Glossae* VI. 1, ed. Ottaviano, p. 178; ed. Geyer, p. 588. 10–11: *Qui etiam modus idem est ille qui est idem praedicatione*, and in *TSum* II, ed. Ostlender, p. 55. 4–5: *ac si diceremus idem praedicatione*. They are distinguished in *LNP*, p. 558. 17–19: *Quae identitas idem videtur esse cum identitate praedicationis quibusdam, quod falsum est*.

written after *TSum*, while the *Glossae*, or rather the source (*x*) on which
Geyer believed they were in part based, had to have been written before
LNP. Geyer did not try to investigate how far the passages in the *Glossae*
parallel to passages in *LNP* were dependent on the missing source *x*
rather than on *LNP*. In the absence of this gloss, Geyer argued that
evidence for the sources of the compilation had to be looked for within
LNP. He justified his decision not to edit the *Glossae* in their entirety on
the grounds that the passages which were significant in that work were
not extensive and did not contribute anything essentially new [30].

A compilation or an evolving gloss?

In a brief, but important comment, Geyer observed that the relationship between *LI* and *LNP* was similar to that between different
versions of the *Theologia* in that *LNP* was a revised version of *LI* [31]. He
also postulated that Abelard wrote another gloss on the *Isagoge* intermediary between *LI* and *LNP*, which provided a source for at least part of
the *Glossae*. The issue which still needs to be examined is how far these
Glossae reproduce the text of this intermediary gloss and what light they
throw on Abelard's method of working.

If a table is drawn up of those passages in the *Glossae* which are
parallel to sections of *LI* and *LNP*, the full extent of the intricate
relationship between these three works can be studied in detail. These
parallels are not always exact, as words or whole phrases are often found
in one gloss which are not found in the same place or are expressed
differently in another. Nonetheless, the number of these parallels is too
great to be ignored.

[30] *Philosophische Schriften*, p. 612.
[31] *Ibid.*, p. 599.

Table I. Parallels between LI, the Glossae and LNP

LI (ed. Geyer, cited by page and line)	Glossae (ed. Ottaviano, cited by chapter and page)		LNP (ed. Geyer, cited by page and line)
1. 5–7	I.	1, 106	
		106–7	505. 13–22, 506. 1–3
		107	506. 13–17
1. 7–11		107	
2. 2–7		108	507. 27–508. 3
1. 11–25	I.	3, 110	
	I.	4, 112	508. 33–509. 8
2. 8–15	I.	5, 113–14	508. 4–9
2. 21–26	II.	1, 115	509. 9–14
2. 26–38	II.	2, 116	
3. 1–6	II.	3, 116–17	509. 29–37, 510. 1–22
4. 14–34, 5. 12–19, 4. 34–5. 11	II.	4, 118–19	510. 23–511. 12 16–29
5. 23–6. 16	II.	5, 120–1	
6. 17–24	II.	6, 121	
6. 25–7. 9	II.	7, 121–2	
7. 9–19	II.	8, 122–3	
7. 21–24	III.	1, 123	511. 31–512. 5
		124–5	524. 32–525. 14
	III.	2, 125–6	525. 15–22
	III.	3, 126–7	525. 23–36,
		127	526. 3–4, 11–13
	III.	4, 128	526. 14–21
		128–9	526. 27–34
	III.	5, 129	526. 35–527. 19
	III.	6, 130	527. 20–29
	III.	7, 130–1	527. 30–528. 8
	III.	8, 131–2	528. 10–16
		132	528. 16–19

LI (ed. Geyer, cited by page and line)	Glossae (ed. Ottaviano, cited by chapter and page)		LNP (ed. Geyer, cited by page and line)
	III.	9, 134	531. 33–532. 3
		135	531. 9–12
	III.	9, 135–6	532. 3–7
		136–7	531. 19–29
		137–8	532. 18–533. 9
8. 26–41		139–40	
9. 1–11		140–1	
30. 34–9	IV.	1, 141–2	528. 28–529. 11
31. 6–21		142	529. 12–21
31. 28–31, 23–27		143	
		144–5	529. 28–37
		146	530. 3–19
	IV.	2, 147	534. 6–16
		147–8	534. 23–30
		149	535. 19–30
		149–50	535. 33–536. 6, 11–16
		150	536. 40–537. 6
	V.	1, 152	541. 5–7, 10–11, 19–28
	V.	4, 156	543. 8–19
	V.	5, 157	544. 13–19
		157–8	545. 5–20
	V.	7, 160	546. 5–9
		161	546. 15–17
		164	547. 6–11
50. 7–14		165	550. 37–551. 7
	V.	8, 165–6	551. 8–10, 14–19
	V.	9, 168–9	552. 8–28, 31–36
57. 14–17	V.	10, 170	553. 1–15
57. 23–35		171–2	553. 16–36
	V.	11, 173	554. 7–15
		173–4	554. 18–24
		174	554. 30–34

LI (ed. Geyer, cited by page and line)	*Glossae* (ed. Ottaviano, cited by chapter and page)		*LNP* (ed. Geyer, cited by page and line)
63. 4–10		175	555. 23–28
63. 10–30		175–6	555. 28–30, 31
			556. 16
65. 12–30		176–7	556. 17–32
65. 31–37	VI. 1,	177–8	558. 1–6
	VI. 2,	179–80	560. 16–40
67. 39–68. 3	VI. 3,	180–1	
69. 30–38		181	
71. 27–35, 72. 1–13		182–3	
73. 36–39	VI. 4,	184	
		184	561. 5–10, 14–16
76. 1–31	VI. 5,	185–6	561. 20–562. 9
76. 32–77. 3	VI. 6,	186	562. 10–16
	VI. 7,	186–7	562. 37–563. 17
	VI. 8,	187–8	562. 16–36
77. 6–14		188–9	563. 18–23
77. 15–41		189–90	563. 24–37
78. 24–26, 31–80. 4	VI. 9,	190–3	564. 1–565. 22
80. 5–81. 2	VI. 10,	194–5	565. 23–566. 25
81. 5–22		195–6	
81. 23–38		196–7	568. 13–37
		197–8	567. 10–17, 19–21, 568. 1–6
81. 39–82. 34		198–9	568. 9–12, 38–569. 31
88. 1–89. 19	VII.	201–2	574. 1–5, 9–12, 25–27, 13–21, 28–35
93. 5–11	VIII. 1,	202	576. 1–5
	VIII. 2,	202–3	576. 5–6, 577. 1–4

One of the most noticeable features of this table is that all the passages which are found in both *LI* and *LNP* also occur in the *Glossae*. According to Geyer's theory, the compiler sometimes borrowed from *LI*, sometimes from *LNP* and sometimes from an intermediary gloss (*x*) written by Abelard after *LI*, but before *LNP*. Geyer did not explain why

II

the compiler should have drawn on so many different sources. A much simpler explanation is to see the text of the *Glossae* as a revision of that of *LI*, while the text of *LNP* as a revision of that of the *Glossae*. The text of the *Glossae* in the Ambrosian library manuscript may not be free from a number of scribal errors, but this does not imply that the original work should not be considered as genuine. Geyer dismissed the possibility that *LNP* might be a revision of the *Glossae* simply by stating that the *Glossae* were not authentic, ‹weil ebenso das Sondergut von *L* gegenüber *A*₂ als echt abaelardisch erwiesen werden kann›[32]. The arguments which he adduced to demonstrate this are, however, far from exclusive. The apparent repetition of a reference to Aristotle in the *Glossae* cannot in itself be used to distinguish the work of a disciple from that of Abelard, while scribal errors within the text of the single extant manuscript may stem only from copying of the work. The reference to *magister noster* within the *Glossae* makes more sense when applied to Roscelin of Compiègne than to Peter Abelard. The textual parallels evident within *Table I* are so numerous as to suggest that the *Glossae* do represent a work written by Abelard after the *Logica ‹Ingredientibus,›* but before the *Logica ‹Nostrorum petitioni sociorum›*.

Abelard may have written other glosses on the *Isagoge* of Porphyry, which may illuminate further the development of the *Glossae* and of *LNP* from the text of *LI*, but these have not survived. There are no clear textual parallels between Abelard's earliest known glosses on the *Isagoge*, found in the *Introductiones parvulorum*, and those of *LI*, although they contain the germ of the ideas developed in detail in later glosses[33]. If the four glosses are compared with each other, a picture emerges of a mind continually rethinking basic issues about language posed by Porphyry in the *Isagoge*. The *Glossae*, far from being a compilation from different sources, represent a stage in Abelard's intellectual development, always in a state of continuous movement.

---

[32] *Ibid.*, p. 612.
[33] *Pietro Abelardo. Scritti filosofici*, ed. M. Dal Pra, Nuova Biblioteca Filosofica, II. 3 (Rome-Milan 1954), pp. 3–42. They are found in the Paris MS, Bibliothèque nationale lat. 13368, ff. 156r–162v.

The evolution of the glosses on Porphyry

Comparison of individual passages in *LI*, the *Glossae* and *LNP* throws light on the way in which Abelard continued to revise what he had written. To take just one of many examples, a sentence in the introduction of *LI* is found in slightly altered form in the *Glossae*, while it is extended further in *LNP*:

LI (ed. Geyer, p. 2. 1–5)

De qua etiam hac ratione conscriptam esse meminit atque eam ad certas argumentationum regulas reductam esse, ne nimium vagos falsis complexionibus in errorem pertrahat, cum id quod in rerum natura non invenitur, rationibus suis videatur astruere et saepe contraria in conditionibus suis colligere hoc modo: ‹Socrates est corpus... etc.›

Glossae (ed. Ottaviano, I. 1, p. 108; ed. Geyer, p. 584. 7–13)

Ad huiusmodi discretionem ergo philosophi laborantes conati sunt ad certas regulas omnes argumentationes reducere ne quis indiscretus in argumentis falsas eorum complexiones pro veris recipiat, atque id quod in natura rerum non invenitur [rerum] concedere compellatur [MS.: appellatur] ac plurimum perturbetur, cum saepe contraria in conclusionibus colligi viderit hoc modo: ‹Socrates est corpus... etc.›

LNP (ed. Geyer, pp. 507. 27–508. 1)

Ad huiusmodi discretionem [Geyer: discretiones] philosophi laborantes conati sunt ad certas regulas argumentationes reducere, ne quis indiscretus in argumentationibus falsas pro veris recipiat. Sicut enim ex similitudine rerum decipimur, ita et in complexionibus contingit. Sicut enim quam plurimos videri pulchros contingit, cum tamen faciat adornatio, ita et versipelles sophistae falsarum complexionum fallacias polientes sophisticis argumentationibus nobis alludunt, atque id quod [est] in natura rerum non invenitur, concedere compellunt, cum saepe contraria in conclusionibus colligi videantur hoc modo: ‹Socrates est corpus... etc.›

The subject of the sentence is changed from Boethius to philosophers in general and a few other phrases changed in the *Glossae*, while a passage highly critical of certain *versipelles sophistae* is added in *LNP*. This may be a reference to Roscelin of Compiègne, whom Abelard criticised indirectly in the *Theologia ‹Summi boni›* as *versipellis sophista, qui auctoritate peripateticorum me arguere niteris*[34].

One indication that Abelard may have deliberately been trying to disassociate himself from the teaching of his former teacher in *LNP* is the change in his description of a universal as a *sermo* rather than as a *vox*, as he had described it in *LI*[35]. John of Salisbury characterised the difference of opinion between Abelard and Roscelin about universals in terms of their definitions of it as a *sermo* and as a *vox* respectively[36]. For Roscelin, a universal was simply a physical sound of human imposition, whereas for Abelard a universal, although just a word, signified something about that which it predicated. Abelard had not always described a universal as a *sermo*. His adoption of the term in *LNP* may reflect his concern to distinguish his own approach more clearly from that of Roscelin.

The major difference between *LI*, the *Glossae* and *LNP* lies in the different ways in which they discuss the problems of universals. While Abelard omitted any detailed discussion of the subject in the *Introductiones parvulorum*, he devoted a long section in *LI* to arguing that a universal was a *vox* rather than a *res*[37]. In the *Glossae*, while the introductory section on the nature of logic was maintained, the discussion of *LI* about universals was omitted and the idea put forward instead that the ques-

---

[34] *TSum* II, ed. Ostlender, p. 52. 10–11. Abelard stated that he wrote this treatise to refute the tritheistic heresy of Roscelin in a letter to the bishop of Paris, *Epist.* 14: ... *multas in me contumelias et mina evomuerit viso opusculo quodam nostro de fide sanctae Trinitatis, maxime adversus haeresim praefatam, qua ipse infamis est, conscripto (PL* 178, 356D–357A).

[35] In *LI*, ed. Geyer, p. 16. 21–22 Abelard stated: *restat ut huiusmodi universalitatem solis vocibus adscribamus;* in *LNP*, ed. Geyer, p. 522. 28–31 he stated: *Sic ergo sermones universales esse dicimus, cum ex nativitate, id est ex hominum institutione, praedicari de pluribus habeant; voces vero sive res nullatenus universales esse, etsi omnes sermones voces esse constat.* On the development of Abelard's terminology about universals see J. Jolivet, *Arts de langage et théologie chez Abélard* (Paris 1969), pp. 69–71, and M. T. Beonio-Brocchieri Fumagalli, *La Logica di Abelardo* (2nd edn. Florence 1969), pp. 49–71. Abelard's approach to universals in general has been expounded in many studies, notably by M. Tweedale, *Peter Abailard and Universals* (Amsterdam-New York-Oxford 1976), L. M. De Rijk, 'The semantical impact of Abailard's Solution of the Problem of Universals, in *Petrus Abaelardus (1079-1142). Person, Werk und Wirkung,* ed. R. Thomas, Trierer Theologische Studien, Bd 38 (Trier 1980), pp. 139–151, and W. L. Gombocz 'Abaelards Bedeutungslehre als Schlüssel zum Universalienproblem' on pp. 153–164 of the same volume.

[36] *Metalogicon* II. 17, ed. C. C. J. Webb (Oxford 1929), p. 92; *Policraticus* VII. 12, ed. C. C. J. Webb (Oxford 1909), II, p. 142.

[37] *LI*, ed. Geyer, pp. 9. 12 – 32. 12; cf. *Scritti filosofici*, pp. 5–6.

tion whether *genera* or *species* existed *in solis et nudis et puris intellectibus* arose from misunderstanding philosophical statements about *genera:*

> In hanc dubitationem inciderant ex locutionibus philosophorum huius-modi: ‹Animal est genus; animal est universale; genus est in pluribus; animal est commune; homo est species; hoc praedicatur de pluribus etc.›, in quibus haec nomina «animal», «homo» et similia in propria et usitata significatione accipientes, animal, id est res huius vocis, animal, quae res est substantia animata sensibilis, et personam hominis, id est animal rationale, genus esse, speciem vel universalem vel communem etc. proponi credebant, – non intelligentes huius praedicta vocabula «homo» et «animal» etc. de personis subiectis, quibus imposita fuerunt, ad se ipsa significanda philo-sophos transtulisse [38].

Abelard included this argument as well as those which follow in the *Glossae* in very similar form in *LNP*, although occasionally rephrasing individual passages. The most important change which he made was to add a long new section in which he argued that a universal was not a *res* or an *intellectus*, but a *sermo* [39]. Abelard's intention was to make more explicit the difference between his own emphasis on what a universal signified and Roscelin's description of it simply as a *vox* [40]. Having defined a universal as a *sermo*, Abelard could then add a long passage in criticism of Roscelin's definition which he claimed was inadequate:

> Vox vero illud non habet, in quo terminatur descriptio et quod per diffi-nitionem copulatur, scilicet praedicabilitatem de pluribus, sed est illud quod praedicatur, quia est sermo praedicabilis. ... Hic sermo «animal» est genus, hoc vocabulum «animal» est genus et universale, et similiter omnes in quibus subicitur vox innuens institutionem, non simpliciter essentiam vel prolationem, sed significationem et praedicans communitatem, sicut est: genus, universale, sermo, vocabulum, dictio, oratio. Vox autem simpliciter innuens essentiam est ut animal, homo, vox, sonus aeris etc. [41].

The remaining discussion about universals in *LNP* appears to have been taken from the *Glossae*, as perusal of *Table I* would suggest. By

---

[38] *Glossae* III. 2, ed. Ottaviano, p. 126. This passage is found in almost identical form in *LNP*, ed. Geyer, p. 525. 16–22.
[39] *LNP*, ed. Geyer, pp. 512. 7 – 524. 31.
[40] *Ibid.*, pp. 522. 10–524. 24.
[41] *Ibid.*, pp. 523. 5–8, 524. 4–10.

comparing the text of the *Glossae* with that of *LNP*, it becomes apparent that Abelard was particularly concerned in the latter work to refute the ideas of Roscelin, while he also incorporated ideas which he had already developed in the *Glossae*.

Abelard took care to introduce his new description of a universal as a *sermo* throughout the text of *LNP* as comparison of individual passages, otherwise very similar, makes clear:

Glossae (ed. Ottaviano, III. 3, p. 127)

> Eadem persona enim appellatur ab universali nomine et a singulari; et nota «subsistant» transferri de rebus ad *voces* pro «appellantur subsistentia» ex adiunctione horum vocabulorum «genus» et «species», quae *vocibus* data sunt ex significatione.

LNP (ed. Geyer, p. 525, 33–36)

> Eadem namque res ab universali nomine et particulari continetur et hoc loco hoc verbum «subsistit» de rebus ad *sermonem* transfertur per adiunctionem horum nominum: genus et species, quae *sermonibus* data sunt.

Later on in the *Glossae* (ed. Ottaviano, VI. 1, pp. 178–9; ed. Geyer, p. 588, 30–32) a similar change is made to the text:

> Illud secundum effectum vel secundum pretium sunt quae idem valent ad efficiendum aliquid, sicut sunt *voces* eiusdem intellectus.

LNP (ed. Geyer, p. 560, 6–8)

> Illud etiam secundum effectum vel secundum pretium dicimus quod idem valet ad efficiendum aliquid, sicut eosdem *sermones* dicimus, qui ad efficiendum intellectum valent.

A sentence in the *Theologia 'Summi boni'* is very similar to the version of this sentence in the *Glossae* in using *voces* rather then *sermones* as in *LNP*.

> Idem secundum effectum aut secundum pretium dicuntur quae idem valent ad efficiendum aliquid, sicut easdem dicimus *voces* quae idem valent ad eumden manifestandum intellectum[42].

---

[42] *TSum* II, ed. Ostlender, p. 57. 1–4.

This provides incidental confirmation of Geyer's hypothesis that *LNP* was written after *TSum*, while suggesting that Abelard may have been drawing from the text of the *Glossae* or a very similar work when he wrote his first treatise on the Trinity. Abelard was thus engaged in dispute with Roscelin on philosophical as well as theological matters at the time of writing the *Theologia 'Summi boni'*[43]. Comparison of *LNP* with the *Glossae* shows, however, that Abelard did not write a gloss on Porphyry quite different from that of *LI* only at this time, but that he revised a pre-existing gloss, itself a revision of *LI* in order to reflect his particular concerns at the time. The development of ideas is less dramatic if the *Glossae* are seen as an intermediary version between *LI* and *LNP*.

The glossae and the Theologia 'Summi boni'

Besides throwing light on the development of Abelard's ideas about universals and the nature of language, the *Glossae* also illuminate his treatment of identity and difference in the *Theologia 'Summi boni'*. Geyer pointed out that this section of *TSum* was closer to the corresponding part of the *Glossae* than to that of *LI* or *LNP*, but he did not explore the significance of this in terms of the literary construction of *TSum* or *LNP*[44]. Comparison of the relevant texts reveals the close relationship between Abelard's writings on logic and those on theology and the continuity of his thought on these two subjects.

Whereas in *LI* Abelard simply stated that the three modes of difference identified by Porphyry – genus, species and number – could be interpreted in various ways, he disregarded this classification in the *Glossae* and spoke of identity and difference as possible in a number of ways: essence, number, definition, similitude, immutability or effect[45]. Abelard wanted to stress that *idem* or *diversum* could have many different meanings, depending on the context in which the terms were used. He enumerated these very same modes of identity and difference in the *Theologia 'Summi boni'* in order to discuss how there could be a diversity of

---

[43] *Philosophische Schriften*, pp. 599–600.

[44] *V. supra*, n. 28.

[45] *Glossae* VI. 1, ed. Ottaviano, pp. 178–9; ed. Geyer, p. 588. 6–39. Cf. *LI*, ed. Geyer, p. 66. 6–28.

persons within the Trinity[46]. The crux of the problem which confronted Abelard was that it did not seem possible to apply any distinct philosophical mode of difference to within God:

> Summa, ut arbitror, omnium quaestionum haec est, quomodo scilicet in tanta unitate individuae ac penitus merae substantiae diversitatem personarum consideremus, cum nullus differentiae modus a philosophis distinctus videatur hic posse assignari secundum quem diversitas valeat ostendi[47].

After a long passage about the transcendence of the divine nature from all human categories, Abelard then proceeded to answer criticism that none of the modes of difference defined by Porphyry applied to the three persons in God by claiming that Porphyry did not describe every mode of difference:

> Quod autem nobis Porphyrium opponunt, qui de differentiis tractans modos differentiarum distinxit, sub quibus modus iste differentiae personarum, quae in Deo sunt, non cadit: nihil impedit. ... Multos etiam alios differentiae modos praeter hos quos Porphyrius distinguit, fateri cogimur, quos omnes ut plenius ac diligentius prosequamur, distinguendum est, quot et quibus modis idem accipiatur, sive etiam diversum, praesertim cum totius controversiae summa ex identitate divinae substantiae et diversitate personarum pendeat, nec aliter ipsa queat terminari controversia, nisi ostendamus hanc identitatem illi diversitati non esse contrariam[48].

The description of the various modes of identity which followed in *TSum* is very similar to that which began the section on difference in the *Glossae*, although it contains more detail. The discussion of the subject in *LNP* is sometimes closer to that of *TSum* than that of the *Glossae*:

---

[46] *TSum* II, ed. Ostlender, pp. 54. 22 – 61. 13. There is some confusion within the text of *TSum* whether Abelard meant that there were six or more modes as stated at the end of the section in all three MSS of *TSum* II, p. 57. 5: Erlangen, Universitätsbibliothek lat. 182, f. 50r; Oxford, Bodleian, Lyell 49, f. 117r; Berlin, Staatsbibliothek Preußischer Kulturbesitz, theol. lat. oct. 95, f. 31v. Ostlender emended the *quinque* to *sex* in his edition (p. 57. 5) to agree with the reference on p. 54. 22. The corresponding sentence in the *Glossae* VI. 1, ed. Ottaviano, p. 179, also has *quinque modis* (*V* on fo. 78rb of the Ambrosiana MS). With Roman numerals scribal errors are easily made.

[47] *TSum* II, ed. Ostlender, p. 47. 9–14.

[48] *Ibid.*, p. 54. 2–17.

Glossae (ed. Ottaviano, V. 1, p. 178; ed. Geyer, p. 588. 6–7)	*TSum* II (ed. Ostlender, pp. 54. 28–55. 5)	*LNP* (ed. Geyer, p. 558. 15–21)
Dicimus enim idem secundum essentiam quorumcumque est eadem essentia, sicut idem est ensis quod mucro, vel substantia quod corpus, sive animal et homo vel Socrates, et album idem quod durum. Qui etiam modus idem est ille qui est idem praedicatione.	Idem esse secundum essentiam dicimus quorumcumque eadem est essentia, ita scilicet ut hoc sit illud, sicut idem est ensis quod mucro, vel substantia quod corpus, sive etiam Socrates, et album idem quod durum; et omnia eadem essentialiter dicuntur quaecumque praedicatione coniungi possunt. Quod tale est ac si diceremus idem praedicatione.	Nam idem dicitur in essentia quorum unumquodque est eadem essentia, ita scilicet ut haec essentia non sit illa, sicut hic homo et Socrates. ... Quae identitas idem videtur esse cum identitate praedicationis quibusdam, quod falsum est, cum multa sint eadem essentialiter et non praedicatione, sicut nomen et verbum et cetera huiusmodi.

The same phenomenon of an argument being extended in *TSum* from its brief form in the *Glossae* and then transferred to *LNP* can be observed by comparing the discussions of identity by number, definition, similitude, immutability and effect in each work[49]. It could be argued that the text of this part of the *Glossae* was abridged from that of *TSum*, but this seems less likely because *TSum* appears to contain a version of the text intermediary between that of the *Glossae* and that of *LNP*.

The importance of this discussion of identity and difference in the *Theologia 'Summi boni'* was that it enabled Abelard to argue that there was a mode of difference, namely that of definition, which could legitimately be applied to the persons in the Trinity without compromising God's essential unity. The originality of Abelard's approach lay in the way in which he discussed a traditional problem of logic, going much further

[49] *Glossae* VI. 1, ed. Ottaviano, pp. 178–9; ed. Geyer, p. 588. 11–32; *TSum* II, ed. Ostlender, pp. 55. 6 – 57. 4; *LNP*, ed. Geyer, pp. 558. 21–27, 559. 5–17, 30–34, 560. 1–2, 6–8.

than Porphyry had done in describing various possible modes of difference. By comparing the corresponding sections in the *Glossae, TSum*
and *LNP*, it becomes apparent that the ideas which Abelard expressed
in *TSum* are an elaboration of those outlined in the *Glossae*. The discussions of difference by essence, number and definition, summarised only
briefly in the *Glossae* were discussed in much more detail in *TSum* because
they were particularly relevant to Abelard's argument about the difference between the persons of the Trinity[50]. The originality of Abelard's
approach to the Trinity was founded on the novelty of his approach to a
problem posed by Porphyry in the *Isagoge*.

If Abelard's argument in *TSum* was more developed than in the
Glossae, his argument in *LNP* was more developed still[51]. As Geyer
correctly pointed out, Abelard revised the idea which he had mentioned
in the *Glossae* and in *TSum* that identity of predication was the same as
identity of essence. He replaced a reference to *voces* with the term
sermones[52]. Abelard also changed the order of his argument in *LNP* so as
to discuss each mode of difference after the corresponding mode of
identity rather than within a separate section as in *TSum* and the *Glossae*[53]. The text of this part of *LNP* would appear to be influenced both by
the *Glossae* and by *TSum*.

Abelard revised his discussion of identity and difference further in
the *Theologia Christiana* in order to omit mention of the mode of effect,
while to add the mode of property because it was particularly relevant to
his discussion of the difference between the three persons of the Trinity[54]. The basic idea which Abelard was putting forward in all his glosses
on the *Isagoge* and in each version of the *Theologia* was the same – that
identity and difference were not absolute concepts, but could be interpreted in a number of different ways, none of which were mutually
exclusive. Things could be technically different and the same at the
same time. Abelard developed this philosophical idea further in the
Theologia Christiana, while in the *Theologia 'Scholarium'* he simplified his
argument by reducing the modes of identity and difference to only three

[50] This is particularly true of the modes of number and definition, *TSum* II, ed.
Ostlender, pp. 57. 27 – 60. 16.

[51] *LNP*, ed. Geyer, pp. 558. 15 – 560. 15.

[52] *V. supra*, n. 29; *LNP*, ed. Geyer, p. 560. 7.

[53] *LNP*, ed. Geyer, pp. 558. 28 – 559. 4, 18–29, 35–36, 560. 3–5, 8–10.

[54] *TChr* III. 138–60, ed. Buytaert, *Corpus Christianorum. Continuatio Mediaeualis*, XII
(Turnhout 1969), pp. 247–254.

– similitude, essence or number and property[55]. His intention here, as throughout the *Theologia 'Scholarium'*, was to eliminate philosophical discussion which did not apply directly to the Trinity. By studying the development of Abelard's approach to identity and difference in both his glosses on Porphyry and in different versions of the *Theologia*, some insight is gained into Abelard's intellectual development as a whole.

Conclusion

This study has been concerned with the close relationships, both textual and thematic, between the anonymous *Glossae secundum vocales*, found in the Milan, Biblioteca Ambrosiana MS. M. 63 sup., ff. 73ra-81vb, and various known writings of Abelard on logic and theology. These anonymous glosses seem to represent a revision made by Abelard of his *Logica 'Ingredientibus'*, while they appear to have been themselves revised in the *Logica 'Nostrorum petitioni sociorum'*. Geyer's argument that they were compiled by a disciple of Abelard from various genuine glosses of his master is unnecessarily complicated and does not fit with the evidence. The text of the *Glossae* as found in the Ambrosian library manuscript may not be free from a number of scribal errors incurred in copying of the work, but this does not mean that the glosses themselves cannot be genuine. Detailed comparison of the work with other writings of Peter Abelard confirms Ottaviano's opinion that the *Glossae secundum vocales* were written by Abelard himself.

---

[55] *Theologia 'Scholarium' (Introductio ad theologiam)* II, ed. Duchesne, *PL* 178. 1065A–66B. The writer is completing a new edition of this work and of *TSum* for the series *Corpus Christianorum*. For study of the relationship between the different versions of *TChr* and *TSch*, see C. Mews, 'The development of the Theologia of Peter Abelard' in *Petrus Abaelardus*, ed. Thomas (v. supra n. 35), pp. 183–198, and 'Peter Abelard's *Theologia Christiana* and *Theologia 'Scholarium'* re-examined' to appear in *Recherches de Théologie ancienne et médiévale*, 52 (1985).

III

MAN'S KNOWLEDGE OF GOD ACCORDING TO PETER ABELARD

«Thinking that there is nothing in heaven or on earth not worth his knowing apart from 'I do not know', he peers at heaven, studies the depths of God and brings back ineffable words which are not given for a man to speak»([1]). This comment of Bernard of Clairvaux sums up his view of Peter Abelard as someone who saw no bounds to the range of human knowledge and tried to reduce the mystery of the Trinity to the domain of reason. Abelard seemed to elevate man's intellectual powers to such an extent as to deny the transcendence of God and reduce the divinity to intellectual formulae. Did Abelard have such an ambitious view of human potential? In this paper I want to examine, not the frequently studied theme of Abelard's use of the secular arts, but what he has to say about man's knowledge of a transcendent, eternal truth — how this knowledge was gained and what were its limitations.

Although there are many different works of Abelard in which one could pursue this theme, I shall concentrate on just one, the *Theologia*, the treatise which came under such criticism during his lifetime. The work is of particular importance because Abelard continued to revise its text over a period of some twenty years, producing three major versions, known successively as the *Theologia «Summi boni»*, the *Theologia Christiana* and the *Theologia «Scholarium»*([2]). Although he was principally concerned in the *Theologia* with the nature of God and how three persons could co-exist in one God, Abelard was also very much concerned with the nature of man's knowledge of the divinity and with his capacity to understand the doctrine of the Trinity. It is on this aspect of the *Theologia* that I wish to concentrate.

([1]) *Ep.* 190, 1, *S. Bernardi Opera*, ed. J. LECLERCQ, Rome, 1977, pp. 17-18.

([2]) *Theologia «Summi boni»* (*TSum*), ed. H. OSTLENDER, *Beiträge zur Gesch. der Philos. und Theol. des Mittelalters*, XXXV, 2-3 (1939); *Theologia Christiana*, ed. E. M. BUYTAERT, Corpus Christianorum Cont. Med., XII, Turnhout, 1969, pp. 71-372; *Theologia «Scholarium»*, shorter recensions (*tsch*), ed. E. M. BUYTAERT, *op. cit.*, pp. 401-455; longer recension (*TSch*), ed. V. COUSIN, *P. Abaelardi Opera*, II, Paris, 1859, pp. 2-149. New editions of *TSum* and *TSch* begun by Buytaert before his death are being completed by the author. References will be to Buytaert's edition of all three versions, with page references to the editions of Ostlender and Cousin in brackets.

420

Abelard's basic theme in every version of the *Theologia* was that the names of Father, Son and Holy Spirit signified three fundamental properties of God, the supreme good: the power by which God could do whatever he willed, the wisdom by which he could discern all things and the bounty or goodness by which he ordered all things for the good, even those which seemed evil([3]). This definition reveals a basic aspect of his approach. Man could understand the Trinity in terms of God's action in the world, not in terms of his transcendent nature. Man's knowledge of God was gained through his perception of creation. In this Abelard differed greatly from Boethius and those twelfth century commentators on the *Opuscula Sacra* who explained the doctrine of the Trinity in abstract terms removed from matter, and was perhaps closer to Augustine in believing that the divine mystery had to be approached through material analogies([4]). There was, however, a fundamental difference of approach between Augustine and Abelard. Whereas Augustine in his *De Trinitate* sought to understand the Trinity by looking at the relationship between memory, intellect and will within an individual, Abelard turned to man's perception of the universe as a whole, through which God revealed himself to man.

Man did not have an innate knowledge of the Trinity, but was able to gain this knowledge by listening to those prophets and philosophers whom God used as a vehicle for his revelation([5]). All knowledge was a divine gift, including that about the properties of the supreme good which constituted the true nature of the Trinity. As Tullio Gregory has so rightly emphasised, Abelard's belief that Plato and other philosophers had understood some aspects of the Trinity was not based on confidence in the powers of unaided reason, but on his conviction that God had revealed himself to the Gentiles through such worldly instruments([6]).

([3]) *TSum* I, 1 (p. 2); *TChr* I, 1; *tsch* 37-39; *TSch* I, 30-32 (pp. 12-13).

([4]) These two approaches are defined by Clarembald of Arras: «Haec i.e. theologia duos habet propriae considerationis modos. Aliquando enim de divinis ratiocinans exemplis utitur quaesitis extrinsecus. Aliquando vero divinam usiam sine subiecta materia curiose intuetur», *Tractatus super librum Boethii De Trinitate*, 14-16, ed. N. HÄRING, *Life and Works of Clarembald of Arras*, Toronto, 1965, pp. 70-72. Cf. S. OTTO, *Augustinus und Boethius im 12. Jahrhundert. Anmerkungen zur Entstehung des Traktates «De Deo uno»*, *Wissenschaft und Weisheit*, XXVI (1963), pp. 15-26.

([5]) *TSum* I, 5, 63 (pp. 4, 24); *TChr* I, 7, 136; *tsch* 75; *TSch* I, 68, 201 (pp. 22, 61).

([6]) *Abélard et Platon*, Peter Abelard, ed. E. M. BUYTAERT, Louvain-The Hague, 1974, pp. 38-64 and *Studi Medievali*, 3ª serie, XIII (1972), pp. 539-562. See also J. JOLIVET's illuminating study, *Doctrines et figures de philosophes chez Abélard, Petrus Abaelardus. Person, Werk und Wirkung*, ed. R. THOMAS, *Trierer Theologische Studien*, Bd. 38, Trier, 1980, pp. 103-120.

Man's first obligation was to heed the teaching of those authorities, pagan or Jewish, who had been so inspired.

Although Abelard saw both prophets and philosophers as instruments of God's revelation to man, he gave far more emphasis in his *Theologia* to the teaching of the philosophers than to that of their Jewish counterparts([7]). In a minor work, the *Soliloquium*, he made the explicit comment that the philosophers expounded the doctrine of the Trinity more fully than the prophets in many aspects([8]). In the *Theologia* «*Summi boni*», Abelard commented that Job, a Gentile, explained the resurrection more clearly than the prophets while elsewhere in the same work he said that the philosophers gave a more satisfactory account of the generation of the Son from the Father([9]). He justified this by arguing that the prophets had to hide their insight because their people were at a primitive stage. By contrast, with the philosophers there was a general zeal for enquiry into the truth and man's understanding of God increased along with his knowledge of creation. The reason why the philosophers were so attuned to understanding the Trinity was not because they had been implanted with some abstract perception about God's nature, but because they gained this understanding through the created world, the medium of revelation. Abelard never tired of citing those verses of the Epistle to the Romans in which St. Paul spoke of the invisible things of God being perceived and understood through those things which had been made: «Invisibilia ipsius a creatura mundi, per ea quae facta sunt intellecta conspiciuntur»([10]). As all human knowledge arose from the senses, knowledge of invisible things was revealed to man, not as a transcendent truth, but through analogy with visible things: «quia cum omnis notitia humana a sensibus surgat, ex rerum visibilium similitudine invisibilium naturam ratio vestigavit»([11]). The philosophers gained their knowledge of God from their observation and thought about the world.

No aspect of God did they understand more fully, in Abelard's mind, than the divine goodness by which all things were ordered in the world, a goodness which Plato described as the world soul and which Christians knew as the Holy Spirit. Abelard cited a number of times the neo-

---

([7]) This can be measured simply by the length of treatment: on the prophets (including Moses) — *TSum* I, 6-29 (pp. 4-11), *TChr* I, 8-53, *TSch* I, 69-93 (pp. 22-28); on the philosophers — *TSum* I, 30-70 (pp. 11-27), *TChr* I, 54-136, *TSch* I, 94-201 (pp. 28-61).

([8]) PL 178, 1877 C.

([9]) *TSum* I, 65 (pp. 24-25), III, 66-67 (pp. 92-93).

([10]) *TSum* I, 32, III, 67 (pp. 11, 93); *TChr* I, 58, II, 6, 12, IV, 7, 85; *tsch* 101, 106; *TSch* I, 94, 98, II, 6, 12, 60 (pp. 28, 29, 64, 66, 83).

([11]) *TSum* III, 67 (p. 93).

Platonic triad of God-mind-world soul as defined by Macrobius, as evidence that Plato and his followers had understood the Trinity, but he concentrated far more on the world soul than on the other two elements of the triad([12]). His discussion of philosophical testimony about divine power and wisdom is relatively brief and unoriginal, being drawn largely from Augustine, unlike his lengthy and original exegesis of the *Timaeus* and of the commentary of Macrobius on the *Somnium Scipionis*([13]). The length of his discussion of philosophical recognition of the goodness which ordered the world reflects Abelard's own devotion, evident in the *Historia Calamitatum*, to the Holy Spirit, which he understood to be the force bringing all things, no matter how bad, to an ultimately good end([14]). Abelard believed that Plato shared the same perception about God's benevolent action in the world, describing it in terms of a world soul. This world soul was not a real thing or entity, but an image used to describe a much more profound truth, beyond definition in human terms([15]). Abelard stressed that Plato was wrong in believing that the world soul was created, but explained his opinion by arguing that he was talking about the effect of the Holy Spirit in the world, rather than about its eternal nature([16]).

Man's knowledge of the Trinity, particularly that gained by the philosophers, was obtained from what man saw and understood of God's action in the world. Abelard shows a clear reluctance to believe that man can gain such knowledge in any other way. His conception that the Holy Spirit proceeded from God to creation was in marked contrast to the traditional view, expressed by Augustine, that the Holy Spirit was the mutual love of the Father and the Son. Abelard discussed this point of view only briefly because it presumed that creation need not necessarily exist([17]). He drew his conception of the Holy Spirit from the goodness which he saw in the world. Similarly the harmonious arrangement of the world illustrated God's power and wisdom, in other words the Father and the Son:

([12]) *TSum* I, 36, 42, III, 66 (pp. 13, 15, 92); *TChr* I, 68, 104, 110-113; *TSch* I, 37, 123, 164 (pp. 14, 36-37, 47).

([13]) *TSum* I, 35, 58-62 (pp. 11-12, 21-24); *TChr* I, 61, 124-132; *TSch* I, 115, 187-196 (pp. 33, 55-59).

([14]) *Hist. Cal.*, ed. J. MONFRIN, Paris, 1978, pp. 94-96, 108.

([15]) *TSum* I, 36 (p. 13).

([16]) *TSum* I, 56, III, 94-96 (pp. 20, 105-106); *TChr* I, 123, IV, 145-147; *TSch* I, 186, II, 175-177 (pp. 55, 111).

([17]) *TChr* I, 152; *TSch* II, 181 (p. 113).

Cuius quoque potentiam atque sapientiam universus mundi ornatus annuntiare non cessat ac praedicare et suo modo laudare et commendare, ex ipsa sui mirabili compositione ac dispositione([18]).

Abelard's Trinitarian theology in fact reveals a great deal about his belief in the order, rationality and goodness of the universe, qualities he thought evident to all men of reason.

Just as man could only know God through those properties which were experienced within creation, so man could never define his true nature. The great error of many dialecticians was that they tried to comprehend the divine nature through their reasoning([19]). Although he does not mention anyone by name, it seems certain that Abelard had his former teacher of logic, Roscelin of Compiègne in mind when he wrote a long polemical passage against pseudo-dialecticians in the *Theologia «Summi boni»*, expanded further in the *Theologia Christiana*([20]). According to a letter to the bishop of Paris, Abelard wrote the *Theologia «Summi boni»* specifically to refute Roscelin's explanation of the distinction between the persons of the Trinity as that between three separate substances within God([21]). The crux of his argument against Roscelin was that God's nature had to be undivided and removed from any substance or indeed from any other logical category([22]). Human language had been instituted by man to describe those created things which man understood and could not therefore be applied to God without a radical change in its meaning([23]). The only difference that man could discern within God was not on the level of his essence, but in the different properties which he could define within God. Central to Abelard's thesis was that these properties were not forms within God, but that they were applied by man to describe different aspects of his nature — namely those of being all powerful, wise in everything and good in all his action([24]). Abelard was here transferring the implications of his own arguments on the philosophical notions of identity and difference, as

---

([18]) *TChr* II, 6 (p. 64); cf. *Comm. Rom.*, I, ed. BUYTAERT, CCCM, XI, Turnhout, 1969, p. 69: «Apparet itaque maxime ex ipsa mundanae fabricae universitate tam mirabiliter facta, tam decenter ornata, quantae potentiae, quantae sapientiae, quantae bonitatis eius artifex sit ...».

([19]) *TSum* II, 19-24 (pp. 33-35); *TChr* III, 33-50.

([20]) Cf. *TSum* II, 75 (p. 52), *TChr* III, 133: «Responde tu mihi, acute dialectice aut versipellis sophista, qui auctoritate peripateticorum me arguere niteris de differentia personarum quae in Deo sunt ...».

([21]) *Epist.*, XIV, PL 178, 356 D-357 A.

([22]) *TSum* II, 31-42 (pp. 38-42); *TChr* III, 71-88.

([23]) *TSum* II, 70-71 (pp. 50-51); *TChr* III, 125-126; *TSch* II, 84-85 (p. 90).

([24]) *TSum* II, 105 (p. 62); *TChr* III, 166.

424

formulated in his glosses on Porphyry's *Isagoge*, to discussion of the Trinity([25]).

Abelard's invective against false dialecticians in the *Theologia «Summi boni»* and the *Theologia Christiana*, far from being in contradiction to his own use of logic to discuss the Trinity, served to distinguish his own approach to logic from that of other dialecticians such as Roscelin. He insisted that human language was limited by its very nature in its capacity to describe an eternal truth. He quoted from the statement attributed to Plato by Macrobius that it was impossible for man to say what God was as the divine nature was so far removed from any human conception([26]). If philosophers did speak about God, they did so only through analogies and examples, such as that of the world soul. Man did not have the capacity to give an objective description of God, as all he could do was to provide his own opinion, itself only a shadow of the truth([27]). Needless to say, the subjectivity of such an approach aroused the criticism of contemporaries who demanded a more dogmatic account of matters of faith([28]). Such subjectivity of man's knowledge of God was, however, consistent with Abelard's view of the limited nature of human language.

As Abelard became increasingly obliged to defend his own use of pagan authors and a dialectical approach to theology, so he changed the emphasis of the *Theologia* away from a critique of false dialecticians such as Roscelin, to a defence of dialectic itself. In the *Theologia «Scholarium»* he abbreviated much of the philosophical detail which had become so elaborate in the *Theologia Christiana*. He also rewrote the prologue which introduced his argument about identity and difference within God so as to address those critics who accused him of adopting an excessively rational approach to the Trinity, omitting those passages in which he criticised other dialecticians([29]). Abelard's failure to mention Roscelin in the *Historia Calamitatum* when describing the genesis of the *Theologia «Summi boni»* may reflect the fact that in 1132-33 when he wrote that autobiographical account he was much more concerned with

---

([25]) *Logica Nostrorum petitioni sociorum*, ed. GEYER, *Peter Abaelards Philosophische Schriften*, Beiträge ..., XXXI, 4 (2nd ed., 1973), pp. 558-568.

([26]) *TSum* II, 21, 66 (pp. 34-35, 48); *TChr* III, 44, 119; cf. *Log. Nost. petit. soc.*, ed. GEYER, p. 516.

([27]) *TSum* II, 26 (p. 36); *TChr* III, 54; *tsch* 5; *TSch* Prol., 5 (p. 3).

([28]) Cf. WALTER OF MORTAGNE, *Epist. ad Abaelardum, Florilegium Patristicum*, XIX, Bonn, 1929, p. 35.

([29]) For a summary of these changes, see my article *The Development of the «Theologia» of Peter Abelard, Petrus Abaelardus* ..., ed. THOMAS, pp. 183-198.

defending the need for any explanation of Christian doctrine to be understood rationally than with engaging in dispute with Roscelin of Compiègne([30]). This change of emphasis, so marked if one compares the *Theologia «Summi boni»* to the *Theologia «Scholarium»*, does not mean that Abelard changed his mind about what he originally said about the impossibility of the human mind comprehending God's nature. He maintained this idea just as strongly in the *Theologia «Scholarium»*, but emphasised more than he had done before that the analogies which man could make about God had themselves to be fully comprehensible to human reason([31]). Rather than saying that man could understand the nature of God through the use of reason, Abelard was saying that any explanations given had to be rational. He commented that there were many doubts and questions about orthodox belief voiced by heretics and non-believers, which the writings of the Fathers had failed to answer, still demanding an adequate reply. He believed, however, that their doubts and questions had to be given a sympathetic hearing and that any solution had to be arrived at rationally, rather than imposed by force([32]).

Although Abelard quoted Augustine frequently to lend authority to his argument, he explicitly rejected the analogy Augustine had suggested and which had been used by Anselm of Canterbury in his treatise against Roscelin, of the Trinity as simultaneously a spring, a river and a pond because the three elements were not of the same substance at the same time. Abelard felt that it was better to look at what philosophers said about the physical world, in particular about the relationship between matter and form or between genus and species in order to understand the Trinity([33]). He compared the relationship between the Father and the Son, in other words between power and wisdom (defined as the power of discernment), to that between matter and form because they were not two separate entities, but two properties of the same substance, one of which depended on the other. In the *Theologia «Scholarium»* Abelard synthesised a number of ideas in a way he had not done in earlier

---

([30]) H. Silvestre argues that this demonstrates the inauthenitcity of the *Historia Calamitatum, Pourquoi Roscelin n'est-il pas mentionné dans l'«Historia Calamitatum»*, *Rech. de Théol. Anc. et Méd.*, XLVIII (1981), pp. 218-224, but he does not take into account the possibility that Abelard himself may not be telling the whole truth about his past. The description in *Hist. Cal.*, II, 695-701, ed. MONFRIN, p. 83 is remarkably close to a passage found only in *TSch* II, 56 (pp. 81-82).

([31]) *TSch* II, 44-60 (pp. 77-83).

([32]) *TSch* II, 36-41 (pp. 74-75).

([33]) *TChr* IV, 83-85; *TSch* II, 119-121 (pp. 99-100).

versions by comparing the three persons of the Trinity to the three properties of a bronze seal: that of being bronze, that of being a seal and that of sealing. As a seal left its image on wax, so man was stamped in the image of God([34]). Abelard used the seal, symbol of the authority and good faith of any medieval lord, to illuminate not just the nature of the Trinity, but the relationship of trust and fidelity which joined man to God. The three persons of the Trinity were not separate transcendent entities, but three properties which man could discern within God's undivided nature by using his powers of reason.

To conclude this brief study, we can summarise Abelard's thought about man's knowledge of God thus: man gained such knowledge through his perception of God's self-revelation in the world. Man could understand the Trinity by observing the power, the wisdom and above all the goodness which ordered creation. The paradoxical co-existence of three persons in one God was not foreign to human reason if man looked at philosophical analogies drawn from the material world. At the same time man could never define God's transcendent nature, as this lay beyond the level of human comprehension. Man's knowledge of God concerned his action in the world. Bernard of Clairvaux thought that Abelard was claiming to understand rationally mysteries beyond the realm of reason. In fact Abelard was saying that the three persons of the Trinity were only names to describe properties of a supreme good ultimately beyond definition. Man had to be content with the evidence with which he was confronted in the world in order to construct his perception of God and so understand the principles which ordered his universe.

([34]) *TSch* II, 112-147 (pp. 97-103).

IV

THE LISTS OF HERESIES
IMPUTED TO PETER ABELARD

Despite the existence of at least forty-five manuscripts which list heretical *capitula* imputed to Peter Abelard, none appears to represent an official record of the council of Sens, held on 2 June 1140. Two lists have, from time to time, been identified with an official list, one of fourteen, known as the *Capitula Haeresum XIV*, the other of nineteen, most frequently found at the end of Bernard's epistolary treatise on the errors of Abelard, *Epist.* 190. Mabillon's hypothesis in favour of the *Capitula Haeresum XIV* has, since the important study of Meyer in 1896, been generally discarded, while attention has focussed on the list of nineteen *capitula* and on Bernard's role in their compilation. [1] Abelard defended himself against this list of nineteen *capitula* in his *Confessio fidei* ' *Universis* ' and in a more detailed manner in his *Apologia*. [2] The most recent editor of the list of nineteen *capitula*, J. Leclercq, has argued that the list was not the work of Bernard of Clairvaux, but rather of the council of Sens itself. [3] The intention of this study is to look again at all the manuscripts of these *capitula*, which vary considerably in number, wording and sequence, in order to establish the interrelationship between the various lists, who compiled the *Capitula Haeresum XIV* and the list of nineteen *capitula* and how these various lists entered into the corpus of

---

1. The *Capitula Haeresum XIV* were edited by Mabillon in 1667 (reprinted in *PL* 182, 1047-54), by E.M. BUYTAERT, Corpus Christianorum. Cont. Med. XII (Turnhout, 1969), pp. 455-80, and again by N.M. HÄRING, *Die Vierzehn Capitula Haeresum Petri Abaelardi*, in *Cîteaux*, xxxi (1980), 35-52. W. MEYER rejected this as the official list in *Die Anklagesätze des hl. Bernhard gegen Abaelard*, in *Nachrichtungen der kgl. Gesellschaft der Wissenschaften zu Göttingen, Phil.-hist. Klasse* (1896), Heft 4, pp. 397-468. The other major studies are by J. RIVIÈRE, *Les 'capitula' d'Abélard condamnés au concile de Sens*, in *Recherches de théologie anc. et méd.*, v (1933), 5-22 ; L. GRILL, *Die neunzehn 'Capitula' Bernhards von Clairvaux gegen Abälard*, in *Historisches Jahrbuch*, lxxx (1961), 230-9 ; J. LECLERCQ, *Les formes successives de la lettre-traité de Saint Bernard contre Abélard*, in *Revue bénédictine*, lxxviii (1968), 87-105, henceforth cited as *Formes*. The edition on p. 103-4 of the article was reprinted with slightly different sigla in *S. Bernardi Opera*, viii (Rome 1977), pp. 39-40.
2. *Confessio fidei* '*Universis*', *PL* 178, 105-8 ; *Apologia contra Bernardum* ed. E.M. BUYTAERT, CCCM XI (Turnhout, 1969), pp. 359-68.
3. *Formes*, 105.

Bernard's correspondence. A new critical edition of the nineteen *capitula* is attached in order that the sources behind the list as well as the variations within their manuscript tradition can be seen at a glance.

*
* *

THE MANUSCRIPTS

J. Leclercq's list of twenty-nine manuscripts of the nineteen *capitula* can be supplemented by others, some of which throw important light on the text of the *capitula*. These include manuscripts of Abelard's *Confessio fidei 'Universis'*, in which the *capitula* occur as rubrics to the work (OP^1P^4Q below) and one which contains an earlier recension of the nineteen *capitula* (*Du* below). Other manuscripts ignored by Leclercq (P^2P^8R below) are less important, but still deserve to be included within a critical edition.

For the sake of consistency, the sigla used here will be those adopted by Leclercq within *S. Bernardi Opera*, while new sigla will be added to denote those MSS which he did not use (*Du OP¹ P²P⁴P⁸QR*). [4] As his descriptions of MSS can in part be corrected or completed (as for $ApCDD^1DuF^1GJLM^2NP^6P^7W^2Y$), brief details of all the known MSS will be given, including the date, the provenance or earliest known owner (where known), as well as which *capitula*, that may be specially marked in some way. The sequence of *capitula* is also given where it differs from that of the edition given at the end of this study, a sequence slightly different from that of Leclercq. The sigla used by Leclercq in his earlier edition, published within the *Revue bénédictine*, lxxviii (1968), 100-105, are given in square brackets, where they differ, as are the sigla used by Monfrin for those MSS described within his edition of the *Historia Calamitatum* ($OP^2P^4P^8$). [5] Reference is also given, where possible, to the most detailed description of each manuscript, most frequently to that within H. Rochais and E. Manning, *Bibliographie Générale de l'Ordre Cistercien : Saint Bernard, La Documen-*

---

4. *S. Bernardi Opera*, viii (Rome, 1977), pp. xi-xiii.
5. J. Monfrin, *Abélard. Historia Calamitatum* (Paris, 1959), pp. 18-19, 23-28.

tation Cistercienne, vol. xxi (Rochefort 1979-83), referred to as
Rochais-Manning. Unless otherwise specified the list always
occurs at the close of Bernard's *Epist.* 190 within collections of
Bernard's correspondence.

A [*A*^{1}] : Douai, *Bibliothèque municipale* 372, t. II, fos. 67^v-
68. — 1162/65 a.d. ; Anchin (OSB), dioc. Arras. *Cap.* 1, 2, 4,
14 marked. Rochais-Manning, no. 3660 ; Leclercq, *La plus
ancienne collection d'œuvres complètes de Saint Bernard*, in *Études
sur S. Bernard et le texte de ses écrits*, *Analecta Sacri Ordinis
Cisterciensis*, ix (1953), 124-33.

A^1 [*A*] : Douai, *Bibliothèque municipale* 372, t. I, fo. 153. —
1162/65 a.d. ; Anchin (OSB), dioc. Arras. *Cap.* 1, 2, 14 marked ;
cap. 8 missing. Rochais-Manning, no. 3659 ; Leclercq, *art. cit.*

Ap : Munich, *Bayerische Staatsbibliothek*, Clm 28363, fos.
132^v-133. — s. xii ; French origin. The *capitula* are quoted by
Abelard at the beginning of his *Apologia* (fos. 132^v-135^v), unfortunately incomplete through the loss of a gathering. Detailed
descriptions by P. Ruf, *Ein neuaufgefundenes Bruchstück der
Apologia Abaelards*, in *Sitzungsberichte der Bayerischen Akademie
der Wissenschaften*, *Phil.-hist. Abt.* (1930), Heft 5, p. 3-9 ; E.M.
Buytaert, *Petri Abaelardi Apologia contra Bernardum*, Corpus
Christianorum. Cont. Med. XII (Turnhout 1969), p. 343-5 ;
D.E. Luscombe, *Peter Abelard's Ethics* (Oxford 1971), p. xliv-
xlv.

Bt [*S*] : St-Omer, *Bibliothèque municipale* 137, fo. 142^v. —
s. xii ; Clairmarais (O. Cist., Clairvaux), dioc. Thérouanne.
Rochais-Manning, no. 4588.

C : Dijon, *Bibliothèque municipale* 191, fo. 66. — s. xiii ;
Cîteaux, dioc. Chalon-sur-Saône. Missing introduction ; placed
after *Epist.* 191. Rochais-Manning, no. 3645 (in which it is
mistakenly placed after *Epist.* 190).

Cs [*K*] : Munich, *Bayerische Staatsbibliothek*, Clm 28195,
fo. 96^v. — s. xii/xiii ; Kaisheim (O. Cist., Morimond), dioc.
Augsburg. Introduction replaced by *He sunt hereses petri abailardi* ; no conclusion ; *cap.* 14 after *cap.* 19 ; occurs after *Epist.*
510. Rochais-Manning, no. 4183.

D : Bruges, *Archief Groot Seminarie* 22-41, fo. 121. — s. xii ;
Dunes (O. Cist., Clairvaux), dioc. Thérouanne. Rochais-
Manning, no. 3450 [*cap.* 1-4, 12, 14 *not* marked as claimed by
Leclercq].

D^1 : Bruges, *Archief Groot Seminarie* 23-48, fo. 106-106^v. —
s. xiv ; Dunes (O. Cist., Clairvaux), dioc. Thérouanne. *Cap.*
1-19 marked. Rochais-Manning, no. 3451.

Du : Durham, *Cathedral Library* B. III. 7, fo. 364^v. — s.
xiii^{ex} ; English provenance (?). Earlier recension of *capitula*,
vid. infra. Described briefly by T. Rud, *Codicum MSS Ecclesiae
Cathedralis Dunelmensis Catalogus* (Durham 1825), p.
150-1 and J. Leclercq, *Notes abélardiennes*, in *Bulletin de philosophie
médiévale*, xiii (1971), 69.

E : Boulogne-sur-Mer, *Bibliothèque municipale* 76, fos. 39^v-
40. — 1174 a.d. ; Mont-Saint-Éloi (canons reg.), dioc. Arras.
Cap. 1, 2, 14 marked. Rochais-Manning, no. 3439.

F^1 : Wolfenbüttel, *Bibliotheca Augusta* 4613, fo. 159-159^v. —
s. xiii ; French origin. *Cap.* 1, 2, 4, 14 marked (not 2, 3, 5, 15
as described by Leclercq and Rochais-Manning) ; *cap.* 11 missing.
Rochais-Manning, no. 4862.

G : The Hague, *Koninklijke Bibliotheek* 70. H. 7, fos. 9^v-10.
— s. xii ; Clairmarais (O. Cist., Clairvaux), dioc. Thérouanne
(erased inscription of Clairmarais visible under ultra-violet light
on fo. 14^v). *Cap.* 1, 2, 4, 14 marked. Rochais-Manning,
no. 3875.

I^2 [*I*] : Cambrai, *Bibliothèque municipale* 252, fo. 184. —
s. xiii ; Saint-Aubert (OSB), dioc. Cambrai. *Cap.* 1, 2, 4, 14
marked ; *cap.* 8 missing. Rochais-Manning, no. 3521.

I^3 [*I*^{1}] : Cambrai, *Bibliothèque municipale* 537, fo. 34. —
s. xiii ; Saint-Aubert (OSB), dioc. Cambrai. *Cap.* 1, 2, 4, 14
marked. Rochais-Manning, no. 3527.

J : Vienna, *Schottenstift* 28, fos. 158^v-159. — 1448 a.d. ;
Schottenstift (OSB), dioc. Passau. *Cap.* 1-19 marked ; *cap.* 8
after cap. 17. Rochais-Manning, no. 4838.

K^1 [*Z*] : Copenhagen, *Det kongelige Bibliotek*, Ny. Kgl. Sml.
119.4^o, fo. 171. — 1478 a.d. ; S. Maria, Bordesholm (canons reg.),
dioc. Bremen. *Cap.* 8 after *cap.* 17. Rochais-Manning, no. 3612.

L : Lilienfeld, *Stiftsbibliothek* 55, fo. 66^v. — s. xiii/xiv ;
Klein Mariazell (OSB), dioc. Passau. *Cap.* 1-19 marked ; *cap.* 8
after *cap.* 17. Rochais-Manning, no. 3942.

L^1 [*B*] : London, *British Library*, Add. 6047, fo. 122. —
s. xv ; Biburg (OSB), dioc. Bamberg. *Cap.* 1-19 marked ; *cap.*
8 after *cap.* 17. Rochais-Manning, no. 3964.

M^2 [*M*] : Douai, *Bibliothèque municipale* 374, fo. 60. — s. xii ;
Marchiennes (OSB), dioc. Cambrai. *Cap.* 1, 2, 14 marked ;
cap. 8 missing. Rochais-Manning, no. 3662 [description slightly
faulty : contents should read *Epist.* 189, 188 (not 337), 190 +
cap.].

N : Munich, *Bayerische Staatsbibliothek*, Clm 727, fo. 113. — 1445 a.d. *Cap.* 8 after *cap.* 17. Rochais-Manning, no. 4120.

O [*Y*] : Oxford, *Bodleian Library*, Add. C. 271, fo. 84ᵛ. — s. xiv ; at Cambrai in 1471. The text occurs in the form of rubrics to the *Confessio fidei 'Universis'*, although without the introduction, conclusion and *cap.* 3 and 16. J. Monfrin, *Abélard. Historia Calamitatum* (Paris 1959), p. 23-25.

P¹ : Paris, *Bibliothèque nationale*, lat. 1896, fos. 192ᵛ. — s. xiv. The text occurs in the form of rubrics to the *Confessio fidei 'Universis'* as in *O* above. R.M. Thomson, *The Satirical Works of Berengar of Poitiers*, in *Medieval Studies*, xlii (1980), 107.

P² [*E*] : Paris, *Bibliothèque nationale*, lat. 2545, fo. 56. — s. xv/xvi ; probably belonged to F. d'Amboise. Missing introduction ; the list occurs after *Epist.* 191 and immediately before Abelard's *Confessio fidei 'Universis'* in a paper manuscript containing letters of and relating to Abelard and Heloise. Monfrin, *Abélard, Historia Calamitatum*, p. 27-28.

P⁴ [*A*] : Paris, *Bibliothèque nationale*, lat. 2923, fo. 49-49ᵛ. — s. xiii ; belonged to Petrarch in 1337. The *capitula* occur as rubrics to the *Confessio fidei 'Universis'* with the same omissions as in *O*. Monfrin, *Abélard. Historia Calamitatum*, p. 18-19.

P⁶ [*P*] : Paris, *Bibliothèque nationale*, lat. 15139, fo. 304. — s. xii ; Saint-Victor, Paris. *Cap.* 3 and 8 missing. The list occurs after an abbreviated version of *Epist.* 190 and is introduced by the concluding phrase, transferred to the beginning of the list. Not in Rochais-Manning ; W. Meyer, *Die Anklagesätze*, p. 431-3.

P⁷ : Paris, *Bibliothèque nationale*, lat. 15698, fo. 36. — s. xiv ; Sorbonne, Paris. The *capitula* occur after *Epist.* 191 without the introduction. Rochais-Manning, no. 4377.

P⁸ [*C*] : Paris, *Bibliothèque nationale*, nouv. acq. lat. 1873, fos. 210ᵛ-211. — s. xv/xvi. The same combination of texts as in *P²* ; similarly without introduction. Monfrin, *Abélard. Historia Calamitatum*, p. 25-27.

Q : Paris, *Bibliothèque nationale*, lat. 14193, fo. 7-7ᵛ. — s. xii ; Saint-Germain-des-Prés (OSB), Paris. The *capitula* occur as rubrics to the *Confessio fidei 'Universis'*, although with a certain degree of modification. Missing introduction, conclusion and *cap.* 3, 16 and 19. L. Van Acker, *Petri Pictoris Carmina*, Corpus Christianorum. Cont. Med. XXV (Turnhout 1972), p. clxi, 48.

R : Prague, *Národní Muzeum* XIII. C. 5, fo. 205ᵛ. — 1470 a.d. *Cap.* 8 after *cap.* 17. Rochais-Manning, no. 4436.

S^1 : St-Omer, *Bibliothèque municipale* 146, fo. 128^v. — s. xii ; Saint-Bertin (OSB), dioc. St. Omer. Rochais-Manning, no. 4593.

Sc [*H*] : Heiligenkreuz, *Stiftsbibliothek* 226, fo. 93-93^v. — s. xiii ; Heiligenkreuz (O. Cist., Morimond), dioc. Passau. *Cap.* 1-19 marked ; *cap.* 8 after *cap.* 17. Rochais-Manning, no. 3819.

T^1 [*T*] : Brussels, *Bibliothèque royale* II.1167, fos. 46^v-47^v. — s. xii [not s. xiii as stated by Leclercq, *Les formes*, 89] ; Saint-Martin (OSB), dioc. Tournai. *Cap.* 1, 2, 4, 14 marked ; *cap.* 8 added to margin of text after *cap.* 7. Not in Rochais-Manning ; A. Boutemy, *A propos d'anthologies poétiques au XIIe siècle*, in *Revue belge de philologie et d'histoire*, xix (1940), 229-33.

V^1 [*V*] : Valenciennes, *Bibliothèque municipale* 40, fo. 121^v. — s. xii ; Saint-Amand (OSB), dioc. Tournai. *Cap.* 1, 2, 4, 14 marked ; *cap.* 8 added below main column of text after *cap.* 17. Rochais-Manning, no. 4794.

W : Munich, *Bayerische Staatsbibliothek*, Clm 22271, fo. 97^v. — s. xii ; Windberg (O. Prem.), dioc. Regensburg. Introduction replaced by *He sunt hereses petri abailardi* ; no conclusion. Occurs after *Epist.* 510. Rochais-Manning, no. 4177.

W^2 [W^1] : Munich, *Bayerische Staatsbibliothek*, Clm 22299, fos. 47-48^v. — s. xii ; Windberg (O. Prem.), dioc. Regensburg. *Cap.* 1-19 marked ; *cap.* 8 after *cap.* 17. Rochais-Manning, no. 4180.

X : Munich, *Bayerische Staatsbibliothek*, Clm 6290, fo. 121. — s. xiii^{in} ; Freising Cathedral (sec. canons). *Cap.* 1-5, 14 marked ; *cap.* 8 after *cap.* 17. Rochais-Manning, no. 4136.

Y : Vienna, *Nationalbibliothek*, cvp 998, fo. 173-173^v. — s. xii^{ex} ; Göttweig (OSB), dioc. Passau. Introduction replaced by *He sunt hereses petri baylardi pauce de multis* ; no conclusion ; *cap.* 3 missing [not *cap.* 14 as stated by Leclercq, *Les formes*, 102]. Occurs after miscellaneous theological notes. Not in Rochais-Manning ; W. Meyer, *Die Anklagesätze*, 134.

DURHAM, CATHEDRAL LIBRARY, B.III.7, FO. 364^v (s. xiii^{ex})

Because *Du* is the only known manuscript to contain a recension of the nineteen *capitula* quite different from that found in the manuscripts cited above, and has not been used in previous editions, *Du* will be described here in more detail. Leclercq noted the list in a very brief description in the *Bulletin de philosophie médiévale*, xiii (1971), 69, but cited both the shelfmark and the contents of *Du* inaccurately.

This large parchment manuscript (ii + 369 fos. ; 355 × 200 mm) has been in the possession of Durham Cathedral since the mid-fourteenth century, when it was given by Robert de Hexham, *hostillarius* to their library in the period when J. Fossor was prior (1342-74). [6] *Du*, written in a single hand, is made up of two parts :

(i) fos. 1-297   *Excerptiones Euipii de libris Augustini*
     fos. 297-309ᵛ   miscellaneous *sententiae* and sermons
     fos. 310ᵛ-311   Gregory Nazianzene, *In apologetico de sacerdotibus*
     (fos. 310, 311ᵛ-312ᵛ blank)

(ii) fos. 312-348ᵛ   Augustine, *Retractationes*
     fos. 348ᵛ-364   Augustine, *De haeresibus ad Quodvultdeum*
     fos. 364-364ᵛ   extract from Guibert de Nogent, *De Vita sua*, III, 17 [7]
     fo. 364ᵛ   *Errores petri abailardi*
     fos. 364ᵛ-365ᵛ   Geoffrey of Auxerre, *Errores gisleberti pictavensis* [8]
     fos. 365ᵛ-369   Index to the works of Augustine

The copyist of *Du* appears to have been working from a copy of Augustine's *De haeresibus*, to which notes had been added on the heresies of a Manichaean sect, described by Guibert of Nogent, of Abelard and of Gilbert of Poitiers, perhaps in the twelfth century.

The extract from Guibert's *De Vita sua*, titled in *Du* as *De haereticis qui gallica lingua dicuntur telier vel deimart* is important because it constitutes an early witness to the text of Guibert's autobiography. The complete text of the *De Vita sua* survives in only one seventeenth century transcription, now PARIS, *Bibliothèque nationale*, Baluze 42, fos. 30-107. This transcript, used by d'Achery for his edition of the work in 1651, was itself copied from a manuscript of the cathedral of Laon which contained many works

---

6. RUD, *Codicum ... Catalogus*, p. 151.

7. *Haeresis ea est ... amplectuntur*, ed. R. LABANDE (Paris, 1981), pp. 428-30.

8. HÄRING, *Das sogenannte Glaubensbekenntnis des Reimser Konsistoriums von 1148*, in *Scholastik*, xl (1965), 55-90 [edition, 86-90] ; *The Writings against Gilbert of Poitiers by Geoffrey of Auxerre*, in *Analecta Cisterciensia*, xxii (1966), 3-83 [edition, 31-35] ; *Texts concerning Gilbert of Poitiers*, in *AHDLMA*, xxxvii (1970), 169-203, partial edition 174-6.

relating to the history of the town in the early twelfth century. [9] d'Achery believed this to have been Guibert's autograph. [10] The extract in *Du* agrees so faithfully with the Baluze transcript, even to sharing a common reading *pennalibus* which the scribe of *Du* explained in the margin as *id est cellerariis* and which d'Achery changed to *penetralibus*, that the original excerptor of *Du* may have copied his text from the same Laon manuscript. [11]

The list of errors of Gilbert of Poitiers, followed by the patristic quotations which refuted his doctrine, the creed agreed at Rheims in 1148 and the list of those present at the council make up the *scriptura* compiled by Geoffrey of Auxerre as a record of the council. The *scriptura* is found in exactly this form in the FLORENCE MS, *Med. Laurenziana*, Conv. soppr. 193, fo. 133-133ᵛ (s. xii) and, with slightly different rubrics, OXFORD, *Bodleian*, lat. Misc. d. 74, fo. 98ᵛ, and OXFORD, *Corpus Christi College* 137, fo. 99ᵛ (both s. xii). [12]

The *Errores petri abailardi*, sandwiched between these two texts on fo. 364ᵛ are of particular interest because although they number nineteen, their sequence is different from that of the list transmitted with Bernard's *Epist.* 190. They do not have *cap.* 3, but include one *capitulum* found otherwise only in the *Capitula Haeresum XIV*. Their sequence is : 1, 2, 7, 4-6, 8-12, *Quod corpus Domini non cadat in terram*, 13-19. The wording of certain *capitula* is also different from that of the established list.

EDITIONS OF THE NINETEEN CAPITULA

In 1616 F. d'Amboise included an edition of seventeen *capitula* from an unspecified manuscript within his *praefatio apologetica*, which replaced Duchesne's introduction, published earlier that year. [13] Although no extant manuscript corresponds exactly to

---

9. Baluze 42, fo. 28 : *ex codice MS ecclesiae Laudunensis*, with a list of its contents, all edited by d'Achery, *PL* 156, 837-1018. See also F. DOLBEAU, *Deux nouveaux manuscrits des 'Mémoires' de Guibert de Nogent*, in *Sacris Erudiri*, xxvi (1983), p. 155-76.
10. *PL* 156, 15AB.
11. Baluze 42, fo. 102ᵛ ; ed. d'Achery, *PL* 156, 951C.
12. HÄRING, *Texts concerning Gilbert of Poitiers*, 176.
13. *Petri Abaelardi ... Opera* (Paris, 1616), fos. b iiᵛ-iii, reprinted *PL* 178, 79-80.

the text of d'Amboise, his edition contains all the errors which are found in two late fifteenth or early sixteenth century MSS, P^2 and P^8, amplified by further errors of transcription and the omission of *cap.* 3 and 15. As d'Amboise owned P^2 (the MS E in Monfrin's account), it seems likely that this was his source. [14] Du Boulay produced in 1665 an almost identical text, reproducing all the erroneous readings of d'Amboise as well as of P^2, but including the two *capitula* which d'Amboise had omitted. [15]

The first attempt to provide a critical edition was that of W. Meyer, who argued that there were originally only eighteen *capitula.* [16] He based his argument on the evidence of the *Confessio fidei 'Universis'*, the text of d'Amboise and the MSS P^6 and Y, making use as well of WW^2V^1, although these included *cap.* 3 about the world soul. Meyer's hypothesis was refuted by J. Rivière who made use of a previously unknown fragment of Abelard's *Apologia*, in which Abelard quoted nineteen *capitula.* [17] In presenting an edition of the *capitula* he did not use any MSS of the list as associated with Bernard's correspondence, even though the sequence in the *Apologia* was slightly different. In 1961 L. Grill produced another edition of the list from a single manuscript (*Sc*), without reference to the study of Rivière. [18]

J. Leclercq published a further edition of the nineteen *capitula* in 1968, using some twenty-nine MSS of the list as found within Bernard's correspondence, but did not follow the example of Meyer or Rivière in using the *Confessio fidei 'Universis'* or *Apologia* as a guide to establishing his text. [19] This edition was reprinted without modification, apart from new sigla, within his edition of Bernard's complete works. [20]

---

14. J. MONFRIN, *Abélard. Historia Calamitatum* (Paris, 1959), pp. 27-8, 39-40.

15. *Historia Universitatis Parisiensis*, ii (Paris, 1665), p. 68. This edition was reprinted by DUPLESSIS D'ARGENTRÉ, *Collectio judiciorum ...* Paris, 1728), i, 21 and MANSI, *Sacrorum Conciliorum collectio ...*, xxi (Venice, 1776), 568-70.

16. MEYER, *Die Anklagesätze*, 431-7.

17. RIVIÈRE, *Les 'capitula' d'Abélard condamnés au concile de Sens*, in *RTAM*, v (1933), 5-22.

18. GRILL, *Die neunzehn 'Capitula' Bernhards von Clairvaux gegen Abälard*, in *Historisches Jahrbuch*, lxxx (1961), 230-9.

19. *Formes*, 100-105.

20. *S. Bernardi Opera*, viii (Rome, 1977), pp. 39-40.

THE LIST OF WILLIAM OF ST-THIERRY
AND THE CAPITULA HAERESUM XIV

Two other lists which have been neglected by previous editors of the *capitula* (with the exception of Meyer) are those drawn up by William of St-Thierry in his letter to Bernard of Clairvaux, and by the author of the *Capitula Haeresum XIV*. Both of these, along with that found in *Du*, shed valuable light on the formation and on the text of the nineteen *capitula*.

William of St-Thierry drew up his list from the heresies which he detected in one or other of two books, *idem paene continentes, nisi quod in altero plus, in altero minus aliquanto invenietur*. [21] One was Abelard's *Theologia 'Scholarium'*, the other, untitled, was a collection of Abelard's *sententiae*, which Abelard would later deny having written himself. He sent these two books to Bernard with the treatise he had written against Abelard's errors and his accompanying letter during Lent of 1140. [22]

The author of the *Capitula Haeresum XIV* used the same two works, but not the list of William, to formulate his own list, to which he added accompanying extracts to justify each accusation. [23] Apart from a final rubric, *Haec sunt capitula Theologiae, immo Stultilogiae Petri Abaelardi*, he refrained from making any comment beyond a carefully worded *capitulum*. [24] While William boldly asserted a little inaccurately, that Abelard taught that the Son was *quaedam potentia* and the Holy Spirit *nulla potentia*, this author, quoting some of the same excerpts as William, simply introduced them with the comment *Horrenda similitudo de sigillo aereo, de specie et genere ad Trinitatem*. The author criticised Abelard's teaching about the limitations to God's power, not mentioned by William, while he ignored opinions about faith as *aestimatio*, the Holy Spirit as the world soul and temptation of the devil through the physical world — all of which William thought were dangerously heretical.

---

21. *Epist.* 326 among the letters of Bernard, ed. LECLERCQ, *Les lettres de Guillaume de Saint-Thierry à Saint Bernard'*, in *Rev. bén.*, lxxix (1969), 377-8.
22. The date of 1140, rather than 1139, is accepted by LECLERCQ, *S. Bernardi Opera*, viii, p. 263.
23. HÄRING, *Die Vierzehn Capitula Haeresum*, 42.
24. Buytaert thought the colophon was a scribal invention, CCCM XII, p. 457, but its authenticity is supported by all the MSS but one.

While the author of the *Capitula Haeresum XIV* followed a
natural sequence for the first thirteen *capitula* (the same number
as in William's list), the first three from the *Theologia 'Scholarium'*, the following ten from the *liber sententiarum*, the fourteenth
about omnipotence belonging *proprie vel specialiter* to the Father
is out of place and seems to have been added to the list only afterwards. The charge is, however, an important one and is exactly
that treated at some length by Bernard of Clairvaux within his
Epist. 190. [25] Buytaert thought that this last *capitulum* might
have been added by Walter of Mortagne because Walter quoted
from the same passage of the *Theologia* in his letter to Abelard as
cited in *cap.* xiv. [26] Walter was quoting from a different recension
of the *Theologia*, however. The excerpt quoted with *cap.* xiv is,
on the other hand, exactly that quoted by Bernard of Clairvaux
within *Epist.* 190 — one of the very few passages of Abelard which
Bernard had not copied from William's treatise. [27] It is possible
that the author added this fourteenth *capitulum* because Bernard
had discussed it in *Epist.* 190, or alternatively Bernard was drawing
here on a later thought of the author of the *Capitulum Haeresum
XIV*. This question will be looked at in studying the relationship
of the list of nineteen *capitula* to *Epist.* 190.

AN EARLIER RECENSION OF THE LIST OF 19 CAPITULA : *Du*

The list of *capitula* in *Du*, introduced simply as *errores petri
abailardi*, contains all the *capitula* mentioned by Abelard in his
Apologia apart from *cap.* 3 about the world soul, while it also has a
capitulum about the eucharist identical (apart from the reading
cadat for *cadit*) to *cap.* ix of the *Capitula Haeresum XIV*. The
capitulum about God's inability to do other than he did is in third
place, as in the *Capitula Haeresum XIV*, rather than in seventh
place as in the traditional list of nineteen. The *capitula* which

---

25. *Epist.* 190, 5-8 (p. 21-24).
26. Buytaert, CCCM XII, pp. 466-7. Walter of Mortagne quoted *TSch Z* 57
in his *Epist. ad Abaelardum*, ed. Ostlender, *Florilegium Patristicum*, xix
(Bonn, 1929), p. 32.
27. *Epist.* 190, 5 (p. 22) quoting *TSch* I, 50 (*PL* 178, 993D), not *TSch* II,
116 as incorrectly cited by Leclercq on p. 22. [References to the *Theologia
'Scholarium'* are to a forthcoming edition being completed from Buytaert's
papers by the author.]

84

are not parallel to those in the *Capitula Haeresum XIV* correspond in part to those mentioned by William of St-Thierry, while were all (apart from one) mentioned by Bernard of Clairvaux within *Epist.* 190 or *Epist.* 188 to the bishops and cardinals of the Curia.[28] *Du* thus appears to have been compiled by extending and modifying the list of the *Capitula Haeresum XIV* with the *capitula* formulated by William of St-Thierry and Bernard of Clairvaux, which was subsequently revised to take the form of *capitula* as quoted within Abelard's *Apologia*. A list of the apparent sources of each *capitulum* of *Du* may be given to make this clear :

Numbering as in established list		*Cap. Haer. XIV*	*William*	*Bernard* (*Epist.*)
1	Q. Pater ... nulla potentia	cf. i	= iii	190
2	Q. Spiritus ... substantia Patris	= ii	cf. iv	190
7	Q. ea solummodo ... non alio	= iii		
4	Q. Christus ... liberaret	= iv	cf. vii	190
5	Q. neque Deus ... trinitate	= v	cf. viii	188
6	Q. liberum arbitrium ... bonum	cf. vi	cf. vi	
8	Q. Deus nec debeat ... impedire	= vii		
9	Q. non contraximus ... tantum	= viii	cf. xi	188
10	Q. non peccaverunt ... ignorantiam	= xi		188
11	Q. non fuerit ... Domini			190
12	Q. potestas ligandi ... eorum	cf. xii		188
	Q. corpus Domini ... terram	= ix	cf. ix	188, 190
13	Q. nec peior ... homo	= x		
14	Q. ad Patrem ... benignitas	= xiv		190
15	Q. etiam castus timor ... vita			190
16	Q. diabolus ... lapidum		cf. x	190
17	Q. adventus in fine ... Patri			
18	Q. anima Christi ... tantum			188
19	Q. neque opus ... exstingui	cf. xiii	cf. xii/xiii	188

As is evident, *Du* is far more influenced by the *Capitula Haeresum XIV* than by the list of William, all of whose *capitula*, apart from his third about the Son and the Holy Spirit, were either modified or rejected completely. The order followed in *Du* was essentially that of the *Capitula Haeresum XIV*, with the single modification that *cap.* ix and x were placed after *cap.* xii, perhaps in order to bring together *cap.* viii and xi, which were both about sin and guilt. *Cap.* xiii was transferred to the end of the list, as in that of William. Between *cap.* x and xiii were added five *capitula*, one of which may have been added to the *Capitula Haeresum XIV* only afterwards, *cap.* xiv. This and three of the four other *capitula* were mentioned

---

28. *Epist.* 190, 10 (p. 25-26), *Epist.* 188, 2 (p. 11).

by Bernard of Clairvaux, either in *Epist.* 190 or in *Epist.* 188. [29]
The one *capitulum* of William retained in *Du*, and not found in the
Capitula Haeresum XIV was the one about the Son as *quaedam
potentia* and the Holy Spirit as *nulla potentia*, which Bernard
emphasised at length within *Epist.* 190.

Du supports certain readings found within the text of the *capitula* as quoted by Abelard within his *Apologia*, but not in MSS
of the list as associated with Bernard's correspondence. One of
the most significant is *cap.* 2, that the Holy Spirit was not *de substantia Patris*. This agrees with the wording of *cap.* ii in the
Capitula Haeresum XIV, but not with that of William of St-
Thierry, who accused Abelard of teaching that the Holy Spirit was
non ex substantia Patris et Filii, sicut Filius est ex substantia Patris.
In the *Apologia*, Abelard stated twice that he was accused of saying
that the Holy Spirit was not *de substantia Patris*, as he also mentioned in the *Confessio fidei 'Universis'*. [30] The addition of *et
Filii* to *de substantia Patris* seems to have been an interpolation
made after Abelard had seen the list, but before it was copied and
circulated with Bernard's correspondence. Again, this may have
been to make the wording of this *capitulum* accord more closely
with what Bernard said within his *Epist.* 190.

Another example where a reading is shared by *Du* and *Ap* is
in *cap.* xiv, *Quod ad Patrem, quia ab alio non est...*, which appears
to be the correct reading, also found in the rubrics to the *Confessio
fidei 'Universis'* in *OP*[4] and in two MSS of the list also containing
Bernard's correspondence, *CsW*. The word *quia* has been corrupted
to *qui* in all other MSS of the list of the nineteen *capitula*.

Given that *Du* is a late thirteenth century manuscript, certain
errors may have crept into its text, but some differences between
Du and the established list suggest that the wording of *Du* may
represent an earlier recension. The wording of *cap.* xii seems to
have been changed from *solis apostolis concessa* to *apostolis tantum
data*. In *Ap*, *OP*[4] and *Y*, this *capitulum* ends *et non successoribus
eorum* rather than with *non etiam successoribus eorum* as in *Du* and

---

29. *Cap.* 15, 16, 18.
30. *Apologia*, 2 and 16, ed. BUYTAERT, p. 359 and 366. *Confessio fidei* ii,
ed. C.H. BURNETT, *Peter Abelard, Confessio fidei 'Universis' : a critical edition
with translation, of Abelard's reply to accusations of heresy*, to appear in *Studi
Medievali*, xxxvi (1985).

all other MSS of the list. Given that the reading of *Du* is maintained in later copies, Abelard may have himself introduced this variant in *Ap*, in turn influencing *OP*[4] and *Y*. The most significant change made to *Du* was the addition of *cap.* 3 about the world soul, a claim made by both William and Bernard, but not by the author of the *Capitula Haeresum XIV*. *Cap.* 7, that God could not do other than he did was transferred to seventh place, immediately before a similar *capitulum* (*cap.* 8) that God could not prevent evil, so providing greater thematic unity. The *capitulum* about the eucharist, apparently taken from the *Capitula Haeresum XIV*, was taken out, perhaps because it was quite different from that about the eucharist made by William of St-Thierry and by Bernard within his *Epist.* 190. [31]

ABELARD'S APOLOGIA AND CONFESSIO FIDEI 'UNIVERSIS'

These two works are important witnesses to the text of the nineteen *capitula* in that they are independent of the textual tradition of the list as contained within Bernard's correspondence. The *Confessio fidei 'Universis'* is less useful than the *Apologia* in that Abelard does not quote the *capitula* with exactly the same precision as in the latter work, but still provides an indication of the sequence and phrasing of certain *capitula*. Abelard did not mention *cap.* 3 about the world soul or *cap.* 16 about the working of the devil, but as he did mention both in the *Apologia*, he seems to have not deemed them worthy of mention in the *Confessio*. *Cap.* 3 does seem to have been added after *Du* had been drawn up, although it is difficult to say whether it had been appended to *cap.* 2 as *immo anima mundi*, as Abelard reported in the *Apologia*, or whether Abelard was himself paraphrasing here. [32]

One other variation between the *Confessio* and *Apologia* on the one hand, and all other MSS of the list, including *Du* on the other, is the separation of *cap.* 12 into two component parts about the

---

31. Bernard, *Epist.* 190, 10 (pp. 25-26), like William, ix (*PL* 180, 280-281A) ; cf. *Cap. Haer. XIV, cap.* ix.

32. Abelard quoted the same charge later in the *Apologia*, 16 (p. 366) without *immo anima mundi*, suggesting that he was paraphrasing first.

guilt of those who crucified Christ in ignorance and about sinning through ignorance in general. As the two ideas are combined in both the *Capitula Haeresum XIV* and *Du*, as well as in other MSS, the division in the *Apologia*, may have been made either by Abelard or a copyist through the simple omission of an *et*. All MSS of the *Confessio* place his response to the second part of *cap.* 12, *Multa quoque per ignorantiam facta...*, between his answers to *cap.* 7 and 8. This may have been a marginal addition in the original exemplar of the *Confessio*, incorrectly copied into the common archetype of all its known MSS. [33]

THE RUBRICS TO THE CONFESSIO IN OP^1P^4Q

Four MSS of the *Confessio fidei* '*Universis*' contain rubrics which correspond to the *capitula* under discussion : Q (PARIS, *Bibliothèque nationale*, lat. 14193, fo. 7-7ᵛ), in which the rubrics often depart quite significantly from the established text, and OP^1P^4 (OXFORD, *Bodleian Library*, Add. C. 271, fo. 84ᵛ ; PARIS, *Bibliothèque nationale*, lat. 1896, fos. 192ᵛ, and lat. 2923, fo. 49-49ᵛ), which contain a more accurate text. All four omit *cap.* 3 and 16, not mentioned by Abelard in the *Confessio*, while Q omits *cap.* 19, implicitly quoted within the *Confessio*, as well.

The presence of the rubrics in Q is significant because Q contains the best extant text of the *Confessio*, with very few faults. [34] The rubrics corresponding to *cap.* 1, 6, 9, 11 and 13 are sufficiently close in wording to the *capitula* that they must have been taken from such a list, while other rubrics tend to paraphrase individual *capitula*. Each begins with *Contra quod...* apart from the first, which begins *Contra primum capitulum quod tale est: Quod ...* . The second rubric conveys the sense of the second charge in *Du*, *Ap* and the *Confessio* itself, rather than of all other MSS of the list : *quod Filius solus sit ex substantia Patris*. This would suggest that the rubrics were taken from a list older than that which circulated with Bernard's correspondence, which has the addition *aut Filii*.

---

33. BURNETT, *Peter Abelard, Confessio fidei 'Universis'.*
34. *Ibid.*

The use of *ex* rather than *de* in *Q* echoes the wording of William of St-Thierry, although in the context *ex substantia Patris et Filii*. Abelard himself was very aware of the distinction between *ex* and *de* and could not have added such a rubric himself to the text of his *Confessio*.[35] The wording of *cap.* 5 and 9 in *Q* is also rather similar to that of William of St-Thierry, suggesting, although not proving that William might have been involved in writing out these rubrics.[36] William, abbot of Signy in the diocese of Rheims, was not far distant from Walter of Mortagne, a teacher in Laon, with whose letters the *Confessio* is associated in *Q*.[37] The rubrics in *Q* seem to have been compiled by someone familiar with the accusations against Abelard, although who felt free to formulate them in quite a loose fashion.

The rubrics given to the *Confessio* in *OP¹P⁴* follow the wording of *Q* in *cap.* 1 and 2 with only slight variation, yet then reproduce the wording of the established list very closely for all the remaining *capitula*, with the introduction *Contra id quod*... *OP¹P⁴* contain the reading *et non successoribus* in *cap.* 12, found in no manuscript apart from *Y* and *Ap*. *OP¹P⁴* also have the correct reading of *quia*, rather than *qui* in *cap.* 14 (found otherwise only in *Du*, *CsW*, *Ap* and *K¹*). The scribe of the common ancestor of *OP¹P⁴* appears to have begun by copying the rubrics of *Q* for *cap.* 1 and 2, but then, as if these were too inaccurate, proceeded to copy the remaining *capitula* from a text very like that which Abelard quoted within his *Apologia*. This scribe might conceivably have been the person responsible for collecting the small dossier of documents within which the rubricated *Confessio* occurs, made up otherwise of Berengar's *Apologia*, his letters against the bishop of Mende and against the Carthusians and Abelard's *Soliloquium*. It is tempting to suggest that this may have been Berengar himself.

---

35. *TSch O* II, 128 (OXFORD, *Balliol College* 296, fo. 39ᵛ) ; cf. H. OSTLENDER, *Die Theologia 'Scholarium' des Peter Abelard*, in *Aus der Geisteswelt des Mittelalters*, in BGPTMA, Supplementband III, 1 (1935), 276-7.

36. *Cap.* 5 in *Q: quod Christus non sit tertia persona in Trinitate*, similar to William, viii : *quod Christus Deus et homo non est tertia ...* while the established list has : *quod neque Deus et homo, neque haec persona quae Christus est, sit tertia ...* . *Cap.* 9 in *Q: quod non contraximus ab Adam culpam, sed poenam* is similar to William, xi : *quod ab Adam ... culpam, sed poenam,* while the normal list has : *quod ... ex Adam, sed poenam tantum.*

37. On Walter of Mortagne, see L. OTT, *Untersuchungen zur theologischen Briefliteratur der Frühscholastik*, in BGPTMA, xxxiv (1937), p. 126-38.

THE LIST WITHIN BERNARD'S CORRESPONDENCE : *CsWY*

Three other MSS which contain the list of nineteen *capitula* at
an early stage of transmission are *C* (MUNICH, Clm 28195, fo. 96ᵛ ;
s. XII/XIII), *W* (MUNICH, Clm 22271, fo. 97ᵛ ; s. XII) and *Y* (VIENNA,
Nationalbibliothek, cvp. 998, fo. 173-173ᵛ) from the monasteries
of Kaisheim, Windberg and Göttweig respectively. The list in all
three MSS is introduced by the phrase *He sunt hereses petri abailardi* [*Y* adds *pauce de multis*], rather than by the sentence about
certain *capitula* being marked with a special sign, as when the list
occurs at the end of *Epist.* 190. There is also no concluding sentence about the books in which the *capitula* had been found. *Y*
omits *cap.* 3, while in *Cs cap.* 14 was added only after *cap.* 19.
In none of these three MSS does the list occur alongside *Epist.*
190, but is rather associated with two other letters, *Epist.* 189
and 194, the letter of Bernard to the pope describing the council
of Sens and the pope's reply. In *CsW* the list is separated from
these two letters by *Epist.* 510 to the archbishop of Trier, while in
Y it occurs immediately before *Epist.* 189 and 194 after some theological notes.

As noted above, *CsW* contain the correct reading of *quia* in
cap. 14, while *Y* agrees with *Ap* and *OP⁴* in *cap.* 12 and shares the
variant *sive* with *Ap* in *cap.* 16. *Y* and *W* in particular both contain a very good text of the *capitula* with few errors. *Y* adds
aut Filii [*CsW* adds *et Filii*] to *de substantia Patris* in *cap.* 2, so
represents a stage later than the text of *Ap* and *OP⁴Q*, which do
not contain this addition.

MSS OF THE LIST ASSOCIATED WITH EPIST. 190

This group of MSS, by far the largest, is characterised by the
presence of the list at the end of Bernard's *Epist.* 190, introduced
by the sentence *Ad capitula tantummodo illa respondimus quae
signo tali ✳ notata sunt.* This sentence refers to the mark placed
against *cap.* 1, 2, 4 and 14 in the best MSS. The list concludes with
a sentence about the books from which the *capitula* were drawn,
as quoted by Abelard within his *Confessio* and *Apologia.* All

90

MSS of this group, like Y, have the variant *qui* for *quia* in *cap.* 14 and have the addition *aut Filii* to *cap.* 2.

Within this group three basic sub-groups can be distinguished. One, which can be denoted as α, contains the sequence of *capitula* found in Ap and W (Cs and Y containing slight variations), all the manuscripts of which come from the region of northern France or Belgium : $ABtCDD^1EF^1GI^3P^2P^6P^7P^8S^1T^1$. A second sub-group of MSS from the same region, which can be classed as β, follows this sequence, but omits *cap.* 8 about God's inability to prevent evil : $AI^2M^2P^6$. A third sub-group (γ) of MSS places *cap.* 8 after *cap.* 17, all, with the exception of V^1 from the region of Germany or Austria : $JK^1LL^1NRScV^1W^2X$.

Following his declared principle that manuscripts from the 'zone of Morimond', namely southern Germany and Austria, contained the earliest form of the text of works of Bernard of Clairvaux (notably the sermons on the Song of Songs, the *De conversione* and the *De consideratione*), Leclercq presumed that the sequence of *capitula* in γ manuscripts was the correct one while those of α and β manuscripts were disturbed. [38] This was despite the fact that not only did most γ MSS date from the thirteenth century or later and contain a consistently poorer text than α or β MSS, but that the sequence given by Abelard in his *Apologia*, and implied within his *Confessio fidei 'Universis'* supported that of α rather than of γ MSS. The position of *cap.* 8 ($=$ no. 17 in Leclercq's edition) in α MSS is also supported by Du and, indirectly, by the *Capitula Haeresum XIV*, where it occupies seventh place.

The faulty sequence of γ MSS can be explained by reference to the MSS A^1 (Douai, *Bibl. mun.* 372, t. I, fo. 153 ; s. xii, Anchin), I^2 (Cambrai, *Bibl. mun.* 252, fo. 184 ; s. xiii, Saint-Aubert), M^2 (Douai, *Bibl. mun.* 374, fo. 60 ; s. xii, Marchiennes) and the closely related *MS* V^1 (Valenciennes, *Bibl. mun.* 40, fo. 121^v ; s. xii, Saint-Amand). $A^1I^2M^2$ contain a very good text of the *capitula*, with only one major fault, the omission of *cap.* 8. A^1 reads *cum* for *quae* in *cap.* 19, while *quae* is omitted in M^2. V^1 contains a similarly near-faultless text, apart from the omission of *quae* in

---

38. *Formes*, 103, reiterated with references to other works in *S. Bernardi Opera*, vii, p. xi. The sequence of *capitula* given by Leclercq is inaccurate for $ApD^1M^2P^6P^7WY$.

cap. 19 and the addition of *cap.* 8 to below the first column of text on fo. 121^v (normally only thirty-eight lines to the page), so placing it after *cap.* 17. V^1 seems to have been based on a faulty exemplar related to $A^1I^2M^2$, but corrected subsequently. The faulty sequence of *capitula* in all the Germanic γ MSS appears to derive from V^1 or a very similar archetype in which the omission of *cap.* 8 was rectified, although incorrectly. The one other fault of V^1, the omission of *quae*, also entered all other Germanic MSS, apart from *JSc* in which it had been corrected.

The context within which the *capitula* occurs in γ MSS also supports the hypothesis that all the Germanic copies of this subgroup ultimately derived from V^1. In A^1M^2 the *capitula* occur after *Epist.* 190 within a dossier of letters sent to Rome, without pope Innocent's reply : *Epist.* 189-188-190-191, while I^2 (a marginally superior text, although s. XIII) contains the *capitula* within an even smaller dossier of *Epist.* 188-190. In V^1 the dossier of A^1M^2 has been slightly revised with the addition of *Epist.* 194, the letter of pope Innocent, to form the dossier : *Epist.* 191-189-188-190-194. This is exactly the sequence of all the Germanic γ MSS, although in these MSS this version of the dossier has often been used to supplement an older collection of letters, classified by Leclercq as 'series I' or *brevior*. [39] *Epist.* 189 in these Germanic MSS, as in V^1 and A^1M^2, does not contain the concluding phrase *quod melius Nicolaus iste meus, immo et vester, viva referet voce*. [40]

Confusion over *quae* in *cap.* 19 occurred at a very early stage in the copying of the *capitula*, not just in all β and γ MSS (apart from I^2 and *JSc*), but also in F^1 and G (before correction) which have the correct sequence of *capitula*. Both F^1 (WOLFENBÜTTEL, *Bibl. Aug.* 4613, fo. 159-159^v ; s. XII, French origin) and G (THE HAGUE, *Kon. Bibl.* 70. H. 7, fos. 9^v-10 ; s. XII, Clairmarais) contain two of the smallest dossiers : F^1 : *Epist.* 190 on its own, and G : *Epist.* 190-194 (followed in the same hand by the sermon of Geoffrey of Auxerre *ad praelatos*, delivered in 1163). [41] Error over *quae*

39. *Formes*, 88-89 ; *S. Bernardi Opera*, vii, p. XI.
40. *Epist.* 189, 5 (p. 16).
41. The Clairmarais origin of fos. 1-14^v of G is evident from an erased inscription on fo. 14^v in the hand which wrote its text : *liber sancte marie de claremareis. Qui abstulerit anathema sit.* Fos. 1-14^v were bound together with the other sections of G in the early nineteenth century when they formed nos. 32-35 of the collection of Lupus of Brussels (d. 1822), which passed into

also occurs in the two copies of the *capitula*, found in the first and second volumes of the oldest known collection of Bernard's complete works, A^1 and A (Douai, *Bibl. mun.* 372, t. I, fo. 153 and t. II, fos. 67ᵛ-68), which can be dated to 1162-65. [42]

A very good text of the *capitula* occurs, however, in manuscript T^1 (Brussels, *Bibl. roy.* II.1167 ; s. xii, St-Martin of Tournai). It is the only one to contain no variant from the established text apart from *qui* for *quia* in *cap.* 14, as in all MSS when the list is attached to *Epist.* 190. The one fault that *cap.* 8 had been omitted from the list has been rectified by the scribe adding *cap.* 8 to the margin after *cap.* 7. The text of T^1 is reproduced with only one further variant in I^3 (Cambrai, *Bibl. mun.* 537. fo. 34 ; s. xiii, Saint-Aubert), a volume possibly copied from T^1 in its entirety. [43]

The dossier in which the *capitula* occur in T^1 has been enlarged from that of all β MSS, by the addition of five further letters of Bernard relative to Abelard, mostly to individual cardinals, so forming the sequence : *Epist.* 187-191, 194-196, 192, 193. This is exactly the sequence found within A, in which they occur within the wider collection of letters that Leclercq has classified as 'series III' or *Perfectior* and was compiled some time after Bernard's death in 1153. The text of the letters within ADT^1 is essentially that of series III, but contains elements of series II and may have been transitional in forming the final collection. [44] *Epist.* 189 in T^1, as in all MSS of the series III collection, includes the additional phrase at the end of the letter to the pope that Bernard's secretary Nicolas would convey further news orally.

The text of *Epist.* 190 in the series III collection, including T^1, contains a number of passages absent from many manuscripts of *Epist.* 190, including $A^1 F^1 G I^2 M^2 P^6 V^1$ from northern France and the

---

the royal library of the Hague in 1819. On Geoffrey's sermon (*PL* 184, 1095-1102), see Leclercq, *Les écrits de Geoffroy d'Auxerre*, in *Recueil d'études sur S. Bernard*, i (Rome, 1962), p. 41.

42. Leclercq, *Études sur S. Bernard et le texte de ses écrits*, in *ASOC*, ix (1953), 124-33.

43. A. Boutemy, *A propos d'anthologies poétiques au XIIᵉ siècle*, in *Revue belge de philologie et d'histoire*, xix (1940), 229-33 corrects the account of Van den Gheyn, *Catalogue des mss de la Bibliothèque Royale de Belgique*, ii (Brussels 1902), 344, including his faulty dating of T^1 to the thirteenth century, followed by Leclercq, *Formes*, 89.

44. Leclercq, *S. Bernardi Opera*, vii, p. xix.

Germanic MSS of the γ group, namely $JK^1LL^1NRScW^2X$. [45] Leclercq thought that there existed only one manuscript which
contained an earlier recension of *Epist.* 190, CHARLEVILLE, *Bibl.
mun.* 67, fos. 122^v-130 (*S*) from the abbey of Signy, where William
of St-Thierry was abbot, but in fact this earlier recension is far
more widespread in the manuscript tradition than his article would
suggest. [46] The later recension of *Epist.* 190 is found in *CsW*, but
the treatise is not associated in these MSS with the nineteen *capitula*, which occur before *Epist.* 510, *Epist.* 189 (in its earlier form)
and *Epist.* 194. [47] The additional passages in *Epist.* 190 give further
force to Bernard's argument, while some give it greater philosophical precision. One phrase, *et item in quadam eius expositione epistolae ad Romanos*, added after *in libro quodam sententiarum ipsius*,
indicated that Bernard had found Abelard's teaching not just in
the book of sentences (which Abelard would deny having written),
but in his commentary on Romans as well. [48] Bernard himself
seems to have been responsible for making or at least accepting
these changes after the list of *capitula* had been attached to *Epist.*
190.

The text of the nineteen *capitula* as found accompanying both
the initial and the subsequent recension of *Epist.* 190 appears to
have originally been disseminated within Benedictine monasteries
in the dioceses of Arras, Cambrai and Tournai. Manuscripts from
monasteries outside this region tend to show relative degradation
in the quality of their text, including most of those found within
a Germanic milieu. Of a subordinate group of MSS, with a good
text apart from the variant of *sufficit* for *sufficiat* in *cap.* 6 only
one, however, is from a Benedictine house (*S*^{1} from St-Bertin),
while four are from Cistercian houses (*BtDD*^{1} from Clairmarais and
Dunes; *C* from Cîteaux) and one from an Augustinian house (*E*
from Mont-St-Éloi). Also related to this subordinate group are
a number of Parisian MSS : *P*^{6} from Saint-Victor (s. XII); *P*^{7} from

---

45. Listed by LECLERCQ, although not from these MSS, *Formes*, 95-97.
The passage *Videt ... maiestatis* (*Epist.* 190, 4, p. 20), written over an erasure
in *S*, is found in all other MSS of the earlier recension.
46. *Formes*, 98.
47. *Epist.* 190, 11 (p. 26).
48. Bernard called Abelard's *Theologia* his *stultilogia* in his preaching, *Epi-
stula Petri Abailardi contra Bernardum abbatem*, ed. R. KLIBANSKY, in *Medieval
and Renaissance Studies*, v (1961), 7 ; the phrase *vel potius stultilogiae* is one
added in *Epist.* 190, 9 (p. 24).

the Sorbonne (s. xiv), related to C in that the *capitula* occur after
Epist. 191 instead of *Epist.* 190 ; P^2P^8 (s. xv^{ex}/xvi^{in}), apparently
based on P^7.

Leclercq commented that the *capitula* were not found attached
to *Epist.* 190 in any of the manuscripts of Clairvaux, but, as he
commented elsewhere, the text of Clairvaux MSS of Bernard's
letters is not particularly reliable, compared to those from northern
France. [49]   The list is not found in any manuscripts of the series
II collection of Bernard's letters, compiled around 1145 by Geoffrey
of Auxerre, and circulated within the twelfth century in Cistercian
houses of the zone of Cîteaux.   *Epist.* 190 in this series had all of the
additional passages of its later recension, but also contained one
phrase, *usque ad senium*, which was deleted in the recension within
the series III corpus. [50]

THE CAPITULA AND EPIST. 190

Leclercq argued that the list of nineteen *capitula* did not form
part of the authentic text of *Epist.* 190 and therefore should not
be considered as the work of Bernard of Clairvaux, but his case
rests on a number of premises which can be questioned. [51]   His
first point was that the *capitula* were missing in most of the repre-
sentative of the series II and series III collections of Bernard's
correspondence.   He did not observe, however, that the earlier
recension of *Epist.* 190 as found in the CHARLEVILLE MS, *Bibl.*
mun. 67, existed in many other manuscripts which did contain
the nineteen *capitula*.   *Epist.* 190 must have been revised before
it entered the series II and III collections with the *capitula* already
attached.   The *capitula* were subsequently excluded from the
series II and some MSS of the series III collections.   The best
MSS of *Epist.* 190 in the series III collection (ADT^1) contain the
capitula, as do those containing the earlier recension of *Epist.* 190.

---

49. *S. Bernardi Opera*, vii, p. xix.   Leclercq has identified the series III
letter collection as occurring in MSS belonging to monastic houses dependent
on Clairvaux (the 'zone' of Clairvaux).   This study, however, would suggest
that the role played by Benedictine monasteries in northern France in the
dissemination of Bernard's letters may have been at least as important as
that of dependencies of Clairvaux or Morimond, if not more so.
50. *Formes*, 98.
51. *Formes*, 105.

The absence of the *capitula* from the Charleville MS can be explained if this manuscript, originally belonging to Signy, the monastery of William of St-Thierry, contained only the initial draft of *Epist.* 190, before the list had been attached. The text of *Epist.* 190 in *S* has itself been considerably corrected. *S* contains a dossier of letters relating to Abelard : *Epist.* 188 (fos. 109-110) - 189 (fos. 110-112ᵛ, 121) - 190 (fos. 113-120ᵛ, 129-132) - 194 (fos. 121-122), occurring after the only known copy of William's treatise with introductory letter to Bernard on the errors of Abelard (fos. 72ᵛ-107ᵛ), and an additional demi-folio (fo. 108), the original of the letter (*Epist.* 327) which Bernard sent in reply. [52] This dossier may have been a source for the series of MSS from northern France which contain the recension of *Epist.* 190 as in *S: A¹GI²M²V¹*, although these have the *capitula* occurring at the end of the letter. Although Leclercq raised the point that the *capitula* occurred after *Epist.* 191, instead of after *Epist.* 190 in two MSS (*C* and *P⁷*), these are late copies, containing a relatively corrupt text. The separation of the list from *Epist.* 190 in *CP²P⁷P⁸* appears to be no more than a fault incurred in the transmission of Bernard's letters. [53]

Another argument raised by Leclercq, was that the sentence *Ad capitula tantummodo illa respondimus quae signo tali * notata sunt*, which follows without any break from *Collegi tamen aliqua et transmisi*, suggested incongruity because it used the first person plural rather than singular as in the preceeding sentence. Bernard, however, uses both singular and plural when referring to himself in his letters, employing the refrain *respondemus* several times within *Epist.* 190. [54] Most of the nineteen *capitula* Bernard either touches on or ignores completely, apart from *cap.* 1, 2, 4 and 14, the ones which are marked with a sign (*) in all the best manuscripts. [55] The signs explain the distinction which Bernard had made immediately beforehand in *Epist.* 190 between the *capitula* which he had discussed and those which he did not have time to deal with, but whose error was evident.

Leclercq suggested that the list might have been the work of the council of Sens, without mentioning that Abelard was himself

---

52. Leclercq, *Notes sur la tradition des épîtres de s. Bernard*, 1. *Une chartula originale?*, in *Scriptorium*, xviii (1964), p. 198-200.
53. *Formes*, 105 n. 2.
54. *Epist.* 190, 18, 19, 21 (pp. 32, 33, 35).
55. Found correctly in *AF¹GI²I³T¹V¹*.

in no doubt that Bernard was the author, or at least propagator of these very *capitula* in both his *Confessio fidei 'Universis'* and his *Apologia.* [56] In both works Abelard appears to be replying indirectly to what Bernard was claiming within his *Epist.* 190 as well as to the individual *capitula*, to defend his position. As in none of these three documents or in the *Disputatio* written by Thomas of Morigny to counter Abelard's argument in the *Apologia* is the council of Sens mentioned, they all seem to have been written before 2 June 1140. [57] Abelard would appeal to the archbishop of Sens that he have the right to defend himself against the accusations which Bernard was making against him, while the council of Sens would only ratify the claims of Bernard of Clairvaux. [58]

THE AUTHORSHIP OF THE NINETEEN CAPITULA

Although it cannot be doubted that Bernard was responsible for propagating these *capitula* as the final part of his *Epist.* 190, the question of who formulated them is more complex. As has already been seen through study of *Du*, an earlier recension of the list of nineteen *capitula*, formulated before the list had been joined to *Epist.* 190, the author of the *Capitula Haeresum XIV* made a particularly important contribution to the drawing up of the final list. His formulations tended to be accepted over those of William of St-Thierry, though not always. Some *capitula* in the final list (*cap.* 11, 15, 18) are not mentioned in the lists of either the *Capitula Haeresum XIV* or of William of St-Thierry, but are cited by Bernard of Clairvaux within either *Epist.* 188 or *Epist.* 190. [59] The assumption can be drawn that the list of *Du* was drawn up by a group of people, including the author of the *Capitula Haeresum XIV* and William of St-Thierry, but under the direction of Bernard

---

56. *Formes*, 105.

57. This is the conclusion of BUYTAERT, CCCM, XII (Turnhout, 1969), p. 461-6, and of Zerbi, *San Bernardo di Chiaravalle e il concilio di Sens*, in *Studi su San Bernardo di Chiaravalle nell'ottavo, centenario della canonizzazione* (Rome, 1975), pp. 49-73, particularly, pp. 53-4.

58. Abelard's initiative is attested by the archbishop of Sens, *Epist.* 337, ed. LECLERCQ, *Autour de la correspondance de S. Bernard*, 1. *La lettre des évêques de France au sujet d'Abélard*, in *Sapientiae Doctrina. Mélanges de théologie et de littérature offerts à Dom Hildebrand Bascour* (Leuven, 1980), p. 185-92.

59. *Epist.* 188, 2 (p. 11), *Epist.* 190, 10 (pp. 25-6).

of Clairvaux, who made some, if not a number of contributions to the list.

The list of *Du* may have been compiled at the meeting which Bernard suggested to William of St-Thierry that they hold after Easter (25 April) 1140 after he had read William's letter and accompanying treatise on the errors of Abelard. [60] Bernard, in the interim, seems to have given the copies of the *Theologia 'Scholarium'* and the book of Abelard's *sententiae*, which William had sent him, to the author of the *Capitula Haeresum XIV*, who used these works to formulate his own list of errors. The absence of the *capitula* from *Epist.* 190 in the Charleville MS (*S*) can be explained if this represents a draft version sent by Bernard to William of St-Thierry, before the list of *capitula*, which Bernard intended to attach to the letter, had been drawn up.

THE AUTHORSHIP OF THE CAPITULA HAERESUM XIV

The question remains of the identity of the person who compiled the *Capitula Haeresum XIV*, which so influenced *Du* and the subsequent revision of the list of nineteen *capitula*. E.M. Buytaert suggested that Walter of Mortagne might have added its last *capitulum* about Abelard's attribution of omnipotence to the Father alone as Walter had mentioned this in his letter to Abelard. [61] As has already been noted, however, the charge might equally well have been added by Bernard of Clairvaux, who quoted the same passage of the *Theologia 'Scholarium'* within *Epist.* 190 as cited within *cap.* xiv of the *Capitula Haeresum XIV*. [62] Bernard may have used *cap.* xiv as a source for his treatise, although it is surprising that this important charge was apparently added to the *Capitula Haeresum XIV* only after its initial redaction and that Bernard did not make more use of the *Capitula Haeresum XIV* if this was the case.

N.M. Häring suggested that the author might be Thomas of Morigny simply on the grounds that one of the oldest manuscripts of the *Capitula Haeresum XIV* (PARIS, *Bibl. de l'Arsenal* 268A,

---

60. *Epist.* 327 (p. 57).
61. *Vid. supra*, n. 26.
62. *Vid. supra*, n. 27.

fos. 248-249^v ; s. xii-xiii) is from the abbey of St-Martin-des-Champs, to which Thomas of Morigny retired in mid-Lent of 1140, and where he stayed until 1144. [63] Although this particular argument is relatively slender, Häring's suggestion merits consideration. Thomas was identified as the author of the *Disputatio catholicorum patrum contra dogmata Petri Abaelardi*, found in the BUDAPEST MS, *Mus. Nat.* Széchényi 16, fos. 1-48 (formerly of Clairvaux) on the strength of a note on fo. 48^v that the first quaternion of the MS was missing and had to be sought *apud morenienses monachos iuxta stampas*. [64] This note corresponds exactly to the description given by Geoffrey of Auxerre of his own defective manuscript of the work in a letter to Cardinal Albinus, in which he promised to contact its author, a certain Benedictine abbot, in order to obtain a complete copy. [65] This abbot could only have been Thomas of Morigny (1080-1145 approx.), abbot of Morigny from 1110 until 1139, when he resigned his position after a series of conflicts with the neighbouring church of Notre-Dame of Étampes and perhaps within his own monastery. He then went into a period of exile, entering the monastery of St-Martin-des-Champs in mid-Lent (around 17 March) 1140. [66] He wrote a plaintive letter to Bernard of Clairvaux around 1144, describing the difficult conditions of his exile in Paris and asking if he should return to Morigny, but did not return there and died not long after in the monastery of Colombes. [67]

---

63. HÄRING, *Die Vierzehn Capitula Haeresum*, 40.

64. M.B. CARRA DE VAUX SAINT CYR, *Disputatio catholicorum patrum adversus dogmata Petri Abaelardi*, in *Rev. des sciences phil. et théol.*, xlvii (1963), 205-20. The work is edited under this title by HÄRING, in *Studi Medievali*, 3a ser. xxii (1981), 299-376. Häring first described the manuscript in *The Writings against Gilbert of Poitiers by Geoffrey of Auxerre*, in *Analecta Cisterciensia*, xxii (1966), 21-28, as did BUYTAERT, CCCM, XI, pp. 345-50.

65. *Epist. ad Albinum*, ed. HÄRING, *The Writings against Gilbert of Poitiers*, 81.

66. The major source for the life of Thomas is the *Chronicon Mauriniacense*, ed. L. MIROT, *La Chronique de Morigny 1095-1152* (Paris, 1909), especially pp. 73-78 on the events leading up to his exile. K. HAMPE suggested that its second book may have been written by Thomas : *Reise nach Frankreich und Belgiën im Frühjahr 1897. iii. Abt Thomas von Morigny als Verfasser des zweiten Buches des Chronicons Mauriniacense*, in *Neues Archiv*, xxiii (1898), 389-98, while MIROT, *op. cit.*, pp. vi-xi, thought it was written by a close friend of Thomas. Two sermons of Thomas survive in PARIS, *Bibl. Mazarine* 771, fos. 153-160^v, and *Bibl. nat.*, lat. 2467, fos. 175^v-176, from which an extract is edited by LE-CLERCQ, *Prédicateurs bénédictins aux XIe et XIIe siècles. ii. Thomas de Morigny*, in *Revue Mabillon*, xxxvii (1943) 65-71.

67. *Epist.* 476 among the letters of Bernard (*PL* 182, 682D-685A).

Thomas of Morigny shows himself in his *Disputatio* to be a
learned, although traditionally minded monk who felt that the
younger generation of students in Paris was being completely
led astray by the teaching of Peter Abelard. [68] He had himself
once written a treatise *De rebus universalibus*, dedicated to a *magister Theodoricus*, in which he seems to have espoused a philosophi-
cally conservative, realist point of view. [69] Thomas read Abelard's *Theologia 'Scholarium'* carefully and quoted only from that
work and the *Apologia* in order to refute Abelard's argument in
the latter work and so defend Bernard of Clairvaux from criticism.
Respecting Abelard's claim that the *liber sententiarum* was not one
of his own writings, Thomas transferred criticism to works, the
authorship of which Abelard could not deny.

While Thomas devoted the first and second books of the *Disputatio* to defending the validity of the first and fifth *capitula* about
the Trinity and about Christ, he launched in the third book into
criticisms which had not been made by either William or Bernard,
but which he claimed to have extracted himself from Abelard's
writings :

> De multis ergo profanis et mortiferis novitatibus quae adhuc
> restant, quas stulte Petrus in *Theologia* sua, stultius in *Apologia*
> sua delirans profudit, tria tantum sequestravi, quae et rempu-
> blicam nostram graviter infestant, atque bonis aemulatoribus
> excitant maiorem zeli, qui candet in domo Dei, fervorem. Unum
> est "quod Filius Dei semper de Deo nascitur". Secundum est
> "quod Deus facere non potest, nisi quod facit, nec alio modo,
> nec alio tempore, nec dimittere quin faciat quod facit". Tertium,
> "quod gratia illa qua salvantur electi, communis est omnibus
> hominibus". [70]

The first point had not been mentioned in any of the previous
tracts and concerned Abelard's interpretation of a certain line in the
psalms. [71] The second, however, corresponds exactly to the third
capitulum of the *Capitula Haeresum XIV*, although it had never

---

68. Cf. *Disputatio*, i, 7 (ed. HÄRING, p. 327) : *O nobilissimi iuvenes ... cur
talia discitis* ; i, 16 (p. 328) : *Expergescimini, qui dormitis lectis eburneis et
lascivitis in stratis vestris* ; i, 25 (p. 330) : *Videtisne, O Parisienses academici ...* etc.
69. *Ibid.*, iii, 75 (p. 367). Thomas praised Aristotle, iii, 64 (p. 365). Cf.
J. JOLIVET, *Sur quelques critiques de la théologie d'Abélard*, in *AHDLMA*,
xxxviii (1963), 44-47.
70. *Disputatio*, iii, 4 (p. 356).
71. *Ibid.*, iii, 6 (p. 356).

been mentioned by either William or Bernard in their respective treatises. Thomas quoted from both the *Theologia 'Scholarium'* and the *Apologia*, including a number of the same extracts as had been quoted in support of *cap.* iii in the *Capitula Haeresum XIV*. [72] The last criticism Thomas made in the *Disputatio* about grace being bestowed on all men parallels *cap.* vi of that list, *Quod Deus non plus faciat ei qui salvatur antequam cohaereat gratiae, quam ei qui non salvatur.* This emphasis on grace in both the *Disputatio* and *cap.* vi was subtly different from the emphasis on free will in the parallel *capitula* of William of St-Thierry and of *Du*, carried over into the final list. In the *Disputatio* Thomas quoted from Abelard's *Theologia* and *Apologia* to support his claim, rather from the *liber sententiarum*, which Abelard denied having written. [73]

The concluding line of the *Capitula Haeresum XIV*, *Haec sunt capitula Theologiae, immo Stultilogiae, Petri Abaelardi*, parallels two derisory comments of Thomas in the *Disputatio*, *in diabologia illa*, and *quas stulte Petrus in Theologia sua, stultius in Apologia sua.* [74] Bernard of Clairvaux added a very similar phrase, *vel potius Stultilogiae*, to qualify *Theologiae* only to the second recension of *Epist.* 190, although he also used the pun in his preaching against Abelard in Paris. [75] There seems to have been a close relationship between Bernard and the author of the *Capitula Haeresum XIV*.

One other possible indication of Thomas of Morigny's influence on the final list of nineteen *capitula* is the reference in the concluding sentence that some had been found in Abelard's *Scito teipsum*. William of St-Thierry knew of the existence of this work, but had not read it. He sent only the *Theologia* and the *liber sententiarum* to Bernard, who was similarly unaware of the *Scito teipsum* in writing *Epist.* 190. Thomas of Morigny, however, had read the *Scito teipsum*, which he knew that Abelard called the *Ethica* and

---

72. *Disputatio*, iii, 41-44 (p. 362) quoting *TSch* III, 35, 36-7, 39, 56 (*PL* 178, 1095CD, 1096AB, 1106C, 1101D) and extracts from the *Apologia*, ed. BUYTAERT, CCCM, XI, p. 368.
73. *Disputatio*, iii, 78-100 (p. 368-72), quoting *TSch* I, 125, 144, 147 (*PL* 178, 1013B, 1018C, 1019B) and the *Apologia*, ed. BUYTAERT, CCCM, XI, p. 366-7. Buytaert attributes these excerpts to Abelard's discussion of the world soul, although their subject matter relates naturally to a discussion of *cap.* 6, about grace and free will.
74. *Cap. Haer. XIV* (ed. HÄRING, p. 52) ; cf. Thomas, *Disputatio*, i, 27 (p. 327) and iii, 4 (p. 356).
75. *Vid. supra* n. 48.

commented on the danger presented by its ideas. [76] The title of *Ethica* does not occur in any manuscripts of the work, which use only the title *Scito teipsum*, but it was used by Abelard to refer to the work in his commentary on Romans, when it had not yet been written. [77] It may not be a coincidence that Bernard should add in his second recension of *Epist.* 190 that he had read of Abelard's doctrine of the redemption in his commentary on Romans as well as *in libro quodam sententiarum.* [78] This addition may have been made after Abelard had denied writing the *liber sententiarum* to give more weight to the accusation being cast, along with other passages which refined Bernard's argument in *Epist.* 190. The hand of Thomas of Morigny, who, living in Paris from March 1140, would have had access to works of Abelard, may again be evident here.

These various points suggest that Thomas of Morigny compiled the *Capitula Haeresum XIV*, and was thus indirectly influential in forming the list of *Du* as well of the subsequent, widely circulated list of nineteen *capitula.* He wrote the *Disputatio* at the suggestion of Hugh of Amiens, archbishop of Rouen, in order to defend Bernard of Clairvaux, not as somebody new to the controversy over Abelard, but as someone already very familiar with Abelard's writings. [79] Thomas, by his own admission, had once been friendly to Abelard and had invited him to be present at the consecration of a new altar at Morigny in January 1131. The author of the second book of the *Chronicon Mauriniacensis*, a close friend of Thomas, writing in 1132, mentioned Abelard's presence in flattering terms immediately after mentioning Bernard. [80] By 1140,

---

76. *Disputatio*, iii, 122 (p. 376).

77. Commentary on Romans, ed. BUYTAERT, CCCM, XI, pp. 126, 293, 307. On the inconsistency between the two titles, see D. LUSCOMBE, *Peter Abelard's Ethics* (Oxford, 1971), p. liv.

78. *Epist.* 190, 11 (p. 26). Other passages added to the initial recension of *Epist.* 190 display a philosophical character which may also be due Thomas's influence, although this is impossible to prove.

79. The role of Hugh of Amiens in the affair over Abelard is obscure, but he was a friend of two of his critics, Bernard and Suger of St-Denis. He was present at the dedication of Suger's new church, 11 June 1140, *Libellus de consecratione Ecclesiae S. Dionysii* (PL 186, 1250C, 1252A). As a cousin of a former prior of St-Martin-des-Champs, Mathew Albano, he may have been influential in allowing Thomas of Morigny to seek exile there. On Hugh's career, see the notice in the *Histoire littéraire*, xii (Paris 1763), p. 647-667.

80. *Chronicon Mauriniacense* (ed. MIROT, p. 54) ; cf. *Disputatio*, i, 63 (p. 337) and iii, 84 (p. 369).

however, Thomas had abandoned Abelard as a friend, while remaining a fervent admirer of Bernard, to whom he would later turn for help in 1144. Thomas's involvement in the affair over Abelard's teaching could be explained by a desire to gain favour with Bernard at a critical time in his career, exiled from his monastery after being its abbot for almost thirty years. Bernard may have given Thomas the books of Abelard's teaching which William had sent him with instructions to draw up a list of errors which would serve as a base for a list of *capitula* to be attached to *Epist.* 190. [81]

One other person possibly involved in drawing up the nineteen *capitula*, although in a limited capacity, could have been Geoffrey of Auxerre. Geoffrey, a former pupil of Abelard, had been converted to the Cistercian life on hearing Bernard preach his sermon *De conversione* in Paris, perhaps on 1 November 1139. [82] Geoffrey quickly became a favourite companion of Bernard, to whom he served as his secretary. The presence of the *errores Petri Abailardi* immediately before Geoffrey's own list of the errors of Gilbert of Poitiers suggests that Geoffrey might have been involved in its formulation. The juxtaposition of texts on Manichaean heretics, Abelard and Gilbert parallels exactly his treatment of these three subjects together in his life of St Bernard, in which he described the council of Sens, the council of Sens and the Henrician heretics whom he encountered in his travels with Bernard to the south of France. [83] Geoffrey's account of the council of Sens contains so many details not found elsewhere that he may well have been an eye-witness. He had read Thomas's *Disputatio* and knew the author.

Geoffrey's involvement is, however, less certain and would only have been limited to a secretarial capacity at the most. The contribution of Thomas of Morigny appears to have been particularly important in drawing up the *Capitula Haeresum XIV* and

---

81. The excerpts from the *Theologia 'Scholarium'* and the book of sentences contain no variation when quoted by all three authors.

82. Geoffrey described his conversion in the *Fragmenta de Vita et Miraculis S. Bernardi*, ed. R. Lechat, *Analecta Bollandiana* 50, (1932), 115-16, and again in the *Vita Prima*, iv, 2 (*PL* 185, 327BC). He related his turning away from Abelard to Bernard in an Easter sermon, ed. Leclercq, *Études sur S. Bernard et le texte de ses écrits*, p. 152-3. On the date of the *De conversione*, see *S. Bernardi Opera*, iv, p. 61.

83. *Vita Prima*, iii, 5-6 (*PL* 185, 310D-313B).

thus in providing the foundation for the list of nineteen *capitula*. William of St-Thierry may have had some say in drawing up the list, although the ultimate responsibility in deciding on which *capitula* were to be included lay with Bernard of Clairvaux himself.

THE MANUSCRIPT TRADITION OF THE CAPITULA HAERESUM XIV

The *Capitula Haeresum XIV* do not occur in any of the official registers of Bernard's correspondence, or indeed in any manuscripts belonging to monasteries of the archdiocese of Rheims, the centre of diffusion of the list of nineteen *capitula*. All the manuscripts are of a relatively late date :

B : BARCELONA, *Archivo de la Corona de Aragón*, Ripoll C 56, fos. 36ᵛ-37ᵛ. — s. XIII-XIV. ROCHAIS-MANNING, no. 3478.

C : LONDON, *British Library*, Royal 8. F. XV, fos. 1-2ᵛ. — s. XII-XIII ; Byland (O. Cist., Clairvaux), dioc. York. ROCHAIS-MANNING, no. 4019.

D : LONDON, *Sion College*, Arc. L 40, 2/L 13, fos. 1-3ᵛ. — s. XIII ; John Grandison, bishop of Exeter (1327-69). N. KER, *Medieval MSS in British Libraries*, i (Oxford 1969), pp. 274-5.

E : OXFORD, *Balliol College* 148, fo. 57-57ᵛ. — s. XIII ; gift of William Grey, bishop of Ely (d. 1478). ROCHAIS-MANNING, no. 4206.

F : OXFORD, *Bodleian Library*, Bodley 375, fos. 44ᵛ-46. — s. XIII ; given to Bodley by William Ballow of Christchurch, 1604. ROCHAIS-MANNING, no. 4214.

G [*A*] : PARIS, *Bibliothèque de l'Arsenal* 268A, fos. 248-249ᵛ. — s. XII-XIII ; St-Martin-des-Champs (OSB), dioc. Paris. ROCHAIS-MANNING, no. 4281.

H : PARIS, *Bibliothèque de l'Arsenal* 502, fos. 103ᵛ-104ᵛ. — s. XIV. ROCHAIS-MANNING, no. 4283.

I [*V*] Rome, Vatican, lat. 663, fos. 3-4. — s. XIV. ROCHAIS-MANNING, no. 4543.

One of the oldest manuscripts, *G*, is from the monastery of St-Martin-des-Champs, where Thomas of Morigny lived in exile 1140-44. *G* stands apart from all other MSS in containing one correct reading not found within any other MS. [84] In *G* the *Capitula*

---

84. *G* is described by BUYTAERT, CCCM, XII, pp. 455-6. Häring does not discuss the textual relationship between *G* and the other MSS in his edition and rejects the phrase *sed potius ... culpa* found only in *G cap.* vi, 2, although it is required by the sense and is accepted by Buytaert (line 139, p. 477).

104

Haeresum XIV does not occur alongside other letters relating to Abelard, but at the end of a manuscript, after a miscellaneous collection of letters of Bernard, many of which relate to the disputed election of York. [85] *G* is also the only Parisian manuscript to contain the initial recension of Bernard's *De conversione* (fos. 112-116v), all others coming from the 'zone of Morimond', apart from one from Marmoutiers. [86]

Although an independent witness to the text of the *Capitula Haeresum XIV*, *G* is far from accurate as a copy of the work. The MS with the fewest faults is *C*, from the Cistercian abbey of Byland, York, written like *G* in either the late twelfth or early thirteenth century. [87] In *C*, as in the related copy of *D*, the list precedes *Epist.* 190, which is in turn separated by various letters from another dossier relating to Abelard : *Epist.* 188-338-337-189-194. *Epist.* 337 is almost always found in the same manuscripts as contain the *Capitula Haeresum XIV*, apart from *G*, and never in any of the official collections of Bernard's correspondence. [88] In four other MSS (*BEFH*), the *Capitula Haeresum XIV* are found within a similar dossier of letters addressed to the pope and cardinals in Rome, all of which include *Epist.* 190 and 337. [89]

Is the combination of the *Capitula Haeresum XIV* and *Epist.* 337 in the same few manuscripts a coincidence? At the end of *Epist.* 337, the archbishop of Sens wrote that he was sending certain *conscripta* :

> Quaedam autem de condemnatis a nobis capitulis vobis, reverende Pater, conscripta transmisimus, ut per haec audita reliqui corpus operis facilius aestimetis. [90]

---

85. *G* was used by C.H. Talbot, *New Documents in the Case of William of York*, in *Cambridge Historical Journal*, x (1950), 1-15. Leclercq mentioned the possibility that *G* may be English, although this is not certain, *Études sur S. Bernard et le texte de ses écrits*, pp. 20-21, a view repeated by Buytaert, CCCM, XII, p. 456.
86. *S. Bernardi Opera*, iv, p. 63.
87. Not mentioned by Häring, but evident from his apparatus.
88. *Epist.* 337 does not occur in Douai, *Bibl. mun.* 374, as claimed by Leclercq, in *Sapientiae Doctrina*, p. 86, and Rochais-Manning, no. 3662, who have confused it with *Epist.* 188. *Epist.* 337 is also found in London, *Sion College*, Arc. L 40, 2/L 13 (s. xiii-xiv), not mentioned by Leclercq or Rochais-Manning. *Epist.* 337 was sufficiently rare in the twelfth century for Otto of Freising to admit that he had not seen it, *Gesta Frederici*, I, 51, ed. Waitz, p. 74.
89. *BF : Epist.* 190-*CH XIV*-188-338-337-189-194 ; *E : Epist.* 189-337-190-*CH XIV*-191-194-195-196-192-193 ; in *H* the sequence has been disturbed and 190 occurs much before *Epist.* 311-*CH XIV*-233-337-338.
90. *Epist.* 337, 4 (ed. Leclercq, in *Sapientiae Doctrina*, p. 190).

Although the *Capitula Haeresum XIV* are not attached directly to *Epist.* 337, they are found in four MSS (*BEFH*) within a dossier addressed to Rome and in three (*CDI*) within the same manuscript. It cannot be proven conclusively, but the *conscripta* sent to Rome could well have been the *Capitula Haeresum XIV*, included among this collection of letters.

There was no official list of *capitula* condemned at the council of Sens beyond the accusations being made by Bernard of Clairvaux between April and June of 1140. Abelard demanded a confrontation with Bernard at the council of Sens in order to defend himself from the accusations of heresy which Bernard was making against him, laid out in the list of nineteen *capitula* which were attached to his *Epist.* 190. The bishops at the Council merely ratified the accusations which Bernard had already been making against Abelard in the preceeding months. Bernard had not himself originated the accusations against Abelard, but had been asked by William of St-Thierry to take up the matter and so give it a far wider hearing than ever William could have done. Bernard appears to have used Thomas of Morigny to prepare an initial list of errors, the *Capitula Haeresum XIV*, separately from that of William of St-Thierry. Nonetheless, Bernard took responsibility for publicising the dangers which he believed were presented by Abelard's teaching. The decision of the council of Sens was simply to support the accusations put forward by Bernard of Clairvaux.

CONCLUSION

The various stages through which the list of heretical *capitula* passed can now be documented. The sigla of the manuscripts used within this study are given in round brackets.

1. William of St-Thierry :
   Epist. 326 and *Disputatio* [Lent 1140] (*S*)

2. Bernard : *Epist.* 190 [1]   Thomas of Morigny :
   (first recension, without list)   *Capitula Haeresum XIV*
   (*S*)   (*cap.* xiv possibly added under
                                     the influence of Bernard)
                                     (*BCDEFGH*)

3. Compilation of 19 *errores*, based on *Capitula Haeresum XIV*, with additions and changes inspired by William of St-Thierry and Bernard [soon after Easter 1140 (25 April)] (*Du*).

4. Revised form of list attached to *Epist.* 190[1]. This list quoted by Abelard within his *Apologia*, indirectly in the *Confessio fidei 'Universis'* and in the rubrics to certain MSS of the *Confessio* [between Easter and Pentecost 1140] (*Ap* and *OP¹P⁴Q*).

5. List quoted within separate list, *Hae sunt haereses...*, with addition of *et Filii* in *cap.* 2 [*aut Filii* in *Y*] (*CsWY*).

6. List quoted at end of *Epist.* 190[1] with *aut Filii* in *cap.* 2 and *qui* for *quia* in *cap.* 14. Circulates among early dossiers of letters about Abelard in northern French MSS (A^1F^1G $I^2M^2P^6V^1$) and, with a disturbed order perhaps dependent on an error in V^1, in Germanic MSS ($JK^1LL^1NRScW^2X$).

7. *Epist.* 190[1] extended into second recension, *Epist.* 190[2], but the list is not changed. This revised text enters the series III collection of Bernard's letters ($ABtCDD^1EI^3S^1T^1$, of which the best MS is T^1).

A number of points worthy of interest emerge from these findings. The role of Thomas of Morigny, a Benedictine abbot exiled from his monastery, appears as particularly important in the formulation of the list of the nineteen *capitula*. Thomas would thus have been Bernard's aide throughout the affair. Bernard was clearly more of a publicist in the controversy with Abelard and did not himself engage in much academic 'research' to refute the opinions of Abelard. Thomas appears to have been a more careful critic than William of St-Thierry, but he was not able to influence the wording of those *capitula* which Bernard incorporated within his *Epist.* 190, itself very dependent on William's *Disputatio*.

By studying in detail all the MSS of the list of nineteen *capitula*, considerable light is thrown on the diffusion of Bernard's letters as a whole. The best MSS all seem to come from Benedictine monasteries in northern France, rather than from Cistercian houses, as might have been expected. Both early dossiers of letters relating to Abelard and the 'official' dossier of the series III collection, compiled after Bernard's death are found in Benedictine MSS, among which the Tournai MS (BRUSSELS, *Bibl. roy.* II.1167) deserves particular attention. The revised form of *Epist.* 190, which Leclercq thought common to all MSS, apart from the CHARLEVILLE MS, *Bibl. mun.* 67, is first found only in the series II and III collections. Many of the Germanic MSS of *Epist.* 190 and the accompanying list appear to depend on a textual tradition from northern France, perhaps directly from VALENCIENNES, *Bibl. mun.* 40 from St-Amand (OSB), rather than from a Cistercian tradition of the 'zone of Morimond'. The list of nineteen *capitula* may have been excluded from MSS of the 'zone of Clairvaux' because the list was not entirely the work of Bernard and had been added to *Epist.* 190 only after the initial redaction of that treatise. Bernard was, however, fully involved in publicising that list with his *Epist.* 190 once it had been drawn up by Thomas of Morigny, William of St-Thierry and himself. The council of Sens simply ratified the accusations which were being put forward by Bernard of Clairvaux.

APPENDIX

THE NINETEEN CAPITULA - A CRITICAL EDITION

Given that the accusations which were made against Abelard were so fluid in nature, it is difficult to identify a specific text as containing a definitive version of the *capitula*. No single manuscript can be used as the basis for a critical edition. The most valuable witness, in certain respects, is MUNICH, Clm 28363, fos. 132v-133 (s. xii), the fragment which contains Abelard's quotation of the list within his *Apologia*. No manuscript survives which gives the list exactly as quoted by Abelard, but the internal evidence, already discussed, would suggest that this list did occur at the end of Bernard's *Epist.* 190. All manuscripts of the list as found with Bernard's correspondence include one addition to *cap.* 2, namely *et Filii* in *CsW*, but *aut Filii* in other MSS. This phrase is given in smaller type to denote the fact that it was added after the initial formulation of the list. Otherwise the text which is given here is that which Abelard read and reacted against in writing his *Confessio fidei 'Universis'* and *Apologia*, based on *Ap*, but controlled by reference to *Du*, the rubrics to the *Confessio* in *OP¹ P⁴Q* and *CsWY*. Apart from the reading *qui* for *quia* in *cap.* 14

108

and the addition in *cap.* 2, this text is found without fault in T^1. Two levels of critical apparatus are given, the first noting deliberate changes in the formulation of individual *capitula*, as found in *Du*, the *Capitula Haeresum XIV* and the list of William of St-Thierry. The orthography adopted is that using *v* and *ae* for *u* and *ę* for the sake of consistency with Leclercq's edition. [91]

CAPITULA HAERESUM XIX

(Bernard, *Epist.* 190) ... Collegi tamen aliqua et transmisi.] Ad capitula tantummodo illa respondimus quae signo tali * notata sunt.

* [1] Quod Pater sit plena potentia, Filius quaedam potentia, Spiritus Sanctus nulla potentia.
* [2] Quod Spiritus Sanctus non sit de substantia Patris aut Filii.
  [3] Quod Spiritus Sanctus sit anima mundi.
* [4] Quod Christus non assumpsit carnem ut nos a iugo diaboli liberaret.
  [5] Quod neque Deus et homo, neque haec persona quae Christus est, sit tertia persona in Trinitate.

Ad capitula ... sunt *om.* $COP^1P^2P^4P^7P^8Q$ ‖ He sunt hereses petri abailardi *add.* $CsWY$, pauce de multis *add.* Y, errores petri abailardi *Du add NX* ‖ illa] ista JK^1LL^1NRSc ‖ respondimus] respondemus K^1LL^1 ‖ notata] nota E ‖ sunt *om.* F^1

[1] = Guilelm., iii ; Bern., *Epist.* 190, 2 ; *Du* i. Cf. *CH XIV*, i : Horrenda similitudo de sigillo aereo, de specie et genere ad Trinitatem. — Pater ... Filius] Filius sit OP^1P^4Q ‖ potentia^3 *om.* Q

[2] = *Du* ii ; *CH XIV*, ii. Cf. Guilelm., iv : De Spiritu Sancto, quod non sit ex substantia Patris et Filii, sicut est ex substantia Patris ; Bern., *Epist.* 190, 2. — Spiritus ... de] solus filius sit ex CP^1P^4 filius solus sit ex Q ‖ sit *om.* N ‖ de *om.* K^1 ‖ aut Filii *om.* $ApDu$ ‖ et filii CsW, an filii EL^1

[3] = Guilelm., v ; Bern., *Epist.* 190, 10. — Quod ... mundi *om.* OP^1 P^4 QY ‖ ¡mmo anima mundi Ap

[4] = *Du*, iv ; *CH XIV*, iv. Cf. Guilelm., viii : Quod Christus non ideo assumpsit carnem et passus est, ut nos a iugo diaboli liberaret ; Bern., *Epist.* 190, 11. — assumpsit] assumpserit Cs

[5] = *Du*, v ; *CH XIV*, vi. Cf. Guilelm., viii : Quod Christus Deus et homo non est tertia persona in Trinitate ; Bern., *Epist.* 188, 2. — Quod ... Trinitate *om.* P^1 ‖ neque^1 ... est] Christus non Q ‖ Deus *om.* F^1 ‖ et] neque $K^1OP^1P^4$ ‖ et homo *om.* P^7 *ante corr.* ‖ Christus est *trp* J

---

91. It remains to thank many librarians who have made this study possible, the *Institut de Recherche et d'Histoire des Textes* of Paris, the *Hill Monastic Microfilm Library* in Collegeville, Minnesota, and C.S.F. Burnett for assistance and encouragement.

[6] Quod liberum arbitrium per se sufficiat ad aliquod bonum.
[7] Quod ea solummodo possit Deus facere vel dimittere vel eo modo tantum vel eo tempore quo facit, non alio.
[8] Quod Deus nec debeat nec possit mala impedire.
[9] Quod non contraximus culpam ex Adam, sed poenam tantum.
[10] Quod non peccaverunt qui Christum ignorantes crucifixerunt, et quod non sit culpae ascribendum quicquid fit per ignorantiam.
[11] Quod in Christo non fuerit spiritus timoris Domini.
[12] Quod potestas ligandi atque solvendi apostolis tantum data sit, non etiam successoribus eorum.
[13] Quod propter opera nec melior nec peior efficiatur homo.
* [14] Quod ad Patrem, quia ab alio non est, proprie vel specialiter

---

[6] = *Du*, iii. Cf. *CH XIV*, vi : Quod Deus non plus faciat ei qui salvatur, antequeam cohaereat gratiae, quam ei qui non salvatur ; Guilelm., vi : Quod libero arbitrio sine adiuvante gratia bene possumus et velle et agere. — sufficiat] sufficit $BtCDD^1EP^2P^6P^7P^8S^1$ ‖ ad *om*. C ‖ bonum] faciendum *add*. K^1 LL^1R

[7] = *Du*, iii ; *CH XIV*, iii. — ea *om*. J. ‖ solummodo] sola Q ‖ possit Deus facere] Deus possit facere J, possit facere Deus I^3LNR, Deus facere possit Q ‖ vel^1] et K^1 ‖ dimittere] quae dimittit *add*. Ap ‖ tantum *om*. Q ‖ quo facit] et Ap *add*. $JOP^1P^2P^4P^8$

[8] = *Du*, vii ; *CH XIV*, vii. — Quod ... impedire *om*. $A^1I^2M^2P^6T^1$ *ante corr*. ‖ *post* ... Patri [16] $JKLL^1NRScV^1W^2X$ ‖ Deus ... impedire] mala impedire non possit Q ‖ nec^1 non L^1P^4 *ante corr*. Y ‖ mala impedire] impedire malum *Cs*, malum impedire W

[9] = *Du*, viii ; *CH XIV*, viii. Cf. Guilelm., xi : Quod ab Adam non trahimus originalis peccati culpam, sed poenam ; Bern., *Epist*. 188, 2. — non] neque K^1 ‖ contraximus] traximus $JK^1LL^1RScW^2$ ‖ culpam ex Adam] ex Adam culpam *Du CH XIV*, ab Adam culpam Q ‖ tantum *om*. Q

[10] = *Du*, ix ; *CH XIV*, xi. Cf. Bern., *Epist*. 188, 2. — non ... ignorantiam] per ignorantiam non peccaverunt Q ‖ peccaverunt qui] peccaverit ut qui P^1 ‖ ignorantes] per ignorantiam P^6 ‖ et *om*. Ap ‖ non sit culpae] sit culpae NR, sit culpae non K^1, non culpae $CP^2P^6P^7P^8$ ‖ ascribendum] inscribendum E ‖ fit per ignorantiam] per ignorantiam fit NX

[11] = *Du*, x. Cf. Bern., *Epist*. 190, 10. — Quod ... Domini *om*. F^1 ‖ in Christo non fuerit] non fuerit in Christo *Du* ‖ fuerit] fuit Ap, fiunt P^4

[12] = Cf. *Du*, xi : Quod potestas ligandi et solvendi solis apostolis concessa sit, non etiam successoribus eorum ; *CH XIV*, xii : De potestate ligandi et solvendi ; Bern., *Epist*. 188, 2. — tantum ... eorum non sit data successoribus apostolorum Q ‖ sit] et *add*. $ApOP^1P^4W^2Y$ ‖ etiam] et *Sc om*. $ApOP^1P^2F^4$ P^8Y ‖ successoribus eorum *trp* W^2 ‖ eorum *om*. P^2P^8 ‖ Quod corpus domini non cadat in terram *add*. *Du*

[13] = *Du*, xiii ; *CH XIV*, x. — nec melior nec peior] nec peior nec melior $DuJK^1LL^1NRX$ ‖ efficiatur] efficitur OP^4, sit Q ‖ homo] quis K^1, *om*. JLL^1NRScW^2X

[14] = *Du*, xiv. Cf. *CH XIV*, xiv : Quod ad Patrem proprie vel specialiter pertinet omnipotentia ; Bern., *Epist*. 190, 10. — ad ... benignitas] sapientia aut benignitas ad patrem non pertineat Q ‖ quia] qui *omnes codices praeter* $ApCsDuK^1OP^1P^4W$

attineat omnipotentia, non etiam sapientia et benignitas.

[15] Quod etiam castus timor excludatur a futura vita.

[16] Quod diabolus immittat suggestiones per appositionem lapidum sive herbarum.

[17] Quod adventus in fine saeculi possit attribui Patri.

[18] Quod anima Christi per se non descendit ad inferos, sed per potentiam tantum.

[19] Quod neque opus neque voluntas neque concupiscentia neque delectatio quae movet eam, peccatum sit, nec debemus eam velle exstingui.

Haec capitula, partim in libro *Theologiae*, partim in libro sententiarum magistri Petri, partim in libro cuius titulus est *Scito teipsum* reperta sunt.

---

attineat] pertineat *J* ‖ omnipotentia] potentia *O*, omnipotentiam L^1 ‖ non²] nec *ES*¹ ‖ etiam] et *add. JK¹LL¹RW²* ‖ et] vel *O om. Du*

[15] = *Du*, xv. Cf. Bern., *Epist.* 190, 10. — Quod ... vita *post* ... exstingui

[15] *Cs, post* ... Domini [11] *OP¹P⁴Q* ‖ etiam castus timor] castus timor etiam *A¹I²M²* ‖ etiam *om. P⁶* ‖ excludatur] excluditur *OP¹P⁴Y om. Q* ‖ vita] exluditur *add. Q*

[16] = *Du*, xvi. Cf. Guilelm., x : Quod suggestiones diabolicas per physicam fieri dicit in hominibus ; Bern., *Epist.* 190, 10. — Quod ... hominibus *om. OP¹ P⁴Q* ‖ suggestiones] malas *add. P⁶* ‖ appositionem] appositiones *CsDuP⁶*, oppositiones *K¹*, passionem *G* ‖ sive] vel *ApP²P⁸Y* ‖ sive herbarum *om. Du*

[17] = *Du*, xvii. — in ... Patri] filii posset attribui patri in fine saeculi *Q* ‖ adventus] filii *add. O* ‖ possit] posset *ApG*

[18] = *Du*, xviii. Cf. Bern., *Epist.* 188, 2. — descendit] descenderit *Y* ‖ sed ... tantum *om. Q*

[19] = *Du*, xix. Cf. *CH XIV*, xiii : De suggestione, delectatione et consensu ; Guilelm., xii-xiii : Quod nullum sit peccatum, nisi in consensu peccati et contemptu Dei. Quod dicit concupiscentia et delectatione et ignorantia nullum peccatum committi et huiusmodi non esse peccatum sed naturam ; Bern., *Epist.* 188, 2. — Quod ... exstingui *om. Q* ‖ neque³ ... exstingui] etc. *OP¹P⁴* delectatio, dilectio *N* ‖ quae] cum *AA¹P²P⁷P⁸*, vel quaecumque *D*, vel cum *interlin. S¹, om. BtF¹G ante corr. K¹LL¹M²NP⁶RV¹W²X* ‖ movet eam *trp CsW* ‖ peccatum sit *trp CsW* ‖ eam velle] ea in velle *K¹ trp Du, om. Y* ‖ exstingui] id est concupiscentiam *add. Du*

Haec ... sunt *om. CsDuOP¹P⁴QWY in initio P⁶* ‖ Haec] Bernardus. Haec *K¹LL¹RW²* ‖ partim¹] reperta sunt *add. J*, partim in libro Theologiae magitri petri *add. ApR om. NX* ‖ magistri Petri] eiusdem *Ap om. R* ‖ Petri] lunbardi *add. P²P⁸* ‖ titulus est *om. K¹ trp JLL¹R*

V

Peter Abelard's *Theologia Christiana*
and *Theologia 'Scholarium'* re-examined

The publication in 1969 of a critical edition, prepared by E. M. Buytaert, of Abelard's *Theologia Christiana* and of the shorter form of the *Theologia 'Scholarium'*, marked an important contribution towards a much-needed critical edition of Abelard's *Theologia*[1]. Unfortunately, Fr Buytaert died before completing his projected edition of the two other versions of the *Theologia*, the *Theologia 'Summi boni'* and the longer form of the *Theologia 'Scholarium'*, scheduled to appear within an accompanying volume in the series *Corpus Christianorum. Continuatio Mediaeualis*[2]. The intention of the present article is to review Fr Buytaert's published editions of the *Theologia Christiana* (*TChr*) and of the shorter form of the *Theologia 'Scholarium'* (*tsch*) and so provide both a guide for their use and a foundation on which edition of the remaining versions of the *Theologia* can proceed.

Fr Buytaert was himself the heir to a long tradition of study of the text of Abelard's *Theologia*. In 1616 A. Duchesne, in conjunction with F. d'Amboise, edited the *Theologia 'Scholarium'* under the title *Introductio ad theologiam* from the *Paris, Bibliothèque nat. MS lat. 14793*, fos. 1-69ᵛ (*P*), while in 1717 E. Martène published his edition of the *Theologia Christiana* from the *Tours, Bibliothèque mun. MS 85*, fos. 133-155ᵛ (*T*)[3]. Working from these printed texts, D. Goldhorn established in 1833 that the *Theologia 'Scholarium'* was

1. *Petri Abaelardi Opera Theologica* ii, *Corpus Christianorum. Continuatio Mediaevalis* [= CCCM] 12 (Turnhout 1969).

2. I am indebted to the editors of *Corpus Christianorum* for allowing me access, through the mediation of Prof. D. E. Luscombe, to Buytaert's typescript editions of *TSum* and *TSch*, which remained incomplete at the time of his death in 1975. I would also like to express my gratitude for assistance given by D. E. Luscombe, C. S. F. Burnett, J. Barrow, numerous librarians throughout Europe and the Hill Monastic Manuscript Library, Collegeville, Minnesota, U.S.A.

3. *Introductio ad theologiam*, ed. A. Duchesne, *Petri Abaelardi ... Opera ...* (Paris 1616), pp. 973-1136. The same collected edition also appeared in 1616 under the

110

a later, much improved version of the *Theologia Christiana*[4]. The basic outline of our present knowledge of three major versions of the *Theologia* was completed by the work of R. Stölzle who published in 1891 an edition of the initial form of this treatise, the *Theologia 'Summi boni'*, or, as he titled it, the *Tractatus de Unitate et Trinitate divina*[5].

This picture was considerably refined by H. Ostlender, who published in 1926 a study of the differences between individual manuscripts of the *Theologia 'Scholarium'*, each of which he classified into one of five 'redactions'. He also produced a new edition of the *Theologia 'Summi boni'*[6]. Ostlender's research and system of classification of the *Theologia* into 'redactions' was the major starting point for the studies undertaken between 1961 and 1965 on the text and chronological succession of the different recensions of the *Theologia Christiana* and *Theologia 'Scholarium'*[7]. This research was synthesised by Buytaert with little major change within his 1969 edition of these two works (the *Theologia 'Scholarium'* in shorter form, *tsch*, only)[8].

name of F. d'Amboise. Duchesne claimed to have used two manuscripts of St Victor, but study of the text shows that he only used the *Paris, Bibliothèque de l'Arsenal MS 265 (St Victor HH 13)* for the title, missing in *P*. D'Amboise only noted the use of one manuscript; cf. J. MONFRIN, *Abélard. Historia Calamitatum* (Paris 1978), p. 46. *Theologia Christiana*, ed. E. MARTÈNE, *Thesaurus novus anecdotorum*, v (Paris 1717), cols. 1139-1369. Both editions are reprinted by Migne, PL 178, 979-1114 and 1113-1330 respectively. V. Cousin's edition of *TSch* and *TChr* was largely derivative of those of Duchesne and Martène, *Petri Abaelardi Opera*, ii, pp. 1-149 and 359-566.

4. D. GOLDHORN, *De summis principiis theologiae Abaelardeae* (Leipzig 1836) and, with fuller chronological arguments, *Abälards dogmatische Hauptwerke "Tractatus de unitate et Trinitate und Theologia"*, in *Zeitschrift für die historische Theologie* 30 (1866) 161-229.

5. R. STÖLZLE, *Abaelards 1121 zu Soissons verurtheilter 'Tractatus de Unitate et Trinitate divina'* (Freiburg i. Br. 1891); see also his study *Abälards verloren geglaubter Traktat 'De Unitate et Trinitate divina'*, in *Historisches Jahrbuch* 9 (1890) 673-686.

6. H. OSTLENDER, *Die Theologia "Scholarium" des Peter Abaelard*, in *Aus der Geisteswelt des Mittelalters*, BGPTMA, Supplementband iii. 1 (1935), pp. 262-281; *Peter Abaelards Theologia 'Summi boni'*, in BGPTMA, xxxv. 2-3 (1939).

7. D. VAN DEN EYNDE, *La "Theologia Scholarium" de Pierre Abélard*, in RTAM 28 (1961) 225-241; *Les Rédactions de la "Theologia Christiana" de Pierre Abélard*, in *Antonianum* 36 (1961) 273-299; E.M. BUYTAERT, *An Earlier Redaction of the "Theologia Christiana" of Abelard*, in *Anton.* 37 (1962) 481-495; *Critical Observations on the "Theologia Christiana" of Abelard*, in *Anton.* 38 (1963) 384-433; *Thomas of Morigny and the "Theologia Scholarium" of Abelard*, in *Anton.* 40 (1965) 71-95.

8. CCCM 12, pp. 7-68 and 375-398. Buytaert summarised the development of ideas in the *Theologia*, in his paper *Abelard's Trinitarian Doctrine*, in *Peter Abelard*.

The work of an editor, however, never stands still. Buytaert's edition of Abelard's commentary on Romans has been reviewed and corrected in many points of detail by R. Peppermüller, while N. Häring has criticised Buytaert's editions of the *Apologia contra Bernardum* and of the *Capitula Haeresum XIV*, and has provided a new edition of the latter work[9]. In a paper offered at the conference held in Trier, 17-19 April 1979, on the 900th anniversary of Abelard's birth, the author has suggested that Buytaert's understanding of the development of different recensions of the *Theologia* needs to be considerably revised if their significance is to be properly understood[10]. The basis of the argument put forward in that paper was that a number of different recensions of *TChr* and *tsch* are simply drafts composed by Abelard to prepare for a major revision of the *Theologia*, the *Theologia 'Scholarium'*. What follows here is a more detailed analysis of the manuscripts of *TChr* and *tsch*, so that Buytaert's edition can be used with both care and profit for understanding the evolution of Abelard's thought about the Trinity.

The manuscripts of the Theologia

Before analysing the MSS of *TChr* and *tsch* in detail, it may be useful to list all the extant MSS of the *Theologia* (exluding seventeenth century transcriptions from known MSS), giving the *sigla* and numbering of each 'redaction' as used by Buytaert, with that of Ostlender in brackets where it differs :

Theologia 'Summi boni' (TSum)

  1 *E*   *Erlangen, Universitätsbibliothek, lat. 182*, fos. 27-65^v; s. xii.
     L   *Oxford, Bodleian Library, Lyell 49*, fos. 101-128^v; s. xii.

Proceedings of the International Conference, Louvain May 10-12, 1971, ed. E. M. BUYTAERT (Leuven-The Hague 1974), pp. 127-152.
9. R. PEPPERMÜLLER, *Zur kritischen Ausgabe des Römerbrief Kommentars des Petrus Abaelardus*, in *Scriptorium* 26 (1972) 82-97. N. HÄRING in a review, *The Thomist* 35 (1971) 319-323 and in *Die vierzehn Capitula Heresum Petri Abaelardi*, in *Cîteaux* 31 (1980) 35-52.
10. C. J. MEWS, *The development of the 'Theologia' of Peter Abelard*, in *Petrus Abaelardus. Person, Werk und Wirkung*, ed. R. THOMAS (Trier 1980), pp. 188-193. These ideas are also developed within a doctoral thesis, *The development of the Theologia of Peter Abelard* (Oxford D. Phil. thesis, 1980), deposited in the Bodleian Library, Oxford.

2 B *Berlin West, Staatsbibliothek Preussischer Kulturbesitz, theol. lat. oct. 95*, fos. 1ᵛ-64ᵛ; s. xii.

Theologia Christiana (TChr)

    D *Durham, Chapter Library of the Cathedral, A. IV. 15*, fos. 57-65ᵛ; s. xii.

(1) 2 R *Vatican, Reginensis lat. 159*, fos. 1-115; s. xii.

(2) 3 C *Monte Cassino, Archivio della Badia 174*, pp. 133-276; s. xii.

(3)   T *Tours, Bibl. mun. 85*, fos. 133-155ᵛ; s. xii.

Theologia 'Scholarium' (tsch)

1 F *Fulda, Priesterseminar 1*, fos. 94ᵛ-98; s. xii.

  H *Heiligenkreuz, Stiftsbibliothek 153*, fos. 82ᵛ-87ᵛ; s. xii.

  Z *Zurich, Zentralbibliothek C. 61*, fos. 53ᵛ-60ᵛ; s. xii.

2 T *Tours, Bibl. mun. 85*, fos. 156-158ᵛ; s. xii.

Theologia 'Scholarium' (TSch)

3 B *London, B.L. Royal 8. A. I*, fos. 3-69; s. xii-xiii.

  D *Douai, Bibl. mun. 357*, fos. 108-139ᵛ; s. xii.

  K *Koblenz-Ehrenbreitstein, Archivbibliothek des Provinzialat der Rheinische-Westfalische Kapuzinerprovinz, cod. 1*, fos. 103-161ᵛ; s. xv.

  M *Berlin East, Deutsche Staatsbibliothek, Magdeburg 34*, fos. 193-261ᵛ; 1452 a.d.

(4) 3' A *Paris, Bibl. de l'Arsenal, lat. 265*, fos. 65-92ᵛ; s. xii.

  P *Paris, Bibl. nat., lat. 14793*, fos. 1-69ᵛ; s. xiv-xv.

(5) 4 O *Oxford, Balliol College 296*, fos. 1-60ᵛ; s. xiv.

To avoid confusion different recensions will not be given numbers, but referred to simply by the *sigla* of the MSS in which they are found, e.g. *TChr CT*, *tsch FH* etc. Individual passages in these works will be cited by the book and paragraph of Buytaert's edition, followed in brackets by the page number of Ostlender's edition of *TSum* or of Cousin's edition of *TSch*, where relevant. Ostlender's edition of *TSum* can be trusted to provide a reasonably accurate text, although a number of readings can be improved by reference to Häring's analysis of the *Oxford MS*, *Lyell 49* (textually very similar to the Erlangen MS)[11]. Cousin's edition of *TSch*, erroneously titled the *Introductio ad theologiam*, is less reliable and only improves on that of Duchesne in correcting certain readings from the same

---

11. N. HÄRING, *A Third MS of Peter Abelard's Theologia Summi boni (MS Oxford, Bodleian, Lyell 49, ff. 101-128ᵛ)*, in *Medieval Studies* 18 (1956) 215-224.

late fourteenth/early fifteenth century MS (*P*) that Duchesne himself used. He also supplied the last part of *TSch*, found only in the *Oxford MS, Balliol College 296*, fos. 58^v-60^v, although this probably through a seventeenth-century transcription, *Oxford, Bodleian Library, Wood Donat. 2*, pp. 148-171[12]. The text of *TSch* on fos. 35^v-41 of the Balliol MS was not given by Cousin, and can be found only in excerpts quoted by Ostlender[13]. The recension of *TSch* in *AP*, the basis of the editions of Duchesne and (apart from the conclusion) Cousin is only marginally different from that of *TSch* in *BDKM*, containing two small passages which have been added to the latter recension[14].

Theologia Christiana : D and R

The recensions of the *Theologia Christiana* found in the MSS *Durham Chapter Library A. IV. 15* (*D*) and *Vatican, Reg. lat. 159* (*R*) are both considerably shorter than that found in the MSS *Tours, Bibliothèque municipale 85* (*T*) and *Monte Cassino, Archivio della Badia 174* (*C*). As Buytaert's descriptions of these manuscripts are not always complete, it is necessary to examine each in turn, looking not just at the text of *TChr*, but at each manuscript as a whole.

The Durham manuscript has already been described by Mynors and by Buytaert, but it may be useful to add and correct certain points here[15]. The codex contains three sections: the first (fos. i-iii, 1-16) was probably written in the third quarter of the twelfth century by a Durham scribe, while the second (fos. 17-56) and third (fos. 57-69) were probably written earlier, in the mid-twelfth century,

---

12. Cousin mentions both MSS on p. 2 of his edition, but the variants he gives are exactly those of the transcription. He used the same transcription, and not the Balliol MS, in order to extend his edition of the *Ethics*, D. E. LUSCOMBE, *Peter Abelard's Ethics* (Oxford (1971), p. lii.

13. *Die Theologia "Scholarium"*, pp. 275-279.

14. *TSch* II, 92 (1072BC; ed. COUSIN, p. 92) *Quod diligenter ... non habet prolem*, also added in part in *TSch* I, 22 (989D; p. 11); *TSch* II, 125 (1072C; p. 101) *Hinc Nicaena ... dicendus est.*

15. R. A. B. MYNORS, *Durham Cathedral Manuscripts to the End of the Twelft Century* (Oxford 1939), pp. 51-52; BUYTAERT, *An Earlier Redaction*, 481-484 and in the introduction to his edition of *TChr* (henceforward cited as *TChr* - Introduction), pp. 10-14.

114

not necessarily at Durham. The second and third sections are of similar parchment, of poorer quality than that of the first section. The single hand which wrote the third section, similar though different to that of the second, is not unlike that which copied *TChr* in the *Tours, Bibliothèque municipale MS 85*, of French origin. The codex was put together in its present form in Durham in either the late twelfth or early thirteenth century[16].

The first section contains the gospel of John, preceeded by the 'Monarchian' prologue, while the second contains glosses on this gospel, attributed in other MSS to Anselm of Laon[17]. The third section contains the first book only of *TChr* (fos. 57-65^v), followed in the same hand by some notes on virtues (fo. 66) and a theological tract (fos. 66^v-67^v) which Buytaert thought were four separate texts, two of which might have been taken from a commentary on the Creed[18].

The tract (*incipit*: *Est una et perfecta unitas ... explicit*: *et in homine Deus*) is clearly, however, a single work, which, although not by Abelard is of interest in itself. The author gives his understanding of the doctrine of the Trinity, followed by a long statement of his belief in the main articles of the Athanasian Creed of his denial of numerous heresies. The author began his explanation by asserting that the names of the three persons of the Trinity were applied to signify properties in God:

> (fo. 66^v). Ad significanda igitur unitatem substantie inuenta sunt nomina opificis, eternus, immensus, bonus et similia, quorum nullum est accidentale. Ad significandam uero proprietatem illorum trium reperta sunt hec nomina : Pater, Filius, Spiritus Sanctus, quorum nullum est substantiale uel accidentale ... et ita data sunt hec nomina, ut habitudo ingenite persone ad genitam dicatur Pater, habitudo uero genite ... etc.

16. Mynors suggests that the first section is mid-twelfth century, and later than the second and third sections, while Buytaert adopts a slightly later dating, *An Earlier Redaction*, 481-482. An inscription of Durham is found in the hand of the copyist of the first section on fo. 1 while there is no such indication on the other sections.

17. The same gloss is found in *Durham Cathedral B. III. 7* and *Cambridge, Trinity College B. I. 10* attributed to Anselm, but is anonymous in *Lincoln Cathedral A. V. 12*.

18. BUYTAERT, *TChr* - Introduction, pp. 12-13.

The author stressed that the Greeks used *substantia* and occasionally *res* to denote what the Latins meant by person :

> (fo. 66ᵛ). Et etiam secundum proprietatem Grece linguae, dicuntur tres *substantie*, que enim est apud Grecos substantia, hoc est apud Latinos sonat persona; et inueniuntur iste tres persone in quibusdam codicibus dici *res*, sed raro. Quod uero apud nos sonat substantia, apud Grecos dicitur usia. ... Dicatur itaque hec nomina relatiua esse, non substantiua, et quamuis substantiam significent, non sunt tamen nomina substantie.

These ideas are similar to those of Abelard's former teacher, Roscelin of Compiègne, who emphasised the distinction between the three persons to such an extent as to compare them to three *res*[19]. Like Roscelin, the author of this tract criticised the idea that Christ was subject to necessity and could not do all that he willed :

> (fo. 67). Anathematizamus etiam illos qui Dei Filium necessitate carnis mutatum esse dicunt, et eum propter assumptum hominem non omnia facere potuisse que uoluit.

The criticism is similar to that made by Roscelin of the teaching Anselm of Canterbury that God was obliged to become man and to suffer everything which he did[20]. In general, however, the purpose of the tract is not polemical, but to assert the author's disassociation from every known heresy :

> (fo. 67). Sin autem hec nostra confessio apostolatus iudicio comprobatur, quicumque uoluerit, se imperitum uel maliuolum uel etiam non catholicum, non me hereticum comprobabit.

If this tract is a *confessio fidei* by Roscelin, it is significant that it should accompany the earliest recension of *TChr*, because *TChr* was written in the immediate aftermath of Abelard's dispute with Roscelin. Abelard amplified in *TChr* many of the indirect criticisms which he had made of Roscelin in *TSum*[21].

The text of *TChr* in *D* is generally good, but unfortunately extends only to the end of the first book, even though the *capitula librorum* at the beginning of *TChr* describe the contents of all five. The copyist of *D* must either have had a deficient exemplar or he decided

---

19. *Epistola ad Abaelardum*, ed. J. REINERS, *Der Nominalismus in der Frühscholastik. Ein Beitrag zur Geschichte der Universalienfrage im Mittelalter*, BGPTMA viii (1910), pp. 72-76.

20. *Ibid.*, pp. 67-68.

21. Cf. *TChr* III, 119-135.

116

not to copy more than the first book, as he changes from *TChr* to other texts within the same gathering. The characteristics of *TChr D* can best be studied by comparing the text of *D* to that of the *Vatican MS, Reg. lat. 159 (R)*.

This manuscript, which contains nothing but *TChr*, was written by a French hand in the second half of the twelfth century[22]. By far the smallest (158 × 110mm) of MSS of *TChr*, *R* seems to have been written and used within a scholastic environment. The lines are not always straight on the page, they vary in number, and there are frequent marks by the text of *TChr* in hard point and in pencil[23]. The early history of *R*, before it was purchased by the Parisian Alexander Petau in 1647 is unknown.

Because the Durham MS does not go further than the first book of *TChr*, it is impossible to gain an accurate idea of exactly how far the text of *D* would have differed from that of *R*. However, because the visible differences between *D* and *R* are relatively few, it may be assumed that the changes made to books II-V in *TChr R* would not have been major. The passages either added to, or modified from the text of *TChr D* extend or revise Abelard's argument only on points of detail :

> *TChr RCT*   I, 27-28   cf. *TChr D* I, 27-28
>   I, 34
>   I, 82-86
>   I, 90
>   I, 120-121

Although it is technically possible that these passages were accidentally omitted by the copyist of *D*, the fact that the text of *D* sometimes agrees with that of *TSum* against all other MSS of *TChr*

---

22. *R* was first described and given a partial edition by C. OTTAVIANO, *Un brano inedito della 'Theologia Christiana' di Abelardo*, in *Giornale critico della filosofia italiana* 11 (1930) 326-332, and subsequently by A. WILMART, *Bibliothecae Apostolicae Vaticanae Codices Manu Scripti*, I : *Codices Reginenses Latini* (Vatican City 1937), pp. 377-378 and BUYTAERT, *TChr* - Introduction, pp. 14-16. Wilmart and Buytaert retained Ottaviano's dating of *R* to the late twelfth century. Not noted by these authors is the absence of any 'gothic' tendency in the script, use of the ampersand alongside the tironian *et* and the running through in red of scriptural passages. There is no cidilla under the *e*.

23. WILMART, *Cod. Reg. Lat.* I, 378. Other MSS of *TChr* are larger than *R* and do not have as much annotation : *D* 237 × 160mm; *C* 230 × 154mm; *T* 312 × 200mm.

as well as the presence of certain irregularities in *R* would suggest that *D* contains an earlier recension of *TChr* than R.

Buytaert describes some of these irregularities in *R*, although not always completely or accurately. The first gathering (fos. 1-8) contains either 30 or 31 lines to the page, apart from the central folios (4-5) which contain 36 lines. These two folios include the passages *TChr* I, 27-28 in revised from from that of *D* and I, 34, absent from *D*. The second gathering (fos. 9-13) is irregularly short, while it contains fo. 12 as an added leaf with only 25 lines on the recto side and 26 on the verso, both sides being written in a darker ink than the surrounding leaves. The same more spacious measure adopted on fo. 12 continues over an erasure for the first two lines of fo. 13 until the line beginning *Illud quoque* ... (*TChr DRCT* I, 87). Fo. 12 contains, after a few lines of *TChr* I, 81, the text of *TChr* *R* I, 82-86 which is missing in *D*. It seems to have been added to accomodate neatly this long additional passage, in exactly the same way as fos. 4-5 apparently replace two earlier folios. The irregularly short second gathering (fos. 9-13) may not be a later addition, as it has been correctly signed with a feint *ii* on fo. 13[v], although when the scribe inked over these signatures, he omitted that of the second gathering, like that of the fifteenth and sixteenth, so causing an irregularity in numbering.

The transposition of the second part of *TChr* I, 120-121 (*-ticeri... reuelaturus esset*), placed after I, 122 in *R*, is difficult to explain unless the passage I, 120-121, which is absent from *D*, was a marginal note in the exemplar of *R* which extended over the page. If this marginal note ended at the bottom of the page with *re-*, the copyist of *R* might have thought this was the end of the marginal addition and so continued to copy his main text. On turning the page of his exemplar, he may have noticed the continuation of the marginal note, which he then incorporated into his text with an appropriate indication to show where it properly belonged.

Although the text of books II-V does not survive in *D*, irregularities in the text of *R* led Buytaert to identify other passages which he thought had been added in *TChr* *R*[24]. One such passage may be

24. BUYTAERT, *An Earlier Redaction*, 490-492; *Critical Observations*, 398-399; *TChr* - Introduction, pp. 30-32.

II, 7, a comment on two psalms, found in the margin of *R*, only the introductory words *Hinc et* existing in the text. These two words could have introduced II, 8 in the original recension. Buytaert suggested that Abelard may have added some extracts of Valerius Maximus in *TChr R* II, 102-103 by analogy with the added passage *TChr* I, 120-121 in which Valerius Maximus is also cited. There are, however, no irregularities in the text of *R* to support this hypothesis, which would logically require *TChr* II, 48, 58, 72, 74 and 107 to have been added as well. One irregularity convincingly identified is a reference to a text of Jerome as *ibidem*, when the preceeding text in *RCT* is one of Augustine, itself placed after the text of Jerome in question. This passage of Augustine (IV, 134) may have been a marginal note in *R*'s exemplar which was incorporated into the main text not just by the copyist of *R*, but also that of *C* and *T*.

Occasionally an irregularity in *C* and *T* may indicate that a passage was new to the recension *TChr R*, even though the copyist of *R* incorporated such an addition into the body of his text. In *TChr* III, 51, *C* follows III, 50 with the first words of III, 52, but then deletes these words to continue with the text of III, 51, a series of quotations from Augustine and Jerome. If the exemplar of *C* had this passage as a marginal note, it is possible that it was also such a note in the exemplar of *R*. The same phrase *Hinc et...* introduces the citation here as another note, found in the margin of *R*, *TChr* II, 7. In both *C* and *T* the major part of *TChr* III, 55, a fuller quotation from Augustine's *De moribus ecclesie contra Manicheos* than that given in III, 1, also occurs in the margin, although this passage has been incorporated into the text of *R*. The common ancestor of *C* and *T*, like that of *R*, seems to have contained a number of marginal texts, which may have been additions to the original text of *TChr*, atthough of this one cannot be certain.

In two places *TChr R* contains the same text as *C* and *T* but placed slightly differently within *TChr*. A sequence of quotations from Gregory, Ambrose and Jerome on the eternal generation of the Word comes after *TChr* IV, 104 in *R*, but after IV, 111 in *T* (and accidentally omitted in *C*). The position of this sequence in *T* makes more logical sense than that in *R*. Similarly the sequence of patristic quotations in *TChr* V, 23, which in *R* interrupts discussion of statements of St Paul, is found in a more natural position in both *C* and *T*. Both of these sequences, which are identical to sequences in the *Sic et Non*, may have been marginal additions in the exemplar of *R*, but which were incorporated by its copyist into the wrong place.

There could be other similar passages in books II-V which were incorporated into the text of *R*, *C* and *T*, but which cannot be identified with certainty without a complete text of *TChr D*. Stylistic markers which may denote the insertion of a passage into, or rather alongside the original text of *TChr* are introductory words like *Hinc et*, *Hinc etiam*, *Vnde* etc., which introduce many of the known additions in *TChr R*. If these passages, often simply series of patristic quotations identical to sequences in the *Sic et Non*, are removed from the main body of the text of *TChr* and read as footnotes for the enquiring reader, Abelard's argument becomes considerably easier to read and follow. Sometimes these patristic texts have the effect of interrupting the flow of the argument, rather than of fitting naturally into the discussion[25].

There are some irregularities in the physical make-up of *R*, like those observed in fos. 4-5 and 12, which suggest that certain folios may have been replaced to contain more neatly an extended or corrected text. In the fourteenth gathering (fos. 98-105), fo. 99 has 30 lines recto and verso and the materially corresponding fo. 104 29 lines, although fos. 98 and 105 have 25 lines (recto and verso) and fos. 100-103^v 23 lines. It is possible that the double folio

---

25. Buytaert's references to the *Sic et Non* are to an unpublished edition. Generally, although not always, his references to *SNlg* correspond to those of B. B. BOYER and R. McKEON, *Peter Abelard. Sic et Non* (Chicago 1976-1977). Some of the clear parallels between *TChr R* and the *Sic et Non* can be given here:

TChr	III,	50-51	= *SN* 18. 12-14; 1. 7-8, 18, 9 (ed. BOYER-McKEON).
	III,	68	= *SN* 8. 33-34 (not in *Z*).
	III,	70	= *SN* 11. 4-5.
	III,	120	= *SN* 9. 8.
	III,	123	= *SN* 9. 4-5.
	IV,	14-15	= *SN* 11. 3; 8. 3, 26-27.
	IV,	27	= *SN* 8. 31-32.
	IV,	28-29	= *SN* 8. 25, 22, 23 (not in *Z*).
	IV,	97	= *SN* 14. 7-10.
	IV,	148-149	= *SN* 24. 8, 10-12, 9 (not in *Z*).
	V,	23	= *SN* 32. 6-7 (not in *ZTCEB*).
	V,	38-40	= *SN* 35. 5-14 (not in *Z*; ʕ not in *ZTCEB*).

99/104 may have replaced an earlier double folio in order to accomodate more neatly new texts such as the citation and discussion of Hilary in *TChr* IV, 136, which begins *Vnde et...* and is extended further in *CT*.

In the sixteenth gathering (fos. 110-115), which has only six rather than the normal eight folios, fos. 110 and 111 have 30 and 31 lines respectively, while the materially corresponding fo. 114 has 31 lines (recto and verso) and fo. 115 only 17. Fos. 112-113ᵛ have 25 lines as does most of the manuscript from the sixth gathering on (fo. 34). By analogy with the irregular collation of the third gathering, Buytaert suggested that fos. 114-115 were rewritten and fos. 110-111 recopied to accomodate new texts[26]. The hand is the same as that which wrote the rest of *TChr*, and not a second hand as claimed by Buytaert. Given the nature of the texts on these folios, and the precedent of other irregularities in *R*, fos. 110ᵛ-111ᵛ may have been rewritten to accomodate the long sequence of quotations from Augustine in *TChr* V, 38-40. The fact that this sequence is one of only two in *TChr R* to be identical to a relatively late recension of the *Sic et Non* would strengthen the possibility that it had been added to an original recension of *TChr*[27]. The other such sequence is *TChr* V, 23, already discussed as likely to have been a marginal note, copied into the wrong place by the copyist of *R*[28].

A clearer example of a correction to the original text of *TChr* leaving traces in *R* was that observed by Buytaert of a change in attribution of the *De orthodoxa fide* from Augustine to Genna-dius[29]. In *TChr D* I, 28 this work is attributed implicitly to Augustine, while in *RCT* the work is attributed correctly to Genna-dius. This correction is incorporated into the new sequence of

---

26. BUYTAERT, *TChr* - Introduction, p. 15.

27. The sequence occurs in this form only in the *versio altera* (*DL*) and in the complete version of *SN* (*MKA*). *TChr* V, 39 includes an apparent passage of Abelard included within *SN DLMKA* 35. 9 (corrupt in *TCEB*) and has variants unique to *DLMKA*, suggesting that Abelard had already composed *SN TCEB* before making the additions in *TChr R* and had quite possibly revised the first part of *SN* into the form *DL* by this time.

28. *TChr R* V, 23 is parallel to *SN DL* 32. 6-7 and has been extended in *CT* with 32. 2 which in *DL*, but not *MKA*, follows 32. 6-7. It is possible that the latter text was part of an original marginal addition but was omitted by *R*. This sequence in *SN DL* is followed by a comment of Abelard on the definition of omnipotence related to the argument of *TChr V* (*SN* 32. 2ª, ed. BOYER-McKEON, p. 614).

texts in *TChr* I, 27-28, found in *R* on fos. 4^v-5, folios apparently replacing others in the original manuscript. Although this passage in *C* takes the same form as in *R*, there is a distortion in the position as well as of the attribution of this passage in *T* which deserves closer examination. *T* contains the longer quotation from Augustine's *Dialogus Quaestionum LXV* which in *R* replaces its indirect quotation in *D*. *T*, however, follows this with the text of the *De orthodoxa fide* introduced as *Item idem*, in other words attributed implicitly to Augustine, exactly as in *D*. He then followed this text with that of Gregory, *Hunc beatus Gregorius ... procedentem*, absent from *D*. The copyist subsequently realised his earlier mistake and wrote *Gennadius* over *Item idem*. Continuing to copy from the improved text, he began to copy the text which he had already included in its old form, but with the new attribution, writing the words *Et Gennadius Massiliensis de orto*, only to break off and continue with the text of Isidore, absent from *D*, which followed. As Buytaert observed, *T* is based here on two versions of the text, one corresponding to *D*, the other to *R* (and *C*)[30]. Either these were separate manuscripts, or more plausibly the exemplar of *T* contained an original recension of *TChr* with a corrected series of texts in the margin. This would be consistent with the exemplars of *R* and *C*, which also contained marginal passages not always correctly understood by the copyists of these manuscripts. The complexity of the corrections made to *TChr* I, 27-28 may explain why the copyist of *R* replaced fos. 4-5 with a neat, although more tightly written double folio.

One further complication in this jig-saw puzzle, which greatly pre-occupied Buytaert, was the same passage in *tsch* 30[31]. In *tsch Z* 30 the sequence of texts is exactly like the apparently mistaken order of *TChr T* I, 27-28, as distinct from that of *R* or *C*, except that the *De orthodoxa fide* is attributed implicitly to Augustine. This is identical to *T*, if the interlinear correction *Gennadius* is ignored. By contrast, *tsch T* (the same manuscript as contains *TChr*) incorporates *et Gennadius* after *Idem* as if to correct the

29. BUYTAERT, *An Earlier Redaction*, 485-492.
30. *Ibid.*, 486.
31. *Ibid.*, 486-490; *TChr* - Introduction, pp. 50-51 and *tsch* - Introduction, pp. 388-389.

error of *tsch* Z. Buytaert was concerned with this point because it seemed to suggest that *tsch* Z, with its implicit attribution to Augustine, was earlier than *TChr* R, in which the same text was attributed to Gennadius. This problem disappears, however, if R is correctly interpreting a correction made to its exemplar, while Z, faced with an exemplar as ambiguous as that of T (*TChr*), does so incorrectly.

In almost all the other places in *TChr* in which the *De orthodoxa fide* is quoted, there is evidence in one or other of the MSS of *TChr* that the name of Augustine has been corrected to that of Gennadius in an original exemplar. In *TChr* I, 114 the work was first attributed to Augustine in R (fo. 17), as in D, but Augustine's name was then erased and replaced with *Gennadius* by the same hand. Both C and T follow D in reading *Augustinus*, although the same passage in *TSch* I, 175 has the attribution to *Gennadius*[32]. This excerpt is quoted in *TChr* III, 117 in fuller form (and therefore not copied from I, 114) in R, where it is attributed to Gennadius (fo. 64). This passage in C and T is also attributed to Gennadius. In *TChr* II, 113 the *De orthodoxa fide* is attributed to Augustine in the text of R (fo. 43ᵛ), but the copyist has subsequently deleted this and has added *Gennadius* above the line.

The same formula *Vnde Gennadius* ... introduces a text in *TChr* III, 23 and, although there is no erasure evident here, the fact that the passage of Augustine which follows immediately is introduced as *Idem*, shows that the preceeding passage had been introduced as of Augustine. The copyists of R and of C subsequently corrected the faulty *Idem*, but not that of T. The same sequence of texts is cited in a slightly different order in *tsch* 9. As noted in *tsch* 30, *tsch* Z 9 has the work attributed to Augustine (perhaps following F and H, MSS to be discussed in due course), while *tsch* T has Gennadius. Again, *TChr* R does not have to be later than *tsch* FHZ if *FHZ* is based on an uncorrected text or simply missed a correction. The copyist of R has incorporated such a correction without trace in *TChr* IV, 28 (fo. 79ᵛ), while in IV, 95 (fo. 92) he was obliged to erase *Idem* in order to incorporate *Gennadius*. C and T omitted *Idem*, but failed to add the new attribution. In *TChr* III, 76 a passage from

Augustine's *Enchiridion* is mistakenly cited as his *De orthodoxa fide*. The same text about God's goodness appears in various forms in *TChr* II, 30, III, 99 and IV, 132. The copyist of *R* initially introduced the text in III, 76 as *Vnde Augustinus* ..., but then erased *Augustinus* and replaced it with *Gennadius* after the erasure (fo. 60), before continuing with his text. This faulty attribution to Gennadius was also copied by *C* and *T*.

What conclusions can be drawn from these corrections within the text of *R*? Besides those passages in book I which are absent from *D*, but are found in *R* (I, 27-28, 34, 82-86, 90, 120-121), the following passages were very likely added to the original recension of *TChr*: II, 7; III, 51, 55; IV, 105 (= *T* IV, 112); V, 23, 38-40. This revises slightly the list given by Buytaert[33]. In addition the *De orthodoxa fide* was attributed to Gennadius instead of to Augustine as it had been in *TChr D*. Most of these new passages supply further *auctoritates*, often identical to passages within the *Sic et Non*, from which some may have been drawn[34]. There may be many other passages which have been added in *TChr R*, not in an earlier recension of *TChr*, but because they have all been incorporated into the body of text by *R* and *T*, they are difficult to identify. Many of these passage provide further authorities to justify Abelard's argument, although they have the effect of interrupting its flow. In reading the *Theologia Christiana*, the nature of the text as a montage of passages which have been added over a period of time, needs to be held firmly in mind.

While *R* contains a very good text of the *Theologia Christiana*, it was the work of a scribe who was having to interpret an exemplar which was not always clear. The copyists of *C* and *T* seem to have been faced with a similar problem. The copyist of *R* replaced the bi-folia 4/5, 98/105, 110/115 and 111/114, so as to contain a more closely written text, added fo. 12 and made a number of erasures, all apparently to contain passages which had been considerably modified or extended from their form in *D*. One explanation which would account for all the irregularities in *R*, as well as those in both *C*

33. *TChr* - Introduction, pp. 30-32.
34. *Vide supra*, nn. 25-28.

124

and *T*, would be that the exemplar of *R* contained many annotations and corrections to an original text, very like that of *D*. Alternatively, the copyist of R came across some new material after he had copied his text, although his first exemplar in itself contained some annotations. The most plausible explanation is that these corrected or additional passages were annotations to an original text, corrections very likely made by Abelard himself.

The manuscripts T and C

These additional passages in *TChr R* can be considered as the work of Abelard because, even if they were suggested by another individual, they were all incorporated by him into the much longer recension of *TChr* found in two manuscripts: *Tours, Bibliothèque municipale 85* (*T*) and *Monte Cassino, Archivio della Badia 174* (*C*). Both manuscripts have been described by Buytaert and by Boyer and McKeon, but because of their importance, it is necessary to look at them again in some detail[35].

The codex which is now in the library of Tours is made up of three sections, all written within the twelfth century: (I) fos. 1-64, 99-158; (II) fos. 65-98; (III) fos. 159-196. The text of the third section, containing mostly works by Hugh of St Victor, is laid out in two columns of 64 lines, with only slight variation in exactly the same dimensions (250 × 164 mm) as the preceeding section which contains glosses on scripture, the *Sic et Non* (fos. 106-118ᵛ) in Abelard's abridgement of Augustine's *Retractationes* (fos. 129ᵛ-132ᵛ), the *Theologia Christiana* (fos. 133-155ᵛ) and a short recension of the *Theologia 'Scholarium'* (fos. 156-158ᵛ). The second section of the codex, which is slightly smaller in size and written in a noticeably different hand from the surrounding text, continues without any break the scriptural glosses on fos. 1-64ᵛ. The similarity in layout

35. *T* is described briefly by M. COLLON, *Catalogue général des manuscrits des bibliothèques en France - Départements*, 37 : *Tours*, i (Paris 1900), pp. 47-51 and more fully in a handwritten notice at the *Institut de Recherche et d'Histoire des Textes* in Paris; by BUYTAERT, *TChr* - Introduction, pp. 16-23 and by BOYER-McKEON, *Sic et Non*, pp. 14-21. *C* is described by L. TOSTI, *Storia di Abelardo e dei suoi tempi* (Naples 1851), pp. 283-315 (with partial edition); by the author of the *Bibliotheca Casinensis*, iv (Monte Cassino 1880), pp. 5-16; by M. INGUANEZ, *Codicum Casinensium manuscriptorum catalogus* (Monte Cassino 1923), pp. 257-258; by BUYTAERT, *TChr* - Introduction, pp. 7-10; by BOYER-McKEON, *Sic et Non*, pp. 21-27.

between the adjacent first and third sections, as well as the very close similarity of hands in both sections would suggest that the codex was assembled by the same group of copyists. One twelfth century hand has added *Nota* throughout the whole codex, including by the *Theologia Christiana* (e.g. fos. 1ᵛ, 2ᵛ, 133).

The earliest indication of ownership of the manuscript is a list on fo. 196ᵛ of the names of some seventy people with the amount of money each had to pay to the priory of St Nicolas of Ploermel in 1254, under the rubric *Hii sunt census prioratus Sancti Nicholai de Ploarmel in festo omnium sanctorum anno MCCL quarto*, written in a hand of that date. St Nicolas was one of the many foundations of Marmoutier established in Brittany through count Conan III (1116-42), the same count as who invited Abelard to St Gildas de Ruys[36]. Although the connection may be fortuitous, St Gildas owned land around Ploermel (some 60 km distant) until 1257 according to a charter of exchange drawn up by John, duke of Brittany[37]. In the fifteenth century the priory of St Nicolas was united to that of St Martin of Josselin, and by 1600 had become a ruin[38]. The manuscript in question had been transferred to Marmoutier by the sixteenth century, where it was given the catalogue number *N 3* and a brief description of the codex added on fo. 1. Dom Martène, who used the manuscript for his 1717 edition of the *Theologia Christiana*, added running titles which identified *TChr* and *tsch* as works of Abelard. The manuscript entered the library of Tours in 1791[39].

The texts of Abelard in *T* were copied with the glosses on scripture as they occur together on both the eleventh (fos. 99-100) and

36. The foundation charter of St Nicolas is edited by S. ROPARTZ, *Notice sur la ville de Ploermel* (Rennes-Paris 1864), p. 186 and by A. DE LA BORDERIE, *Recueil d'Actes inédits des ducs et princes de Bretagne (XIᵉ, XIIᵉ, XIIIᵉ siècles)* (Rennes 1888), no. xxxiv, p. 74.

37. Ploermel is mentioned among many possessions of St Gildas in the charter edited by DE LA BORDERIE, *Recueil*, no. cxxx, pp. 206-207. See also LE MÉNÉ, *L'abbaye de Rhuys*, in *Bulletin de la Société polymathique du Morbihan* (1902) 76-77. This charter, like all other documents about St Gildas de Rhuys, is known only through the history of the monastery, compiled by Dom Noël Mars c. 1653 and found on pp. 635-676 of a long history of St Gildas and its abbots, written by an anonymous Maurist of St Gildas in 1668, now *Paris, Bibliothèque nationale fr. 16822*.

38. ROPARTZ, *Notice*, p. 160 and DE LA BORDERIE, *Recueil*, p. 75.

39. On the shelfmarks and history of the library of Marmoutiers, see COLLON, *Catalogue*, pp. vi-vii.

twelfth (fos. 111-138) gatherings. On fos. 99ra-106ra there is a gloss on the *Song of Songs*, followed on fos. 106rb-118vb by the *Sic et Non*, attributed to Abelard by the copyist. The *Sic et Non* is incomplete through the loss of a folio, while the same scribe has added on fos. 119ra-129rb excerpts from Bede, with passages parallel to the *Glossa Ordinaria*. They cover the only two historical books (not including the Pentateuch) which are not glossed on fos. 1-49 and were probably added here, because the copyist had forgotten to include them earlier in his manuscript[40]. He then returned to texts of Abelard by copying on fos. 129va-132vb the abridged version of Augustine's *Retractationes* intended to accompany the *Sic et Non*, followed by the *Theologia Christiana* on fos. 133ra-155vb, incomplete through the loss of a folio, and a short form of the *Theologia 'Scholarium'* on fos. 156ra-158vb (hence referred to as *tsch T*). The copyist stopped writing the latter work ... *quod nihil sit quod non sensum habeat in Deum* (*tsch* 111) a quarter of the way down the second column of fo. 158^{v}.

The *Monte Cassino MS, Archivio della Badia 174* (*C*) is similar to *T* in that, after containing Augustine's *Enchiridion de spe et caritate*, preceeded by its *capitula*, on pp. 1-51, and the complete text of Augustine's *Retractationes* on pp. 53-132, it contains the *Theologia Christiana* on pp. 133-276 and the *Sic et Non* on pp. 277-451. As in *T*, *TChr* is anonymous while the *Sic et Non* is attributed to Abelard, although the sequence of the two works is reversed. Each of the four works in *C* occurs in a separate section of the codex, although all are written by hands of the same school at the same period of time in the late twelfth or early thirteenth century[41]. One hand copied the two works of Augustine, while another copied both the *TChr* and, with the help of one other, the *Sic et Non*. The *TChr* and the *Sic et Non* were originally separate manuscripts, as shown by the signatures to the gatherings of both works, but the rubrics to these works, as to those of Augustine, were all written by one hand, who used the same style of decoration throughout. Although there is no firm indication, the codex may

---

40. *Expositio allegoricae in Ezram et Nehemiam* (PL 91, 807C-924B) and the *Glossa Ordinaria* (PL 113, 691D-726B).
41. BOYER-MCKEON, p. 15.

well have been written at Monte Cassino, where it has always remained[42].

The Sic et Non in T and C

Before proceeding to analyse the text of the *Theologia Christiana* in *T* and *C*, it may be worthwhile to summarise and comment on the observations of Boyer and McKeon in their admirable analysis of the text of the *Sic et Non*, as found in these two manuscripts[43]. The sixty-seven questions in *T* correspond almost identically to those of *C* if allowance is made for the fact that the *Sic et Non* in *T* is incomplete and that *T* seems to have been copied from an exemplar in which a series of adjacent questions (62, 68, 63, 72, 48, 78, 84, 106, 158, 107, 110-113, 115) was missing[44]. The copyist of *T* has added a sign on fo. 11[va] indicating such a lacuna between *SN* 80, 33 and *SN* 47, 11. The missing section is found not only in *C*, but in two other manuscripts which also contain the same recension, although in truncated form, of the *Sic et Non*: *Brescia, Biblioteca Queriniana A. V. 21*, fos. 14-64[v] (*B*) and *Einsiedeln, Stiftsbibliothek 300*, pp. 1-74 (*E*). The text of the *Sic et Non* in these two manuscripts, however, breaks off within q. 117, a long series of quotations about the eucharist[45]. A complete text of q. 117 in the same form as in *TC*, and *EB* as far as can be judged, is found on its own as a *Tractatus Magistri Petri Abaielardi de sacramento altaris*, in the *Turin, Biblioteca Nazionale MS E. V. 9*, fos. 168-174 (*S*)[46].

Boyer and McKeon classified the recension of the *Sic et Non*

---

42. BUYTAERT, *TChr* - Introduction, p. 7.

43. BOYER-McKEON, *Sic et Non*, pp. 14-27.

44. *Ibid.*, p. 16.

45. *Ibid.*, pp. 28-43. *B* also has a mutilated porton containing qq. 56, 139, 136 and 137 with the Gelasian decree and Abelard's abridgement of Augustine's *Retractationes* in an initial two gatherings *ibid.*, p. 35.

46. Not used by Boyer-McKeon. Described briefly by F. COSENTINI, *Inventari dei manoscritti delle Biblioteche d'Italia*, ed. G. MAZZATINTI, 28 Torino, no. 749, p. 76. The fragment is written in a fourteenth century hand. According to an unpublished study of Julia Barrow, to whom I am grateful for communicating her research, the text of *S* is closely related to that of *TCEB* in q. 117, while is not directly derivative of any one of these MSS. It is particularly close to that of q. 117 in *B* for as far as can be ascertained.

128

found in *TCEB* as a *versio prima*, transitional between a draft recension found in the *Zurich, Zentralbibliothek MS Car. C. 162*, fos. 23-38^v (*Z*) and a *versio altera* found in two truncated MSS, *Douai, Bibliothèque municipale 357*, fos. 140-155^v (*D*) and *London, British Library, Royal 11. A. V*, fos. 73-98^v (*L*). This latter version is itself anterior to the final form of the *Sic et Non*, containing one hundred and fifty-eight questions, found in three manuscripts (excluding a sixteenth century transcription): *Munich, Staatsbibliothek Clm 18926*, fos. 14^v-105^v (*M*), *Cambridge, University Library, Kk 3, 24*, fos. 67^v-159 (*K*) and *Avranches, Bibliothèque municipale 12*, fos. 132-207 (*A*)[47].

The sequence of questions discussed in *TCEB* is quite different from that of the final form of the *Sic et Non* and reflects more clearly than *MKA* a division into questions about faith in God and the Trinity (qq. 1-6, 8-9, 11-18, 27, 19, 23-24, 7), about Christ (66, 64, 75, 67, 42, 41, 70-71, 35-36, 79, 69, 80, 62, 68, 63, 72-73, 48, 78, 84), about the sacraments (106, 158, 108, 110-113, 115-135) and about sin or the lack of charity (56, 139, 136-137, 140, 138, 141-144, 149, 145-147, 31, 148, 151, 153-154, 157). The subject matter of *TCEB* represents a major development from that of *Z*, which was concerned only with the Trinity apart from the final question about the person of Christ[48]. The significance of this grouping of questions into the broad categories of faith, sacraments and charity in the manuscripts *T* and *C* will become clear in due course.

Although the sequence of questions in *T* and *C* is almost identical, there are three questions and some thirty-odd quotations in *C* (and in *EB*, where the text is not deficient) which are not found in *T*[49]. Because the text of *T* sometimes corresponds to that of *Z* rather than to that of *CEB*, Boyer and McKeon have argued that

---

47. The contents and sequence of *TCEB* are described by BOYER-McKEON, *Sic et Non*, pp. 577-612, that of *DL*, pp. 613-615.

48. *Z*, described on pp. 7-14 of Boyer-McKeon's edition, contains after the prologue, qq. 1, 5, 6, 8, 9, 11-19, 23, 24, 7 and 66.

49. *SN* 4, 27, 79 and 139. Individual quotations not in *T* include: *SN* 1. 16; 2. 5; 3. 3; 5. 8; 9. 14^{abc}; 17. 2; 18. 9-11; 24. 12^a; 66. 7; 67. 22^a; 42. 5; 41. 1-1^a; 71. 3^{ab}; 117. 47, 56, 86, 120-121; 125. 20; 131. 4; 138. 21^{ab}, 46; 141. 3^a; 142. 11-12. The texts with a suffix *a, b* or *c* are those not included in *DL* or *MKA*.

T represents an initial recension of the *versio prima*, extended slightly in *CEB*. Occasionally *C* omits a quotation found in *T* or *EB*, but this seems to be no more than accidental omission[50]. The most interesting and important difference between *T* and *C* occurs at the end of *SN* 141, about whether or not works of mercy are of benefit to unbelievers. Where *T* has a quotation from *Luke* 17, 7-10 about the unfaithful servant, *C* has a long discussion on the subject introduced with the rubric *Abaelardus* and in complete harmony with Abelard's teaching about the priority of intention in matters of charity[51]. This passage, not transferred into the final version of the *Sic et Non*, is found only in *C* (*E* and *B* are unfortunately deficient at this point) and seems to have been a comment by Abelard himself. The absence of this passage from *T* would suggest that the text of Luke was changed only after *T* or its exemplar had been copied.

The 'Theologia Christiana' in T and C

The text of the *Theologia Christiana* in *T* and *C*, like that of the *Sic et Non*, also seems to derive from a common exemplar. Van den Eynde, following a brief comment of Ostlender, thought that *T* and *C* might represent separate redactions of *TChr*, both later than that of *R*, but Buytaert questioned this and argued convincingly that the few differences between *T* and *C* in *TChr* could be explained in terms of passages having been omitted by one copyist of another[52]. The most striking similarity between *T* and *C* is the presence of numerous passages separated from the main body of text in *TChr* in both MSS, either in the margin in *C* or placed within parentheses or, from book II on, within a box inserted into the column of the text of *T*. Some passages are also placed in the margin or between the two columns of text of *T*. These marginal passages in *C* have been added after the main text of *TChr* had been written, and are clearly distinguishable by the colour of their ink from words or phrases which have been accidentally

---

50. BOYER-MCKEON, *Sic et Non*, p. 21. *C* omits only *ZT* 75. 13[a]; *TEB* 116. 15[d]; 117. 3-4; *T* 142. 10[abc].

51. Ed. BOYER-MCKEON, pp. 609-610, discussed on p. 27.

52. VAN DEN EYNDE, *Les Rédactions de la "Theologia Christiana"*, 293; BUYTAERT, *Critical Observations*, 428-431.

omitted in copying of the text. Likewise in *T*, these passages have not been accidentally omitted, but the copyist would, from the second book on, begin by writing such a passage within a box and only subsequently fill the rest of his column with text. Both scribes seem to have been copying from an exemplar in which there were frequent marginal annotations and additional passages, although they did not always agree on which passages should remain separate from the main body of text of *TChr*.

The text of *TChr* in *T* and *C*, when compared to that of *R*, posed many problems to the two scholars who studied *TChr* in these manuscripts, Van den Eynde and Buytaert. Not only is the text in *T* and *C* much longer than that in *R*, but they contain many passages which seem to be repetitious, out of context or simply incomplete. The most difficult of these passages in *CT* to explain were those which contained only the *incipit* and sometimes the *explicit* of passages which occurred in full in the *Theologia 'Schola-rium'*[53]. As these passages fitted awkwardly into the text of *TChr*, often duplicating passages elsewhere in the same work, but made perfect sense within *TSch*, Van den Eynde assumed that these abbreviated passages must have been added to *TChr* in *C* and *T* by Abelard after he had written the passages in full in the *Theologia 'Scholarium'*[54]. This was despite the fact that many other

---

53. The abbreviated passages in *CT* can be listed with the passages they duplicate in *TChr* and *TSch*:

TChr CT	II,	13[b]	=	*TChr RCT* III,	1-2	=	*TSch* II, 14-15 (1039CD; pp. 66-67)
	II,	125[a]	=	*RCT* I,	54-55	=	II, 26-27 (1043B-44A; pp. 70-71)
	III,	2[b]	=	*RCT* III,	53	=	II, 17 (1040AB; p. 67)
	IV,	66[b]	=	*CT* I,	16[a]	=	*tsch* 67, *TSch* I, 60 (996AB; p. 19)
	IV,	66[c]	=	*RCT* I,	19-21	=	*tsch* 68-70, *TSch* I, 61-63 (996B-97A; pp. 19-20)
	V,	30[a]	=	*RCT* V,	35	=	*TSch* III, 30 (1094AB; p. 72)
also	III,	8[d]	=	*SN* Prol. 27-30, 37-43		=	*TSch* II, 34-35 (1046C; pp. 73-74)
	IV,	74[c]	=	*SN* 1. 22, 19-20, 23		=	*TSch* II, 42 (1048D-49B; p. 76)

54. *Les Rédactions de la "Theologia Christiana"*, 295-296.

passages found in C and T seemed quite clearly to have been written before *TSch*, in which they were improved or completely rewritten. Although this process of revision of *TChr* by the addition of texts from *TSch* seemed to him to be hasty and superficial, Van den Eynde thought that Abelard must have made these changes himself because so many of these additions paralleled passages in Abelard's other writings [55].

Buytaert, in general, accepted Van den Eynde's conclusions about the complex inter-relationship between *TChr CT* and *TSch*, and modified his argument only in judging C and T to be copies of the same common ancestor rather than separate redactions of *TChr* [56]. Many of the peculiarities of C and T he attributed to the fumbling and mistakes of scribes in copying the work. Buytaert believed that *TChr CT* was not a proper 'redaction', but rather a form of *TChr* drawn up by Abelard for his private use, to which he added and substituted many passages, often in abbreviated form, over a long period of time. He also revised Van den Eynde's chronology of *TChr* by arguing that *TChr R* was much later in date than had previously been thought [57]. An alternative interpretation of all these abbreviated passages, which I have already outlined elsewhere, is to see *TChr CT* as a draft of the *Theologia 'Scholarium'* [58]. In order to understand the text of C and T in this light, it is necessary to look closely at the passages in C and T absent from R, in detail in order to determine how they are related to the wider whole.

The first abbreviated passage in C and T is doubly complicated because it is followed by a passage which Martène, Cousin, Van den Eynde and Buytaert all thought must be extraneous to the text of *TChr* [59]. The whole passage (*TChr CT* II, 12-13-13^{ab}-13)

55. *Ibid.*, 296-297.
56. BUYTAERT, *An Earlier Redaction*, 495; *Critical Observations* 429-432; *TChr* - Introduction, pp. 32-41.
BUYTAERT, *An Earlier Redaction*, 495; *TChr* - Introduction, pp. 50-52.
58. *Vid. supra* n. 10.
59. Cf. the notes of Martène (PL 178, 1172D); COUSIN, *P. Abaelardi Opera*, ii, pp. 405-406; VAN DEN EYNDE, *Les Rédactions de la "Theologia Christiana"*, 277-278; BUYTAERT, *Critical Observations*, 408-409 and his edition of *TChr*, p. 138. Buytaert's transcription of C and T here, as elsewhere, is not wholly accurate.

132

is best reproduced in the form in which it is found in *T*, with the paragraph numbers of Buytaert's edition in square brackets :

T fo. 138ra ; *C* pp. 164-165

... *Inuisibilia enim ipsius a creatura mundi, per ea que facta sunt, intellecta conspiciuntur. Sempiterna quoque eius uirtus ac diuinitas* etc. [13a] Ex quibus
5 aperte Apostolus docet eis quoque mysterium Trinitatis fuisse revelatum. [13a] Sed hec quidem uerba Apostoli nobis in sequentibus exponenda occurrent. [13b] Nunc autem aduersus
10 tam hereticorum quam philosophorum obiectiones pluribus de fide sancte Trinitatis collectis atque expositis testimoniis, superest aperire →

→ quibus rationibus defendi possit quod testimoniis confirmatum est. Omnis quippe controuersia, ut in *Rhetoricis* suis Tullius meminit, aut in scripto aut in ratione uersatur et, beato attestante Augustino, in omnibus auctoritatem humane anteponi rationi convenit, maxime autem in his que ad Deum pertinent, tutius auctoritate quam humano nitimur ingenio. Hinc est illud quod ait, capitulo primo libri *De moribus ecclesie contra Manicheos* : "Nature quidem ... ascribunt.

quomodo una penitus permanente substantia, tres in ea persone distingui
15 queant, quarum nullatenus una sit alia? Deinde, quomodo hec persona genita, illa procedens dicatur? Primo itaque disserendum occurrit quot modis 'persone' nomen accipi solet, ut diligenter a ceteris hec significatio distinguatur. Aliter autem in rhetorica, aliter in grammatica atque aliter in theologia personam accipimus.
20   [13] Quod enim dictum est *Inuisibilia Dei* fuisse revelata ...

---

1 a] que *add. del.* C [col. altera] possit] posset *T Buytaert*   5 quoque *add. del. T*
9 [col. altera] pertinent] pertinere *CT* [col. altera] tutius *om. T*   13 [col. altera]
quidem ... ascribunt] quidem ascribunt *T* quidem *C*   15 nullatenus *inter lin. T*
ut *inter lin. T*   17 hec significatio] hoc signo *Buytaert*

Although Buytaert, following earlier writers, thought that the passage *quomodo ... accipimus* was an extraneous accretion to the text, this passage reads in *T* as the continuation of the sentence *Nunc autem aduersus ... aperire* and is interrupted only by a mark like an arrow →, which refers to the passage inset within the column of text *quibus rationibus ... ascribunt*. In *C* this latter passage has been added to the main body of text after the truncated abbreviation *Nature quidem*. Because the copyist of *T* must have written the inset passage before he wrote the surrounding text, this passage must have been separated similarly within *T*'s exemplar, while *C* tried to combine it into his main text. Buytaert could not explain why the passage *quomodo ... accipimus* should announce the argument of the third and fourth books of *TChr* or of the second book of *TSch* in the middle of commentary on Romans I, 19-20. Following Van den Eynde, he thought that the abbreviated passage mentioned at the end of te inset, *Nature quidem ... ascribunt* had been copied from the complete version of this passage in *TSch* II, 14-15 (1039CD; ed. Cousin, pp. 66-67), duplicating for no reason the text of *TChr* III, 1-2[60].

Both passages make sense, however, if they represent successive drafts for this part of the *Theologia 'Scholarium'*. If the inset passage is interpreted as a reference to the passage in *TChr RCT* III, 1-2 which guided Abelard to turn to this part of *TChr* when copying out the beginning of the second book of *TSch*, then the duplication is fully explained. The passage *TChr* III, 1-2 has itself been extended with another additional section (III, 2[a-b]; in the margin of *C*, but within the text of *T*) which concludes with the words *in eos conuerso, robur eorum*. This ungrammatical ending is an abbreviated reference to *TChr RCT* III, 53, which continues the draft text of *TSch* II, 1-17 (1035A-1040B; pp. 62-67). Both passages, which must have been marginal in Abelard's exemplar, were added by Abelard to indicate which parts of books two and three of *TChr* he wished to incorporate into the *Theologia 'Scholarium'*.

In the second book of *TChr* Abelard had launched into a long defence of his use of classical writers by describing the virtue of their lives as well as the validity of their ethical teaching. By contrast, in the third book of *TChr* he had extended the second book of *TSum*, the beginning of which he had consecrated to an attack on false logicians like Roscelin of Compiègne. As this section of *TChr* had become longwinded and somewhat off the point, he 'summarised' the basic points which he had made in the second book of *TChr* and the first part of book III (III, 1-58) within a new prologue to the argument of the second book of the *Theologia 'Scholarium'*. Abelard added passages to his text of *TChr* at II, 13[a-b] and III, 2[a-b] in order to help effect this summary.

Having included the beginning and end of his prologue in book III of *TChr*, he then turned to the end of its second book (*TChr* II, 117), which contained a very similar discussion about the

60. *Vid. supra* n. 59.

encouragement patristic writers gave to study of secular disciplines, and extended this further in *CT*. He added an abbreviated reference to a passage from the middle of the second book of *TChr* which he wished to incorporate (*TChr CT* II, 125ᵃ = *RCT* II, 54-55) and concluded with a reference to a passage in book three (*TChr CT* II, 125ᶜ = *RCT* III, 6-8) on the theme that no true knowledge could ever be wrong to know. This passage he in turn extended with an attack on the ignorance of those who criticised his philosophical approach to religion, to which he appended abbreviated references to texts in the prologue of the *Sic et Non* (*TChr CT* III, 8ᵈ = *SN* Prol. 27-30, 37-43). There was one last section in *TChr* which Abelard wished to incorporate into the second book of *TSch*, namely *TChr* IV, 72-74. This too he extended with a passage incorporating further abbreviated references to the *Sic et Non* (*TChr CT* IV, 74ᶜ = *SN* 1. 22, 19-20, 23).

By means of these additional passages and abbreviated references added to his text of *TChr* Abelard marked out those sections which he wished to include within *TSch*. He wanted to emphasise his idea that all knowledge was fundamentally good and that philosophical and religious truth was ultimately identical. He therefore excluded passages of *TChr* which were no longer relevant to this theme, particularly those directed against the garrulity and arrogance of false dialecticians. Other passages in praise of pagan virtue within the second book of *TChr* were not directly relevant to his argument in *TSch*, although he would develop such ideas in other writings, notably the *Collationes*, the commentary on Romans and the *Ethics*.

If the passage *quibus rationibus … ascribunt* (*TChr* II, 13ᵇ), inset within *T*, is an abbreviated reference to *TChr* III, 1-2, then the passage *quomodo … accipimus*, found within the text of both *C* and *T* as the continuation of *superest aperire* becomes comprehensible as an earlier draft of the first part of *TSch* II. The only way both passages make sense grammatically is if the passage inset in *T*, and introduced with an arrow, is an alternative text to the passage which occurs immediately after a corresponding arrow in the main body of text. The addition *Sed hec quidem uerba … accipimus* (*CT* II, 13ᵃ⁻ᵇ) is out of context within the discussion of *TChr* II, 12-13, but makes complete sense as a draft passage which would have concluded the prologue to the argument of the second book of

TSch as well as have introduced the subsequent discussion. The wording of the passage Buytaert thought to be inauthentic is, in fact, very close to that of the beginning of Abelard's philosophical argument about the Trinity in *TSch* II, 68 (1057BC; p. 85). The argument which follows in *TSch* II, 69-93 (1057C-1064D; pp. 85-93) is very largely taken from *TChr CT* (III, 72ᵃ, 74, 73, 105, 119-129, 132, 130, 133-134) about the unity of the divine substance and the incapacity of human language to define it fully. Then follows in *TSch* II, 94 (1064D-1065C; p. 93) a passage even more similar to the 'inauthentic' text :

> Querunt autem quomodo una penitus in Deo permanente substantia uel essentia, aliqua ibi proprietatum sit diuersitas secundum quas Trinitas personarum constat? Vel quomodo possit esse ... Quot quidem, ut diligentius fiat, premittendum est quot modis 'idem' et quot 'diuersum' accipiatur.

This passage concludes a much more developed prologue to the argument of book II of *TSch*, replacing a fairly short original prologue in which Abelard had intended to pass relatively quickly over his defence of classical writers in order to enter his philosophical argument more quickly. The manuscript *T* records with remarkable fidelity, a correction which Abelard introduced to his text of *TChr* to allow him to use much more of *TChr* in *TSch* than he had previously planned.

The differing approach of the copyists of *T* and *C* to this section of *TChr* raises the question of how accurately the material separated from the main text in *T* and *C* reflects the format of their common ancestor. As already mentioned, the passage *Sed hec quidem uerba ... accipimus* (*CT* II, 13ᵃ⁻ᵇ) (the original text which would have connected the prologue to the main argument of book II of *TSch*) occurs within the body of the text of both *T* and *C*, although it interrupts the surrounding text. Abelard may have originally appended this passage as a marginal addition to his text of *TChr*, although correcting this in turn by another passage. Of the passages which have been added or changed in *TChr CT* to create the text of *TSch* II, 1-42 (1035A-1049B; pp. 62-76: *TChr CT* II, 13ᵃ⁻ᵇ; II, 2ᵃ⁻ᵇ, 54-55; II, 117ᵃ, 118ᵃ, 119ᵃ, 123-124ᵃ, 125ᵃ⁻ᶜ; II, 8ᵃ⁻ᵉ; IV, 72, 74ᵃ⁻ᵈ), all occur within the text of *T* and *C*, apart from III, 2ᵃ⁻ᵇ and II, 118[a] in the margin of C^{61}. The copyists of T and C seem to have copied most, although not all of the additions which Abelard applied to his original text of $TChr$, particularly when their wording followed naturally from that of the text which immediately preceeded such an addition. By contrast, additions in CT which break up the flow of Abelard's argument, notably almost all new patristic quotations are left separate from the main text by the copyists of T and C^{62}.

The textual differences between T and C can all be explained in terms of errors made by one or other scribe. Besides differing occasionally in whether a passage was placed within the main text or not, or in the position of such a passage C might omit a marginal passage included in T^{63}. The latter manuscript omits very few passages - patristic quotations in $TChr$ III, 72[a] and IV, 131 and a summary of II, 123 found in C, and copied into $TSch$ II, 25 (1042D; p. 70). In this passage the copyist of T has included the account of Jerome's dream found in $TChr$ R II, 123, although he went on to copy Abelard's revised discussion of this dream, in which Jerome was accused of being a Ciceronian rather than a Christian, in $TChr$ CT II, 125[b]. The copyist of C on the other hand has here correctly understood his exemplar and has replaced $TChr$ R II, 123 with a short bridging sentence as well as adding the new text II, 125[a-c] which Abelard added as part of his draft for $TSch$ II, 25-29 (1042D-1046C; pp. 70-71).

The same phenomenon of C and T incorporating both the original

---

61. Buytaert is incorrect in saying that II, 118[a] occurs only in T, $TChr$ - Introduction, p. 35 and p. 185. The additional phrase has been added to the margin of C, as he correctly reports in *Critical Observations*, 410-411. This phrase in C is added as if it had been accidentally omitted from the text (perhaps because it was outside the main text in C's exemplar), not as a marginal entry like other passages in the margin of C.

62. Within these marginal entries in C and T, the most quoted authors are Augustine (I, 16[a], 193[a]; II, 106[a]; III, 52[a]; IV, 65[a], 96[a]) and Jerome (I, 87[a]; II, 49[a], 65[a], 67a, 69[a], 76[a]). Also quoted are Ambrose (I, 1[a]; IV, 115[a], 134[a]), Cassiodorus (I, 15[a], 104[a]), Chrysostom (IV, 95[a], 103[a]), Ephraem (IV, 112[a]), Gregory I (III, 47[a], 123[a]; IV, 117[a]), Hilary (III, 72[a]), Ivo of Chartres (IV, 126[a]) and Seneca (I, 133[a]). Other excerpts may also have been marginal entries in the exemplar of C and T but were incorporated by the copyist of C and T into their main text.

63. E.g. within I, 1[a]; II, 113; III, 13; IV, 112-113 [Buytaert not clear here, $TChr$ - Introduction, p. 37 and pp. 320-321]; IV, 120; 134[a]; 135[a]; V, 25[a].

version of a text as in *R* and an alternative version intended for use in *TSch* occurs in *TChr* III, 131, a passage in which Abelard addresses Roscelin *Responde tu mihi, acute dialectice aut uersipellis sophista*, omitted in *TSch*. At the same time both *C* and *T* replace *TChr R* III, 132 and the first words of III, 133 with a more general address, included in part in *TSch* II, 89 (1063C; pp. 91-92), *Attendite fratres et uerbosi amici*. Similarly both *C* and *T* contain the text of *TChr* IV, 132, although according to *TSch* II, 154-161 (1076B-1078B; pp. 104-106), this was intended to be replaced by the series of texts in *TChr CT* IV, 126-131. There are thus several different layers evident within the text of *C* and *T*, which can be distinguished only by comparison with *TSch*.

Not all additions or corrections in *TChr CT* appear in *TSch*. Most of the passages separated from the main body of text in *C* and *T* fall into this category, apart from a few patristic quotations (I, 16^a, 87^a, 133^a; III, 72^a, 123^a) and the 'signpost' additions already discussed (II, 13^b; III, 2^{a-b}). These patristic marginalia might have been added after Abelard had copied out *TSch* from his text of *TChr CT*, although they might equally represent an earlier stage in the development of *TChr* than that of the draft for *TSch*. In the same way as Abelard added authorities to an already established text of *TChr*, which were subsequently included as an integral part of *TChr* by *R*, so he continued to add more such texts after *R* had been copied. These may have been more for his own reference than for including in a finished work such as *TSch*. Other changes within *CT*, not incorporated into *TSch*, show an intermediate stage in the development of his ideas for the latter work (*CT* I, 16; II, 13^b; III, 62, 71, 114, 132; IV, 7, 85, 92, 95-96). These passages reveal how Abelard tried to improve a passage in his draft for *TSch*, but might then revise what he had written in more radical fashion in *TSch*. In an effort to simplify his argument about the difference between the three persons and about the generation of the Word from the Father, Abelard rewrote a great deal of what he had written in books III and IV of *TChr*, even in the form *CT*.

The additions found in the fifth book of *TChr CT* provide either a draft text or notes for the beginning of the third book of *TSch*. Abelard used almost the whole of *TChr* V, 1-29 in *TSch* III, 1-27 (1085C-1094A; pp. 119-123), but at the point at which he had mentioned the difficulties inherent in his own approach, he added an abbreviated reference (*CT* V, 30ᵃ) to *TChr* V, 35, where he would resume his text. Here he added a long passage developing his argument about the goodness of all God's action (V, 35ᵃ⁻ᶠ). The remainder of the text of *TChr* V, although copied out by *C* and *T*, Abelard would completely rewrite in *TSch*, developing ideas sketched out in notes (V, 33ᵃ and 34ᵃ) attached to the section which he would rewrite.

In the passage *TChr CT* V, 35ᵇ Abelard referred to a text of Jerome, *Absit ergo in Filio Dei ... temporalis agnoscitur*, as one that he had already mentioned in his first book, *sicut in primo libro prefati sumus*. Van den Eynde followed, without acknowledgement, the opinion of Robert, Cottiaux and Ostlender that this must have been a reference to *TSch* I, 48 (993BC; p. 16) in which exactly this text is cited as it does not occur at all within the first book of *TChr*[64]. Neither Van den Eynde nor Buytaert after him considered which recension of *TSch* might have been thus referred to, in particular whether it could have been the same passage in *tsch* 55, nor could they explain why Abelard should so confuse *TSch* with *TChr*. The reference is explained, however, if it is taken to refer to a work written, rather than to a complete work already in existence. When adding new passages in *TChr CT* V, Abelard already had a clear idea of the contents of the first book of *TSch*. Study of two very short manuscripts (*FH*) of the *Theologia 'Scholarium'* makes this clear.

tsch FH and tsch Z : early drafts of the Theologia 'Scholarium'

The text of *TSch* found in two MSS, *Fulda, Priesterseminar 1* (formerly Fritzlar, no shelf-mark), fos. 94ᵛ-98 (*F*) and *Heiligenkreuz, Stiftsbibliothek 153*, fos. 82ᵛ-87ᵛ (*H*) was interpreted by Van den Eynde, following Ostlender, as an abbreviation of *TSch* found in the *Zurich, Zentralbibliothek MS C. 61*, fos. 53ᵛ-60ᵛ (*Z*)[65]. Buytaert

---

64. VAN DEN EYNDE, *Les Rédactions de la "Theologia Christiana*, 292, following the argument of G. ROBERT, *Les écoles et l'enseignement de la théologie pendant la première moitié du XIIᵉ siècle* (Paris 1909), p. 193. Robert's argument was also taken up by COTTIAUX, *La conception de la théologie chez Abélard*, in *Revue d'Histoire ecclésiastique* 28 (1932) and by OSTLENDER, *Die Theologia "Scholarium"*,ʼ 371-372.

65. OSTLENDER, *Die Theologia "Scholarium"*, 267 and 281 n. 89; VAN DEN EYNDE, *La "Theologia Scholarium" de Pierre Abélard*, 227.

modified Van den Eynde's view slightly by arguing that *tsch FH* was an abbreviation of a 'proto-redaction' of *tsch*, as *FH* often contained a text superior that of *Z*. He nonetheless retained Ostlender's hypothesis that the text of *tsch* in *FH* had been abbreviated by a copyist rather than by Abelard himself[66]. However, there are many features of *F*, *H* and *Z* which merit more attention than given by Buytaert in his edition of *tsch*. As his descriptions of these manuscripts, which all contain a wide range of twelfth century theological literature, are not always complete, the contents of each will be noted as well as the text of *tsch* studied in more detail.

The *Fulda, Priesterseminar MS 1* (formerly known as the 'Fritzlar-codex', no shelfmark), belonged to the library of the former cathedral of Fritzlar, in the diocese of Mainz, until recently, when it was bought by the library of Fulda[67]. Buytaert was unable to locate the original manuscript in preparing his edition of *tsch*, making use of a microfilm of the relevant folios only, so could not comment on the manuscript as a whole. As existing descriptions are not fully accurate, its contents may be listed here:

fos. 1-13 Hilary of Poitiers, *De synodis.*

fos. 14-33ᵛ Rupert of Deutz, *De officiis* [*F* not listed by R. Haacke in his edition, CCCM VII].

fos. 34-43ᵛ William of St Thierry, *Liber de corpore et sanguine Domini* preceeded by his letter to Rupert (PL 180, 341-366).

fos. 44-51ᵛ Hugh of St Victor, *Dialogus de sacramentis legis naturalis et scripte* (PL 175, 17-42).

fos. 52-62 Bernard of Clairvaux, *De gratia et libero arbitrio* (ed. Leclercq, *Opera*, iii, 157-203).

fos. 62-65 Hugh of St Victor, extracts from *Miscellanea* (PL 177, 469-900): I, 186, 193; II, 3; I, 18.

fos. 65-70 extracts from the *Summa Sententiarum* (PL 176, 41-174).

---

66. BUYTAERT, *tsch* - Introduction, pp. 385-386.

67. Various items in *F* were first identified by A. LANDGRAF, in *Scholastik* 9 (1934) 227 and again in *Werke aus dem Bereich der Summa Sententiarum und Anselmus von Laon*, in *Divus Thomas* 14 (1936) 215. The manuscript had passed from Fritzlar to Fulda when H. Weisweiler published a brief list of its contents within a book review, *Scholastik* 31 (1956) 474-475. This is generally more accurate than the description given in by H. ROCHAIS and E. MANNING, in *Bibliographie générale de l'Ordre Cistercien: Saint Bernard*, in *La Documentation Cistercienne*, 21 (Rochefort 1979-83), no. 3763. See also VAN DEN EYNDE in *La "Theologia Scholarium" de Pierre Abélard*, 227-228 and BUYTAERT, *tsch* - Introduction, pp. 375-377.

V

140

fos. 70-72 Hugh of St Victor, *Miscellanea*, including I, 78, 160, 8 and Bernard, *Sermo* 92 (ed. Leclercq, *Opera*, vi, 346-348).
fos. 72ᵛ-83ᵛ *Non queso arrogantie ... quod potui, feci.* (a tract on original sin).
fos. 84-85ᵛ Hugh of St. Victor, *Miscellanea* I, 173.
fos. 85ᵛ-88 Hugh of St. Victor, *De quinque septenis* (PL 175, 405-14).
fos. 88-89 Hugh of St. Victor, *De Sacramentis* (beginning only; PL 176, 183-5).
fos. 89-94 Hugh of St. Victor, *De beate Marie uirginitate* (extract only; PL 176, 859C-72A).
fos. 94ᵛ-98 Peter Abelard, *tsch*.
fos. 98-99ᵛ tract on Christ (*Cum ubique solliciti esse ... subsistit*) [also found in *Escorial, Real Biblioteca Q. III. 9*, fo. 5][68].
fos. 99ᵛ-100ᵛ Augustine, *De diuersis questionibus ad Simplicianum* (extracts).
fos. 100ᵛ-101 small texts on the sacraments.

The fragmentary nature of these texts suggests that *F* is a copy of a student's workbook, compiled in the mid-twelfth century. The *Heiligenkreuz, Stiftsbibliothek MS 153* (*H*) is written in a single hand, not dissimilar to that which wrote *F* and contains an equally complicated collection of texts[69]. Buytaert did not analyse the contents of *H* in detail, or its relationship to *F*, but relied on the description of Gsell, itself based on rather inaccurate fourteenth century running titles added to the manuscript. Van den Eynde thought that *tsch H* may have been copied from *tsch* in *F*; in fact fos. 69ᵛ-91ᵛ of *H* corresponds exactly to fos. 84-101 of *F* and fos. 91ᵛ-109 of *H* to fos. 70ᵛ-83ᵛ of *F*, from which *H* may have been copied[70]. The contents of *H* may be broken up into its many constituent parts:

fos. 1-54ᵛ *Glose super Apocalypsim* (*Apocalipsis subauditur, haec est. ... cum omnibus uobis fidelibus. Amen*). [Found in a shorter version, without the prologue, in *Paris, Bibl. nat. lat. 17251*, fos. 1-29ᵛ (s. xii²), *lat. 689*, fos. 39-71 (s. xiii), *Würzburg, Univ. Bibl. M.p.th.q. 72*, fos. 84-101 (s. xii²) and *Bologna, Univ. 2545*, fos. 1-97.].

68. G. ANTOLIN, *Catálogo de los códices latinos de la Real Biblioteca del Escorial*, iii (Madrid 1913), p. 425.
69. B. GSELL, *Verzeichniss der Handschriften in der Bibliothek des Stiftes Heiligen-kreuz*, in *Xenia Bernardina, Pars secunda : Handschriften Verzeichnisse der Cister-cienserstifte*, i (Vienna 1891), pp. 159-160; BUYTAERT, *tsch* - Introduction, pp. 377-379.
70. VAN DEN EYNDE, *La "Theologia Scholarium" de Pierre Abélard*, 225-227.
71. STEGMÜLLER, *Repertorium biblicum medii aevi*, vii (Madrid 1961), nos. 10331 and 10662. Coincidentally, *Paris, Bibl. nat. lat. 17251*, from Notre-Dame, contains on fos. 33ᵛ-46 Abelard's *Expositio in Hexaemeron*, preceeded on fos. 31-33ᵛ by an abbreviated version of the same work. Buytaert identifies incorrectly the commentary in *H* with another, quite different commentary found in *Paris, Arsenal 64* (cited

V

fos. 55-68 *De ecclesie ordinibus* (*Legitur in ecclesiastica historia ... in omnibus. Amen* [Also found in *Paris, Arsenal 371*, fos. 92ᵛ-95 and *Zurich, Zentralbibl., Rh. 147*, fos. 14ᵛ-25].

fos. 68-68ᵛ *Expositio orationis dominice* (*Prima petitio est Pater*).

fos. 68ᵛ-69ᵛ *De uerbis Grecis baptizerii* (*Baptizo te, id est intinguo te ... donatus eterne. Amen*).

fos. 69ᵛ-71ᵛ = *F* fos. 84-85ᵛ.
fos. 71ᵛ-75ᵛ = *F* fos. 85ᵛ-88.
fos. 75-76   = *F* fos. 88-89.
fos. 76-82ᵛ = *F* fos. 89-94.
fos. 82ᵛ-87ᵛ = *F* fos. 94ᵛ-98 (*tsch*).
fos. 87ᵛ-89ᵛ = *F* fos. 98-99ᵛ.
fos. 89ᵛ-91 = *F* fos. 99ᵛ-100ᵛ.
fos. 91-91ᵛ = *F* fos. 100ᵛ-101.
fos. 91ᵛ-94 = *F* fos. 70ᵛ-72.
fos. 94-109 = *F* fos. 72ᵛ-83ᵛ.

fos. 109-110ᵛ Bernard, *Sermo* 104 (*... ad eius similitudinem reformari*, ed. Leclercq, *Opera*, vi. 374-375).

fos. 110ᵛ-111 Thierry of Chartres, extract from *Expositio in Hexaemeron*, introduced by *Magister Tirricus super locum illum: Posuit de firmamentum in medio aquarum. Aere ex superius ...* (ed. Häring, *Commentaries on Boethius*, p. 558)[72].

fos. 111-111ᵛ gloss on *Exodus* 32, 10, attributed to Augustine (*Permitte me ... sententiam, non consilium*).

fos. 111ᵛ-112 [*V*]*ox ecclesie ad sponsum. Omnia poma uetera ...* [*Cant.* 7, 13] *Per poma noua intelligitur lex noua ... alia competunt inducenda.*

fos. 112-119ᵛ Paragraphs on personalities of the Old Testament (*Legitur in ueteri testamento in tabernaculo Domini mensam habuisse ... et ascendit super cherubim et u. u. s. p. u.* [*Ps.* 17, 11]).

fos. 119ᵛ-121 *Pascite quod in uobis est ... protegamur, ipso praestante, Qui uiuit et regnat* (on duties of priests).

fos. 121-121ᵛ *Cum ualde occulta sint Dei iudicia ... ad exteriora deriuatur* (on judgement).

---

as 65), fos. 180-187 and in *Chartres, Bibl. mun. 288*, fos. 99-101 (since destroyed), attributed tentatively to Stephen Langton by STEGMÜLLER, *Repertorium*, v (Madrid 1955), no. 7935. G. Lobrichon identifies the author of the commentary in *H* with a French, perhaps Parisian master teaching c. 1125-1150, *L'apocalypse des théologiens au douzième siècle* (doctorat du 3ᵉ cycle, EHSS-Paris X, 1979), ii, p. 56.

72. R. W. SOUTHERN, in *Platonism, Scholastic Method and the School of Chartres*, Stenton Lecture (University of Reading, 1979), pp. 33-34, has argued that this extract is a *reportatio* of Thierry's teaching, but the differences between *H* and Thierry's text are so minor as to make this uncertain.HÄRING, *The Commentaries on Boethius by Thierry of Chartres and his School*, in *Studies and Texts*, 20 (Toronto 1971), p. 46 describes the passage as an excerpt. I am grateful to J. S. Barrow for help in analysing fos. 109ᵛ-132 in *H*.

fos. 121ᵛ-122 *Gregorius. Non sine magno misterio quinquagenarius numerus ... et gloria excipiat in octaua.*

fos. 122-128 *De corpore Domini. Sacramentum dominici corporis et sanguinis quod eucharistia appellatur ... sicut per baptismum membra Christi efficimur.*

fos. 128-128ᵛ *Attende quod quadam ratione sicut Deus ... nisi a quo dari potuit, reddi non potest* (on free will).

fos. 128ᵛ-132 *Quatuor sunt quibus omnis dictanti scientia plene colligitur, inuentio ... nisi per ea que apud nos sunt uisibilia et nota nobis erudiamur* (notes on various subjects, including the words *theologia, philosophia, hierarchia, symbolum* and *analogia*).

fo. 132 *Est ratio cur altaris pars dextra ... Sub mundi fine fideles* (note added to fill in space).

As is evident from this break-down, *H* contains a complex collection of theological notes and extracts, among which Abelard's *tsch* is tucked away as an anonymous tract on the Trinity. The *Zurich, Zentralbibliothek MS C. 61* (*Z*), written in either the late twelfth or early thirteenth century, contains a similar collection of works, apparently compiled by a student of theology some time in the mid-twelfth century, perhaps 1130-40[73]. Again Buytaert's analysis of the manuscript is deficient in that he does not take into account a number of important early scholastic works, which occur immediately before *tsch* in *Z*, described in some detail by Weisweiler[74]. As with *F* and *H*, these works illuminate the milieu in which Abelard's teaching circulated :

fos. 1ᵛ-39 *Summa Sententiarum* (PL 176, 42-174).

fos. 39ᵛ-40ᵛ Geoffrey Babion, *Sermo* cxi (attributed to Hildebert of Le Mans in PL 171, 873-877).

fos. 40ᵛ *Ex duobus constat ecclesia* (note on predestination).

fos. 40ᵛ-43 *Non est Pater lumen de lumine ... uel sterilitatem culpam esse dicamus* (discussion of the Trinity, etc. with extracts from Augustine, Isidore, Hilary and Origen.

fos. 43ᵛ-44ᵛ *Primum queritur quare peccator ... nisi priuatio boni* (based on Ps-Alcuin, *Interrogationes et Responsiones in Genesim*, PL 100, 515-568, discussed with partial edition by Weisweiler, *Das Schrifttum*, pp. 162-165).

---

73. Described by C. MOHLBERG, *Katalog der Handschriften der Zentralbibliothek Zürich*, I : *Mittelalterliche Handschriften* (Zurich 1952), pp. 34, 355-356; A. BRUCKNER, *Scriptoria Medii Aevi Helvetica*, III : *Schreibschule der Diözese Konstanz. St Gallen* (Geneva 1938), p. 125.

74. H. WEISWEILER, *Das Schrifttum der Schule Anselms von Laon und Wilhelms von Champeaux in deutschen Bibliotheken*, BGPTMA 8 (1936) pp. 261-288.

fos. 44ᵛ-45ᵛ *Quare cum eadem fide ... absque palea* (ed. Weisweiler, pp. 281-283).
fo. 45ᵛ Patristic quotations (ed. Weisweiler, p. 165).
fos. 45ᵛ-50ᵛ *Augustinus. Nichil semper fuit ... Lazarum solvendo* from the circle of Odo of Ourscamp, discussed by Weisweiler, pp. 166-171. On fo. 46 is quoted an opinion of Abelard, identified as *Magister Petrus*, about the power of the Church to bind and loose sins, ed. Weisweiler, pp. 268-269.
fos. 50ᵛ-53ᵛ *Potest queri quid sit peccatum ... sicut est in istis* (ed. Weisweiler, pp. 259-269).
fos. 53ᵛ-60ᵛ Peter Abelard, *tsch* (mutilated at end), titled *Tractatus utilis de sancta Trinitate.*

The text of *tsch* in *FH* is much shorter than, and occasionally quite different from that of *tsch* in *Z*, but has a number of features which are difficult to explain in terms of an abbreviation made by a copyist. The passages of *tsch Z* which are not found in *FH* are very often exactly those which occur in either *TChr CT* or the *Sic et Non*. All the passages of *tsch Z* which introduce the argument of the complete *Theologia 'Scholarium'* (*tsch* 34-35, 59, the first part of 60, the first and last sentences of 74) are similarly absent from *FH*. If allowance is made for the occasional omission caused by homoioteleuton in *FH*, a list can be drawn up of all those passages found in *tsch Z* which do not occur in *FH*:

lines	*tsch Z*	
254-255	20	
344-362	30	= *TChr RCT* I, 27-28.
383-415	33-35	= *SN* 8. 35, 2; 18. 6 (+ text of Abelard).
456-460, 462-463	41-42	= *TChr RCT* I, 6 (+ text of Abelard).
465-558	42-49	Cf. *TChr RCT* I, 8, 9, 104, 12, 25
584-586	51	
616-632	55-56	Cf. *TChr CT* V, 35ᵇ; *SN* 15. 23.
706-709	59	
738-741	61	= *TChr RCT* IV, 64.
754-761	62	
789-815, 819-820	66-68	= *TChr CT* IV, 66ᵃ⁻ᶜ with references to *TChr CT* I, 16ᵃ and I, 19.
839-840	70	= *TChr CT* I, 21.
857-863	72	Cf. *TChr RCT* I, 32-33.
893-896, 902-903	74	
904-947	75-78	Cf. *TChr RCT* I, 8-9.
955-1013	80-85	= *TChr RCT* I, 12-15, 22, 38.
1025-1061	85-88	= *TChr RCT* I, 38-41.
1071-1490	90-123	= *TChr CT* I, 43-70.

144

A feature of *FH* not noticed by Buytaert is that the paragraph divisions in both MSS correspond exactly to the sections of the text which are found in extended form in *tsch Z*, listed above. These paragraph marks define the essential body of argument in the opening of the *Theologia 'Scholarium'*, and indicate where *tsch Z* would expand *tsch FH*. The text of *tsch FH* contains only a prologue in which Abelard justifies the orthodoxy of his approach, brief definitions of faith, charity and sacrament, followed by a long discussion of the content of faith which draws in part on ideas formulated in the third and fourth books of *TChr* (*RCT* III, 18-19, 23, 58, 60, 62-63; IV, 65-66). *tsch FH* concludes with passages from the beginning of book I of *TChr* (*RCT* I, 19-20, 18, 33, 36, 10), but does not go any further than brief mention of scriptural testimony about the Trinity. At the end of *tsch FH* there occur two passages, separated from the preceeding text by the same paragraph marks as occur throughout *FH* (*tsch FH* 80 and 46, lines 963-968, 505-510), which Buytaert thought had been accidentally forgotten by the copyist and added at the end of *FH* because both occur much earlier in the text of *tsch Z*[75]. He could not explain why only these paragraphs should have been remembered and added at the end of *FH* and not others of *tsch Z*.

Buytaert acknowledged that in some respects *FH* contained a better text than that of all other MSS of *TSch*, as for example the correct order of certain patristic quotations, also found in the *Sic et Non*, and was compelled to argue that *FH* was an abbreviation of a 'proto-redaction' of *tsch*[76]. He did not comment that sometimes a passage 'abbreviated' in *FH* corresponded exactly to the text of *TChr*, while *Z* had a longer version of the text than *TChr* (as in *tsch FH* 62-63 = *TChr RCT* IV, 66).

One passage in *tsch FH* cannot have been abbreviated from *tsch Z* 66 as it is quite different in content. The significance of this passage in *FH* can best be appreciated by comparing the text of *tsch FH* 66-70 with that of both *tsch Z* 66-70 and *TChr* IV, 66[a-c], which in turn contains abbreviated references to *TChr CT* I, 16[a] and I, 19 :

---

75. BUYTAERT, *tsch* - Introduction, pp. 376-377.
76. *Ibid.*, pp. 385-386.

FH 66. Logos itaque Filius Dei cum dicitur, id est Verbum, secundum illam significationem sumitur secundum quam 'logos' apud Grecos ipsum mentis conceptum seu rationem mentis significat, non uocis prolationem. *Aliter. Verbo Domini celi firmati sunt.* Verbum Domini Filius est Patris, sicut scriptum est : *In principio erat Verbum*; quod ideo dicit *Verbum*, quia sicut est uerbum manifestatio intellectus latentis, ita Christus ueniens in mundum fuit ostensio Patris, secundum illud : *Pater, manifestaui nomen tuum hominibus quos* ... [68] *Ego uox clamantis in deserto*. Iohannes *uox* a propheta uocatus est quia Verbum preibat. Quod est dicere, sicut uerbum audibile in auditore precedit intelligibile, quia uidelicet prius uox sonat ut postmodum ex ea intellectus concipiatur. [69] Verbum itaque ... [= *TChr* I, 20, 18] ... intelligentie [70] Hanc autem intellectualem Dei locutionem, id est eternam sapientie sue ordinationem, Augustinus, *De ciuitate Dei*, libro XVI, capitulo VI commemorat : 'Est incommutabilis ratio, que non habet sonum strepentem atque transeuntem, sed uim sempiterne manentem et temporaliter operantem'.

Z 66. Logos itaque ...
= *tsch FH, TChr CT* IV, 66ª.

... prolationem.
Unde Boethius, *In Categorias Aristotelis*, libro II :
'Quoniam Greca oratione logos dicitur etiam animi cogitatio et intra se ratiocinatio ... [= *TChr CT* IV, 66ª] ... addidit : 'que fit cum uoce'. [67] Vnde et beatus meminit Augustinus ... [= *TChr CT* IV, 66ʰ] ... et rationem significat; ... ratio dicitur' [= *TChr CT* I, 16ª]. Idem in libro *Contra quinque haereses* : '*In principio erat Verbum*. Melius Greci 'logos' dicunt. Logos quippe uerbum significat et rationem. '[68-70] De quo quidem Verbo Dei, scilicet intelligibili, quod ut dictum est, eius sapientie intelligitur, beatus Gregorius ... operantem'. [= *TChr CT* IV 66ᶜ = *TChr CT* I, 19-21]

Buytaert thought that the passage in *tsch FH* introduced by *Aliter* was inauthentic because it was so different from the corresponding section in *tsch Z*[77]. However, if *tsch FH* is read as a complete text, it is evident that it contains a continous argument about the identity of *Logos* with the Son and connects the argument of *TChr RCT* IV, 66 with that of *TChr RCT* I, 20, 18, 21. The text of *tsch Z*, on the other hand, presents a more developed version of the same argument, incorporating the passage *TChr CT* IV, 66ᵃ⁻ᶜ at exactly the point where *FH* is marked with the comment *Aliter*.

77. *Ibid.*, p. 427.

146

This additional passage in *CT* is quite out of context within *TChr* IV, 66-67, but makes complete sense if it is intended to revise the part of *TChr* IV, 66 which Abelard wished to use in the opening part of the *Theologia 'Scholarium'*. He included within this addition in *CT* two abbreviated references, one to a passage he had added to the margin of book I (*TChr CT* I, 16ᵃ), the other to a longer passage, *TChr CT* I, 19-21. The text of *tsch FH* contains an earlier draft of ideas for the *Theologia 'Scholarium'*, subsequently modified within *TChr CT* and *tsch Z*. The *Aliter* which had been copied into the text of *F* and *H* is likely to have been a marginal note of Abelard which indicated his intention to change this part of *tsch*.

Abelard thus composed *tsch FH* before this part of *TChr CT*. His intention in writing *tsch FH* was to outline ideas for the first part of *TSch*, which was to be quite different from the beginning of *TChr*, while the intention of *TChr CT* was to indicate which parts of *TChr* he would use. Abelard compiled *tsch Z* by adding to *tsch FH* further texts from *TChr CT*, in particular to improve the transition in his argument from that of the fourth to the first book of *TChr*. The paragraph marks in *FH*, like the word *Aliter*, indicate Abelard's intention to extend or revise specific sections of *tsch FH*. When he added the reference to a text of Jerome *sicut in primo Libro prefati sumus* in *TChr CT* V, 35ᵃ⁻ᶜ, Abelard had already referred to this text in *tsch FH* 55. He might have already added the complete text of Jerome in *tsch Z* 55 before he made the reference to it in the fifth book of *TChr CT*. Not all the additional passages in *TChr CT* may have been added at the same time, as some could have been added after *tsch Z*, particularly where they did not concern this part of the *Theologia 'Scholarium'*.

The question arises as to how these private drafts of Abelard for the *Theologia 'Scholarium'* have survived within neatly written manuscripts like *F*, *H* and *Z*. The most likely solution is that these drafts were copied by students eager to obtain a written text from Abelard, into notebooks in which they collected a wide range of miscellaneous theological texts. Such notebooks were then copied out more neatly as these students entered religious communities, notably in a Germanic or Austrian environment[78]. A copy of *tsch* either very

78. P. CLASSEN, *Zur Geschichte der Frühscholastik in Oesterreich und Bayern*, in *Mitteilungen des Instituts für Oesterreichische Geschichtsforschung*, 67 (1959) 249-277.

similar or identical to *tsch Z* was shown to Walter of Mortagne by students of Abelard. Although it contained only the first part of the *Theologia 'Scholarium'*, it did mention Abelard's promise to discuss in detail the generation of the Son from the Father and the procession of the Holy Spirit[79]. The passages quoted by Walter in his letter to Abelard correspond exactly to parts of *tsch Z*, but not to the corresponding parts of *tsch FH* or *tsch T*. It is just possible that Abelard sent the text of *tsch Z* deliberately to Walter of Mortagne for comment. Walter's letter is not written in the harsh tones of William of St Thierry or Bernard of Clairvaux and resembles rather these letters which he sent to Alberic of Rheims and other *magistri*, discussing their opinions. Walter says that he had heard Abelard teach in person and had discussed some matters recently with him[80]. Abelard seems to have allowed these early drafts to circulate and provide a basis for discussion before proceeding to the next stage of writing the *Theologia 'Scholarium'*.

tsch T and the complete text of the Theologia 'Scholarium'

Abelard expanded or revised in *tsch T* exactly those passages of *tsch Z* which Walter of Mortagne cited in his letter, presumably in direct response to Walter's criticisms[81]. The longest new passage in *tsch T* was one (2-5) in which he emphasised that he had turned to elucidating problems posed by Christian belief in a rational manner because he had been begged to do so by disciples. He also rewrote a passage that Walter had criticised in which he spoke of the Son as a 'portion' of divine omnipotence and added new material to his arguments about the attribution of power to the Father and wisdom to the Son (*tsch T* 57-59; 49, 53, 65). These corrections and additional passages seem to have been added to an original draft of *tsch*, in turn incorporated within the main text of *tsch T*.

The co-existence of *tsch T* in the same manuscript as *TChr T*

---

79. *Epist. ad Abaelardum*, ed. H. OSTLENDER, in *Florilegium Patristicum*, 19 (Bonn 1929), p. 34, referring to *tsch Z* 74. Ostlender believed Walter saw a copy of *tsch* like that of *H* in his edition of the letter; see also OSTLENDER, *Die Theologia "Scholarium"*, pp. 266-269.

80. *Epist. ad Abaelardum*, ed. OSTLENDER, p. 40.

81. *Ibid.*, pp. 35-36 citing *tsch Z* 1-5, 57 and 58.

is itself significant because the scribe who copied both works (which occur within the same gathering) seems to have been following the pattern of texts in his exemplar. The sequence *TChr-tsch* does not occur in *C*, but that may be because its copyist (or that of its immediate exemplar) had felt that it was unnecessary to include such an incomplete work. The two texts *tsch T* and *TChr CT* provide complementary drafts for all three books of *Theologia 'Scholarium'*. By copying out *tsch T* as far as it went, and then copying from the parallel place in the first book of *TChr CT*, Abelard had put together the text of the first book of *TSch* almost in its entirety.

Abelard created the second book of the *Theologia 'Scholarium'* by selecting the passages in the second, third and fourth books of the *Theologia Christiana* which he had marked out in *CT*, while completely rewriting his discussion of the generation of the Son from the Father. He had originally intended to introduce his philosophical argument with only a short prologue, defending his use of classical writers, but he subsequently extended this by adding a patchwork of texts taken from various places within *TChr CT*. Although he had made some modifications to his argument about the generation of the Son within *TChr CT*, he simplified his explanation drastically when writing out this part of the *Theologia 'Scholarium'* and drew together a number of previously disparate ideas into a homogeneous whole (*TSch* II, 94-147; 1064D-1075A; pp. 93-103). His discussion of the procession of the Holy Spirit was, by contrast, very largely based on the draft text formulated in *TChr CT* IV, 117-160. Abelard likewise began the first part of book III of the *Theologia 'Scholarium'* by copying out from *TChr CT* V, 1-35f, but he then abandoned his draft and developed his argument much more fully in the remaining part of the third book (*TSch* III, 37-120; 1096A-1114B [incomplete]; pp. 125-149).

Abelard might well have produced further drafts in preparing his *Theologia 'Scholarium'* which have not survived, but of these nothing can be said. Those which do survive, notably *tsch FH*, *TChr CT*, *tsch T*, combine to throw a great deal of light on the literary construction of the *Theologia 'Scholarium'*.

TChr CT, tsch T and the Sic et Non

One other work which may also throw light indirectly on the

Theologia '*Scholarium*' is Abelard's *Sic et Non*. The presence of this work in the two manuscripts *C* and *T* is itself significant and deserves further comment. As has already been shown, the *Sic et Non*, Abelard's abridgement of Augustine's *Retractationes*, *TChr* and *tsch* were all copied together in *T*[82]. In the Monte Cassino manuscript *TChr* follows a complete text of Augustine's *Retractationes* and is in turn followed by the *Sic et Non*. Although all three works were originally separate manuscripts, they were copied and rubricated at the same time[83]. In a list of books bequeathed by Cardinal Guy of Castello to the church of Città di Castello on his death in 1144, the same combination occurs of the *Sic et Non* and a *Theologia cum libro Retractationum*[84]. Abelard intended his collection of excerpts from Augustine's *Retractationes* to be attached to the *Sic et Non*, as they are in some manuscripts of that work, although in *T* they are separated from the *Sic et Non* by a series of comments on scripture based on Bede[85]. What is the relationship between *T*, *C* and the works owned by Guy of Castello, later pope Celestine II?

In the library list of Città di Castello, itself in a thirteenth century hand, the *Sic et Non* is separated from the *Theologia cum libro Retractationum* by two works of Augustine (*De octo quaestionibus* and *De fide et operibus*), one of Cicero (*Rhetorica* or *De inventione*) and one of Seneca. This may, however, simply reflect a librarian's desire to distinguish patristic works, including the *Sic et Non* as a patristic anthology, from classical works, and these in turn from more contemporary treatises and commentaries. Although it cannot be proven, the association of the *Retractationes* with the *Theologia* rather than with the *Sic et Non* would suggest that *C* and *T* were textually related to Guy's copy, although copied some fifty or more years later. Guy's copy of the *Sic et Non* may also have been

---

82. *Vid. supra*, n. 35.
83. One hand, however, rubricated all the works in *C*, suggesting that they were all copied at the same time.
84. A. WILMART, *Les livres légués par Célestin II à Città di Castello*, in *Revue bénéd.* 35 (1923) 98-102; LUSCOMBE, *The School*, p. 88.
85. *Sic et Non*, Prol. 348-350. The interruption in *T* may have been because the copyist wished to complete his series of glosses on the historical books of the O.T., *vid. supra*, n. 40. Abelard's abridgement is also found in *B*, *M* and *K*, BOYER-MCKEON, p. 51 and edited pp. 529-576.

150

related to that found in the MSS *Brescia, Biblioteca Queriniana A. V. 21 (B), Einsiedeln, Stiftsbibliothek 300 (E)*, (both of the twelfth century) and *Turin, Biblioteca Nazionale E. V. 9 (S)*, containing the complete text of *SN* q. 117, (of the fourteenth century) as these three MSS contain the same recension of the *Sic et Non* as C^{86}. Città di Castello, roughly equidistant between Brescia and Monte Cassino, could have been a centre of diffusion of the work. In *CEBS* as in *T* the *Sic et Non* is attributed to Abelard, unlike *TChr* in both *C* and *T*. The *Retractationes* are not associated with the *Sic et Non* in these MSS apart from being separated by *TChr* as in *C*, or in a separate, initial section of the MS, along with a mutilated portion of late questions from the *Sic et Non*, as in *B*. In *C* Abelard's abridgement of the *Retractationes* has been replaced with a complete text of the work.

The same displacement of the *Retractationes* from the *Sic et Non* is evident in *T*, although this manuscript cannot be identified with the common ancestor of *CEBS* as *T* is itself based on a deficient exemplar in which a whole series of questions were missing. Certain passages seem to have been added to the *Sic et Non* after *T*, or rather its exemplar had been copied, but before the copying of the common ancestor of *CEBS*[87]. Like that of *TChr* the text of the *Sic et Non* in this common ancestor seems to have had numerous annotations to its text, some of which are found in *EB*, but not C^{88}. The common ancestor of *T* and *CEBS* appears to have been none other than Abelard's own workbook, in which existed the *Sic et Non*, his abridgement of the *Retractationes*, *TChr* and quite likely

---

86. *Vid. supra*, n. 46. The Einsiedeln MS, which contains on pp. 75-128 five sermons of Abelard, was written at Einsiedeln in the late twelfth century, G. MEIER, *Catalogus codicum mss. qui in bibliotheca monasterii Einsidlensis OSB servantur*, I (Einsiedeln-Leipzig 1899), 274-275. Because of its geographical proximity, it may have been related to the copy of the *Sic et Non* (with unspecified sermons adjacent), belonging to the neighbouring monastery of Engelberg, listed in a catalogue compiled by its abbot Frowin between 1148-1178, P. LEHMANN, *Mittelalterliche Bibliotheks-kataloge Deutschlands und der Schweiz*, I (Munich 1918), 32; see LUSCOMBE, *The School*, pp. 78, 81.

87. BOYER-MCKEON, *Sic et Non*, p. 21.

88. E.g. *SN EB* 15. 1ª, 7ª; 18. 7ª; 66. 15ᵃᵇ; 67. 29ª, 31ª etc. These may have been omitted by *C*, or alternatively were added to an exemplar at a later stage. *B* in particular has much additional material, BOYER-MCKEON, *Sic et Non*, p. 38.

tsch. Of this workbook *T* is perhaps the most faithful copy, although probably not a direct one. *C* likewise seems also to have been based on a heavily annotated exemplar, perhaps even the copy owned by Guy of Castello, but this can only be speculated upon.

The association of the *Sic et Non* with two drafts of the *Theologia 'Scholarium'*, *TChr CT* and *tsch T*, in *T* and thus quite possibly in Abelard's own workbook is significant because the patristic quotations being evaluated in the *Sic et Non* are grouped into the broad divisions of faith, sacraments and charity, the same outline as is discussed briefly in the beginning of the *Theologia 'Scholarium'*[89]. Abelard quoted and discussed many of the same *catenae* of patristic quotations in *TChr CT*, *tsch ZT* and the complete *Theologia 'Scholarium'* as he included within the *Sic et Non*. In *TChr CT* he made abbreviated reference to particular passages in the *Sic et Non* so that he could use them when writing out the complete text of the *Theologia 'Scholarium'*[90]. In this respect the *Sic et Non* also deserves to be considered as a source for the *Theologia 'Scholarium'*.

The question of whether Abelard intended to discuss the whole range of issues mentioned in the *Sic et Non* within his *Theologia 'Scholarium'* is too complex to be broached here and needs to be discussed within the context of the collections of *sententie* of Abelard's teaching on faith, the sacraments and charity[91]. For the moment, it may simply be noted that the *Theologia 'Scholarium'*, as it survives in both draft and final form, provides the vantage point from which to study Abelard's mature thought on the issues he raised at the beginning of the *Sic et Non*, on faith, the Trinity and the nature of God.

Dating of TChr and tsch

One question which has not so far been raised in this review of Buytaert's edition is that of his dating of *TChr* and *tsch*. There

---

89. *Vid. supra*, n. 47.
90. *TChr CT* III, 8^d and IV, 74^c.
91. *Epitome Theologiae Christianae*, ed. RHEINWALD, PL 178, 1685-1758; *Sententiae Florianenses*, ed. OSTLENDER, in *Florilegium Patristicum*, 19 (Bonn 1929), pp. 1-33; *Sententiae Parisienses*, ed. LANDGRAF, *Écrits théologiques de l'école d'Abélard* (Louvain 1934), pp. 5-60.

seems little doubt of his dating of the initial recension of *TChr*, in the present state of our knowledge *TChr D*, to the period 1122-1125, namely some time after the council of Soissons, held in March or April 1121, and possibly after his escape to the territory of Champagne and establishment of the oratory dedicated to the Paraclete [92]. In this Buytaert was following the opinion of Stölzle, Robert, Cottiaux and Van den Eynde although none had been aware of the recension of *TChr* in this particular manuscript [93]. There are many references in *TChr* to criticism of his theology and to the worldly life of many monks and abbots, coupled with much eulogy of the asceticism of the ancient philosophers and of the fructifying power of the Holy Spirit which would correspond to the period in which Abelard was teaching at the Paraclete [94]. Abelard cannot have composed *TChr* too long after the council of Soissons, because he also included many arguments directed against Roscelin of Compiègne, with whom he had been in debate before 1121. Roscelin had himself been condemned for heresy in 1092/3 and cannot have survived for very long after 1121 [95].

Buytaert drew on arguments first put forward by Robert in 1909, based on tentative identification of certain teachers mentioned within *TChr* IV, 77-80 and *TSch* II, 63-66 (1056B-1057B; pp. 84-85) to establish a *terminus ante quem* for *TChr D* [96]. While some indivi-

92. BUYTAERT, *TChr* - Introduction, pp. 44-50.

93. STÖLZLE, *ed. cit.*, n. 5; ROBERT, *Les écoles*, p. 198; COTTIAUX, *La conception de la théologie*, 262; VAN DEN EYNDE, *La "Theologia Scholarium" de Pierre Abélard*, 232.

94. His criticisms in *TChr* II, 57 and 71 recall those made of St Denis, *Hist. Cal.*, ed. MONFRIN, 11.654-660. Abelard quoted from *TChr* II, 38, 39, 67, 96-97, 101 in *Hist. Cal.* 11. 514-522, 523-524, 504-506, 539-545, 453-464.

95. Cf. *TChr* III, 119-135. On Roscelin, see F. PICAVET, *Roscelin philosophe et théologien, d'après la légende et d'après l'histoire* (Paris 1911), J. REINERS, *Der Nominalismus in der Frühscholastik*, BGPTMA 8. 5 (1910) and E.-H. W. KLUGE, *Roscelin and the Medieval Problem of Universals*, in *Journal of the History of Philosophy* 14 (1976) 405-414. The main sources, his letter to Abelard (ed. REINERS, pp. 63-80) *Epist.* XIV of Abelard (PL 178, 355-358), the letter of Walter of Honnecourt to Roscelin (ed. G. MORIN, *Revue bén.* 22 (1905) 165-180) and their relationship to *TSum* will be discussed by the author in a forthcoming study, as also the problem raised by H. SILVESTRE, *Pourquoi Roscelin n'est-il pas mentionné dans l' "Historia Calamitatum"?*, in RTAM 48 (1981) 218-224. The author is grateful to H. Silvestre for comments on the subject.

96. BUYTAERT, *TChr* - Introduction, pp. 48-49, drawing on the observations of ROBERT, in *Les écoles*, pp. 198-202. The identity of these teachers is also discussed by J. G. SIKES, *Peter Abailard* (Cambridge 1932), pp. 263-267.

V

duals can be identified with some certainty, like Alberic of Rheims and Ulger of Angers, others are less easy to identify. It is possible, but not certain, that Abelard was referring to Bernard of Chartres (who died before 1130) as one who believed in the efficacity of a sacramental formula independent of its user. He is identified in *TChr* as a brother of someone who believed in the eternity of the world, possibly Thierry of Chartres[97]. Buytaert followed Robert in thinking that Abelard was referring to Joscelin of Soissons as the teacher in Bourges who believed that things could turn out differently from the way God foresaw, although there is no evidence that Joscelin, who lived in Soissons from 1115 and became bishop of that city in 1126 ever taught in Bourges or held that doctrine[98]. Buytaert's argument that Abelard would not have dared to attack directly a bishop like Joscelin or Ulger (bishop of Angers from 1125), even if based on a correct identification of these individuals, accords ill with Abelard's known attitude to the episcopate, notably to William of Champeaux.

A *terminus post quem* for *TChr D* may perhaps be provided by a more general judgement that the initial form of *TChr* is not likely to have been written too long after the council of Soissons, given the directness with which Abelard replied in *TChr* both to Roscelin and those who criticised his philosophical approach to the Trinity. Abelard may have begun to collect further patristic

97. *TChr* IV, 80. J. PARENT denies that Thierry ever held this doctrine, in *La doctrine de la création dans l'école de Chartres* (Paris - Toronto 1938), pp. 96-99. Otto of Freising described Bernard and Thierry as brothers from Brittany, *Gesta Frederici Imperatoris I*, 48, ed. WAITZ-SIMSON (Hannover 1912), p. 68, but it is not certain if this Bernard was the chancellor of Chartres, as noted by R. W. SOUTHERN, *Humanism and the school of Chartres*, in *Medieval Humanism and other Studies* (Oxford 1970), p. 70 n. See also J. CHÂTILLON, *Les écoles de Chartres et de Saint-Victor*, in *La scuola nell' Occidente ...*, *Settimani di studi ...* (Spoleto 1972), ii, p. 800. John of Salisbury spoke of Bernard, chancellor of Chartres, and of Thierry without describing them as brothers, *Metalogicon*, I, 5, ed. C. WEBB (Oxford 1929), pp. 16-17. Bernard must have died by 1130, but Thierry did not die until 1156, A. VERNET, *Une épitaphe inédite de Thierry de Chartres*, in *Recueil de travaux offerts à M. Cl. Brunel* (Paris 1955), ii, pp. 660-670.

98. *TChr* IV, 79; *TSch* II, 66 (1056B; p. 85); BUYTAERT, *TChr* - Introduction, p. 49. On Joscelin, see the entry in the *Histoire littéraire de la France*, xii (Paris 1763), 412-417. Joscelin is not mentioned in the list of *scholastici* drawn up by Y. RIBAULT, *Les écolâtres de Bourges au XIIe siècle*, in *Enseignement et vie intellectuelle. Actes du 95e Congrès national des sociétés savantes* (Reims 1970), p. 91.

material to add to the *Theologia* '*Summi boni*' even while at St Denis. He seems to have been compiling the *Sic et Non* at the same time, as many *catenae* of quotation in this work are also used in *TChr*[99].

Buytaert's dating of the recension of *TChr* found in *R* to 1134-1135, more than ten years later than the date of 1122-1125 proposed by Van den Eynde, seems very difficult to hold, given that this recension differs from *TChr D* only by the addition of a few passages[100]. Buytaert opted for a late date for *TChr R* when he first studied the text of *D* and thought that *TChr R* may have been written after *tsch Z*, on the grounds of the attribution in the latter of a text of Gennadius to Augustine[101]. He subsequently modified his opinion to admit that *TChr* might have been prior to *tsch Z*, although he continued to prefer a late date on the grounds that a series of quotations in *TChr* V, 38-40 paralleled a similar sequence found in identical form only in a 'late' recension of the *Sic et Non* (*DL*, Buytaert's fourth recension)[102]. This argument proves little, however, as it is not known when this recension of the *Sic et Non* was written. Abelard did not change in *TChr R* any of those passages which referred to Roscelin. Comparison of *TChr R* with the extant text of *TChr D* does not reveal any major development in Abelard's thought, but simply the refinement of certain points of detail. *TChr R*, like *TChr D*, would appear to belong to the period in which Abelard was teaching at the Paraclete, i.e. 1122-1126.

The dating of the drafts *tsch FH*, *TChr CT*, *tsch Z* and *tsch T* is more difficult because of the complexity of their interrelationship.

---

99. Abelard was engaged in comparing the different accounts of the life of St Denis in 1121, shortly after the council of Soissons, *Hist. Cal.*, 11.942-961. Unlike *TChr*, *TSum* has few *catenae* of quotation parallel to those within the *Sic et Non*, but there are sufficient to suggest that *TSum* and the initial recension of *SN Z* may have been composed at about the same time: *TSum* I, 35 (pp. 12-13) = *SN* 15. 16; II, 24 = *SN* 1. 1; 18. 12-14; II, 33 (p. 39) = *SN* 13. 3-4; II, 68 (p. 50) = *SN* 9. 3; II, 104 (p. 62) = *SN* 9. 12; III, 6 (p. 70) = *SN* 8. 29. On parallels with *TChr*, *vid. supra*, n. 25.

100. BUYTAERT, *TChr* - Introduction, pp. 50-52; VAN DEN EYNDE, *Les Rédactions de la "Theologia Christiana"*, 298.

101. BUYTAERT, *An Earlier Redaction*, 485-490, 495.

102. *TChr* - Introduction, p. 52. Buytaert acknowledged the weakness of the *Gennadius* argument on p. 32 n. 17 and admitted that *TChr R* was more likely to be earlier than *tsch Z* on p. 392.

V

One *terminus post quem* is provided by a text of Augustine quoted inaccurately in *TChr D, R* and *sermo* I, preached to the nuns of the Paraclete, but given correctly in *tsch FH, TChr CT* and subsequent recensions of *tsch* and *TSch*[103]. This would place *tsch FH* after 1129, while the references Abelard made in its prologue to the requests of his students would suggest that it was composed while he was teaching. Abelard was certainly teaching, and had engaged in debate with Walter of Mortagne before he had drafted *tsch Z*[104].

Abelard's movements in the 1130's are obscure because his account in the *Historia Calamitatum* stops in 1132/33 in a period when he had exiled himself from St Gildas, although he was still their abbot — a title which he retained until his death in 1142[105]. Abelard was present at the dedication of a new altar at Morigny in the diocese of Sens on 20 January 1131, in company with pope Innocent II, Bernard of Clairvaux and other notable figures, including Guy of Castello, a cardinal sympathetic to Abelard and owner of the *Sic et Non* and the *Theologia Christiana*. The author of the chronicle of Morigny, writing in 1132, described Abelard as both an abbot and an outstanding *rector scolarum* to whom students came from the whole latin world[106]. Abelard travelled extensively in the period 1129-1131 while establishing his foundation of the Paraclete for Heloise and succeeded in obtaining papal protection for the community through the mediation of the bishop of Troyes in November 1131[107]. Abelard was teaching on the Mont St Geneviève in 1136, when John of Salisbury studied under him, but left soon after, perhaps in 1137[108]. In an extremely illuminating study of political factions within Paris in this period, R.-H. Bautier has suggested that Abelard's presence in Paris corresponds very closely to the periods in which Stephen Garland, a known patron and

103. Incorrect form in *TSum* I, 16 (p. 7), *TChr DR* I, 21 and *sermo* I (*PL* 178, 387A); correct form *TChr CT* I, 21, *tsch* 70, *TSch* IV 63 (997A; p. 20).

104. *tsch* 1, *Scholarium nostrorum petitioni prout possumus satisfacientes* ...; cf. *Epist. ad Abaelardum*, ed. OSTLENDER, pp. 34, 40.

105. Abelard was succeeded as abbot of St Gildas by William in 1142, according to the *Chronicon Ruyense*, ed. LOBINEAU, *Histoire de Bretagne* (Paris 1707) II, col. 370.

106. *Chronicon Mauriniacensis*, ed. L. MIROT, *La Chronique de Morigny, 1095-1152* (Paris 1909), p. 52.

107. *Hist. Cal.* 11. 1313-1345.

108. *Metalogicon* II. 10, ed. WEBB, p. 78.

156

friend of Abelard, occupied a position of power within the capital[109].
Stephen Garland, deacon of the abbey of St Geneviève from 1111,
last exercised political influence, after a period of exile, from 1132 to
August 1137, when he was ousted by his great rival, Suger
of St Denis[110]. This would point to the period of Abelard's re-
establishment as a teacher, and therefore the planning and writing
of the *Theologia 'Scholarium'*, as between 1132 and 1137.

Certain parallels between *TChr CT* and Abelard's correspondence
would suggest that this draft of the *Theologia 'Scholarium'* belongs
to the early rather than the mid-1130's. In his *Epist.* VII, written
before the rule of the Paraclete, Abelard quoted certain patristic
and classical texts in such a combination and form that he seems
to have been quoting from *TChr CT* I, 126-128; II, 104, 106-106ª[111].
There are noticeable parallels in interpretation of *I Corinthians* 14,
1-20 between a long passage only found in the complete text of the
Theologia 'Scholarium' and part of Abelard's rule for the Paraclete,
attached to *Epist.* VIII[112].

Within the *Theologia 'Scholarium'* one teacher who can be identified with certainty as Alberic of Rheims is described as teaching
in Francia. Alberic taught in Rheims until 1136, when he was
consecrated archbishop of Bourges[113]. If Abelard was referring
to Gilbert the Universal in both *TChr* and *TSch* as the teacher
in Burgundia who believed that divine properties were separate from

109 R.-H. BAUTIER, *Paris au temps d'Abélard*, in *Abélard en son temps. Actes
du colloque international organisé à l'occasion du 9ᵉ centenaire de la naissance de
Pierre Abélard (14-19 mai 1979)* (Paris 1981), pp. 21-77, especially pp. 53-77.

110. *Ibid.*, pp. 63, 77.

111. *Epist.* VII, ed. J.T. MUCKLE, *The Letter of Heloise on Religious Life and
Abelard's First Reply*, in *Medieval Studies* 17 (1955) 271-272, 276-277. While some of
these passages also occur in *TSum* I, 60-61 (pp. 23-24) and most in *TChr DR*,
only *TChr CT* has them all. A minor variant of *TChr* I, 128 in *TSch* I, 191 (1031C;
p. 57), the reading *que Cumaea siue Cumana*, not found in *Epist.* VII, 272, shows
that Abelard was not quoting from *TSch* in *Epist.* VII; VAN DEN EYNDE, *La
"Theologia Scholarium" de Pierre Abélard*, 237.

112. *Epist.* VIII, *regula sanctimonialium, Abelard's Rule for Religious Women*, in
Medieval Studies 18 (1956) 286-287; cf. *TSch* II, 52-55 (1052D-54A; pp. 80-81).
The image of the blind leading the blind, used in the *Hist. Cal.* 11. 690-701 to
defend the rational approach of *TSum*, appears in the same context only in *TSch* II,
56 (1054A; p. 81) and not at all in either *TSum* or *TChr*.

113. *TChr* IV, 78; *TSch* II, 63-64 (1056BD; p. 84). On Alberic's career, see J.R.
WILLIAMS, *The Cathedral School of Reims in the Time of Master Alberic, 1118-1136*,
in *Traditio* 20 (1964) 93-114.

God, that Christ was born fully grown and that monks and nuns could marry after taking their religious vows, then he could not have made the criticism long after 1128 when Gilbert became bishop of London, let alone after 1134 when he died[114]. According to a letter attributed to Walter of Mortagne, a pupil of Gilbert did hold just the opinion about the marriage of monks and nuns criticised by Abelard[115]. However, as commented earlier, identification of individuals in *TChr* is difficult as Abelard may have been far from accurate in the claims he made.

In conclusion, it may be suggested that Abelard planned the *Theologia 'Scholarium'* through the drafts *tsch FH, TChr CT, tsch Z* and *T* (and possibly others no longer extant) in the early 1130's, tentatively 1132-1135. The *Theologia 'Scholarium'* represented a major revision of the *Theologia Christiana*, as contained in *R*, and may have been the fruit of many years work. Abelard composed his commentary on Romans after *TChr CT*, but before the third book of the *Theologia 'Scholarium'*; he wrote the *Ethica* or *Scito teipsum* only after he had finished its third book[116].

Conclusion

The results of this review of Buytaert's edition of the *Theologia Christiana* and of the shorter form of the *Theologia 'Scholarium'* may be summarised as follows :

(1) The different manuscripts of the *Theologia Christiana* and the *Theologia 'Scholarium'*, rather than being 'first', 'second' or 'third' redactions of one or other work, each represent the attempt of a

---

114. *TChr* IV, 80; *TSch* II, 63, 65 (1056BD; p. 84). On Gilbert, see B. SMALLEY, *Gilbertus Universalis, Bishop of London (1128-1134) and the Problem of the "Glossa Ordinaria"*, in RTAM 7 (1935) 235-262.

115. Ed. MARTÈNE-DURAND, *Veterum scriptorum ... collectio* (Paris 1724) I, cols. 839-843. This letter is discussed by L. OTT, *Untersuchungen zur theologischen Brief-literatur der Frühscholastik*, BGPTMA 34 (1937), pp. 292-313.

116. In his commentary on Romans, ed. BUYTAERT, CCCM 11 (Turnhout 1969), pp. 68, 69, 70-71 and 152-153 Abelard referred to *TSch* books I and II, perhaps still only in draft form on pp. 75-76, 225, 259-260, 281-282 he reffered to the arguments of *TSch* III about free will and God's grace as still to be written. In the *Ethica*, ed. LUSCOMBE, p. 96 he referred to his discussion of *TSch* III, 117-120 (pp. 148-149) as already written.

copyist to reproduce the state of Abelard's text, with all its annotations, as it stood at the time it was copied. Abelard was in the habit of continually making additions and corrections to his text. The *Vatican, Reginensis MS lat. 159* (*R*) may be a direct copy of an annotated exemplar belonging to Abelard.

(2) The MSS *Monte Cassino, Archivio della Badia 174* (*C*) and *Tours, Bibliothèque municipale 85* (*T*) both contain copies of the *Sic et Non* and the *Theologia Christiana* ultimately dependent on an exemplar used and annotated by Abelard himself. This exemplar contained the text of the *Theologia Christiana* which Abelard used to provide a draft for the main body of his argument in the *Theologia 'Scholarium'*. The apparent confusion of the text of *TChr* in *C* and *T* can be explained as the result of scribes reproducing at the same time both the original text of *TChr* and the extensive corrections and notes Abelard added to his copy.

(3) The shorter forms of the *Theologia 'Scholarium'* found in the MSS *Fulda, Priesterseminar 1* (*F*) and *Heiligenkreuz, Stiftsbibliothek 153* (*H*) are copies of Abelard's draft of the opening section of *TSch*, while that found in *Zurich, Zentralbibliothek C. 61* (*Z*) and the *Tours MS* (*T*) are later drafts dependent on both *tsch FH* and *TSch CT*. These drafts of *TSch*, *tsch FH*, *TChr CT*, *tsch Z* and *tsch T*, may be dated tentatively to the period 1132-1135.

VI

The *Sententie* of Peter Abelard

What is the status of the text edited by F.H. Rheinwald under the title *Petri Abaelardi Epitome Theologiae Christianae*, frequently referred to as the *Sententie Hermanni*, and recently re-edited by S. Buzzetti under the title *Sententie magistri Petri Abelardi*?[1] What is its relationship to the *Sententie Florianenses*, *Sententie Parisienses* and *Liber sententiarum magistri Petri*, all conventionally attributed to the school of Peter Abelard?[2] How are these different sentence collections related to Abelard's *Theologia "Scholarium"*? While the appearance of Buzzetti's new edition of the unjustly neglected *Sententie* can only be welcomed, these questions remain to be answered. Buzzetti suggests that Abelard may be the author of these *Sententie*, and that a pupil called Hermann later produced a revision of the work[3]. He does not explain the significance of the many variations between the different manuscripts of the *Sententie*, or comment on its relationship either to other sentence collections or to the writings of Abelard[4].

1. *Petri Abaelardi Epitome Theologiae Christianae, Anecdota ad historiam ecclesiasticam pertinentia* 2, Berlin 1835, reprinted with Rheinwald's introduction, *PL* 178, 1685-1758 and in part only by V. Cousin, *Petri Abaelardi Opera* 2, Paris 1859, p. 567-92; S. Buzzetti, *Sententie magistri Petri Abelardi (Sententie Hermanni)*, Florence 1983. It is to be regretted that Buzzetti does not use the correct latin spelling *Abaelardus*, used by the author himself as an example within the *Dialectica*, ed. L.M. De Rijk, Assen 1970[2], p. 114[30], 566[26] (*Paris, Bibl. nat. lat. 14614*, ff. 127[v], 197) or in signing a charter of Notre-Dame du Ronceray, Angers (*Arch. dép. de Loire-Atlantique, H 351*, *pièce 1*); *ae* is written separately and pronounced as two vowels (as in *Israel*) in these and other manuscripts. This accounts for the variety of forms of his name also met with : *Abaialardus, Abaielardus, Baiolardus* etc. Poets always scan his name as five syllables; see B. Geyer, *Peter Abaelards Philosophische Schriften*, in *Beiträge zur Geschichte der Philosophie und Theologie des Mittelalters* 21, 1 (1919), p. v.
2. *Sententiae Florianenses*, ed. H. Ostlender, *Florilegium Patristicum* 19, Bonn 1929; *Sententie Parisienses*, ed. A. Landgraf, *Écrits théologiques de l'école d'Abélard*, in *Spicilegium Sacrum Lovaniense. Études et documents* 14, Louvain 1934, p. 3-60; *liber sententiarum magistri Petri*, ed. C.J. Mews, at the end of this study.
3. Buzzetti, p. 5-6.
4. There are numerous deficiencies in the technical aspects of the edition. Apart from scriptural texts, not one quotations, either of Abelard or of a patristic author is identified. For correction of comments on the description of manuscripts, see below,

VI

This study, originally written quite independently of Buzzetti's research, is not intended to be a review of the new edition, but rather to answer those questions which still need to be dealt with. His criticism of the argument of Ostlender that the *Sententie* should be attributed to an otherwise unknown Hermann, concides with conclusions which I myself had arrived at [5]. To focus argument, however, on the question of whether or not the work was *written* by Abelard or a disciple is to miss the significance of the text. In the absence of an autograph, every manuscript containing a work attributed to Abelard reflects the intervention of a copyist in the transmission of its text. As I have shown elsewhere, each manuscript of the *Theologia* represents an individual scribe's interpretation of the often very complicated text with which he was confronted [6]. The manuscripts of the *Sententie* present a similar problem to those of the *Theologia* in the variety of alternative readings which they present. Two related questions need to be asked of these manuscripts : how far has a disciple (or a forger) developed and perhaps modified

nn. 19-29. The editor does not explain what principles he follows in presenting the text, many important variants being included within the apparatus, others, often unmarked, within the body of text. Much of the text of the first section would have been elucidated by comparison with that of the *Theologia "Scholarium"*. Errors of transcription are numerous, sometimes entire phrases being omitted (see below, nn. 48-58); references are to the chapter, the same as in *M* and thus as in *PL* 178, and the line of Buzzetti's edition. The following errors, taken out of the first three chapters (there are thirty-eight) concern only the main body of text or the reading to be adopted : 1) 14 refertur *ad*; 35 Sacramentum *vero CP*, *TSch*; 2) diligent*ius*, *pro*positam *CSP*, *TSch*; 15 nemo *enim*; 16 apparentia *esse*; 29 appare*re*; 47 Sed *si*; 3) 5 divin*itatis*; 4) 25-26 spirit*us* sanct*i*; 30 in*quit*; 33 aliqu*id* (aliquem *CP*); 40 cum *ipse*; 44 capite *ii* (v *M'Pr*); 48 de*itatis*; 60 ind*ividuam*; 5) 19 nisi *quoniam* (quia *SP*); 30 *qua* scilicet; 31 possi*nt*; 34 qui *omnia*. All extracts quoted in this article have been checked against the manuscripts, variants being signalled only when important. I am grateful to C.S.F. Burnett and J.S. Barrow for being able to consult a version of the text they have under preparation and to D.E. Luscombe for discussion of ideas in this paper.

5. C.J. MEWS, *The Development of the Theologia of Peter Abelard*, D. Phil. thesis, Oxford 1980. The conclusions of Ostlender's unpublished thesis, *Peter Abaelards Theologia und die Sentenzenbücher seiner Schule*, Breslauer Kath.-theol. Diss. 1926, were first summarized by B. GEYER, *Die Patristische und Scholastische Philosophie*, Berlin 1927, p. 225-6, but were given in more detail in Ostlender's article, *Die Sentenzenbücher der Schule Abaelards*, in *Theologische Quartalschrift* 117 (1936) 208-52.

6. MEWS, *Peter Abelard's Theologia Christiana and Theologia "Scholarium" re-examined*, in *RTAM* 52 (1985) 109-158.

ideas of Abelard, and what is their significance for our understanding of the evolution of the thought of Abelard himself? Controversy surrounds the *Sententie* because Abelard denied that he had ever written a certain *liber sententiarum magistri Petri*, which William of Thierry and Bernard of Clairvaux had used as evidence for his teaching of heresy[7]. This particular text, originally untitled but which became known as the *liber sententiarum*, is different from the *Sententie Abaelardi* as edited by Rheinwald and Buzzetti, while similar in structure and argument. When Bernard mentioned the *liber sententiarum magistri Petri*, he seems to have meant a book of the teachings of master Peter. Abelard denied that *liber sententiarum* was a book like *Theologia* or *Scito teipsum*[8]. The *liber sententiarum* seems to be of a different status to these literary works, but does it contain ideas distinct from those of Abelard?

Interpretations of the Sententie

Rheinwald thought that the *Sententie* were either written or dictated by Abelard himself[9]. He pointed out that the first part of the *Sententie*, far from being a simple abbreviation of the *Theologia "Scholarium"* contained an original synthesis of Abelard's teaching, sometimes more developed than in *TSch*. In addition he noticed that a reference by the author to an earlier commentary on a passage in the Epistle to the Romans (*Jacob dilexi* etc., *Rom.* 9, 13) corresponded exactly to the passage in Abelard's commentary on Romans about God's love for Jacob and his enmity for Esau[10].

---

7. *Confessio fidei "Universis"* (*PL* 178, 107-8): *Quod ... amicus noster concluserit* "*... partim in libro sententiarum eiusdem ... reperta sunt*" *non sine admiratione suscepi, cum nusquam* {not *numquam* as in A. Duchesne *PL* 178} *liber alicuius qui sententiarum dicatur a me scriptus reperiatur*; *Apologia contra Bernardum* 3, ed. BUYTAERT, *Petri Abaelardi Opera theologica* 1, CCCM 12, Turnhout 1969, p. 360-1 : *Deo autem gratias quod in his libris asserit reperiri, ubi cum reperiri non possint aut mea scripta non fuerint ...* See too C.S.F. BURNETT, *Peter Abelard, Confessio fidei "Universis" : A Critical edition of Abelard's reply to accusations of heresy*, in *Mediaeval Studies* 48 (1986) and C.J. MEWS, *The lists of heresies imputed to Peter Abelard*, in *Revue bénéd.* 95 (1985) 73-110.
8. See below, n. 136.
9. Rheinwald's important discussion is printed *PL* 178, 1685-94.
10. *Ibid.* 1688A; see below, nn. 94-95.

VI

In order to reconcile the evident affinity of the arguments of the *Sententie* to those of Abelard with his denial that he had ever written a *liber sententiarum*, D. Gieseler argued that the *Sententie* contained a report of his oral teaching, taken down by a pupil[11]. This view was later countered by H. Denifle, who judged the *Sententie* to be so carefully written that it had to have been composed by a disciple summarising a much larger work[12]. Denifle sought to identify this literary source with a *cursus theologiae*, of which the *Theologia "Scholarium"* was the introduction, but of which the rest did not survive in manuscript. Eager to emphasise Abelard's scholastic influence, he also thought that this *cursus theologiae* inspired the author of the *Sententie Florianenses*, as well as Roland and Omnebene, who both produced independent collections of *sententie*[13].

Some aspects of Denifle's hypothesis were criticised by Ostlender, in particular the assumption that the *Theologia "Scholarium"* originally dealt with the incarnation, the sacraments and charity as well as with faith in God. He thought that Abelard never completed his treatise and that an anonymous disciple, author of the *liber sententiarum*, was the first to extend his master's thought into a systematic body of doctrine[14]. This *liber sententiarum* he believed to have inspired the authors of the *Sententie Abaelardi*, *Sententie Parisienses*, *Sententie Florianenses*, Roland and Omnebene. He argued from certain references within some manuscripts of the *Sent. A.* that its true author was called Hermann[15]. The implication of his argument was that these writings did not represent a reliable report of Abelard's teaching, as they all depended on a work composed by another disciple.

A number of scholars expressed doubts about individual aspects of Ostlender's hypothesis, but never in a consistent manner or

11. D. GIESELER, *Über Abaelard's Sententiae*, in *Theologische Studien und Kritiken* (1837) 366-9.
12. H. DENIFLE, *Die Sentenzen Abaelards und die Bearbeitung seiner Theologia vor Mitte des 12 Jahrhunderts*, in *Archiv für Literatur- und Kirchengeschichte des Mittelalters* 1 (1885) 402-69, 584-624.
13. DENIFLE, 420-69; see A.M. GIETL, *Die Sentenzen Rolands*, Freiburg 1891, and the *Sententie* of Omnebene, currently being edited by J.S. Barrow.
14. OSTLENDER, *Die Sentenzenbücher*, 242-50.
15. *Ibid.*, 210-12.

dealing with his argument as a whole. The abrupt style of the *Sent. Florianenses* suggested to several scholars that it was more likely to be a report of Abelard's oral teaching, an opinion held by Landgraf with respect to the *Sent. Parisienses*[16]. Landgraf effectively demolished Ostlender's argument in the introduction to his edition of the *Commentarius Cantabrigiensis*, which he showed was a *reportatio* of Abelard's lectures on the Pauline epistles, but did not develop his ideas about the nature of the different sentence collections. A further inconsistency in Ostlender's argument was identified by Blomme, who noted that the definition of sin as consent to a wrong will corresponded to Abelard's teaching in the *Ethica*, and was more developed than that in the *Sent. A.* of sin as *mala voluntas*, also found in Abelard's earlier writings[17]. While commenting that the *liber sententiarum* could not be the source of the other sentence collections, he did not use the discovery to re-assess the relationship between these texts and the writings of Abelard. The weakness of Ostlender's argument for the attribution of the *Sent. A.* to Hermann and assumption that its author modified some aspects of Abelard's theology in reaction to the controversy of 1139-40 is criticised by Buzzetti in the introduction to his edition[18]. He makes no attempt, however, to relate the *Sent. A.* to the other sentence collections, but asserts that it may have been composed by Abelard on the grounds that its arguments are "fin troppo abelardiana". A second recension found in three manuscripts (*M'M"Pr*) he judges to be a revision made by a pupil called Hermann. Although there has been no lack of isolated comments on these various *sententie*, it is evident that some effort must be made to relate them, and the *Sententie Abaelardi* in particular, to

---

16. In book reviews by F. PELSTER in *Scholastik* 5 (1930) 451, by H. WEISWEILER, *ibid.* 12 (1937) 434-5, by A. LANDGRAF, *Die Abhängigkeit der Sünde von Gott, ibid.* 10 (1935) 176, by E. BERTOLA, *Le "Sententiae Florianenses" della scuola di Abelardo,* in *Sophia* 18 (1950) 377; see also LANDGRAF, *Écrits théologiques de l'école d'Abélard,* p. xxxiv-xxxix and (after publication of Ostlender's article) his introduction to *Commentarius Cantabrigiensis in Epistolas Pauli e Schola Petri Abaelardi* 1, Notre-Dame, Indiana 1937, p. xx-xxxiii. D.E. LUSCOMBE interpreted these texts as works of different authors, *The School of Peter Abelard,* Cambridge 1969, p. 143-72.

17. R. BLOMME, *La doctrine du péché dans les écoles théologiques de la première moitié du XIIe siècle,* Louvain 1958, p. 229-35, 245, 263 n. 2, 267 n. 3, 290 n. 1.

18. BUZZETTI, p. 15-16.

the writings of Peter Abelard in order to determine their full value and significance.

The manuscripts of the Sent. A.

Before evaluating the text of the *Sent. A.*, the major known manuscripts need to be listed. The sigla used by Buzzetti are given in brackets when they are different from those used here.

A (Pr): *Princeton, University Library, R. Garrett 169*, ff. 83-151^v; s. XII. Probably copied at Admont (formerly Stiftsbibliothek 729). The text breaks off at the same point as *M*, ... *graviter est puniendus* (*PL* 178, 1758D) and is titled *Sentencie petri baiolardi*[19].

C: *Carpentras, Bibliothèque Inguimbertine 110*, ff. 55-65^v; s. XIII. The provenance and early history of the MS is unknown. The text, anonymous in *C*, is longer than that of other MSS, and concludes half-way down f. 65^v: ... *Per hos, inquam, duos effectus due claves dicuntur*[20].

M (M'): *Munich, Bayerische Staatsbibliothek, Clm 14160*, ff. 1^v-39; s. XII. *M* belonged to the church of St Emmeram in Regensburg in the twelfth century, but may have been copied at the abbey of Prüfening in the same diocese. The work, titled the *sentencie magistri petri abelardi*, breaks off at the same point as *A* and *N*[21].

N (M"): *Munich, Bayerische Staatsbibliothek. Clm 16085*, ff. 104-142^v; s. XII. *N* belonged at an early date to the canons of St Niklaus

---

19. S. DE RICCI, *Census of Medieval and Renaissance Manuscripts in the United States and Canada* 2, New York 1937, no. 2295. Copied in a similar hand is the *Theologia* "Summi boni", within *Oxford, Bodleian Library, Lyell 49*, 101-128^v, also from Admont.

20. M. DUHAMEL, *Catalogue général des manuscrits des bibliothèques publiques en France. Départements 34, 1*, Paris 1901, p. 57-8. To Buzzetti's note, add J.R. WILLIAMS, *The Twelfth Century Theological «Quaestiones» of Carpentras 110*, in *Medieval Studies* 28 (1966) 300-6. Its final section is edited by LUSCOMBE, *The School*, p. 312-15.

21. The Prüfening origin of *M* is suggested by A. BOECKLER, *Die Regensburg-Prüfeninger Buchmalerei des XII-XIII Jahrhunderts*, Munich 1924, p. 120 and is discussed by LUSCOMBE, *Peter Abelard's Ethics*, Oxford 1971, p. xli-xliv. Rheinwald's edition is based on *M*, which is the only manuscript to divide the text into chapters. As its text is the least reliable, these divisions seem unlikely to be authentic.

vor Passau. The *Sent. A.*, anonymous in *N*, breaks off at the same point as *A* and *M*[22].

P : *Pavia, Biblioteca Universitaria, Aldini 49*, ff. 73-88[v]; s. XII. The provenance of *P* is unknown. Titled *sententie magistri Petri abaialardi de fide et caritate et sacramento*, the text breaks off accidentally within the section on charity ... *Christo sane asserimus* (1755A)[23].

Pa : *Paris, Bibliothèque nationale lat. 18108*, ff. 76[v]-77[v]; s. XII. The first gathering belonged to St Denis of Rheims, but not necessarily the codex, which belonged to the abbey of St Martin-des-Champs, in Paris[24]. The anonymous fragment contains the text of chapters 12-18 only (1714D-1722A).

S : *St Gallen, Stiftsbibliothek 69*, pp. 417-448; s. XII. *S* was copied at St Gallen. The text, anonymous in *S*, breaks off accidentally near the beginning of the section on charity: ... *qui eum diligunt, non* (1748C)[25].

A fragment of the chapter on the eucharist, titled *De specie panis et vini*, occurs in two related MSS : *Cologne, Historisches Archiv, W 137*, ff. 5-5v (s. XII) in the possession of the canons of Niederwerth, near Vallendar in the diocese of Trier; *Trier, Stadtbibliothek 591*, ff. 114[v]-115 (s. XII) in the possession of St Eucherius of Trier in 1243[26]. Also should be mentioned is the partially erased text of the beginning of the *Sent. A.* on f. 179 of the Cologne MS (*Historisches Archiv, W 137*). Although it is titled *theologia pet{ri} baylardi* in a 14th century hand, as in an initial list of contents on f. 1, the text corresponds to the beginning of the *Sent. A. (Tria sunt ...)*

22. H. WEISWEILER, *Un manuscrit inconnu de Munich sur la querelle des investitures*, in *Revue d'Hist. ecclés.* 34 (1938) 245-69.

23. L. DE MARCHI, *Inventario dei manoscritti della R. Biblioteca Universitaria di Pavia* 1, Milan 1894, p. 21-22. A fourteenth century inscription has been erased from the flyleaf (verso), and is barely visible: *f... h... Liber ... ini.* Another has been erased from f. 1.

24. Described by LANDGRAF, *Écrits théologiques*, p. xiii-xxvi. As with the other manuscripts, Buzzetti confuses provenance of a manuscript with its ownership, particularly misleading in the case of a composite codex like *Pa*.

25. A. BRUCKNER, *Scriptoria Medii Aevi Helvetica* 3 : *Schreibschulen der Diözese Konstanz. St Gallen* 2, Geneva 1938, p. 47 and 63.

26. WEISWEILER, *Eine neue Bearbeitung von Abaelards « Introductio » und der Summa Sententiarum*, in *Scholastik* 9 (1934) 366-8 and *Un manuscrit inconnu* (*supra* n. 22) 265.

VI

and not that of *TSch* (*Scholarium* ...). The list of contents on f. 117ᵛ also corresponds to that of the *Sent. A.* rather than of *TSch*[27]. Another fragment of the *Sent. A.* not mentioned by Buzzetti occurs in the MS *Vienna, Nationalbibliothek, cvp 998*, f. 177; s. XIIᵉˣ, which belonged to the abbey of Göttweig, in the diocese of Passau, where it may have been copied. The fragment is given under the rubric : *Petrus Abaielardus in theologia sua*[28]. Mention should also be made of copies of the *Sent. A.* now lost, belonging to the abbeys of Prüfening, St Peter's of Salzburg, Engelberg and possibly of Beinwil[29]. The geographical location of these manuscripts suggests that one centre of diffusion of the *Sent. A.* was within the dioceses of Constance (St Gallen, Engelberg) and

---

27. In *Peter Abelard's Following*, unpublished Ph.D. thesis, Cambridge University 1964, p. 114-21, Luscombe studies the text erased on f. 179, which he judges to be that of the *Theologia "Scholarium"*, following P. CLASSEN, *Zur Geschichte der Frühscholastik in Österreich und Bayern*, in *Mitteilungen des Instituts der Österreichischen Geschichtsforschung* 67 (1959) 255. The partly erased list of contents on f. 117ᵛ, gives certain sections found in *Sent. A.*, but not *TSch* (marked *): *De christiane fidei religione. Testimonia trinitatis de veteri testamento. Testimonia de prophetis de filio. Testimonia de spiritu sancto. Testimonia philosophorum de deo. De spiritu sancto inter nos et grecos. De predicatione nominum*. Quid philosophi de spiritu sancto senserint. De excommunicatione*. De clavibus*. De sacramento meritoque (?) videndum (?) restat. Demum (?) ... contrahere presit**. Only f. 179ᵛ remains, as it was the last leaf of its gathering and the same copyist followed on ff. 180-222ᵛ with the *Elucidarium* of Honorius Augustodunensis. The contents of this manuscript are described in detail in the handwritten catalogue of Dr Kelleter in *Cologne, Historisches Archiv, Findbuch Handschriften (Theol. Trakt.) 1*, ff. 170-2.

28. Identified by W. MEYER, *Die Anklagesätze des hl. Bernhard gegen Abälard*, in *Nachrichten der k. Gesellschaft der Wissenschaften zu Göttingen, phil.-hist. Klasse*, Göttingen 1898, 4 Abhdlg., p. 434 n. 2 (equivalent to 21, 53-62 in Buzzetti's edition).

29. Prüfening, according to catalogues of 1165 and 1347, owned a copy of the *Sententie Petri Baiolardi* and *Ethica* (probably related to *M*), C.E. INEICHEN-EDER (ed.), *Mittelalterliche Bibliothekskataloge Deutschlands und der Schweiz 4. 1*, Munich 1977, p. 425²²⁴, 431¹³⁴. St Peter's, Salzburg, owned a copy of the *Sententie Petri Bailardi* in the twelfth century, G. BECKER, *Catalogi Bibliothecarum Antiqui*, Bonn 1885, p. 237 and G. MÖSER-MERSKY, H. MIHALIUK (ed.) *Mittelalterliche Bibliotheks-kataloge Österreichs 4*, Graz-Vienna-Cologne 1966, p. 71. Engelberg owned a copy *Liber magistri Petri de fide et caritate et de sacramentis* and the *Sic et Non*, according to a catalogue drawn up 1147-78, P. LEHMANN and P. RUF (ed.) *Mittel-alterliche Bibliothekskataloge Deutschlands und der Schweiz 1*, Munich 1918, p. 32. Beinwil owned c. 1200 *duo parium sententiarum magistri Petri A.*, P. LEHMANN, *Die Bibliothek des Klösters Beinwil*, in *Zeitschrift für Schweizerische Kirchengeschichte Freiburg* 44 (1950) 1-16, reprinted in *Erforschung des Mittelalters. Ausgewählte Abhandlungen und Aufsätze 2*, Stuttgart 1959, p. 157-70; this could also be the *Sic et Non*.

Basle (Beinwil), while another was further east, within the dioceses of Regensburg (St Emmeram, Prüfening), Passau (Admont, Göttweig) and Salzburg (St Peter's). The provenance of the Carpentras and Pavia manuscripts is unfortunately unknown.

The role of Hermannus

Ostlender's argument that the *Sententie* were written by a pupil of Abelard called Hermannus rested on his interpretation of a passage, found only in *AMN* and not in *S, C* or *P*[30] :

> Diverso vero tempore prolata idem significant[1], ut si quis diceret[2] heri[3], "Hermannus {iste *S*; Petrus *CP*} leget cras", qui idem hodie[4] dicat "Hermannus {iste *S*; Petrus *CP*} legit[5] hodie" et cras idem dicat "Hermannus {iste *S*; Petrus *CP*} legit heri[6], idem enim significat[7] : scilicet quod ego hodie legerim. Idem namque est me heri fuisse lecturum hodie[8] et me hodie legere et cras me hodie legisse.

1 significat *N*   2 dixisset *P Buzzetti*, dicat *M*   3 *om. M*   4 hodie *om. AMN*   5 leget *CS*   6 cras idem ... heri *om. M*   7 significant *Rheinwald, Buzzetti*   8 *om. P, ante* lecturum *AMN*

Hermannus is mentioned further on in *AMN*, but not in *C* (*S* and *P* being deficient at this point)[31] :

> Item, si Hermannus[1] eandem habet voluntatem[2] cum magistro suo Petro[3], et uterque pecuniam ad faciendam domum pauperibus paravit[4], et alter edificet cui pecunia[5] remanet, alter vero minime cum ei pecunia ablata sit, non qui edificat quam qui[6] hoc non facit maioris meriti apud Deum esse debet.

1 *om. C*   2 eadem voluntatem habet *C*   3 *P.* suo *C*   4 paratam *C*
5 pecuniam *C*   6 quod *C*

While Ostlender thought that *AMN* contained the correct version of the text and that *C, S* and *P* were more corrupt, comparison of the first part of *SCP* with the text of the *Theologia* "*Scholarium*" shows that these manuscripts contain a version of the *Sententie* distinctly earlier than *AMN*, a conclusion arrived at by Buzzetti without reference to *TSch*[32].

30. *Sent. A.*, 1, ed. BUZZETTI, 21, 27-32.
31. *Ibid.*, 34, 49-54.
32. BUZZETTI, p. 10. Comparing the *Sent. A.* with *tsch*, ed. BUYTAERT, CCCM

VI

Buzzetti's conclusion, however, that *SCP* represents a single recension, of which Abelard was the author, and which was subsequently revised by a pupil called Hermann, leaves some questions unanswered. Are the important differences between *S, C* and *P* all to be attributed to the imagination of copyists? *AMN* (which can be treated as a single recension) incorporates a number of additional passages not found in *SCP* or in the *Theologia "Scholarium"* which illuminate Abelard's argument in the latter treatise. Either Hermann had so fully absorbed the thinking of his master that he had become an *alter ego*, or the different forms of the text of the *Sententie* reflect changing or new arguments of the master himself. Hermann may have inserted his own name into two examples, but what evidence is there for Buzzetti's claim that Hermann was responsible for all the changes to the text of the *Sententie* in *AMN*? No other composition of this Hermann is known to survive[33]. One can never ignore the influence of any copyist on a text of which the autograph is no longer extant; the question, however, which needs to be asked is not whether Hermann added his name to the text or not, but what light the manuscripts of the *Sententie* throw on the thought of Abelard himself.

12, p. 401-51, the following passages occur in *AMN*, but not *SCP* or *tsch*: *Sent. A.* 2, 65-66: *vel catholica fides ideo dicitur universalis scilicet quod nos unum facit vel quod nos unit Deo*; 5, 22-25: *hoc est ita in potestate eius sunt omnia posita quod de omnibus que ipse vult ordinare vel facere, non est aliquis qui possit eius voluntatem impedire*; 28: *Dei sapientia genita*; 43: *divini cultus perfectionem vel religionem*; 9, 32-33: *Hinc et Augustinus: "Deus quidem unus est sed non singularis"* ... *a legislatore* (referring back to the sentence before *Augustinus*).

33. According to a notice by N. RHEINHARDT, *Lexicon für Theologie und Kirche* 5, Freiburg i.B. 1960, p. 254, this Hermann wrote the commentaries in the *St Gall MSS 64* and *1716*. There is no indication within either manuscript, both of which are anonymous, of authorship by this Hermann: *St Gall 64*, p. 13-267 contains literal, interlinear and marginal glosses on the Pauline epistles based on Augustine and Jerome, while *St Gall 1716*, p. 1-288 is a commentary on the catholic epistles, which begins on p. 1-2 with the same introduction as Abelard's commentary on Romans (ed. BUYTAERT, CCCM 11, Turnhout 1969, p. 41[5]-43[85]), but continues *In argumentum Iacobus sanctum instruxit clerum* ... Its authorship deserves further investigation. On these two MSS, see BRUCKNER, *Scriptoria* ... *3. St Gallen 2*, p. 62 and 113.

The Sententie Abaelardi and the Theologia "Scholarium"

The value of the *Sent. A.* as a record of Abelard's teaching can best be assessed by comparing the first part of this work with the *Theologia "Scholarium"*. Ostlender thought that the first eleven chapters of the *Sent. A.* formed an abridgement of what he called the second redaction of the *Theologia "Scholarium" (tsch T)*[34]. More detailed research led Van den Eynde to comment that some passages of the *Sent. A.* were closer to an earlier draft (*tsch Z*, Ostlender's first redaction), while others were closer to *tsch T*, apart from two short passages which betrayed the "influence" of *TSch*. He suggested that Hermann made use either of a combination of *tsch Z* and *tsch T* or of a version intermediate between the two, plus a copy of *TSch*[35]. Buytaert followed up this line of argument by suggesting that Hermann could simply have combined parts of *tsch Z* with parts of *TSch*, but he could not explain why parts of the *Sent. A.* corresponded exactly to *tsch T* rather than to either *tsch Z* or *TSch*[36]. Neither of these scholars were aware that the main passage which suggested the "influence" of *TSch* occurred only in the manuscripts *AMN* of the *Sententie*[37]. Just as *SCP* corresponded to a recension of *tsch* between *Z* and *T*, so *AMN* had been revised in the same place as Abelard had modified *tsch*, when writing out the complete *Theologia "Scholarium"*.

All these hypotheses are vitiated by the assumption that this part of the *Sent. A.* is derivative of the *Theologia "Scholarium"*. Its first eight chapters, found in *S, C, P* and *AMN*, present a text very similar to the beginning of *tsch* in a version transitional between *Z* and *T*, but with some important differences. The *Sent. A.* begins, not with the preface (*Scholarium nostrorum petitioni prout possumus*

---

34. OSTLENDER, *Die Sentenzenbücher*, 217.

35. D. VAN DEN EYNDE, *La « Theologia Scholarium» de Pierre Abélard*, in *RTAM* 28 (1961) 229-31.

36. BUYTAERT, CCCM 12, p. 381-3.

37. *Sent. A.* 11, 72-77 (a passage from Claudian) found only in *AMN* occurs in *TSch* I, 99 (*PL* 178, 1005D-6A); the other passage thought to be "influenced" by *TSch*, *Sent. A.* 5, 30-31 (*qua scilicet eo modo vult omnia provenire quo melius possint*) is only an alternative to the reading in *tsch* 39 : *qua videlicet optime cuncta vult fieri seu disponi*. In *TSch* I, 32 (989D) the versions of *tsch* and *Sent. A.* are combined and expanded.

satisfacientes, aliquam sacre eruditionis summam quasi divine Scripture introductionem conscripsimus ...) as in *tsch* and *TSch*, but with the beginning of its first book : *Tria sunt, ut arbitror, in quibus humane salutis summa consistit, fides videlicet, caritas et sacramenta*[38]. After brief definitions of faith, charity and sacrament, Abelard says in the *Theologia "Scholarium"* that each needed to be discussed in relation to man's salvation, particular those aspects which gave rise to the greatest difficulty, while in the *Sent. A.* he says he will discuss each of these subjects :

> Nunc autem, tribus suprapositis breviter assignatis atque descriptis, {scilicet fide, caritate et sacramento *add. TSch*} de singulis diligentius agamus {agendum est *TSch*} quantum ad propositam {suprapositam *AMN*} humane salutis summam pertinere videtur {pertinet summam *TSch*}, et de his precipue que maioribus questionibus implicita videntur; ac primum de fide, que naturaliter ceteris prior est tanquam bonorum omnium fundamentum[39].

Abelard gives no indication either in the *capitula librorum* preceding the first book of *TSch* or within his text that he intended to deal with the redemption, the sacraments or charity beyond saying *de singulis diligentius agendum est*[40]. The promise *agamus* in the *Sent. A.* is carried out, as, unlike *TSch*, the *Sententie* cover all the main aspects of faith, sacraments and charity, although not in the detail which Abelard devotes to the Trinity in *TSch*.

The variants between *tsch-TSch* and the *Sent. A.* are of interest for our appreciation of the main thrust of Abelard's argument. A long series of patristic quotations in *tsch* is summarised : *His ergo et aliis multis que inducere possemus testimoniis* ..., while an example of immaterial belief, *vel si credamus Christum huius vel illius stature fuisse vel non, vel in illa civitate predicasse vel non* not found in *tsch* occurs in the *Sent. A.*[41]. Sometimes *AMN* contains additional phrases or commentary which elucidates further the text of *TSch*[42].

---

38. *tsch* 11, *TSch* I, 1 (981C). *Sent. A.* 1, 2 has *sacramentum* rather than *sacramenta* in *SCP*.

39. *tsch* 17-18, *TSch* I, 1-2 (984B); cf. *Sent. A.* 2, 1-6.

40. The two aspects of faith in God and in his benefits to man are defined in *tsch* 24, but no promise is made to deal with the latter.

41. *Sent. A.* 2, 50-53 in place of the patristic texts cited in *tsch* 19-20; 2, 58-60 added to the examples in *tsch* 22.

42. See above, n. 32.

Ostlender thought that the omission in the *Sent. A.* of a passage about *sapientia Dei* as *quedam potentia* indicated that the author wished to "tone down" a controversial aspect of Abelard's argument. The passage "omitted", however, is only an elaboration of the argument firmly put forward in the *Sententie* that power belonged properly to the Father, wisdom being described as *quedam potentia* in later discussion of the generation of the Word[43]. A quotation from a commentary of Haymo on Ephesians, not found in *tsch* or *TSch*, has been added at precisely the point in Abelard's argument in which, having been criticised by Walter of Mortagne, he sought to clarify his attribution of omnipotence to the Father[44]. Other passages which are different in *Sent. A.* from *tsch-TSch* provide a new formulation of Abelard's central and controversial argument about the different properties of the three persons of the Trinity[45]. Rather than being an abridgement of the corresponding part of *TSch*, the *Sent. A.* presents a thoughtful restatement of its main ideas.

The major difference between the manuscripts of the *Sententie* lies in the way in which Abelard's argument is justified through citation of auctoritates. In *S* there is only a brief justification of the preceding argument based on a few passages of scripture and not at all on philosophical testimony[46]. Is this an accidental omission by a copyist or does *S* represent a recension of the *Sententie* earlier than *C*, *P* and *AMN*? The "omission" in *S* occurs at exactly the point in *tsch* at which Abelard begins to reproduce auctoritates previously cited in the *Theologia Christiana*[47]. Is it an accident that the copyist of *S* should omit exactly that section of the *Sententie* which is given in two different forms in *CP* and *AMN*? One explanation for this is that *S* is a copy of an original recension, to which the "missing" section was added. While this is the only major difference between *S* and *CP*, there are small corrections in

43. OSTLENDER, *Die Sentenzenbücher*, 214; cf. *Sent. A.* 10, 74-77 (omitting *tsch* 89), but 15, 1-14 expounding the same doctrine is retained.

44. *Sent. A.* 5, 98-107; cf. *tsch T* 48; *tsch Z* 48-59 is revised at a number of places in *tsch T*, perhaps in reponse to the criticisms made by William of Mortagne of this very passage (as it stood in *Z*), *Epist. ad Abaelardum*, ed. OSTLENDER, *Florilegium Patristicum* 19, Bonn 1929, p. 34-6.

45. *Sent. A.* 6, 14-33; 6, 12-19.

46. *Sent. A.* 8, 1 - 4, 9; 9, 4 - 11, 162 is omitted in *S*.

47. *tsch* 74; from *tsch* 75, the text is based on *TChr* I, 7-70.

S and *C* which suggest that they derive from a common exemplar to which marginal corrections had been added over a course of time—not all of which were noticed by copyists[48].

Unlike *S*, *C* and *P* contain some of the arguments from scriptural and philosophical authority found in *TChr* and reproduced in the drafts of the first book of the *Theologia "Scholarium" (tsch Z and T)*. They include the same commentary on texts of Genesis as *tsch T*, but a summary only of its exegesis of the Psalms, Proverbs, Wisdom and Ecclesiasticus. *C* and *P* conclude with a passage not found in *S* or *AMN*, similar to part of *tsch*, with the unmistakeable ring of Abelard summarising his argument in the *Theologia*:

> De Spiritu quoque Sancto[1] aliquos non lateat quam manifeste et pro-
> phetas et alios[2] esse locutos. ... Cum et alia innumera scripturarum
> suppeditent testimonia, hec[3] ad presens sufficiant, et his indubitanter
> tam Verbum Dei quam Spiritum[4] eius Deum esse cum Patre liqueat.
> Nunc, post hec[5] prophetarum et aliorum testimonia, aliquantula[6] quo-
> que ad idem confirmandum inducamus exempla philosophorum[7], quos
> ad unius Dei intelligentiam ipsa tantum[8] philosophie ratio perduxit,
> quia iuxta Apostolum: "Invisibilia ... etc."[49].

> 1 quod s. *C*   2 per prophetas et per alios *P*   3 hoc *C*   4 spiritus *P*
> 5 *om. P*   6 aliqua *P*   7 *post* aliquantula *C*   8 tamen *CAN*

C and *P* then include a brief defence of pagan wisdom followed by a section of philosophical testimony about the Trinity, in part identical to *tsch Z* 114-115 (or *TChr* I, 61) and in part a summary of the main ideas of the first book of *TChr* (later included in *TSch*).

---

48. *Sent. A.* 6, 19 = *tsch* 52 (*benignitate*) in *S*, but not *CPAMN*; there are no major places where *S* is otherwise closer to *tsch* than *CPAMN*. The omissions in *S* (e.g. 13, 4-6; 14, 1-6; 17, 55: *et e converso S*) may be accidental. *Sent. A.* 18, 2-10 and 23, 34-37 present different readings of the text in *S*, but again perhaps a different interpretation due to a copyist. In 20, 180 *SCP* share an original reading *unicum et omnimodum omnibus solatium*, but *S* and *C* add *eventibus* as a correction. *AMN* give a longer version still: *unicum remedium et omnimodum in omnibus eventibus solatium*, as if *eventibus* was the first part of a marginal addition, not noticed by *P*. Similarly, in 8, 104-5 *C* adds as a correction a line omitted in *SP*, but found in *AMN*; in 21, 10 *S* adds a line (*hoc excepto ... recipiunt*) which seems to have been a marginal annotation in his exemplar, as it occurs in the correct place in 21, 45-47 in *AMNP*, but omitted here in *SC*. Buzzetti's critical apparatus is deficient in these last three examples.

49. *Sent. A.* 10, 205-9; 11-1-2 (divided between the critical apparatus and the text; the first sentence is omitted entirely and should be added to 10, 167, before *Intelligant* ...; there are five further errors of transcription in this extract alone).

AMN, on the other hand, do not cite the philosophical testimony given in *C* and *P*, but reproduce the complete text of the full version of the *Theologia "Scholarium"* (as distinct from the earlier drafts) about the testimony of the prophets and the much enlarged defence of pagan wisdom, based on patristic texts[50]. Just as *TSch* is more careful than *tsch* in its justification of recourse to pagan wisdom, so the recension *AMN* of the *Sententie* has a greater scriptural and patristic emphasis than *C* or *P*. Is the modification due to a copyist deciding to omit part of his original text, so as to include a longer extract from *TSch*? If he did so, he was reproducing a change of emphasis in the mind of Abelard himself. As already mentioned, there are other passages found only in *AMN* (sometimes consigned to the critical apparatus of Buzzetti's edition, other times left unnoticed within the main body of text, only occasionally in italics) which expand on ideas of Abelard in such a way as to follow the gist of his thought with great fidelity[51]. There is no evidence of any student introducing ideas of his own, different from those of his master. While one cannot exclude such initiative on the part of a scribe, the significance of such modification lies in the development and re-formulation of arguments by Abelard himself. One explanation for the fact that chapters 9-11 in *AMN* (omitted in *S*) has so much more literal quotation than the other chapters of *AMN*, or anywhere in *S* or *CP*, is that Abelard suggested a student turn to the relevant part of *TSch* as it contained some new ideas, not found in *tsch*.

While *P* generally contains the same text as *C*, it also includes a number of additional phrases or passages not found in any other manuscript of the *Sententie*, which are of considerable interest for our understanding of the ideas expressed in the text. These are unfortunately generally left unremarked in the critical apparatus

50. The text of *CP*: 11, 12-21, 24-33 (based on *tsch* 101-106) and 37-71 (based on *tsch* 114-15, *TChr* I, 72 and I, 126; this section is *not* found in *AMN*, not mentioned by Buzzetti). The text of *AMN* on the prophets: 10, 1-237 (based on *TSch* I, 75-93 (99D-1004D) or *tsch* 82-100); justification of pagan wisdom: 11, 1-36, 72-162 (based on *TSch* I, 94-108 (1004D-7C), not in *tsch*).

51. To the examples in n. 32 above, add the modifications in *Sent. A.* 12, 19-21; 20, 61-62: *sicut bonum est, id est utile est bonum esse, ita bonum est, id est utile, malum esse*; 21, 39-41: *AMN* adds *Augustinus tamen pro prescientia quandoque predestinationem ponere solet.*

of the new edition. Some of the additional phrases in *P* have the character of brief comments added into the reading of a text, such as *ut beatus Augustinus ait, omnes actiones agere*[52], *ut iam diximus*[53], *ut ait Boethius*[54], *ut ait Augustinus*[55], while others provide a little extra commentary on a passage found unchanged in the other manuscripts[56]. In four places *P* includes a sentence or phrase identical to the text of *tsch T*, even though all the other manuscripts shorten the corresponding text in *tsch*; one such passage in *P* is identical to *tsch T*, while *CAMN* corresponds exactly to *tsch Z*[57]. Most of the passages found only in *P* occur in the section of the *Sententie* which is not textually related to *tsch*. It may be significant that those phrases and sentences unique to *P* in the first part should reproduce parts of *tsch T* not found in *SCAMN*, as if the author decided to add more ex tempore remarks after departing from a fixed text.

One of the longer new passages in *P* introduces the discussion of philosophical analogies of the Trinity, unlike the previous section, not textually related to *tsch* or *TSch*. This discussion, which presents a fresh and independent formulation of the main arguments of the second book of *TSch*, is also found in the *Paris MS, Bibl. nat. lat. 18108*, ff. 76ᵛ-77ᵛ (*Pa*), alongside the *Sententie Parisienses*. Whereas in *SCAMNPa* this section begins with the statement *Illud igitur ad presens inquiri sufficiat qualiter unum et trinum Deum esse cognoverint* (a reference to the philosophers), it begins in *P* rather differently:

> Cum igitur et adhuc huiuscemodi multa contra infidelium impugnationes ad fidei nostre defensionem afferre possemus, illud amodo inquiri sufficiat qualiter Pater de se Filium gignat, qualiter quoque Spiritus Sanctus ab utroque procedat. Verum, ut dicta memorie melius inhereant et dicenda facilius appareant, quodammodo que dicta sunt ex parte sub brevitate

---

52. *Sent. A.* 5, 22.
53. *Ibid.* 14, 2 (replacing *ut iam superius assignavimus*).
54. *Ibid.* 14, 10 (omitted by Buzzetti; add after *enim*).
55. *Ibid.* 15, 64.
56. *Ibid.* 17, 22-23, 29-30; 18, 47; 19, 1; 20, 1-2; 20, 14; 24, 30-32; 24, 41; 26, 2; 26, 38; 26, 67-70, 74-75; 27, 14, 19, 63; 28, 89; 31, 74; 32, 13. None of the passages or phrases in *P* are distinguished from scribal errors in the apparatus of the new edition, while some are treated as an omission of *SCAMN*.
57. *Sent. A. P* 8, 65 (*tsch ZT* 67); *P* 9, 4-9 (*tsch T* 74); *P* 9, 12-13 (*tsch T* 75; *CAMN* like *tsch Z* 75); *P* 9, 34-36 (*tsch T* 77).

repetamus. Hoc ergo prius diligentius inquiramus qualiter unum Deum et trinum esse cognoverint [58].

The first sentence of the new introduction in *P* contains a reference to many other arguments which could be raised in defence of Christian belief against hostile criticism—such as were given in more detail in the *Theologia "Scholarium"*. In the second sentence a slight inconsistency in *SCAMN* is rectified: having already explained in the previous section how the philosophers understood the trinitarian nature of God, the author intended to follow arguments from authority with arguments culled from philosophical analogies, so that a certain repetition was inevitable. The repeated reference to *dicta* needing to be absorbed into the memory parallels the frequent mention *ut diximus* added elsewhere in *P*. The impression given is that these passages in *P* record the spoken comments of Abelard, perhaps introduced in a fresh reading of a prepared text, or incorporated into the margin of an existing text of the *Sententie* as additions and corrections.

There are a number of ideas in *Sententie*, not found in exactly the same form in the *Theologia "Scholarium"*, which illuminate the argument of the latter work. Ostlender's claim that because the examples of *aurum* and *anulus* are used in the *Sententie*, the author was tempering a controversial image of Abelard misses the significance of the analogy, used here to describe how something could be one in number while two in property. The image of the Trinity as a bronze seal is introduced in the *Sententie*, but placed at an earlier stage in the argument than in *TSch* [59]. The discussion of the generation of the Word from the Father is combined with that of the procession of the Holy Spirit, rather than made separately. In every version of the *Theologia* Abelard gave a fresh account of the relationship between the Son and the Father. That given in the *Sententie* may not be as detailed as that in *TSch*, but it provides a succinct introduction to the major themes of his argument.

A small story, not found in *TSch*, which explains how the schism

58. *Sent. A.* 12, 1-2 (*Verum ... appareant* omitted by Buzzetti).
59. OSTLENDER, *Die Sentenzenbücher*, 213; *Sent. A.* 12,3-9. See the discussion of difference *TSch* II, 95-102 (1065A-67C), a simplified version of *TChr* III, 119-35. The image of the seal is given in *Sent. A.* 12, 34-41 and 17, 60-75; cf. *TSch* II, 112-117 (1068D-1070C) on the seal analogy.

arose between the Eastern and Western Churches about the procession of the Holy Spirit, gives concrete illustration of a point made
in more learned terms in the *Theologia* : the division between East
and West arose when Pope Paschasius became afraid of the cunning
of some Greek theologians who came to Rome; he subsequently
refused to give them an audience. The schism arose from the refusal
of one party to talk to another, not because of any basic contradiction between their doctrines[60]. The anecdote introduces a summary
of Abelard's teaching that the Holy Spirit proceeded to creation
from the wisdom and power of God, in which the patristic arguments of *TSch* are only referred to, rather than quoted in full[61].

There then follows a discussion, again absent from *TSch*, of
how names were applied to God's essence (*substantialiter*) and
to the properties of individual persons (*relative*)[62]. Ostlender thought
that because in an earlier passage some names were referred to as
naturalia rather than *substantialia*, the author of the *Sententie* was
copying blindly from a literary source, but had failed to make his
argument consistent[63]. This source, he argued, must have been
the same as that used by the author of the *Sententie Florianenses*
(who mentions *nomina secundum substantiam*), Omnebene (who
refers to *nomina essentie*) and Roland (who uses *nomina substantialia*)[64]. According to Ostlender, Hermann changed *substantialia*
to *naturalia* the first time he came across the word, but left it
unchanged when he came across the term again. While there may
be some inconsistency in the vocabulary of the *Sententie*, not such
a carefully composed work as the *Theologia "Scholarium"*, there
is no suggestion of any lack of intellectual cohesion. The phrases
about divine names in the different sentence collections are too
diverse to offer clear proof that they all depend on a common literary
source, a claim for which Ostlender could adduce no supporting
evidence beyond some vague similarities of argument. The distinction between names applied to God as a whole and names applied
to individual persons provides a new way, perhaps formulated in

60. *Sent. A*. 16, 14-29.
61. *Ibid*. 17, 1-31; cf. *TSch* II, 157-65 (1077A-80B).
62. *Sent. A*. 17, 42-18, 13.
63. Ostlender, *Die Sentenzenbücher*, 230-1, referring to 14, 1-10.
64. *Sent. Florian.*, p. 6; *Sent. Rolandi*, p. 43.

spoken teaching, of clarifying the basic argument of every version of the *Theologia* about the inexactitude of identifying the Father with the Son. Like the bronze and the seal in a bronze seal, they were the same in essence, but could not properly be identified with each other[65].

The arguments of the *Sententie* differ most from those of *TSch* when they concern the power, wisdom and goodness of God, although, as in the preceding section, the underlying theme is not different. Discussion of what God "could" and "could not" do occurs within an introductory section, rather than within analysis of God's power, as in *TChr* and *TSch*[66]. One opinion put forward in the *Sententie*, not mentioned in *TSch*, but for which Abelard would be criticised, is that Christ's descent into hell refers to the efficacy of the suffering which Christ endured in his soul and not to any physical descent[67]. The passages from Cicero, Augustine and Plato, quoted at length in *TChr* and *TSch* are referred to indirectly, or quoted loosely, as if from memory[68]. There is a slightly fuller account of how God could allow evil to exist in the world. Abelard's conclusion about the ultimately rational basis of suffering and evil is placed at the end of the section on God's power rather than in that on his goodness, as in *TSch*[69]. The text of this part of the *Sententie* is basically the same in the different manuscripts, although some further clarification is present in *AMN*. Some of these additional phrases could have been marginalia in an original exemplar of *S*, *C* and *P*, not always noticed by a scribe in copying out a text[70]. Certain variants, such as the use of *Petrus* or *Hermannus* in place of *iste* in the example of "X is reading today", identical to "X will be reading tomorrow" said the day previously, may be the result of the invention of a scribe, or could equally well be due to Abelard imagining a new example in order to give life to his lecture[71]. The difference in points of detail between this part

65. *Sent. A.* 17, 52-59.
66. *Ibid.* 19, 1-96; cf. *TChr* V, 18-28, *TSch* III, 18-26 (1091C-93D).
67. *Sent. A.* 19, 93-96; cf. *Expositio Symboli* (*PL* 178, 626D).
68. *Sent. A.* 20, 6-23; cf. *TChr* V, 6-8, *TSch* III, 6-8 (1087B-8C).
69. *Sent. A.* 20, 144-90; cf. *TSch* III, 117-18 (ed. COUSIN, *P. Abaelardi Opera* 2, p. 148-9).
70. See above, n. 48.
71. See above, n. 30; similar arguments occur in glosses on Aristotle, *Logica "Ingredientibus"*, ed. GEYER, p. 350-1 and *TSch* III, 61 (1103AB).

of the *Sententie* and the corresponding section of *TSch* is not proof that the former work does not reflect Abelard's thought, but rather serves to highlight a desire to present his teaching in a fresh and comprehensible way.

The incarnation

Whereas *TSch* deals only with faith in God, the *Sententie* also discuss faith in Christ, the sacraments and charity. The section corresponding to the argument of *TSch*, occupying over half the length of the *Sententie*, provides the bedrock for the subsequent discussion of these other subjects. Although not as detailed as the commentary on Romans or the *Ethica*, this part of the *Sententie* illuminates the ideas about sacrament and charity outlined at the beginning of *TSch* as well as Abelard's thinking on a number of specific questions not covered in the two other works.

There are parallels with the interpretation of Christ's redemption in the commentary on Romans, but Abelard's theme is put more bluntly in the *Sententie*, with the first person used in the singular rather than the plural:

> Ego vero econtra dico et ratione irrefragibili probo quod diabolus in hominem nullum ius habuit. Neque enim quia eum {fraude maligna *add. C*} decipiendo a subiectione Domini sui alienavit, aliquam potestatem super eum debuit accipere, potius si quam prius haberet, debuit amittere[72].

Some of the arguments then brought forward are slightly different from those of the commentary[73]. The message is the same, that Christ did not become incarnate to free man from any legitimate yoke to the devil, but to fill man with the love of God.

The discussion of the two natures of Christ in the *Sententie* elaborates an idea mentioned in less detail in *TSch* that, just as "body" and "soul" were not separate entities within one person, so Christ's humanity and divinity were not separate things within Christ[74]. The difference between God's Word being present in the

---

72. *Sent. A.* 23, 21-25; cf. *Comm. Rom.*, p. 115.
73. *Sent. A.* 23, 25-36; cf. *Comm. Rom.*, p. 114-15.
74. *Sent. A.* 24, 1-27; cf. *TSch* III, 77-81 (1107C-9A).

blessed Virgin or in the saints and in Christ was that while the Holy Spirit might dwell in the former for a while and then depart, everything that Christ did emanated from his soul and thus from the Word of God. Statements that "Christ was man" and "Christ was God" were both linguistically imperfect expressions of the more correct statement, "Christ was God and man"[75].

Considerable attention is paid to Christ's experience of human anxieties and pain[76]. As in the preceding section, the discussion of the will of Christ is framed around analysis of the patristic arguments quoted at much greater length in the *Sic et Non*, the opinions of Hilary, who emphasised the purely transitory nature of Christ's suffering being singled out for particular criticism[77]. The argument put forward, that his suffering was never willed for in itself, but endured for the love of God, is similar to that made in the *Ethica* about hardship in general. The fact that a series of questions about Christ is interrupted with an important digression on the divine will in exactly the same sequence as the order of questions in the shorter recension of the *Sic et Non* (*TCEB*) suggests that Abelard may have being using his collection of patristic *sententie* as the basis for his own lectures[78].

There are a number of additional sentences in the text of *P*, not found in any other manuscript of the *Sententie* which refine points of detail. One such passage touches on the immaculate conception :

> In beata namque Virgine, ut beatus ait Augustinus, sic fuit quod ab omni peccato eam mundavit, nec ullum postmodum contagium eam inquinavit, utpote quam totam replevit et repletam inhabitavit. In multis quoque aliis per inhabitationem dicitur inesse, ut eorum spiritus cum Spiritu Dei, iuxta Apostolum, < unus > efficiatur[79].

75. *Sent. A.* 24, 70-90, referring to texts used in the *Sic et Non* (*SN*) 66. 1-3, 10, ed. B. BOYER - R. McKEON, Chicago-London 1976-77.

76. *Sent. A.* 25, 1-73.

77. *Ibid.* 25, 9-34, commenting on *SN* 80. 1-34, contrasted with *SN* 80. 50. Abelard dwells on the reality of Christ's suffering in his sermon 11 on Good Friday (468A-9C). See too *Ethica*, p. 8-10.

78. *Sent. A.* 26, 1-75; cf. *SN* 35-36, which occur in *TCEB* after *SN* 71 on the divinity of the Son. Similar ideas on the divine will occur in *TChr* II, 26-28, *TSch* II, 24-26 (1093B-D) and *Comm. Rom.* p. 207.

79. *Sent. A.* 24, 30-32; *SCAMN* read : In beata namque Virgine sic fuit Spiritus Sanctus quod totam eam replevit et in multis aliis ... Similar arguments occur in sermon 2 (390BC).

Another comment added in *P* to a discussion of how God could have allowed Judas to betray Christ brings in an idea also made in the commentary on Romans—that more use came from the disobedience of Judas than from the obedience of Peter :

> Petrus obedivit, Iudas non, quia non voluit {quia non disposuit Deus *P*} ut obediret; et sicut rationabilis causa fuit quare voluit ut obediret Petrus et salvaretur, sic rationabilis causa fuit quare noluit ut Iudas obediret et damnaretur {et plus, dicam, utilitatis secutum est ex inobedientia Iude quam ex Petri obedientia *add. P*}[80].

A statement left unchanged in *SCAMN* about the irrationality of any creature, even Christ, being equal to God in knowledge—quod irrationabile esse videtur—is replaced in *P* with a justification of this argument :

> Dicunt tamen quod non erat equalis, quia Verbum per se illam habebat, anima vero illa< m > non a se, sed a Verbo. Sed similiter posset dici Filium non esse equalem Patri, quia non habet a se esse. Simiter possum dicere istos non esse equales in possessione una quorum unus dono, alter vero eam pretio possidet; vel non esse equales in scientia una, quorum alter ab altero eam didicit. Quod quam sepe contingat in promptu habetur[81].

These and other passages found only in *P* convey with particular immediacy comments on specific issues, apparently by Abelard himself. If they were composed by a disciple, then he had absorbed his master's thought and phraseology to a remarkable degree.

The sacraments

Abelard seems to have written no specific treatise on the sacraments, but sufficient of his ideas are known through his sermons for an assessment to be made of this part of the *Sententie*[82]. The

---

80. *Sent. A.* 26, 67-70; cf. *Comm. Rom.*, p. 239 : *Multo profecto utilius est operatus in nequitia Iude quam in iustitia Petri.* On Abelard's sympathy for social outcasts, *Sent. A.* 26, 45-49, *Problemata Heloissae* 9 (691CD) and *Ethica*, p. 28-30.

81. *Sent. A.* 27, 19; cf. *SN* 81. 5; 83. 14; 44. 4.

82. *Sent. A.* 28, 1 - 31, 95. For an excellent summary of Abelard's thinking, see R. E. WEINGART, *Peter Abailard's Contribution to Medieval Sacramentology*, in *RTAM* 34 (1967) 159-78.

treatment of baptism is very similar to that given in Abelard's sermon, or rather small tract on Christ's circumcision, as well as in the commentary on Romans. Baptism, did not confer salvation in itself, but was rather the Christian form of circumcision, which had the advantage of applying to both men and women, Jews and Gentiles. The merit of water was that not only was it used for washing, but it was also available to both rich and poor[83]. The eucharist also performed a social function, binding together Christians into the body of Christ, the Church, without being a guarantee of salvation in itself[84]. Its inner purpose, to nurture man in the love of God through being a memorial of Christ's passion, was ultimately more important than its external form, as its efficacy lay in the devotion with which it was received[85]. The discussion of other sacraments, notably confirmation, unction and marriage is more perfunctory, but consistent with Abelard's comments in other writings[86].

Charity

The introduction to the section on charity in the *Sententie* is strikingly similar to the passage which Abelard incorporated into the full text of *TSch*, but not found in *tsch T*[87]:

{*Sent. A*} Caritas, ut supra diximus, est amor honestus, id est amor qui ad eum finem ad quem referri debet retorquetur. Est autem amor bona voluntas erga aliquem propter ipsum. Si enim diligam aliquem propter aliquam utilitatem, non est amor ad ipsum, sed ad meam utilitatem. Unde si optem etiam vitam eter-	{*TSch*} Caritas vero est amor honestus, qui ad eum finem dirigitur ad quem oportet, sicut e contrario cupiditas amor inhonestus ac turpis appellatur. Amor vero est bona erga alterum propter ipsum voluntas. ... ... Sepe namque contingit ut, aliquem odientes et ab eo quoque modo nos liberare volentes, opte-

83. *Sent. A.* 28, 14-47; cf. *Comm. Rom.*, p. 93 and sermon 3 (403A-4A). The text of *SN* 101. 2 on the desire to receive baptism is discussed in *Sent. A.* 28, 70-91.
84. *Sent. A.* 29, 19-49.
85. *Sent. A.* 29, 6-14, 159-66; cf. *Probl. Hel.* 6 (686B).
86. *Sent. A.* 31, 1-95; cf. *TChr* II, 87-105 and *Probl. Hel.* 14 (701B-D), *Historia Calamitatum*, ed. J. MONFRIN, Paris 1959, p. 75-8 and *Epist.* V, ed. J.T. MUCKLE, *The Personal Letters between Abelard and Heloise*, in *Mediaeval Studies* 15 (1953) 88-93.
87. *Sent. A.* 31, 99-106; *TSch* I, 3 (981D-2C); cf. *tsch T* 13-15.

nam alicui non propter se, sed quia ab eo liberarer, iam vellem ut in paradiso esset, non eum diligo, sed aliquod de morte sua commodum mihi desidero.

mus eum ad celestia iam transferri et superna illa gloria frui, quo melius ei contingere nihil potest. Nec id tamen eius amore gerimus quia pro nobis id potius quam pro ipso agimus, nec tamen illius utilitatem quam nostram in hoc intendentes.

One small difference is that the first person singular is used more frequently in the *Sententie*, while the first person plural occurs more consistently in the corresponding passage in *TSch*. Given that the first part of the *Sententie* in *GCP*, which has no connection with the complete text of *TSch* and seems rather to be based on a draft transitional between *tsch Z* and *T*, the possibility should be considered that Abelard used this part of the *Sententie*—or similar lecture notes—as the basis for the additional passage added in *TSch*. The final text of the *Theologia "Scholarium"* would thus be dependent on the *Sententie* rather than the other way round.

The central argument of this part of the *Sententie* is that charity is the love of one's neighbour for God, not for oneself, and that it was defined by intention rather than outward form. Virtue, as taught by Aristotle, was a habit of mind[88]. A similar classification of the virtues into justice, fortitude and temperance, all of which were rooted in charity, occurs as in the second book of *TChr* and the *Dialogue* between a philosopher and a Christian[89]. While there is a similar distinction to that made in the *Ethica* between those vices which existed in the inclination of human nature and those which could properly be called sins, the definition of the difference between vice and sin is less precise than in the *Ethica*[90]. As Blomme noted in his penetrating study of the evolution of Abelard's thought on sin, the definition of sin in the latter work as consent to a *mala voluntas* —also found in the *liber sententiarum magistri Petri*—masks a distinctly later stage in his thought than the definition of sin as *mala voluntas*, found in the *Sententie*, the commentary on *Romans* and *TSch*[91].

88. *Sent. A*. 32, 80-88; cf. *Ethica*, p. 128.
89. *Sent. A*. 32, 106-34; cf. *TChr* II, 64; *Dialogus inter philosophum, Iudaeum et Christianum*, ed. R. THOMAS (Stuttgart-Bad Canstatt 1970), ll. 2065-2291 : *SN* 137: 2, 138. 23.
90. *Sent. A*. 33, 26-40; cf. *Ethica*, p. 2-4, 12-14 etc.
91. *Comm. Rom.*, p. 279; *TSch* III, 107 (ed. COUSIN, p. 145); cf. BLOMME, *op. cit.* (see above, n. 17).

The role of grace is not denied in the *Sententie*, as has been claimed, but the emphasis is that grace can do nothing if man does not respond. The same analogy of a sick man having to accept medicine from his doctor occurs as in the commentary on *Romans*[92]. Without the detail of the latter work, the theme is the same; unless loving and cleaving to God came from man's will, grace would render merit useless[93]. There then follows a reference to a previous discussion of the passage in *Romans* about God's love for Jacob and his enmity for Esau :

> quod quidem quia in epistola ad Romanos super eum locum : "Iacob dilexi etc.", diligenter expressi, hoc quasi notum pretereundem existimo[94].

Ostlender argued that Abelard's commentary on that verse (*Romans* 9, 13) was too brief to be that referred to in the *Sententie*, but the reference fits perfectly clearly if it is to this section of the commentary rather than to a single verse[95]. At the same time it could be a reference to oral exegesis of the Epistle, such as recorded in the *Commentarius Cantabrigiensis*, a text which contains a number of arguments in common with the *Sententie*[96]. There seems no reason to postulate that the commentary of some disciple is being referred to, rather than the teaching of Abelard himself.

The last part of the *Sententie* deals with the forgiveness of sins, confession, satisfaction and the power of a priest to give absolution, in the same sequence as in the *Ethica*[97]. The analysis of confession is more organised than in one of Abelard's sermons, but not quite as developed as in the later treatise[98]. His central argument is un-

---

92. *Sent. A.* 34, 65-71; *Comm. Rom.*, p. 240.

93. *Sent. A.* 34, 71-74. LUSCOMBE in *The School*, p. 162-3 argues that the author of the *Sent.* (Hermann) restricts the role of grace more than Abelard does in the commentary on Romans; although human initiative is emphasised, grace is not denied.

94. *Sent. A.* 34, 74-77.

95. OSTLENDER, *Die Sentenzenbücher*, 214-15; cf. *Comm. Rom.*, p. 232-42, correctly commented on by BUZZETTI, p. 5. The division of scripture into verses was, of course, unknown to Abelard.

96. *Comm. Cantab.*, ed. LANDGRAF 1, 119-35. As in the written commentary, Abelard's exposition of the words *Jacob dilexi* is brief, but the discussion of God's love for Jacob is of great importance in the commentary on Romans as a whole.

97. *Sent. A.* 35, 1-38, 50; cf. *Ethica*, p. 76-126.

98. *Sent. A.* 36, 1-54; cf. Sermon 8 (439B-44D) and *Ethica*, p. 76-88.

changed—that the purpose of confession was to develop humility and devotion, and that if a priest was not available, the sacrament itself was not necessary if there was true remorse[99]. The priest's power lay not in conferring salvation or damnation, but in opening the door of the Church to sinners. His role was to symbolise the social aspect of the sacrament rather than to administer control over the gates of heaven[100].

As has become clear from the preceding discussion, there can be little doubt that the *Sententie* not only reports quite accurately the teachings of Peter Abelard, but as a work is not dependent on any single one of his writings. There is no evidence for Ostlender's hypothesis that the text was composed by a pupil of Abelard, both developing and reacting against ideas of his teacher. The work provides a coherent account of Abelard's doctrine on all those aspects essential to salvation, as outlined at the beginning of the *Theologia "Scholarium"*. In terms of intellectual content, the *Sententie* deserves to be read alongside—or before *TSch*, the commentary on *Romans* and the *Ethica*—as a valuable introduction to Abelard's teaching as a whole. At the same time, the work does not fall into quite the same categories as these other writings. While based in part on a written text, or notes, there also seems to be an element of ex tempore commentary in the *Sententie*, and a desire to avoid excessive citation of patristic texts. The differences between the manuscripts, S, C, P and *AMN* may be due, not to the imagination of copyists, but to different "readings" by Abelard of the same body of text or to comments delivered at different occasions and scribbled into the margin of an existing text by eager students. Strands of oral and literary transmission are both woven inextricably into the text which now survives as the *Sententie Abaelardi*.

The Sent. Florianenses and the Sent. Parisienses

Besides the different recensions of the *Sententie* already discussed, there survive two anonymous accounts of Abelard's teaching about

99. *Sent. A*. 36, 9-13; texts quoted in *SN* 151. 4, 7 are then discussed; cf. *Ethica*, p. 100-4.
100. *Sent. A*. 38, 45-50; cf. *Ethica*, p. 112-26.

faith, the sacraments and charity (again not mentioned in Buzzetti's edition) which are less well written, but nonetheless important : the *Sententie Florianenses* (*St Florian, XI. 264*, ff. 147-163ᵛ; s. XII) and the *Sententie Parisienses* (*Paris, Bibl. nat. lat. 18108*, ff. 70-75ᵛ; s. XII)[101]. As already mentioned, Denifle thought that the *Sent. Florianenses* was based on a lost *cursus theologiae* of Abelard, of which *TSch* was the beginning, while Ostlender thought both works were dependent on the lost *liber sententiarum*, quoted by his critics in 1140. Ostlender's theory was criticised by a number of scholars, all of whom thought that the *Sent. Florianenses* was an oral report of Abelard's teaching, but no-one formulated this view in any detail apart from Landgraf, with reference to the *Sent. Parisienses*[102]. He commented that the imperfections of expression, the jerky style and the frequent use of direct address in that work could only be explained if it was a *reportatio*[103]. Ostlender doubted Landgraf's argument, suggesting that the absence of certain definitions in the *Sententie Parisienses* indicated that it was not composed by Abelard, but by another master[104]. As with his arguments about the *Sententie Abaelardi*, such selective comments depend on a very narrow interpretation of Abelard's theology and fail to come to grips with the underlying identity of conception between his written works and the various collections of sententie. Each of these collections provides a similar but clearly independent report of his teaching.

The doctrine of the Trinity is expounded quite briefly in both the *Sent. Florianenses* and the *Sent. Parisienses*. Patristic and pagan writers are barely cited at all beyond occasional vague reference to Augustine, Hilary, Plato or *philosophi* in general. As in the recension *S* of the *Sententie*, there is no section about the testimony of the prophets and the philosophers. There is more discussion in the *Sententie Parisienses* about the distance of God from any human category than about the relationship between the three persons in

---

101. See above, n. 2.

102. See above, n. 16; cf. *Sent. Florian.* 4, p. 2 : *Modo de fide plenius, postea de caritate, deinde <de sacramento? > dicit*, a sentence which seems to be a clear reference to oral teaching.

103. LANDGRAF, *Écrits théologiques*, p. xxxiv-viii.

104. OSTLENDER, *Die Sentenzenbücher*, 220-1.

God. Many of its ideas and references to scripture and other writers occur in the second book of *TSch*, but not in the *Sententie Abaelardi*[105]. Some ideas are expressed more bluntly than in the other collections, such as that philosophers might say that they did not believe in the Father, Son or Holy Spirit, but this was because they did not use those terms or *voces*, although they knew God through natural reason[106]. The *Sent. Florianenses* gives a little more attention than the *Sent. Parisienses* to the relationship between the persons of the Trinity, compared to a bronze seal, as in the *Sententie A.* and *TSch*, although the explanation is less elaborate, only the term *sigillum* being used, rather than *sigillabile*[107]. The Son is described as *ex portione Patris*, an expression used in *tsch FH* and *Z*, but removed in *tsch T* and *TSch* after it had been criticised by Walter of Mortagne[108].

Similar ideas about divine grace are found in the *Sent. Florianenses* as occur in the other collections, although sometimes at a different place in the overall argument. The analogy of grace as medicine given to a sick man is contrasted with one Abelard found more appropriate, of grace as a precious object offered to the industrious and the lazy alike. The same contrast occurs in Abelard's commentary on Romans, the *Sent. Parisienses*, the *Commentarius Cantabrigiensis* and the *liber sententiarum*, although in each text details are slightly different[109].

Within the section on God's power in the *Sent. Parisienses* there occurs a passage without parallel in any other work, but which bears the imprint of Abelard's argument:

> Item opponitur. Nullum temporale est causa eterni. Solutio. Temporale non dicitur nisi res. Eventus non est res. Oppositio. Fuit, quando non fuit eventus.
> Male dixisti, quia eventus perpetui sunt; qui Petrum modo sedere, hoc verum fuit a principio mundi, et verum etiam post diem iudicii me

---

105. *Sent. Paris.*, p. 5-7; cf. *TSch* II, 68-91 (1057A-64A), especially II, 76-77, 70, 80 (1060A, 1058B, 1061AB).

106. *Sent. Paris.*, p. 10-11.

107. *Sent. Florian.* 16, p. 7.

108. *Ibid.* 15, p. 6. The text of *tsch Z* 58 was criticised by Walter of Mortagne, *Epist. ad Abaelardum*, ed. OSTLENDER, removed in *tsch T* 58.

109. *Sent. Florian.* 27, p. 13; cf. *Comm. Rom.*, p. 241; *Sent. A.* 34, 64-71; *Sent. Paris.*, p. 60, *Comm. Cant.* 1, 98.

sedisse hic. Adhuc opponit ... Opponitur. Si Deus fecisset Petrum melio-
rem et illud ratio esset. Responsio. Similiter posses dicere : si Deus lapis
esset, et illud ratio esset[110].

The extract seems to record Abelard's spoken comments, and perhaps
the interjections of a student as well. One can observe the close
interplay between Abelard's linguistic and theological teaching in
the conversation, which makes allusion to the example given a
little more formally in the *Sententie "Petrus (Hermannus) legit hodie"*
etc. Abelard seems to have used a basic stock of arguments, but
frequently changed details or its format depending on the situation.
Another example of how he could use a familiar argument for a
new purpose occurs immediately after discussion of the two natures
in Christ :

> Opponetur. Ergo quedam persona est in quadam persona? Solutio. Per-
> sona alio modo accipitur in grammatica, alio in rhetorica, alio in theo-
> logia ... Quando tu dicis : illa persona que est Verbum, hic accipitur
> diverso modo[111].

Abelard had often used this argument about the multiple meanings
of persona in the context of the Trinity, but not in discussing the
person of Christ. Because this question and answer interrupts a
flow of argument, it is possible that it was a response to an un-
expected interjection.

There is less of immediate interest in the section of the *Sent.
Parisienses* about the sacraments, which do not appear to have
prompted the same critical debate as Abelard's exposition of the
Trinity and the incarnation. The text of this section is generally
identical to the corresponding part of the *Sententie A.*, but small
differences between the two works make it impossible for one to
have been copied from the other[112]. Their respective treatments
of marriage are virtually identical, although their positioning of this
section is slightly different[113]. The discussion of charity in the
Parisienses (unfortunately missing from the manuscript of the *Sent.*

---

110. *Sent. Paris*, p. 22.
111. *Ibid.*, p. 30.
112. LANDGRAF, *Écrits théologiques*, p. xxxiii, xxxviii-ix.
113. *Sent. Paris.*, p. 44-48; cf. *Sent. A.* 30, 1-54.

Florianenses) is similarly related to that of the *Sententie A.*, though less detailed [114].

The nature of the Sententie

The interplay between the colloquial and the more ordered parts of the *Sententie Parisienses* throws light on the nature of the *Sententie* as a whole. The hypothesis of a common literary source—like the *liber sententiarum*—must be discarded, the common source being the teaching or lectures of Abelard himself. The student who compiled the *Sententie Parisienses* transcribed what he could of those lectures, based in part on a prepared text, but delivered with some freedom of expression. He may not have been present for the entire course—redemption is passed over very briefly with a reference to comment elsewhere on Romans, while the section on the relationship between the three persons of the Trinity is also very deficient [115]. For this reason that same student copied the section of the *Sententie* (*Pa* : chapters 12-18 of the printed text) into the following two leaves of his workbook.

What then is the status of the *Sententie Abaelardi*, as found in that fragment and in *S, C, P* and *AMN*? One solution which springs to mind is that its text is a verbatim report of his teaching, while another is that it is the text which Abelard used as the basis for his lectures—lecture notes in other words, copied by students at different times for their own use. The first part of the *Sententie A.* betrays many features of a written text, such as a number of patristic and scriptural quotations, and corresponds textually to a draft transitional between *tsch Z* and *T*. All manuscripts of the *Sententie* repeat an error found in *tsch Z* and *T*, copied into *TSch*—the erroneous interruption of an extract from Gregory the Great with other passages from Gregory and Augustine [116]. The error would easily be

114. *Sent. Paris.*, p. 48-60. This section is studied in detail by Ph. DELHAYE, *L'enseignement moral des Sententiae Parisienses*, in *Mélanges E.R. Labande*, Poitiers 1974, p. 197-207.

115. *Sent. Paris.*, p. 29 : *De qua satis in lectione dictum, ibi Ut quid etc.* (*Romans* 5, 6); on the Trinity, *ibid.*, p. 10.

116. *Sent. A.* 2, 30-39 interrupts the quotation of Gregory, 2, 26-42 as in *tsch ZT* 19, *TSch* I, 12 (985AB), correct only in *tsch FH* 19. On *tsch FH* and this passage, see MEWS, *Abelard's TChr*, 138-47.

made by Abelard himself if the additional passages had been added into the margin of his text. The correct sequence appears only in the earliest known draft of the *Theologia "Scholarium"—tsch FH*. Although there is not quite as much citation of patristic texts as in *tsch*, this introductory section of the *Sententie* (equivalent to the argument of book I of *TSch*) is still more detailed than what follows, the text of which is not related directly to *TSch*.

A good description of the way such *Sententie* were compiled is given by Laurence, a student of Hugh of St Victor, who describes how he was asked by other students to take down Hugh's *sententie* and would bring his text to Hugh every week for correction. Hugh then used these *sententie* in writing his major treatise, the *De sacramentis* :

> Qui cum sentencias de divinitate dicere incepisset, rogatus sum a plerisque sociorum, qui quidem officium, quod michi imponebant, multo facilius ipsi perficerent, si non aliis fortasse impedirentur negociis, rogatus, inquam, sum, quatenus ad communem tam mei quam aliorum utilitatem easdem sentencias scripto et memorie commendarem. ... Qui {Hugo} et hoc onus scribendi nobis iniunxit et fiduciam perficiendi magna quadam alacritate promisit. ... Et ne quis vel iuste reprehendencium vel invide mordencium calumpnie pateret introitus, semel in septimana ad magistrum Hugonem tabellas reportabam ut eius arbitrio, si quid superfluum esset, resecaretur, si quid pretermissum, suppleretur, si quid vitiose positum, mutaretur, si quid vero quandoque forte fortuitu bene dictum, tanti viri auctoritate comprobaretur. ... Non enim me huius operis auctorem, sed quodammodo artificem profiteor[117].

The passage is worth quoting at length for the detail which it provides about how a master could authorise a student to take down his *sententie* and supervise his work. Abelard very likely had such an amanuensis responsible for the redaction of the *Sententie*. The differences between *S, C, P* and *AMN* can be accounted for if passages were added to an original text over a course of time, students making personal copies from this text at different occasions. Comparison with the structure of the *Sent. Florianenses* and *Sent. Parisienses*, in which there is no section corresponding to "testimony of the prophets and philosophers", confirms the hypothesis that

117. B. BISCHOFF, *Aus der Schule Hugos von St Viktor*, in *Aus der Geisteswelt des Mittelalters*, BGPTMA Supplementband 3, 1 (1935) 246-50, reprinted in *Mittelalterlichen Studien*, Stuttgart 1967, 2, 182-7.

S represents the original form of the *Sententie*. Little is changed in *C* except for the addition of a passage about these testimonies— that on the prophets an abbreviation of part of *tsch*, that on the philosophers a re-formulation of ideas in tsch, in all likelihood by Abelard himself. The text of *P* was based on a text like *C*, to which further annotations had been made—perhaps corrections by Abelard in the same way as those made by Hugh to Laurence's copy, or maybe taken down in re-delivery of the same *sententie*. The original exemplar of *AMN* seems to have been a revised version of *C*, in which a new section of testimonies had been added, based on *TSch*, replacing the equivalent section in *C*. Given that other additions in *AMN* are so close to Abelard's thought, one can only assume that this long section was also added under his inspiration.

The difference between the *Sententie Abaelardi* on the one hand, and the *Sententie Florianenses* and *Parisienses* on the other is that while the former represents a more "official" version, the other two texts report his teaching on two other occasions, either delivered more freely or taken down less accurately—probably indeed a combination of the two. The student who took down the *Sententie Parisienses* had recourse to the more authoritative text to cover the argument which he had not taken down.

The earliest of these reports is the *Sententie Florianenses*, which contains some expressions, such as *ex portione Patris*, not used after *tsch Z*. Because it contains the analogy of the Trinity as a bronze seal, not found in *TSum* or *TChr* (including *TChr CT*), it would probably date to a period in the early 1130's, before the drafting of the *Theologia "Scholarium"* had reached an advanced stage—such as when Walter of Mortagne wrote his letter to Abelard[118]. The redaction of the earliest recension of the *Sententie* (*S*) would have taken place after *tsch* had reached the stage recorded in *Z*, and perhaps after Walter had made his comments, but before *tsch T*. The *Sententie* thus record Abelard's thinking about the Trinity after *TChr CT*, but before the completion of the *Theologia "Scholarium"*. The recension found in *C* (and with some modifications in *P*) incorporates some of the prophetic and philosophical testimony found in the *Theologia Christiana* and *tsch ZT*, but nothing

118. See above, n. 108.

which is only found in the *Theologia "Scholarium"*, so *C* could have been produced before the latter's completion. The fact that the beginning of the *Sententie* is textually so close to the draft *tsch ZT*, while there is no direct correspondence with the second and third books of *TSch* is explained if these two books had not yet been written. Abelard had already drafted their content by making extensive annotations to his working copy of the *Theologia Christiana* (*CT*), but may have developed the ideas unique to *TSch* only after he had prepared its subject matter within his teaching.

In all manuscripts of the *Sententie* (excluding *S* and *P*, unfortunately deficient at this point) Abelard refers to earlier commentary on Romans 9, 13 (*Jacob dilexi* etc.). Does this mean that he had already written his famous commentary, or is he talking about earlier lectures? Buytaert thought that the commentary on *Romans* had to have been written between the second and third books of *TSch* because in that commentary Abelard promises to deal with certain subjects—which are covered in *TSch* III—while refers to others as already dealt with in the *Theologia* which are covered in its first and second books[119]. If these passages are scrutinised in detail, it emerges that all the references to existing discussion could refer to *TChr* or *tsch*. The one reference which Buytaert took as applying to *TSch* II, about philosophical analogies of the Trinity, occurs after a discussion which does not include mention of the analogy of the seal, developed in full only in the second book of *TSch* and not before[120]. Although he says that he has discussed philosophical analogies in its second book, he may have been referring only to its draft form in *TChr CT*—to which the comments

119. BUYTAERT, CCCM 11, p. 27-32.
120. References to *TSch* III, *Comm. Rom.*, p. 75, 225, 259-60, 282; to *TSch* I, *ibid.*, p. 68, 69, 152-3; to *TSch* II, p. 70-71, thought to refer to *TSch* II, 112-16 (1068C-70B). Abelard referred to having discussed another subject in the first book of *TSch* within his draft *TChr CT* V, 35b, even though he had not written out the finished text of the first book from his draft. The fact that he refers to the second book of *TSch* in the past tense in the commentary could mean that he then considered the second book written in draft (which it was), while the new ideas of the third book of *TSch* had not been drafted. This hypothesis is supported by the fact that the passage in *TChr* IV, 85-90, similar to the ideas mentioned in the commentary, has been revised in *TChr CT*, but, unlike the other revisions in *CT*, was not incorporated into *TSch*, as if representing an earlier version of *TSch* II, not in fact used.

in the commentary are closer. The analogy of the seal does occur in the *Sententie*, which might suggest that Abelard had written the commentary before making the reference to *Jacob dilexi*[121]. The written commentary on Romans may also only be the fruit of oral exegesis of all the Pauline epistles, as reported in the *Commentarius Cantabrigiensis*.

Abelard seems to have used the text of these *Sententie* as a basis for completing the *Theologia "Scholarium"*—rather like Hugh used the notes of his student Laurence to produce the *De sacramentis*. Mention has already been made of the passage about charity introduced into the full version of *TSch*, which is so similar to part of the *Sententie*[122]. This chronology would also explain the reason behind a new recension of the *Sententie*, as found in *AMN*. When writing out the final text of the first book of *TSch* out of the draft *tsch T* (or some similar draft) Abelard added a few new passages—not just about charity, but also further justification of Christian use of pagan texts, inserted between the sections about prophetic and philosophical testimony[123]. It seems most likely that a student or amanuensis copied from this new version of the first book in order to update the *Sententie*. He may have been the Hermann mentioned in a couple of examples in the text, but there is no evidence that this Hermann was responsible for introducing ideas of his own rather than those of Abelard. The recension *AMN* can thus tentatively be dated to after the completion of at least the first book of *TSch*. The *Sententie Parisienses* presuppose the existence of the *Sententie A.*, of which they are a variation, delivered by Abelard himself. The extract from the *Sententie* (*Pa*) which the copyist prefixed to his text corresponds to the recension *AMN*. This coupled with the fact that there is allusion to ideas of *TSch* suggests that the *Sententie Parisienses* were produced after *TSch* had been completed, although this report is definitely earlier than the *liber sententiarum*, the moral teaching of which is closer to that of the *Ethica*.

121. See above, n. 59.
122. See above, n. 87.
123. This passage had been expanded slightly in *tsch T* 107-109, but was developed much more in *TSch* I, 99-114 (1005A-9C).

The Sic et Non, Sententie and the idea of a summa

The structure on which Abelard based his teaching was that of the *Sic et Non*. In, the earliest "draft" version of the work (*SN Z*), Abelard only discussed questions about faith in God with one final question about the person of Christ [124]. In a subsequent version, found in the manuscripts *TCEB*, the patristic texts were organised into questions about faith in God, the redemption and person of Christ, the sacraments and charity. This basic structure was expanded upon in points of detail, with certain re-arrangement, in subsequent recensions (*DL* and *AKM*) [125]. If the *Sententie* "depend" on any written source outside an early draft of the *Theologia "Scholarium"*, it is the *Sic et Non*, used as a basis for discussion in lectures. The *Sententie Abaelardi* form a commentary on the collection of often contradictory patristic sententie collected in the *Sic et Non*, in which the methodology outlined in its prologue was applied to many different questions of great contemporary interest. As with the manuscripts of the *Sic et Non*, those of the *Sententie* should not be used as evidence that Abelard wished to produce a specific number of recensions. As he was always refining his arguments on points of detail, adding new authorities as he thought fit, so every manuscript records his ideas at a particular moment in time—often subject to the limitations of an individual copyist. The basic structure of his teaching, however, remained the same.

The form of the *Sententie Abaelardi* throws important light on the genesis of the *Theologia "Scholarium"*. In the earliest version of that treatise, the *Theologia "Summi boni"*, Abelard's major emphasis had been on the trinitarian nature of the supreme good, which was God. He had been prompted by a desire to use the skills of dialectic to refute the ideas of his former teacher, Roscelin of Compiègne, about the nature of the difference between the three persons in the divine nature. Such concerns were still dominant when he extended this work into the *Theologia Christiana*, probably in the years following the council of Soissons, 1121, although in countering criticism he was obliged to develop his ideas about

124. Described by BOYER-MCKEON, *Peter Abailard's Sic et Non*, p. 7-14.
125. The sequence of texts as printed by Boyer-McKeon is that of *AKM*. They list that of *TCEB* and *DL* on p. 577-615.

ethical and other issues. A major change is evident in the *Theologia* *"Scholarium"* : discussion of the Trinity is placed within the context of what man needed for salvation—faith, charity and sacraments. If, as has been argued, the *Sententie* formulate Abelard's teaching on these subjects before he had completed the *Theologia* *"Scholarium"*, then the change from *TChr* to *TSch* becomes much less abrupt. Abelard decided to modify the introduction to his *Theologia* in order to situate the argument of an existing treatise (*TChr*) within the context of his teaching on all the questions relevant to salvation.

The early drafts of this new *Theologia*, in particular one transitional between *tsch Z* and *T*, served a dual purpose—for outlining the introduction of the new *Theologia* *"Scholarium"* and as notes for the initial part of his course of teaching. The subtle difference in wording between the statement of *tsch-TSch*, *Nunc autem, tribus suprapositis breviter assignatis atque descriptis, ... de singulis diligentius agendum est*, and that of the *Sententie*, *Nunc autem ... de singulis diligentius agamus*, was deliberate [126]. In the preface attached to the *Theologia* *"Scholarium"*, not found in the *Sententie*, Abelard assured his reader that he had no intention to contradict religious orthodoxy, but that he had been asked to write a summa of sacred learning at the request of his pupils :

> Scholarium nostrorum petitioni prout possumus satisfacientes, aliquam sacre eruditionis summam quasi divine Scripture introductionem conscripsimus [127].

He outlined the contents of this *summa* in the list of chapters inserted between the preface and book I in the complete version of the *Theologia* (*TSch*) :

> Primus iste liber Theologie breviter comprehendit summam totius predicti tractatus, in fide scilicet et caritate et sacramentis : quid sit fides, quid spes, quid caritas, quid sacramentum; quomodo proprie sive improprie fides dicatur; que sit fides catholica; positio sententie de fide sancte Trinitatis sive unitatis ... [128]

While Abelard thus covered briefly all the essentials to salvation, his emphasis in the *Theologia* (*TSch*) was on faith in God rather

126. See above, n. 39.
127. *tsch* 1, *TSch Prol.* (979A).
128. *TSch Cap. libr.* (981-2), an authentic part of the text.

than on other questions. This was not because he had not developed his thinking on these other subjects. The *Theologia* would cover this topic; other subjects would be dealt with elsewhere.

Abelard used the word *theologia* as the title of a treatise about the divine nature, not (at least within his writings) as study of the divine nature and never in the modern sense of "theology" to embrace redemption, sacraments and ethics as well[129]. When writing his commentary on Romans he referred in passing to a number of works which he wished to write : the *Theologia* (already prepared in draft through revision of the *Theologia Christiana*), an *Anthropologia* and the *Ethica*[130]. The *Anthropologia*, which he may

129. The one known occasion in which Abelard uses *theologia* in the sense of discussion, as distinct from a treatise title, is reported in the *Sententie Parisienses*, p. 29 : *Diximus illa, que pertinent ad theologiam. Nunc dicendum est de his que pertinent ad beneficia, quia fides catholica in duobus consistit, in cognitione divine essentie et beneficiis.* The term *theologia* does not occur at all in the earlier *Sent. Florianenses* or *Sententie A.* The use of *theologia* as a title for two fragments of the *Sent. A.* (the Vienna and Cologne MSS, *supra*, nn. 27-28) or to denote both *TSch* and the *liber sententiarum* in MSS of the *Capitula Heresum XIV* (*infra* n. 142) does not have foundation in the best MSS or in Abelard's use of the term. Abelard replaced *divini* and *spiritualis doctor* in *TSum* II, 110, 112, 34 (ed. OSTLENDER, p. 64[13, 23], 39[22]) with *theologi* in *TChr* III, 178, 181, 75, a term he had previously used in the sense known to Augustine of pagan writers about deity, *Logica "Ingredientibus"*, ed. GEYER, 51[15]. He did not introduce *theologia* into *TChr* except as a title. J. Rivière rightly pointed out that it was only a title, but incorrectly assumed that it meant a systematic study of all sacred science, *Theologia*, in *Revue des Sciences religieuses* 16 (1936) 5-22. There is much misconception on this; cf. H. SANTIAGO-OTERO, *El termino «teologia" en Pedro Abelardo*, in *Rivista española de teologia* 36 (1976) 251-60 and G.R. EVANS, *Old Arts and New Theology*, Oxford, 1980, p. 33.

130. The *Anthropologia* is promised in *Comm. Rom.*, p. 215 (*Atropologia* in one MS) as a treatise on the incarnation. Buytaert assumed (CCCM 11, p. 36) that this work was different from that promised on the same subject, titled *Tropologia* in two MSS and *Theologia* in two other MSS, in *Comm. Rom.*, p. 118. Given the divergence between these readings, it seems more likely that both are corruptions of *Anthropologia*, a non-latin word the copyists may not have understood the first time they came across it. *Tropologia*, a more familiar word meaning a way of speaking, makes no sense related to the redemption. This could be one of the works referred to by William of St Thierry in his *Epist. ad Bernardum*, ed. J. LECLERCQ, *Les lettres de Guillaume de Saint-Thierry à S. Bernard*, in *Rev. bén.* 79 (1969) 378 : *Sunt autem, ut audio, adhuc alia eius opuscula, quorum nomina sunt : Sic et Non, Scito teipsum et alia quedam, de quibus timeo, ne sicut monstruosi sunt nominis, sic etiam sint monstruosi dogmatis; sed sicut dicunt, oderunt lucem, nec etiam quesita inveniuntur.* If Abelard followed the sequence of the *Sententie A.* then he would have written the *Anthropologia* before the *Ethica*. The fragments of the *liber sententiarum* about the redemption may well give an indication of its argument. Abelard promises the *Ethica* in *Comm. Rom.*, p. 126, 293, 307; he uses this title at the beginning of its second book (*Ethica*, p. 128), but it is titled in the MSS *Scito teipsum*.

VI

have written, but has since been lost, was to deal with the incarnation and redemption. Its argument would have continued themes of the commentary on Romans. The *Ethica*, also known as the *Scito teipsum*, corresponds in subject matter to the third section of the *Sententie*, about vice and virtue. The fact that its second book, about virtue, survives in an introductory fragment only makes the comments of Abelard in the *Sententie* all the more important as a source for our knowledge of his teaching on the subject. The *Theologia, Anthropologia* and *Ethica* were intended as independent treatises which covered in much greater detail the ideas outlined in his lectures—as recorded in the *Sententie*. He used unfamiliar Greek titles for books about traditional subjects, presented in a new way : the nature of God, God made man and how man should behave.

The originality of the structure of his teaching is evident when it is compared to that of his influential contemporary, Hugh of St Victor, who composed the *De sacramentis* in about the same period as Abelard was drafting the *Theologia "Scholarium"*—namely the early to mid-1130's[131]. Hugh made frequent reference to ideas which are found in the various collections of Abelard's *sententie*, without ever identifying Abelard by name or quoting from his writings. Following a tradition set by Anselm of Laon and William of Champeaux, Hugh opened his treatise by talking about God, then dealing with the angels, the creation of the world and of man, the fall, the incarnation, the redemption and concluded, in imitation of the *City of God* with a meditation on the heavenly city, man's final end. His theme was that man came to knowledge of God through the different sacraments given to him through history. Such a framework, moving from past to future, laid implicit emphasis on original sin and on man's need to be redeemed from his fallen state, as well as on the role of the Church as mediator of divine sacraments.

---

131. On the date of the *De Sacramentis*, see VAN DEN EYNDE, *Essai sur la succession et la date des écrits de Hugues de S. Victor*, in *Spicilegium Pontificii Athenaei Antoniani* 13, Rome 1960, p. 100-3, and on the date of *TSch*, MEWS, *Abelard's "TChr"*, 152-7; the drafting of the *Theologia "Scholarium"* probably took a longer time than I indicated in the preceding article, as I had not taken into account the writing of the commentary on *Romans* or the redaction of the *Sententie*. Hugh's knowledge and criticism of Abelard's teaching is discussed by LUSCOMBE, *The School*, p. 183-97.

Abelard did not make such a clear-cut distinction between events or thinkers before and after the time of Christ. The doctrine of the Trinity, in his view, was accessible to all men and women of reason, provided thay had been inspired by the Holy Spirit. He understood the redemption to have been achieved by Christ through the example of his life and death, freeing man from servititude to sin rather than from any legitimate yoke to the devil and enabling him to come to the perfect love of God. Again he reflects a tendency not to draw too great a divide between those who lived before Christ and those who came after. While not denying the reality of the incarnation, he thought that some Old Testament figures came to the full love of God [132]. The fact that the account of sacraments in the *Sententie Parisienses* reports so little debate compared to the discussion of the Trinity and the incarnation, and stuck so much more closely to the text of the *Sententie A.*, reflects Abelard's own relative lack of interest in the subject. While not disparaging the role of sacraments, he was much more concerned with questions of interior morality and devotion. He did not give sacraments the importance accorded by Hugh of St Victor. Abelard interpreted faith, charity and sacraments as subjects capable of being analysed in terms of reason rather than in terms of man's sinfulness and his need for redemption.

The liber sententiarum magistri Petri Abaelardi

Criticism of Abelard's ideas came to a head in 1140 when William of St Thierry came across a copy of the *Theologia "Scholarium"* and a collection of his *sententie*, commonly known as the *liber sententiarum* :

Casu nuper incidi in lectionem cuiusdam libelli hominis illius, cuius

---

132. *Comm. Rom.*, p. 117-18. A similar doctrine was criticised by Bernard of Clairvaux in his *Epist.* 77 (*De baptismo*), written to Hugh c. 1127 in criticism of ideas akin to those of Abelard, *S. Bernardi Opera* 7, Rome 1974, 184-200; Hugh incorporated part of *Epist.* 77 into the *De sacramentis*, WEISWEILER, *Die Arbeitsweise Hugos von St Viktor*, in *Scholastik* 20/24 (1949) 63-64 and L. OTT, *Untersuchungen zur theologischen Briefliteratur der Frühscholastik*, BGPTMA 34 (1937) 495-548.

VI

titulus erat Theologia Petri Abaelardi. Fateor, curiosum me fecit titulus ad legendum. Duo autem erant libelli idem pene continentes, nisi quod in altero plus, in altero minus aliquanto invenietur. Ubi cum aliqua invenirem, que multum moverent me, notavi, et cur moverent subnotavi, et cum ipsis libellis misi vobis; utrum recte me moverint, iudicii vestri sit[133].

While William did not give it a title, Bernard referred to the second text within his *Epist.* 190, *sicut in libro quodam sententiarum legi,* and in *Epist.* 188 as *alium, quem dicunt sententiarum eius*[134]. It was mentioned again at the end of the list of nineteen *capitula,* attached to *Epist.* 190 :

> Hec capitula partim in libro Theologie, partim in libro sententiarum magistri Petri, partim in libro cuius titulus est Scito teipsum reperta sunt[135].

Abelard quoted this passage verbatim in his *Apologia* and *Confessio fidei* with one significant change : he placed *magistri Petri* after *libro Theologie* and added *eiusdem* after *libro sententiarum*[136]. This change, not supported by any manuscript of the *capitula,* he seems to have made deliberately in order to lend weight to his interpretation of the sentence as implying that he had written the *liber sententiarum,* as he had the *Theologia* and *Scito teipsum.* Bernard seems only to have meant a book "of the opinions of master Peter", differentiating it from the other two texts by adding this qualification. The retort had its effect, however, as Thomas of Morigny made no mention at all of the *liber sententiarum* in his *Disputatio,* written to defend Bernard of Clairvaux from the accusations made in the *Apologia*[137].

Ostlender used Abelard's denial as evidence that he could not have been responsible for making the statements which William and Bernard found so abhorrent in the *liber sententiarum.* If some of its ideas were heretical, this was the fault of a disciple, not of the master himself[138]. Although Ostlender was anxious to read into

133. *Epist. ad Bernardum,* ed. LECLERCQ, 377.
134. *Epist.* 190, 11, ed. LECLERCQ, *SBO* 8, 26; *Epist.* 188, 3, *SBO* 8, 11.
135. *Epist.* 190, ed. LECLERCQ, *SBO* 8, 39-40; a new edition is given in MEWS, *The lists of heresies,* 108-110.
136. *Confessio fidei "Universis"* (*PL* 178, 107-8); *Apologia contra Bernardum,* ed. BUYTAERT, CCCM 11, p. 360.
137. Edited by N.M. HÄRING, *Thomas von Morigny «Disputatio catholicorum patrum contra dogmata Petri Abailardi",* in *Studi Medievali* 3ª ser. 22 (1981) 299-376.
138. OSTLENDER, *Die Sentenzenbücher,* 248-50.

the *liber sententiarum*, as into the other sentence collections, ideas which were different from those of Abelard, none of their arguments are inconsistent with those of his writings. The hypothesis that a pupil was responsible for extending unfinished ideas of Abelard into a systematic whole does not stand up to the evidence of a number of different independent collections of *sententie*, all of which indicate that Abelard was himself responsible for incorporating his teaching into a systematic framework. While none of these collections can be disassociated from the activity of students copying down Abelard's sentences, they ultimately depend on his inspiration.

There were students who did use Abelard's teaching—oral and written—as a source of ideas, without being completely committed to his ideas. Into this category fall *magistri* like Omnebene, Roland, the author of the *Isagoge in theologiam* and the authors of a number of other works[139]. They do not concern us here because they all have an identity distinct from that of Abelard. There is no specific evidence that the *liber sententiarum* provided a source of stimulation for their ideas. This particular work was only one of a number of such collections which reported his *sententie*.

If the extracts of the *liber sententiarum* quoted by William of St Thierry, Bernard of Clairvaux and the author of the *Capitula Heresum XIV*—whom I have identified elsewhere as Thomas of Morigny—are put together, a not inconsiderable portion of its text can be reconstructed[140]. William did not distinguish between the *Theologia* and *liber sententiarum* in his *Disputatio*, but as he did not have in his possession any other text, one needs only to eliminate those extracts taken from *TSch*. These were similarly the only two texts used by Bernard in his *Epist.* 190, although in a later recension he added that he had also come across some of the same doctrines in Abelard's commentary on Romans, without giving any

---

139. *Isagoge in theologiam*, ed. LANDGRAF, *Écrits théologiques*, p. 63-285; *Die Sententiae Quoniam misso aus der Abaelardschule*, ed. J. TRIMBORN, Cologne 1962; H. WEISWEILER, *Eine neue Bearbeitung von Abaelards "Introductio" und der Summa Sententiarum*, in *Scholastik* 9 (1934) 346-71; these and other works are described by LUSCOMBE, *The School*, p. 168-72, 224-60.

140. WILLIAM OF ST THIERRY, *Disputatio contra Petrum Abaelardum* (*PL* 180, 249-82); *Epist.* 190, ed. LECLERCQ, *SBO* 8, 17-38; N.M. HÄRING, *Die Vierzehn Capitula Heresum Petri Abaelardi*, in *Cîteaux* 31 (1980) 35-52. On the authorship of the latter, see MEWS, *The lists of heresies*, 97-103.

VI

new extracts from this work[141]. They are also the two sources used in the *Capitula Heresum XIV*, whose author may have thought that they all formed part of the same *Theologia*[142]. Bernard seems to have given these two texts to its compiler, Thomas of Morigny, before he had produced the initial recension of *Epist.* 190, and the list of nineteen *capitula* had been drawn up. This list was produced by combining the *Capitula Heresum XIV* with that of William of St Thierry[143]. Unlike William or Bernard, Thomas of Morigny had read the *Ethica* or *Scito teipsum*, and perhaps under his authority this work was also mentioned as a source of the heretical *capitula*, although all the nineteen charges were originally based only on two texts—the *Theologia "Scholarium"* and the *liber sententiarum*. Bernard added reference to the commentary on Romans within the text of *Epist.* 190 after the list of nineteen *capitula* had been drawn up and attached to that letter-treatise, perhaps because Abelard had denied that the *liber sententiarum* was one of his writings[144].

The arguments of the liber sententiarum

The only part of its initial section about the Trinity which was quoted against Abelard is an extract in which it is argued that the names of Father, Son and Holy Spirit were applied *improprie* to God as a whole, as each name properly described only an aspect of his nature, namely his power, wisdom and goodness[145]. Although the term *improprie* does not occur in the *Theologia "Scholarium"* in this context, the idea that the three persons were names predicated of God each according to a different capacity was fundamental to his thought[146]. Abelard was not denying the divinity of the three persons, as William of St Thierry thought, but was making

141. *Epist.* 190, 11, *SBO* 8, 26.
142. *Cap. Her.* 14: *Hec sunt capitula theologie, immo stultilogie Petri Abaelardi* (found in all but one MS; authenticity uncertain).
143. MEWS, *The lists of heresies*, 83-86 and in my introduction to *TSch* (forthcoming).
144. *Ibid.*, 101-241.
145. Appendix, *Fragm.* 1.
146. E.g. *tsch* 39, *TSch* I, 32 (989D-990A).

the linguistic point that the concept of a person in the Trinity was not identical to the concept of God, even though one notion might elucidate the other. As has been observed in the *Sententie Parisienses*, Abelard seems to have been rather more daring in his spoken teaching than in his written works. This statement in the *liber sententiarum*, definitely compiled after the *Theologia "Scholarium"* had been completed (as evident from study of its ethical doctrine), provides an interesting insight into the general direction of his argument about the Trinity, although not expressed with the caution of the *Theologia.*

Much more survives of the section of the *liber sententiarum* about the redemption and person of Christ. Some of the extracts quoted are textually identical to the discussion of the subject within Abelard's commentary on Romans, while others are very similar in argument[147]. They cannot be extracts from the commentary, however, as William would have mentioned that he had three texts of Abelard rather than two. Was the *liber sententiarum* compiled by a student copying some extracts from this commentary, others from oral teaching? While not impossible, this explanation does not account for the evident continuity between those passages identical to parts of the commentary and those which are not. A simpler parallel can be observed with the *Sententie A.*, the first part of which is often textually identical to a draft of the *Theologia "Scholarium".* Abelard may have used the text of the *quaestio* on the redemption in his commentary (or in the *Anthropologia*) in lectures taken down by an amanuensis, perhaps corrected by reference to lecture notes or to his writings.

One passage, quoted by all three critics, re-iterated Abelard's argument that the devil had no legitimate rights over man and ended with the statement: *nec Filius Dei, ut hominem a iugo diaboli liberaret, carnem assumpsit*[148]. Both William and Bernard omitted the crucial phrase *a iugo diaboli* (although it was retained by Thomas of Morigny and in the final list of *capitula*), thus distorting the original meaning of Abelard's argument—according to which the purpose of Christ's incarnation and death was not to free

---

147. Appendix, *Fragm.* 2-9.
148. *Ibid., Fragm.* 3.

man from a legitimate yoke to the devil, but to bring man, tied in the condition and bondage of sin, to the love of God[149]. When quoted out of context, Abelard's argument could easily be made to seem more daring and heretical than in fact it was.

The discussion of grace and free will was similar, but not identical to that in the commentary on Romans, and considerably more elaborate than in the other collections of *sententie*[150]. In the section on charity, the arguments advanced are close to those of the *Ethica*, in particular with regard to the definition of sin as consent to a wrong will, rather than as a wrong will itself[151]. The doctrine of the *liber sententiarum* is, in this respect, more advanced than that of the commentary on Romans or of the *Theologia "Scholarium"*. There are also close parallels to the teaching of the *Ethica* in the discussion of why God rewarded intention rather than achievement, and why those who crucified Christ did not sin if they kept true to their conscience[152]. Even an argument of the *Ethica* about how the devil could incite temptation through magnetic stones and aphrodisiac plants, not found in other sentence collections, occurs in the *liber sententiarum*[153]. It is impossible to say which was produced before the other, but the *liber sententiarum* must have been compiled after the *Theologia "Scholarium"* had been completed.

Conclusions

The *liber sententiarum magistri Petri* is only one of a number different collections of Abelard's sententie. It can be compared most closely to the *Sententie Abaelardi* in the precision with which his argument is presented—part of its discussion of the redemption is identical to the *quaestio* on the subject in Abelard's commentary on *Romans*, in the same way as the *Sententie* reproduce parts of a draft of the *Theologia "Scholarium"*. Both may have been compiled by an amaneuensis either from dictation or from Abelard's lecture

149. *Ibid., Fragm.* 8.
150. *Ibid., Fragm.* 15-17.
151. *Ibid., Fragm.* 18-25.
152. *Ibid., Fragm.* 21-23.
153. *Ibid., Fragm.* 20.

notes (or from both). The differences between manuscripts of the *Sententie A.* may result from an original text having been corrected over a period of time by students adding spoken comments and in the case of *AMN*, a long passage from the *Theologia "Scholarium"*. The *Sententie Florianenses* and *Sententie Parisienses* are less careful productions, perhaps taken down in haste by students in a lecture room. Abelard seems to have used a draft of the beginning of the *Theologia "Scholarium"* for the beginning of his lectures, while basing the structure of his discussion of faith, the sacraments and charity on the *Sic et Non*. He subsequently used some of the arguments of the *Sententie* as a basis on which to complete the *Theologia "Scholarium"*, a detailed study of the first part of his course. The *Ethica* developed that part of his teaching about charity, while the *Anthropologia* (if completed) would have covered that about redemption. The *Sententie Florianenses*, *Sententie Abaelardi*, *Sententie Parisienses* and *liber sententiarum magistri Petri* (in that chronological order) do not belong to his strictly literary compositions, but they should be differentiated from those texts which combine ideas of Abelard with those of other teachers. To group all such works under the loose umbrella of "the school of Peter Abelard" is to misunderstand the significance of those which reproduce his teaching alone. The four texts mentioned shed important light on the ideas of Abelard about faith in God and in Christ, the sacraments and morality, not on the thinking of his disciples.

APPENDIX

LIBER SENTENTIARUM MAGISTRI PETRI

The following edition of the *liber sententiarum magistri Petri* is based on the *Disputatio* of William of St Thierry, *Epist.* 190 of Bernard of Clairvaux and the *Capitula Heresum XIV*, probably compiled by Thomas of Morigny. In the absence of a complete manuscript of the work, any edition must depend on quotations made by critics of Abelard, the accuracy of which cannot be verified, except by comparing different versions of the same extract.

S   *Charleville, Bibliothèque municipale 67*, s. XII.

This manuscript is an important witness to the text of the *liber sententiarum* because it contains both the *Disputatio* of William of St Thierry (not known

VI

in any other manuscript) and the initial recension of Bernard's *Epist*. 190. It was copied in the twelfth century at the abbey of Signy (diocese of Rheims), where William of St Thierry lived from 1136 until his death in 1148[154]. A composite manuscript, it contains on ff. 1ᵛ-71 the *In laudibus Virginis Matris*, *De gradibus humilitatis* and *De laude nove militie* of Bernard of Clairvaux and on ff. 140ᵛ-147 the *Oratio pro Ligorio* of Cicero. The second, ff. 72-139, contains a dossier of texts principally about Abelard :

ff. 72ᵛ-74	Letter of WILLIAM OF ST THIERRY to Geoffrey of Chartres and Bernard of Clairvaux, ed. J. LECLERCQ, *Rev. bén.* 79 (1969) 377-8.
ff. 74-107ᵛ, 108	WILLIAM OF ST THIERRY, *Disputatio adversus Abaelardum*, *PL* 180, 249-82.
f. 108	BERNARD, *Epist.* 327, ed. J. LECLERCQ, *S. Bernardi Opera* 7 (Rome 1977) 263.
ff. 109-110	BERNARD, *Epist.* 188, ed. J. LECLERCQ, *SBO* 8, 263.
ff. 110-112, 121	BERNARD, *Epist.* 189, ed. J. LECLERCQ, *SBO* 8, 12-16
ff. 121-122	INNOCENT II, *Epist.* 194, ed. J. LECLERCQ, *SBO* 8, 46-48, followed by a brief note about the sentence, ed. J. LECLERCQ, *Rev. bén.* 79 (1969) 379.
ff. 122ᵛ-128ᵛ, 113-120ᵛ, 129-32	BERNARD, *Epist.* 190, ed. J. LECLERCQ, *SBO* 8, 17-38.
ff. 132-138ᵛ	WILLIAM OF ST THIERRY, *De erroribus Guillelmi de Conchis*, ed. J. LECLERCQ, *Rev. bén.* 79 (1969) 382-91.
ff. 138ᵛ-139	Hymns : *Te Matrum laudamus* ..., ed. J. LECLERCQ, *Fragmenta Mariana, Ephemerides liturgicae* 72 (1958) 293-4; *Clemens et benigna* ..., ed. DREVES, *Analecta Hymnica* 47, 35.

The slight irregularity of folios is due to the misbinding of ff. 113-120ᵛ. According to Leclercq, f. 108 (a demi-folio) may be the original of the letter (*Epist*. 327) sent by Bernard in response to William's letter and accompanying treatise about the errors of Abelard[155]. The text of *Epist*. 190 in *S* is that of an initial recension, without a number of additional passages which Bernard inserted only later. Although, as has been demonstrated elsewere, *S* was the only manuscript to contain this initial recension, *S* does seem to contain the most reliable text of *Epist*. 190. The list of nineteen *capitula* had not been attached to *Epist*. 190 in *S*, as found in other manuscripts of this earlier recension[156]. Bernard may have sent his initial draft of *Epist*. 190 to William, whose treatise inspired much of his own argument, prior to drawing up the list of nineteen *capitula*. This would explain why the original version of *Epist*. 190 occurs in a manuscript belonging to the abbey of Signy, William's monastery.

---

154. The manuscript is described by J. LECLERCQ, *Notes sur la tradition des épitres de S. Bernard. I. Une chartula originale?*, in *Scriptorium* 18 (1964) 198-200, reprinted in *Recueil d'études sur saint Bernard* 3, Rome 1969, p. 308-10.

155. *Ibid.*

156. J. LECLERCQ, *Les formes successives de la lettre-traité de saint Bernard contre Abélard*, in *Rev. bén.* 78 (1968) 87-105; see MEWS, *The lists of heresies*, 94-96.

The Capitula Heresum XIV

The other major source for the text of the *liber sententiarum* is the list of fourteen *capitula*, with accompanying extracts, probably drawn up by Thomas of Morigny. In general Thomas quoted from the *liber sententiarum* more accurately and more extensively than either William or Bernard. Buytaert's edition of the *Capitula Heresum XIV*, based only on two manuscripts (*GI*), has been superseded by that of Häring, who uses all eight manuscripts known to survive, but even this edition is not free from error[157]. None of these manuscripts date from before the late twelfth century[158]:

B   Barcelona, *Archivio de la Corona di Aragon, Ripoll C 56*, ff. 36ᵛ-37ᵛ; s. XIII-XIV.
C   London, *British Library, Royal 8. F. XV*, ff. 1-2ᵛ; s. XII-XIII.
D   London, *Sion College, Arc. L 40, 2/L 13*, ff. 1-3ᵛ; s. XIII.
E   Oxford, *Balliol College 148*, ff. 57-57ᵛ; s. XIII.
F   Oxford, *Bodleian Library 375*, ff. 44ᵛ-46; s. XIII.
G   Paris, *Bibliothèque de l'Arsenal 268*, ff. 248-249ᵛ; s. XII-XIII.
H   Paris, *Bibliothèque de l'Arsenal 502*, ff. 3-4; s. XIV.
I   Vatican, *Biblioteca Apostolica, lat. 663*, ff. 3-4; s. XIV.

Häring does not discuss the relationship between these various manuscripts, but analysis of the variants suggests that *C*, from the Cistercian abbey of St Mary, Byland (diocese of York), contains the most reliable version of the text. There are two main groups of manuscripts, which go back to a common exemplar, *BCDF* (of mainly English provenance) and *EHI* (with a common source of French origin), of which the latter is generally the less reliable. The manuscript *G*, from the abbey of St Martin des Champs, Paris, is one of the oldest and seems to be quite independent of the other two groups. Despite many errors, it sometimes is alone to contain a reading which is supported by the version given by William and Bernard. The *Capitula Heresum XIV* were not incorporated into any of the standard registers of Bernard's correspondence circulated in the twelfth century, but were included in a much less copied dossier of documents about Abelard, which included the letter of the archbishop and bishops of Sens to Innocent II (*Epist.* 337 in the later corpus), also absent from the twelfth century registers[159]. Thomas of Morigny lived in the abbey of St Martin des Champs 1140-44; Paris may thus have been the original centre of its diffusion.

157. BUYTAERT, CCCM 12, p. 473-80 and HÄRING, see n. 140.
158. Häring supplies a full bibliography for these manuscripts, to which can be added the descriptions in H. ROCHAIS and E. MANNING (ed.), *Bibliographie générale de l'ordre cistercien: Saint Bernard*, in *La documentation cistercienne* 21, Rochefort 1979-82, nos. 3478 (*B*), 4019 (*C*), 4206 (*E*), 4214 (*F*), 4281 (*G*), 4283 (*H*), 4543 (*I*).
159. Ed. J. LECLERCQ, *Autour de la correspondance de S. Bernard: 1. La lettre des évêques de France au sujet d'Abélard*, in *Sapientiae Doctrina. Mélanges de théologie et de littérature médiévales offerts à Dom Hildebrand Bascour*, Leuven 1980, p. 185-92; see MEWS, *The lists of heresies*, 103-5.

The edition

As the *Capitula Heresum XIV* generally gives better quotations from the *Theologia "Scholarium"* than the treatises of William or Bernard, its text of the *liber sententiarum* has normally been followed, where possible. To avoid over-burdening the critical apparatus, reference to individual manuscripts is only given when the editions of Häring (*Cap. Her.*) and Leclercq (*Epist.* 190) have not been followed. The sequence of fragments has been established by the order in which they are quoted, combined with using the *Sententie A.* as a guide. Also included are those *capitula* for which no text was ever quoted, but which must have been based on passages in the *liber sententiarum*.

{*LIBER SENTENTIARUM MAGISTRI PETRI*}

Fragm. 1. (*S* 75) Notandum quod ista tria nomina, Pater et Filius et Spiritus Sanctus, quamvis sicut et alia nomina de Deo improprie dicantur, tamen ad commendationem summi boni in descriptione ipsius convenienter sunt apposita, per que potentia Dei designatur, et sapientia et benignitas. Si enim omnipotens esset et non omnisapiens, summe bonus non esset. Iterum, si benignus non esset, eius potentia perniciosa et inutilis esset.

E Guil., Disp. 2 (*PL* 180, 250D-51A); cf. *tsch* 39, *TSch* I, 32.

Fragm. 2. (*S* 118ᵛ) Cum solos electos liberaverit Christus, quomodo eos diabolus possidebat, sive in hoc seculo, sive in futuro magis, quam modo? Numquid etiam pauperem illum, qui in sinu Abrahe requiescebat, sicut et divitem damnatum, diabolus cruciabat, aut etiam in ipsum Abrahe dominium habebat, ceterosque electos?

E Bern., Epist. 190, 18 (ed. LECLERCQ, *SBO* 8, 32-33). Cf. *Comm. Rom.* (ed. E. M. BUYTAERT, p. 114).

Fragm. 3. (*S* 95, 128) Sciendum est quod omnes doctores nostri[1] qui post apostolos fuerunt[2] in hoc conveniunt quod diabolus dominium et potestatem habebat super hominem et iure eum possidebat, ideo scilicet quod homo ex libertate arbitrii quam habebat, sponte diabolo consensit. Aiunt namque quod si aliquis[3] aliquem vicerit, victus iure victoris servus[4] constituitur. Ideo, sicut dicunt doctores, hac necessitate incarnatus est Filius Dei, ut homo qui aliter liberari non poterat, per mortem innocentis iure (S 128ᵛ) liberaretur a iugo diaboli[5]. Sed, ut nobis videtur, nec diabolus umquam ius aliquod in hominem[6] habuit et iure eum possidebat[7], nisi forte[8], Deo permittente, ut[9] carcerarius, nec Filius Dei ut hominem a iugo diaboli[10] liberaret, carnem assumpsit.

E Cap. Her. iv, 1-2; *Guil., Disp.* 7 (269D); *Bern., Epist.* 190, 11 (p. 26). Cf. *Sent. Florian.* 30 (ed. OSTLENDER, p. 41); *Sent. A.* (ed. BUZZETTI, 23, 21-36); *Comm. Rom.* (pp. 114-15).

1 doctores nostri} *trp Cap. Her. BCDEFHI*   2 qui ... fuerunt} *post* apostolos *Guil.*, *Bern.*   3 aliquis} quis *Bern.*   4 victoris servus} *trp Guil.*   5 ideo scilicet ... diaboli} *om. Cap. Her.*   6 in hominem} super hominem *Cap. Her.*, in homine *Guil.* (*Epist.* 190, ed. Leclercq)   7 et ... possidebat} *om. Guil.*, *Bern.*   8 forte} fortassis *Cap. Her.*   9 ut} sicut *Guil.*   10 a iugo diaboli} *om. Guil.*, *Bern.*

Fragm. 4. (*S* 95, 119) Que itaque[1] necessitas, aut[2] que ratio, aut[2] quid[3] opus fuit, cum sola iussione (S 119ᵛ) sua divina miseratio liberare hominem a peccato posset[4], propter redemptionem nostram Filium Dei, carne suscepta, tot et tantas inedias, opprobria, flagella, sputa {et sicut paulo post dicit, viderit ipse unde acceperit: spineam coronam (*S* 95ᵛ) capiti eius usque ad cerebrum impressam *add. Guil.*} denique ipsam crucis asperrimam et ignominiosam[5] mortem sustinere et[6] ut[7] cum iniquis patibulum sustineret?

E Guil., Disp. 7 (270A); *Bern., Epist.* 190, 19 (p. 33). Cf. *Comm. Rom.* (p. 116), *Sent. A.* (23, 63-68).

1 itaque} *om. Guil.*   2 aut} *om. Guil.*   3 quid} quod *Bern.*, *Guil.*   4 cum ... posset} *om. Guil.*   5 asperrimam ... ignominiosam} *trp Bern.*   6 et} *om. Leclercq*   7 ut} *om. Guil.*

Fragm. 5. (*S* 95ᵛ, 120ᵛ) Quomodo nos iustificari vel reconciliari[1] Deo per mortem Filii sui[2] dicit Apostolus[3], qui tanto amplius[4] adversus hominem irasci debuit, quanto amplius homines[5] in crucifigendo Filium suum[6] deliquerunt, quam in transgrediendo primum[7] eius preceptum[8] unius pomi gustu[9]? Quo enim amplius per homines multiplicata sunt peccata, irasci Deum hominibus amplius iustum fuerat[10]... Quod si tantum fuerat illud Ade peccatum, ut expiari non posset nisi morte Christi, quam expiationem (*S* 129) habebit ipsum homocidium quod in Christo commissum est, et tot et tanta scelera in ipsum vel in[11] suos commissa[12]? Numquid mors innocentis Filii in tantum Deo Patri[13] placuit, ut per ipsam reconciliaretur nobis qui hoc peccando commisimus propter quod innocens Dominus est occisus? nec nisi hoc maximum fieret peccatum, illud multo levius potuit ignoscere? nec nisi multiplicatis malis tantum bonum facere? in quo etiam iustiores facti sumus per mortem Filii Dei quam ante eramus, ut a poenis iam liberari debeamus?[14]

E Cap. Her. iv, 3; *Guil., Disp.* 7 (270B); *Bern., Epist.* 190, 21 (p. 35); *Comm. Rom.* (pp. 116-17).

1 nos ... reconciliari} apostolus reconciliari hominem *Guil.*   2 sui} eius *Cap. Her.*, Dei *Guil.*   3 dicit Apostolus} *om. Guil.*   4 amplius} plus *Guil.*   5 hominem} *om. Cap. Her.*   6 suum} eius *Guil.*   7 primum} *om. Guil.*   8 eius preceptum} *trp Cap. Her.*   9 gustu} *ante* unius *Guil.*   10 Quo enim ... fuerat} *om. Bern.*   11 in} *om. Cap. Her. BCDEFHI, Häring*   12 et tot ... commissa} *om. Bern.*   13 in ... Patri} tantum Deo *Cap. Her.*   14 Quo enim ... debeamus} *om. Guil.*; nec nisi multiplicatis ... debeamus} *om. Bern.*

Fragm. 6. (*S* 129ᵛ) Cui vero non crudele in iniquum videtur, ut sanguinem

VI

innocentis in[1] pretium aliquod quis requisierit, aut ullo modo ei placuerit innocentem interfici, nedum Deus tam acceptam Filii mortem[2] habuerit[3], ut per ipsam universo reconciliatus sit mundo? Hec et his similia non mediocrem movere questionem nobis videntur, de redemptione scilicet et de[4] justificatione nostra per mortem Domini nostri Iesu Christi. Nobis autem videtur quod in hoc sumus *iustificati in sanguine* Christi et *Deo reconciliati* {*Rom.* 5, 9-10} quia[5] per hanc singularem gratiam nobis exhibitam quod Filius suus nostram suscepit naturam et in ipsa nos tam verbo quam exemplo instituendo usque ad mortem perstitit, nos sibi amplius per amorem adstrinxit, ut tanto divine gratie accensi beneficio, nihil iam tolerare propter ipsum vera reformidet caritas. Quod quidem beneficium antiquos etiam patres, hoc per fidem expectantes[6], in summum amorem Dei tamquam homines temporis gratie[7] non dubitamus accendisse[8].

E *Cap. Her.* iv, 4; *Bern., Epist.* 190, 22 (p. 36); *Comm. Rom.* (pp. 117-18).

1 in} et *Cap. Her.*   2 Filii mortem} *trp Bern.*   3 habuerit} habuit *Cap. Her.*   4 et de} vel *Comm. Rom.*   5 quia} quod *Comm. Rom.*   6 hoc ... expectantes} per hoc fidem excitantes *Häring*   7 gratie} illius *Cap. Her. G,* om. *BCDEFHI, Häring*   8 Hec et his similia ... accendisse} om. *Bern.*

Fragm. 7. (*S* 130) ... dicat totum esse quod Deus in carne apparuit, nostram de verbo et exemplo ipsius institutionem, sive ut postmodum dicit instructionem; totum quod passus et mortuus est, sue erga nos caritatis ostensionem vel commendationem.

E *Bern., Epist.* 190, 22 (p. 36).

Fragm. 8. (*S* 101ᵛ, 130ᵛ) Patet ergo quod consilium et causa incarnationis[1] Domini fuit ut luce sapientie sue[2] mundum illuminaret et ad amorem suum accenderet, tamquam posset provocari homo superbus ad amorem Dei, nisi primo humiliaretur ab amore sui, et nisi prius sacramento redemptionis solveretur, ligatus a conditione et vinculo peccati[3].

E *Guil., Disp.* 7 (276B); *Cap. Her.* iv, 5; *Bern., Epist.* 190, 23 (p. 37). Cf. *Sent. Florian.* 32 (pp. 15-16), *Sent. A.* (23, 5-12).

1 incarnationis} et passionis *add. Guil.*   2 sapientie sue} *trp Bern., Cap. Her. BCDEFHI*   3 tamquam ... peccati} om. *Bern., Cap. Her.*

Fragm. 9. (*S* 131) Redemptio itaque nostra est illa summa in nobis per Christi passionem[1] dilectio.

E *Bern., Epist.* 190, 24 (p. 37); *Comm. Rom.* (p. 118).

1 Christi passionem} *trp Comm. Rom.*

Fragm. 10. Quando dico "Christus est tertia persona in Trinitate", hoc volo dicere quod Verbum quod ab eterno tertia persona in Trinitate fuit, tertia persona sit in Trinitate; et ita patet quod locutio figurativa est. Si enim eam propriam diceremus esse, cum hoc nomen "Christus" idem sonet[1] quod

"Deus et homo", tunc talis esset sensus : "Deus et homo est tertia persona in Trinitate"; quod penitus falsum est.

E Cap. Her. v, 1. Cf. Sent. A. (24, 1-10).

1 sonet} sonat Häring

Fragm. 11. (S 102) Et[1] sciendum est[2] quod[3], quamvis[4] concedamus quod Christus est tertia[5] persona in Trinitate, non tamen concedimus quod hec persona (S 102^v) que Christus est, sit tertia persona in Trinitate.

E Cap. Her. v, 2; Guil., Disp. 7 (276D-7A).

1 Et} om. Guil.   2 sciendum est} trp Cap. Her. G, Häring   3 quod} om. Häring   4 quamvis} licet Guil.   5 est teria} tertia sit Guil.

Fragm. 12.
(a) {Quod in Christo non fuerit spiritus timoris Domini.}
(b) {Quod etiam castus timor excludatur a futura vita.}
(c) {Quod adventus in fine seculi possit attribui Patri.}
(d) {Quod anima Christi per se non descendit ad inferos, sed per potentiam tantum.}

E cap. 11 (a); 15 (b); 17 (c); 18 (d) (ed. MEWS, 109-110). Cf. Bern., Epist. 188, 2 (p. 11) (a, d); Epist. 190, 10 (p. 25) (a, b : timorem Domini castum).

Fragm. 13. De speciebus panis et vini queratur si sint modo in corpore Christi sicut prius erant in substantia panis et vini que versa est in corpus Christi, an sint in aere? Sed veresimilius est quod sint in aere potius quam sint in corpore Christi, cum corpus Christi sua lineamenta et quam speciem habeat sicut alia corpora humana. Species vero iste, scilicet panis et vini, fiunt in aere sicut et sapor panis et vini fit in ore ad celandum et obtegendum corpus Christi.

E Cap. Her. ix, 1; cf. Guil., Disp. 9 (280C), Bern., Epist. 190, 10 (pp. 25-26). Cf. Sent. Florian. 70 (p. 31); Sent. A. (29, 131-153); Sent. Paris. (p. 43).

Fragm. 14. Hic autem queritur de hoc quod quandoque videtur esse muscidum—unde etiam precipitur quod a sabbato usque ad sabbatum servetur, sicut de panibus propositionis factum fuisse legitur {I Paral. 9, 32}—a muribus etiam corrodi videtur et de manu sacerdotis vel diaconi in terram cadere; et ideo queritur quare Deus permittat ista fieri in corpore suo? An fortassis non ita fiat in corpore, sed tantum ita faciat apparere in specie? —Ad quod dicimus quod revera non est sic in corpore, sed Deus ita in speciebus ipsis propter negligentiam ministrorum reprimendam apparere facit; corpus vero suum, prout ei placet et ubi placet, reponit et conservat.

E Cap. Her. ix, 2. Cf. Sent. A. (29, 153-158); Sent. Paris. (pp. 43-44).

Fragm. 15. (S 92) Hic iterum solet queri illud quod a quibusdam dicitur, scilicet[1] utrum omnes homines ita sola misericordia Dei salventur, ut nullus sit qui bonam voluntatem habere possit, nisi gratia Dei preveniente que cor moveat, et bonam voluntatem inspiret et inspiratam multiplicet et multiplicatam conservet. Quod si ita est, scilicet[2] ut homo ex se nihil[3] boni operari possit, ut aliquo modo ad divinam gratiam suscipiendam per liberum arbitrium sine auxilio gratie se erigere[4], prout dictum est, non possit, non videtur ratio quare, si peccat[5], puniatur. Si enim non potest ex se aliquid boni facere[6], et talis factus est ut pronior sit[7] ad malum quam ad bonum, (*S* 92ᵛ) nonne, si peccat, immunis est a culpa? Et[8] numquid Deus qui ita[9] eum infirmum et fragilis nature[10] fecit, laudandus est[11] de tali creatione? Immo si ita esset, nonne potius culpandus videretur[12]?

> *E Cap. Her.* vi, 1; *Guil.*, *Disp.* 6 (266D-7A). Cf. *Comm. Rom.* (p. 240); *Sent. A.* (34, 71-81); *Sent. Paris.* (p. 59).

> 1 Hic ... scilicet} Queritur etiam *Guil.*   2 scilicet} *om. Cap. Her.*   3 nihil} *post* homo *Guil.*   4 se erigere} *post* dictum est *Guil.*   5 peccat} peccaverit *Guil.*   6 boni facere} *trp Guil.*   7 ut ... sit} qui sit pronior *Cap. Her.*   8 culpa? Et} peccato *Guil.*   9 ita} talem *Guil.*   10 infirmum ... nature} *om. Guil.*   11 laudandus est} *trp Cap. Her.*   12 Immo ... videretur} et non potius culpandus *Guil.*

Fragm. 16. (*S* 92ᵛ) Quod si ita esset ut homo ad divinam gratiam percipiendam se erigere sine auxilio alterius gratie non posset, non videtur esse ratio quare homo inculparetur et Deus in gratiam haberetur, sed potius in auctorem ipsius culpa[1] refundenda videretur[2]. Sed quia ita non est, sed longe aliter, dicendum est prout rei[3] veritas se habet. Dicendum est igitur quod homo per rationem a Deo quidem datam gratie apposite cohere potest, nec Deus plus facit isti qui salvatur, antequam cohereat gratie, quam illi qui non salvatur. Ita enim se habet Deus erga homines quemadmodum mercator qui pretiosos habet lapides[4] venales, qui videlicet exponit eos in foro et eque omnibus ostendit, er per ostensos[5] desiderium in eis ad emendum excitat[6]. Qui prudens est, sciens se eis indigere, laborat ut habeat, acquirit nummos et emit eos. Qui deses est et piger, etsi desiderium habeat, quia tamen piger est non laborat, etiamsi fortior sit alio corpore, nec emit eos; et ideo culpa sua est quod caret illis[7]. Similiter Deus gratiam suam apponit omnibus, et consulit scripturis et doctorum[8] exemplis provocat[9], ut homines[10] per libertatem arbitrii quam habent, gratie cohereant. Qui prudens est, providens sibi in futuro ex libertate[11] arbitrii quam habet[12], coheret gratie. Piger vero et carnalibus desideriis implicatus, etiam si desideret beatificari, tamen quia non vult laborare compescendo se a malis, sed negligit[13], quamvis per liberum arbitrium possit coherere gratie, ab omnipotenti Deo negligitur[14]. Quod autem sicut mortuus Lazarus non potuit reviviscere nisi Deo suscitante, sic ad bene volendum non posse surgere hominem, nisi gratia vivificante, dicitur aut creditur; ideo vivificatio ista attribuitur gratie, quia ratio qua homo discernit et intelligit a malo abstinendum et bene agendum, est a Deo. Et ideo hoc inspirante Deo agere dicitur, quia Deus per rationem, quam dedit homini, facit eum peccatum ipsum agnoscere[15].

E Cap. Her. vi, 2; *Guil.*, *Disp.* 6 (267AB). Cf. *Comm. Rom.* (p. 241); *Sent. A.* (34, 37-74); *Sent. Florian.* 27 (p. 13); *Sent. Paris.* (p. 60).

1 sed ... culpa} potius in auctorem ipsius *Cap. Her.* BCDEFHI, *Häring* 2 Quod si ... videretur} *om. Guil.*   3 rei} *om. Guil.*   4 Ita enim ... lapides} Sed sicut qui lapides preciosos exponit *Guil.*   5 qui videlicet ... ostensos} et *Guil.*   6 in eis ... excitat} videntium excitat ad emendum *Guil.*   7 Qui prudens ... illis} *om. Guil.*   8 doctorum} *om. Guil.*   9 provocat} *om. Cap. Her.*   10 homines} *om. Cap. Her.*   11 providens ... libertate} per libertatem *Guil.*   12 quam habet} sui *Guil.*   13 vero ... negligit} et carnalis *Guil.* 14 cohere ... negligitur} negligit et ideo negligitur a Deo *Guil.*   15 Quod autem ... agnoscere} *om. Cap. Her.*

Fragm. 17. In primis videndum est quid sit consentire malo et quid non. Ille equidem malo consentire dicitur qui cum debeat illud prohibere et possit, non prohibet. Si autem debeat et non possit, et e converso si possit et non debeat, non est reus. Si vero nec debet, nec potest, multo minus reus censendus est. Et ideo Deus a consensu malorum est alienus qui nec debet nec potest mala impedire. Ideo non debet quia cum res per benignitatem illius eveniat[1] eo modo quo melius possit[2], nullo modo contra hoc velle debet. Ideo autem non potest quia bonitas illius, electo minori bono, illi quod maius est impedimentum minime parare potest.

E Cap. Her. vii. Cf. *Sent. A.* (26, 63-75).

1 eveniat} eveniant *Cap. Her.* BCDFI, *Häring*   2 possit} possunt *Cap. Her.* BCDEFHI, possent *Häring*

Fragm. 18. Sciendum est quod quando dicitur "originale peccatum est in pueris", hoc dicitur pro pena temporali et eterna que debetur eis ex culpa primi parentis.

E Cap. Her. viii, 1; cf. *Guil.*, *Disp.* 9 (281D). Cf. *Comm. Rom.* (p. 171); *Sent. Florian.* 54 (p. 26); *Ethica* (pp. 20-22).

Fragm. 19. Similiter dicitur *in quo omnes peccaverunt* {*Rom.* 5,12}, ideo scilicet quia seminarium omnium erat in illo qui peccavit. Non tamen inde provenit quod omnes peccassent, quia non erant et qui non est, non peccat.

E Cap. Her. viii, 2. Cf. *Comm. Rom.* (p. 157); *Sent. Florian.* 54 (p. 26).

Fragm. 20. (*S* 106ᵛ) De suggestione diaboli solet queri quomodo possit suggerere hominibus, cum nec verbis nec signis hoc faciat. Ad quod dicimus quod[1] facit hec per physicam rerum, lapidum vel herbarum, quia sicut in natura quorumdam lapidum est ferrum trahere vel libidinem exstinguere, ita quidam lapides sunt vel herbe, quibus libido, ira et cetera vitia excitantur. Quando ergo diabolus vult suggerere alicui libidinem vel iram vel alia vitia, apponit ei lapidem illum sive herbam quam scit talem habere virtutem.

E Guil., *Disp.* 10 (281AB); cf. *Bern.*, *Epist.* 190, 10 (p. 26). Cf. *Ethica* (pp. 36-38).

1 quod} quia *Guil.*

Fragm. 21. Solet queri quid a Deo remuneretur, opus an intentio seu utrumque? Auctoritas autem videtur velle quod opera a Deo eternaliter remunerentur. Ait namque Apostolus : *Reddet Deus unicuique secundum opera sua* {*Rom.* 2, 6}, et Athanasius sit : "Et reddituri sunt de factis propriis rationem"; et paulo post ait : "Et qui bona egerunt, ibunt in vitam eternam, qui vero mala, in ignem eternum" {*Symbolum "Quicumque"*}. Nos vero dicimus quod sola voluntas a Deo eternaliter remuneretur, sive ad bonum sive ad malum, nec propter opera vel peior vel melior efficitur homo, nisi dum operatur fortassis in aliquo eius voluntas augmentetur. Nec est contra Apostolum vel alios auctores, quia cum Apostolus dixit : *Reddet unicuique* etc., ibi effectum pro causa posuit, opera scilicet pro voluntate seu intentione.

E Cap. Her. x. Cf. *Ethica* (p. 58); *Sent. A.* (34, 37-49).

Fragm. 22. Opponitur de Iudeis qui Christum crucifixerunt, et de aliis qui martyres persequendo *obsequium se* putabant *prestare Deo* {*Jn.* 16, 2}; et de Eva etiam dicunt quod non egit contra conscientiam quando seducta est, et tamen certum est eam peccasse.—Ad quod nos dicimus quod revera illi simplices Iudei non agebant contra conscientiam, sed potius zelo legis sue Christum persequebantur nec putabant se male agere, et ideo non peccabant. Nec propter hoc aliqui eorum damnati sunt, sed propter precedentia peccata, merito quorum in istam cecitatem devoluti sunt. Et inter istos erant electi illi pro quibus Christus oravit dicens : *Pater dimitte illis quia nesciunt quid faciunt* {*Lk.* 23, 34}. Nec oravit ut hoc peccatum eis dimitteretur, cum hoc peccatum non esset, sed potius peccata precedentia.

E Cap. Her. xi; cf. *Guil.*, *Disp.* 13 (282B). Cf. *Ethica* (pp. 54-56).

Fragm. 23. (*S* 107ᵛ) Propter quod Iudei qui Stephanum lapidaverunt et Dominum crucifixerunt non peccaverunt; immo plus peccavissent si contra conscientiam estimationis sue ei pepercissent.

E Guil., *Disp.* 13 (282B).

Fragm. 24. (*S* 107ᵛ) Concupiscere alienam uxorem sive concumbere cum alterius uxore non est peccatum, sed solus in hoc consensus et contemptus Dei peccatum est.

E Guil., *Disp.* 12 (282A). Cf. *Ethica* (p. 14).

Fragm. 25. (*S* 107ᵛ) Dicit concupiscentiam et delectationem carnis non esse in nobis occidendam, sed odiendam, sicut precepit Dominus patrem et matrem odiendos propter Deum {*Lk.* 14, 26}, non occidendos, ut semper habeamus contra quod pugnemus. Quod enim cum labore et (*S* 109) certamine bene agitur, hoc est quod coronam et premium meretur; quod vero cum pace et delectatione, nihil meretur.

E Guil., *Disp.* 13 (282BC).

Summary

Often attributed to a certain Hermannus, the work titled in manuscripts the *Sententie Petri Abaelardi* (also known as the *Epitome Theologiae Christiane*) report the teaching of Abelard himself, and not that of a disciple, on faith, the sacraments and charity. They have recently been re-edited by S. Buzzetti as *Sententie magistri Petri Abelardi (Sententie Hermanni)*, Florence, La Nuova Italia, 1983, but many aspects of the work are not touched on in that edition. The article analyses the significance of the different versions of the *sententie* found in the extant manuscripts and of their relationship to the *Theologia 'Scholarium'*. The changes made to the *Sententie* echo those made to the *Theologia* and thus should be considered as modifications made by Abelard himself in the course of his teaching. The *Theologia 'Scholarium'* provides a more advanced study of the first part of his course, to be grasped only after the *Sententie* had been fully understood. Abelard's denial that he wrote the *liber sententiarum* quoted against him by his critics does not mean that he never taught the doctrines it contained. Rather, it is more likely that this work, like the *Sententie* edited by Buzzetti, was taken down by an amanuensis from lectures, perhaps themselves based on written notes. The extant fragments of the *liber sententiarum magistri Petri* are edited in an appendix.

ON DATING THE WORKS
OF PETER ABELARD

Any attempt to assess the evolution of the thought of Peter Abelard (1079-1142) must be based on a firm grasp of the sequence of his various writings on logic and theology. The studies which follow concentrate on two works: the *Dialectica* and the *Dialogus inter philosophum, Iudaeum et Christianum* or *Collationes*. While a number of scholars have attempted to date individual works of Abelard, there has not yet emerged any clear consensus of opinion about the overall chronology of his writings[1]. By looking again at the *Dialectica* and the *Dialogus* in relation to his other writings on logic and theology it is hoped to gain a clearer picture

(*) For abbreviations, see pp. 133-4.

(1) V. Cousin, *Ouvrages inédits d'Abélard pour servir à l'histoire de la philosophie scolastique en France* (Paris, 1836), pp. xxxi-xxxvi, cxiv-cxvi and in the introduction to individual editions within *Petri Abaelardi Opera* 2 vols (Paris, 1849, 1859); Robert, pp. 187-211; Sikes, pp. 258-71; Cottiaux, 250-69; Geyer, pp. 591-633; H. Ostlender, 'Die Theologia "Scholarium" des Peter Abaelards', *Aus der Geisteswelt des Mittelalters*, BGPTMA Supplementband 3, 1 (1935), pp. 262-81; L. Nicolau d'Olwer, 'Sur la date de la Dialectica d'Abélard', *Revue du moyen âge latin* 1 (1945), 375-90; D. Van den Eynde, 'La "Theologia Scholarium" de Pierre Abélard', *Recherches de théologie ancienne et médiévale (RTAM)* 28 (1961), 225-41; 'Les Rédactions de la "Theologia Christiana" de Pierre Abélard', *Antonianum* 36 (1961), 273-99; 'Le Recueil des sermons de Pierre Abélard', *ibid.* 37 (1962), 17-52; 'La Chronologie des écrits d'Abélard à Héloïse', *ibid.* 337-49; 'Les écrits perdus d'Abélard', *ibid.* 467-80; 'Détails biographiques sur Pierre Abélard', *ibid.* 38 (1963), 217-23; E. M. Buytaert, 'An Earlier Redaction of the "Theologia Christiana" of Abelard', *ibid.* 37 (1962), 481-95; 'Critical Observations on the "Theologia Christiana" of Abelard', *ibid.* 38 (1963), 384-433; 'Thomas of Morigny and the "Theologia Scholarium" of Peter Abelard', *ibid.* 40 (1965), 71-95; 'Thomas of Morigny and the "Apologia" of Abelard', *ibid.* 42 (1967), 25-54; 'Abelard's Collationes', *ibid.* 44 (1969), 18-39; Buytaert, CCCM 11, pp. xxii-xxv. See also C. J. Mews, 'The development of the *Theologia* of Peter Abelard', *P. Abaelardus*, Trier, pp. 183-98; 'Peter Abelard's *Theologia Christiana* and *Theologia 'Scholarium'* re-examined, *RTAM* 52 (1985) 109-58; 'The lists of heresies imputed to Peter Abelard', *Revue bénédictine* 95 (1985), 73-110; 'The *Sententie* of Peter Abelard', *RTAM* 53 (1986).

74

of the development of his thought and so provide a perspective which is not to be found in the *Historia Calamitatum*[2].

I. The *Dialectica* and related texts

The *Dialectica* is found in a single manuscript, Paris, Bibl. nat. lat. 14614, ff. 117-202 (s. xii), from which the introductory section is missing. Various dates have been put forward for this text: 1140-42 (Cousin); 1120-21 (Robert); 1133-37 (Geyer); begun before 1121, but completed after 1134 (Cottiaux); after 1135, but two earlier recensions, no longer extant, dating to before 1118 and 1121-23 respectively (Nicolau d'Olwer)[3]. Geyer thought that the *Dialectica* contained the most mature formulation of Abelard's logic; Beonio-Brocchieri, on the other hand, has judged some of its passages to have been written before Abelard's other major work of logic, the glosses on Porphyry and Aristotle, edited by Geyer under the title *Logica 'Ingredientibus'*[4]. If the Paris manuscript contains a recension produced in the mid- or late 1130's, as Geyer and Nicolau d'Olwer have claimed, then not only did Abelard fail to revise certain 'out-dated' passages, but he showed very limited knowledge of the new works of Aristotle being used in the teaching of logic as early as 1132[5]. A firm date for the *Dialectica* is essential for a correct understanding, not only of the evolution of his thought, but of the development of logic in this period as a whole.

The literal glosses and the Introductiones parvulorum.

One of the earliest known writings of Peter Abelard (possibly a text taken down from spoken commentary) is a set of short "literal" glosses

(2) The authenticity of the *Historia Calamitatum* was doubted by R. BENTON, 'Fraud, fiction and borrowing in the correspondence of Abelard and Héloïse', *P. le Vén.-P. Abélard*, p. 469-506, but largely re-affirmed in his later communication, 'A reconsideration of the authenticity of the correspondence of Abelard and Heloise', *P. Abaelardus, Trier*, pp. 41-52. Although Benton's earlier position is still supported by H. SILVESTRE, 'Pourquoi Roscelin n'est-il pas mentionné dans l'*Historia Calamitatum*', *RTAM* 48 (1981), 218-24 and in *Bull. TAM* 13 (1983), 420-23, no solid arguments have yet, in the author's opinion, been put forward to justify the hypothesis of a forgery. In consequence its authenticity is accepted.

(3) COUSIN, *Ouvrages inédits*, pp. XXXI-XXXVI; ROBERT, pp. 188-90; GEYER, pp. 606-9; COTTIAUX, 263-7; NICOLAU D'OLWER, *art. cit.* De RIJK supports the views of Nicolau d'Olwer, with some reservations, *Dialectica*, pp. XXII-XXIII.

(4) GEYER, p. 606: 'Ohne zweifel die reifste der uns bekannte, also auch zeitlich die letzte'. M. BEONIO-BROCCHIERI FUMAGALLI, *La Logica di Abelardo* (Florence, 1964, 1969²), pp. 9-11, 68-70, 76-99; this brings together 'Note sulla logica di Abelardo', *Rivista di filosofia neo-scolastica* 13 (1958), 12-26, 280-90; 14 (1959), 3-27; 15 (1960), 14-21; 18 (1963), 131-46, and is translated into English, *The Logic of Abelard* (Dordrecht, 1969).

(5) See below, p. 102-4.

on the *Isagoge* of Porphyry, the *Categories* and *Periermeneias* of Aristotle and the *De divisione* of Boethius. In the one manuscript in which they occur, Paris, Bibl. nat. lat. 13368, ff. 128-167v (s. xii), the glosses on Porphyry and Aristotle are each described as an *Editio*, perhaps in imitation of the commentaries of Boethius[6]. Because Abelard is more concerned to expose the literal meaning of the text than his own opinion on individual questions of logic, these glosses are believed to date to an early period of his career, between 1102 (when he first started teaching at Corbeil) and 1113-14 (date of his return to Notre-Dame)[7]. The brevity of his comment on the passage of the *Isagoge* about genus and species, which he used as a point of departure for his debate with William of Champeaux on the nature of universals, would suggest that this gloss was composed before the disputation, that is before 1108-9[8].

While Geyer expressed caution on the point, Dal Pra and de Rijk have assumed that these literal glosses are identical to the *Introductiones parvulorum* to which Abelard makes frequent reference within the *Dialectica*[9]. Most of the references are to discussions of forms of argument and cannot be matched to identifiable passages in the literal glosses. John of Salisbury quotes a comment of Abelard about the popularity of such *Introductiones*, designed for popular instruction, from which it is clear that these were independent treatises and not commentaries on the ancients[10]. It is thus unlikely that the *Introductiones parvulorum* were glosses. The veracity of John of Salisbury's report is testified by a number of such *Introductiones* which survive in manuscript, including one probably by William of Champeaux[11]. This latter work might have provided a model for Abelard to emulate.

(6) There is no title to the gloss on the *Categories* (of which the beginning and end is missing), but one can assume it would have been titled *Editio* by analogy with the accompanying glosses on the *Isagoge* and *Periermeneias*. That the gloss on Boethius is titled *De divisionibus* in the MS, not *Editio*, may be a deliberate choice, reflecting a desire not to place Boethius on the same level as the other authors. The gloss on the *De differentiis topicis* (not part of the literal glosses), is simply titled *super Thopica glose* (see below n. 14).

(7) DAL PRA, *Scritti di logica*, pp. xv-xvi.

(8) *Ed. sup. Por.* 5-6; cf. *Hist. Cal.* 70-100. On the chronology of Abelard's early career, see R.-H. BAUTIER, *Abélard en son temps*, p. 54 (21-77).

(9) GEYER, p. 609; DAL PRA, p. xvii (preferring the title *Introductiones dialecticae*); de RIJK, p. xi n. 1. The *Introductiones* are mentioned in *D.* III, 269, 329, 352; IV, 482 (no parallels to literal glosses). De Rijk relates *D.* II, 174 to *Ed. sup. Per.* 113-124 and *D.* II, 232 to both *sup. Top.* 320 and 329, although *sup. Top.* is not part of the literal gloss, as Dal Pra shows, pp. xxxi-xxxv. Abelard describes only the gloss on Porphyry as an *Introductio ad Categorias, Ed. sup. Por.* 4, never the glosses as a whole.

(10) *Metalogicon* III, 4, ed. C. C. J. WEBB (Oxford, 1929), p. 136-7. The *liber fantasiarum* (*D.* III, 448, 3-4) may have been another independent treatise written before the *Dialectica*.

(11) De RIJK, *Logica Modernorum. An Introduction to the History of Early Terminist Logic* 2 vols. (Assen, 1962, 1967), 2, 1, pp. 167-70; the *Introductiones dialectice secundum Wilgelmum* are partially edited on pp. 130-39.

76

The "Logica".

Much more developed than the literal glosses are the *Glosse super Porphyrium, super Predicamenta* and *super Periermeneias Aristotelis,* found in the Milan MS, Bibl. Ambrosiana M 63 sup., ff. 1-72 (s. xii), known as the *Logica "Ingredientibus"*. The gloss on the *Periermeneias* is incomplete in this manuscript, but exists *in toto* in the Berlin MS, Preussischer Kulturbesitz, lat. fol. 624, ff. 97-146 (s. xii)[12]. A revised form of the *Glosse* on Porphyry, entitled *Glossule super Porphyrium,* occurs in the Lunel MS, Bibl. mun. 6 (s. xiii), a work which Geyer thought was the beginning of another recension of the same *Logica*, which he distinguished by its incipit, *Nostrorum petitioni sociorum.* Geyer's hypothesis was that the *Dialectica* of the Paris MS represented a third recension of this same *Logica*, later than the other two because it supposedly contained the fullest formulation of Abelard's logic, in the form of an independent treatise rather than of a commentary[13]. The late date which he attributed to the *Dialectica* (1133-37) served to justify his argument.

Also to be associated with the glosses on Porphyry and Aristotle in the Milan MS are the glosses on the *De differentiis topicis (super Topica Glosse),* found in the Paris MS, Bibl. nat. lat. 7493, ff. 168-84 (s. xii). Like these other glosses, those on Boethius are characterised by long digressions on individual aspects of logic. Dal Pra has convincingly demonstrated that this text is not to be grouped with the literal glosses as had been thought, but had to have been written after the *Glosse super Periermeneias*[14].

What is the evidence for the argument that the four glosses on Porphyry, Aristotle and Boethius form part of a single *Logica*? Nowhere in their text is there any mention of such a *Logica* or *Dialectica* of which they formed a part. Geyer's hypothesis of an organic unity to the *Logica* is based on the fact that in each gloss Abelard refers to other glosses in either the past or future tense[15]. We can conclude from these references that Abelard composed his *Glosse* on the *Isagoge,* the *Predicamenta* and

---

(12) The last section of the gloss on the *Periermeneias* in the Milan MS (ed. GEYER, 497-503), does not occur in the Berlin MS; MINIO-PALUELLO thinks that this small tract on modal propositions is not by Abelard, *Twelfth Century Logic II*, pp. xvi-xxi.

(13) GEYER, p. viii (writing in 1919), and pp. 597-8, 606-7.

(14) DAL PRA, pp. xxxi-xxxix. A fragment of this gloss occurs in the Paris MS, Arsenal 910, ff. 120 vb-121 rb (s. xii), identified by N. J. GREEN-PEDERSEN, 'The doctrine of the "maxima propositio" and "locus differentiae" in commentaries from the twelfth century on Boethius' Topics', *Studia Mediewisticyzne* 18 (1977), 127-8 (125-63).

(15) Abelard refers to *sup. Pred.* in *sup. Por.* 36, 86, 87, 96; he refers to *sup. Per.* in *sup. Por.* 27 and (in the past tense), *sup. Top.* 226; he refers back to *sup. Por.* in *sup. Pred.* 141, 174, and *sup. Per.* 316, 368; he promises a study *in hypotheticis* in *sup. Pred.* 291, *sup. Per.* 389 and *sup. Top.* 325, but it is not known if this was ever written; he promises *sup. Top.* in *sup. Per.* 327.

De differentiis topicis in that order, but not necessarily that they all formed part of a single work. While the Lunel *Glossule* certainly contain a revision of the *Glosse* on Porphyry, they contain no promise of any further discussion of Aristotle or Boethius. As no manuscript survives containing any such revised glosses corresponding to the revision of Porphyry, it seems more prudent to speak only in terms of those glosses which survive, rather than of this hypothetical *"Logica"*.

The glosses on Porphyry.

Besides observing that the *Glossule (L)* were a revised form of the *Glosse* on Porphyry (*A*[1]) at the beginning of the Milan MS, Geyer also noticed that the anonymous *Glosse super Porphyrium Secundum vocales* (*A*[2]), found on ff. 72v-81v of the same Milan MS contained a text closely related to both *A*[1] and *L*[16]. Although he used *A*[2] to correct the readings of *L*, he argued that *A*[2] was the compilation of a pupil, drawing from certain lost glosses of Abelard, transitional between *A*[1] and *L*, as well as from both *A*[1] and *L*. Its discussion of identity and difference is virtually identical to that of the *Theologia 'Summi boni'*, though transitional between those of the other two glosses on Porphyry[17]. It makes more sense to interpret the *Glosse secundum vocales* as another revision of glosses on Porphyry composed by Abelard himself, a revision of *A*[1], in turn revised further in *L*. Like both other glosses, *A*[2] is not free from errors of transcription, perhaps the result of being taken down from dictation, but this does not mean that it should be treated as the composition of a pupil rather than of Abelard.

Geyer dated the three *Glosse* (his *Logica "Ingredientibus"*) to before 1120 and the *Glossule* to 1122-25[18]. He argued that in the *Glossule* Abelard redefined a universal as a *sermo* rather than as a *vox* in order to distinguish his own position more clearly from that of Roscelin, with whom he was engaged in controversy at the time of writing *TSum*. By comparing the discussions of identity and difference in *TSum* and the *Glossule*, he concluded that the latter had to have been written after *TSum*, but before the *Theologia 'Scholarium'*[19].

In arriving at the sequence *Editio-Glosse-TSum-Glossule* Geyer seems to be correct. While Abelard outlines his theme in the *Editio* on Porphyry that all modes of difference were *voces* and did not refer to things, he still preserves Porphyry's classification of difference into that

---

(16) Discussed by GEYER, pp. 610-12. For the editions, see the list of abbreviations (*Gl. sec. voc.*) at the end of this article.

(17) MEWS, 'A neglected gloss on the "Isagoge" by Peter Abelard', *Freiburger Zeitschrift für Philosophie und Theologie* 31 (1984), 35-55.

(18) GEYER, pp. 599-600.

(19) GEYER, pp. 602-3.

which was *communis, propria* and *magis propria*[20]. He mentions these latter modes of difference in passing in the *Glosse*, but suggests that all modes of difference fell under the category of common difference[21]. The Porphyrian classification is completely passed over in the *Glosse secundum vocales*, in which Abelard suggests that there are as many modes of difference as of identity, namely: by essence (equated with identity by predication), number, definition, similitude, incommutability and effect[22]. Because this classification is reproduced and expanded upon in *TSum*, the *Gl. sec. voc.* would most likely have been produced either shortly before or perhaps not long after *TSum*. As Geyer noted, Abelard explicitly repudiates in the *Glossule* the statement made in the *Gl. sec. voc.* that identity of essence was the same as that by predication, so the *Glossule* must be the later work. A major new element in his argument in *TChr* is that the three persons could not be predicated of each other[23]. One can also observe that the list of possible modes of difference in the *Glossule* is closer to that of *TSum* than to that of *TChr*, in which the mode of effect (mentioned in both *TSum* and the *Glossule*) is omitted in *TChr*[24]. As the earliest recension of the *Theologia Christiana* must have been written by 1125-26, the *Glossule* on Porphyry would most likely have been composed before this date, but after 1120-21 — a conclusion which Geyer arrived at, although based on a faulty dating of the *Theologia 'Scholarium'*.

The Dialectica and the Theologia 'Summi boni'.

The five treatises which make up the *Dialectica* were conceived from the outset as parts of a whole. Abelard states his intention to cover the subject matter of all seven texts of the old logic *(Isagoge, Categories, Periermeneias, De differentiis topicis, De syllogismo categorico, De syllogismo hypothetico* and *De divisione)* in the prologue to the second treatise[25]. The frequent cross-references within the *Dialectica* to other parts of the work leave no doubt that it was conceived as a whole[26]. Abelard dedicated the *Dialectica* to his brother Dagobert, at whose suggestion the work was

(20) *Ed. sup. Por.* 23-25.

(21) *sup. Por.* 65-69.

(22) *Gl. sec. voc.* (ed. GEYER, 588; ed. OTTAVIANO, p. 178); cf. *TSum* II, 81-102 (ed. OSTLENDER, pp. 54-61).

(23) *Glossule* 558, 17-21; cf. GEYER, p. 601.

(24) *TChr* III, 172-3, 176, 186; IV, 39-5.

(25) D. II, 145-146.

(26) De RIJK (p. XXII) thought that the fifth treatise *(De divisione)* might have been added to the *Dialectica* only later, because of the statement in D. IV, 498, 20: *in syllogismis vero disiunctarum operis nostri laborem finiemus.* This might, however, only refer to the fourth treatise. Abelard states his intention to deal with the subject matter of the fifth treatise in D. II, 146, 16 and III, 447, 7.

written[27]. The question remains of what chronological relationship the *Dialectica* has to the sequence of texts already proposed: *Ed. sup. Por.*; *Glosse sup. Por.*; *Gl. sec. voc.* / *TSum.*; *Glossule*; *TChr.*

Abelard refers in the *Theologia 'Summi boni'* to a *Dialectica* which he had already written:

Sunt et alie consimilis dispositionis argumentationes, quibus propter terminorum dispositionem premissa regula <*scil.* quotiens aliquid predicatur de aliquo, quicquid predicatur de illo predicato et de subiecto > competere videtur, cum a sensu verborum longe sit. Quales sunt huiusmodi complexiones : hic homo est hoc corpus ; sed hoc corpus est semper ; ergo hic homo est semper. ... Item, hic miles est hic citharedus, et hic citharedus bonus est vel laudandus ; ergo hic miles, Sed de hic in *Dialectica* nostra latius prosecuti sumus[28].

Is this *Dialectica* the same work as found in the Paris MS? Geyer thought that the reference in *TSum* was too vague for such a conclusion to be drawn[29]. Yet Abelard is clearly referring to a work of logic. Does it survive?

Abelard mentions this *Dialectica* at the end of a long series of answers to various objections which could be made against the logic asserting that God could be three persons; he then follows with a different discussion of relationships within the Trinity[30]. Throughout the preceding section of *TSum* III Abelard had emphasised that identity of essence had to be distinguished from identity of property or definition and that Aristotle's rule about predication of a subject as of a predicate only applied in the former kind of identity. In the paragraph quoted above, Abelard was referring to an important theme of the *Dialectica*, that errors of reasoning often arose from a false recognition of the meaning of a combination of terms. The example of *citharedus bonus* (taken from the *Periermeneias*) as a single name, in which *good* did not refer to an inherent goodness, but to being a good harp-player, was used a number of times in the *Dialectica* to illustrate this theme[31]. Attentive study of the *Dialectica*, particularly of the first two treatises, illuminates Abelard's argument in the third book of *TSum*. The reference could thus be to the work in the Paris MS, but further evidence is needed to be more certain.

(27) Dagobert is mentioned in *D.* II, 146 and III, 447.

(28) *TSum* III, 43 (pp. 83-84); *TChr* IV, 59.

(29) Geyer, p. 617.

(30) *TSum* III, 1-43 (pp. 42-47) answers the objections posed in *TSum* II, 43-63 (pp. 42-47) ; III, 44-86 (pp. 84-102) answers those in II, 62 (pp. 46-47).

(31) *D.* I, 115-117 ; II, 166-167, 170-171, 224-226, 249.

Signification and the meaning of a vox.

Comparison of Abelard's discussion of signification in the *Dialectica* with that in his glosses on the *Isagoge* and the *Periermeneias* is instructive. According to the *Glosse sup. Por. ('Ingredientibus')* and the *Gl. sec. voc.* a *vox* was both a natural sound and a vehicle capable of signification. In the *Glossule*, however, Abelard insisted on avoiding this ambiguity by defining a *vox* as a sound of natural origin, inherently devoid of meaning, reserving the word *sermo* to mean a word of human institution and a carrier of meaning[32]. If otherwise identical passages in the *Gl. sec. voc.* and *Glossule* are compared, it is evident that Abelard deliberately substituted *sermo* for *vox* when revising his gloss on the *Isagoge* in order to make his meaning clearer and avoid the ambiguity implicit in the term *vox*[33].

A single sentence, which begins in the same way in the *Gl. sec. voc.* and *Glossule* (not found in *TChr*) illustrates this change of terminology[34]:

Idem secundum effectum vel secundum pretium sunt, que idem valent ad efficiendum aliquid,

[*Gl. sec. voc.*] sicut sunt voces eiusdem intellectus.

[*TSum*] sicut easdem dicimus voces que idem valent ad eundem intellectum manifestandum.

[*Glossule*] sicut eosdem sermones dicimus, qui ad efficiendum eundem intellectum < idem > valent.

Abelard's concern to refine his terminology is also evident from the changes which he made in *TChr* (given in italics) to a passage of *TSum*:

Sed cum Aristotiles vester dicit in I *Periermeneias*[35] voces < *sermones sicut* > et litteras non easdem < *eosdem* > omnibus esse, sed diversas < *diversos* > diversis, secundum officium significandi id dixit < add. *quod est sermonum et litterarum* >, non secundum < add. *ipsam vocum* > prolationem, quia cum sit prolatio vocum naturalis omnibus, significandi officium apud omnes non tenetur, sed apud eos solummodo qui earum impositionem non ignorant. Qui etiam postmodum cum in II *Periermeneias*[36]

---

(32) *Glossule* 522, 18-21 : *Hoc enim quod est nomen sive sermo, ex hominum institutione contrahit. Vocis vero sive rei nativitas quid aliud est quam nature creatio, cum proprium esse rei sive vocis sola operatione consistat?*

(33) MEWS, 'A neglected gloss', 43-45. Among the fragments edited by Geyer one can compare *Gl. sec. voc.* 586, 11 and 588, 31 with *Glossule* 508, 33 and 560, 7 *(vox* to *sermo)*; cf. *Gl. sec. voc.*, ed. OTTAVIANO, p. 179 with *Glossule* 560, 21-32 *(vox* to *vocabulum)*. Although he states *voces sunt emule rerum* in the *Glossule* 537, 5-9, when glossing the phrase of Boethius *in voce predicatur*, he then adds *Ut enim primo loco substituitur substantia accidentibus, sic nomen significans substantiam ... ponitur.*

(34) *Gl. sec. voc.*, ed. GEYER, 588, 30-32; *TSum* II, 88 (p. 57, 1-4); *Glossule* 560, 6-8.

(35) *Periermeneias* I, 16a, *transl. Boethii,* ed. MINIO-PALUELLO, *Aristoteles Latinus* II, 1-2 (Bruges-Paris, 1965), p. 5.

(36) *Ibid.* I, 18a, *ed. cit.*, II, p. 13.

ait vocem esse unam et affirmationes multas, aut cum Priscianus[37] dixit multa nomina incidere in unam vocem, ' multa ' seu ' diversa ' accipiuntur secundum hoc quod diversos intellectus efficere valent < hoc quod... valent : *ipsum significandi officium ad diversos intellectus constituendos unde affirmationes vel nomina dicuntur. Vocem vero unam dixit ex ipsa prolationis et soni forma, non ex officio, cum videlicet ' vox ' hoc nomen ex qualitate soni, non ex officio significandi datum sit*>[38].

In both *TSum* and *TChr* Abelard is addressing Roscelin directly and challenges his argument about the variety of names which might be applied to God. According to Roscelin, this variety was one of usage and not of meaning, while Abelard emphasised that Aristotle's comment about a plurality of terms concerned their capacity to signify. By modifying the Boethian translation of an important phrase in the *Periermeneias* *(nec litterae omnibus eaedem, nec eaedem voces)* to use *sermo* rather than *vox*, he indicated his frustration with the terminology of existing debate, so much conditioned by the language of Boethius. He also added in *TChr* a comment that a *vox* was so named after its physical rather than significative aspect, as in the *Glossule*.

What is the position which Abelard adopts in the *Dialectica*? In every discussion of *vox* in this work he retains the idea that it was both a physical entity and capable of signification, never making any special distinction between *vox* and *sermo*. This is evident from his discussion of signification in the first treatise:

> Est autem significare non solum vocum, sed etiam rerum. ... Nunc etiam per signa aliquid innuimus et he quidem rerum proprie significare dicuntur que ad hoc institute sunt, sicut et voces, ut significandi officium teneant, quemadmodum supraposite. ... Alii enim omnia quibus vox imposita est, ab ipsa voce significari volunt, alii vero ea sola que in voce denotantur atque in sententia ipsius tenentur. Illis quidem magister noster V. favet, his vero Garmundus consensisse videtur ; illi qui< dem > auctoritate, his vero fulti sunt ratione. Quibus enim Garmundus annuit rationabiliter ea sola que in sententia vocis tenentur < significari, sustinentur > iusta definitione ' significandi ', que est intellectum generare. ... Liquet autem ex suprapositis significativarum vocum alias naturaliter, alias ad placitum significare. ... Naturales quidem voces, quas non humana inventio imposuit, sed sola natura contulit, naturaliter < et non > ex impositione significativas dicimus, ut ea quam latrando canis emittit, ex qua ipsius iram concipimus[39].

(37) *Institutiones grammaticae* II, 5, ed. KEIL, *Grammatici Latini* 2-3 (Leipzig, 1855, 1859), I, pp. 74-75.

(38) *TSum* II, 102 (p. 61), modified in *TChr* III, 162.

(39) *D.* I, 111, 13, 18-21; 112, 24-31; 114, 16-18, 20-23. On the identity of *magister noster V.*, see below, n. 54.

Abelard assumes a similar ambiguity in his discussion of the different meanings of *vox* in the fifth treatise of the *Dialectica*[40]. He also comments in passing that *vox* took its name from *vocando, id est significando*, a complete contrast to the etymology proposed in *TChr* in the passage quoted above[41]. Given the care which Abelard took to replace *vox* with *sermo* in the *Glossule* and *TChr*, it seems hard to believe that he should have reverted to an earlier position in the *Dialectica* or have neglected to revise his discussion. The *Dialectica*, as found in the Paris MS must have been written before the *Glossule*, but was it written before or after his glosses on Aristotle?

There are some important differences between the ideas expressed in the *Dialectica* and in the *Glosse sup. Per.*, as the following passage reveals:

Nam latratus natura artifex, id est Deus, ea intentione cani contulit, ut iram eius representaret ; et voluntas hominum nomina et verba ad significandum instituit nec non etiam res quasdam, ut circulum vel signa quibus monachi utuntur. Non enim significare vocum tantum, verum etiam rerum. ... Similiter unaqueque vox... non ideo significativa dicenda est, quia per nullam institutionem hoc habet... Significativum vero magis ad causam quam ad actum significandi pertinet, ut sicut non omnia significativa actualiter significant, ita non omnia actu significantia sint significativa, sed ea sola que ad significandum sunt instituta. ... Sicut enim ' rident ' per adiunctionem ' prata ' mittit ad florere, cum dicitur ' prata rident ', sed non ita cum dicitur ' homo ridet ', ita cum dicitur ' homo est vox vel nomen ' per adiunctionem predicatorum significantium voces tantum mittit ' homo ', hec vox, ad se ipsam, sed quia translatio huiusmodi nullius est proprietatis... non est inde hoc nomen ' homo ' significativum iudicandum, quia hoc per accidens habet, non ex propria accomodatione[42].

Whereas in the *Dialectica* Abelard acknowledges that *voces* signify as well as things, in the gloss he asserts that *voces* in themselves do not have any meaning, unless they were instituted for this purpose. His terminology is more careful: the barking of a dog represents the anger of a dog, while nouns and verbs signify through the imposition of a human will. Although he acknowledges that barking does signify through nature, he comments that not all *significantia* were in fact *significativa*, a notion which applied to the purpose rather to than the act of signification. Absent from the *Dialectica* is the discussion of the meaning of 'man' when used

(40) *D.* V, 562, 8-574, 10. This point is made by Beonio-Brocchieri, *La Logica*, pp. 49-60 and J. Jolivet, *Arts du langage et théologie chez Abélard* (Paris 1969), pp. 26-27.

(41) *D.* I, 128, 4.

(42) *sup. Per.* 335, 32-36; 336, 3-5, 9-12, 20-26. I am grateful to K. Jacobi for permission to consult the critical edition which he is preparing.

to mean that word. Abelard insisted in the gloss that such a *vox* signified only through a process of *translatio*, not through any intrinsic property of the word. This concept of transference of meaning, not discussed in the *Dialectica*, has an important place in the glosses on the *Categories* and *Periermeneias* as well in every version of the *Theologia*[43].

The position which Abelard adopts in the *Dialectica* is in fact closer, in some respects, to that which he follows in the *editio* on Porphyry. Here he is even more faithful to the language of Boethius in stating that every *vox* is significative because it generates an intellection in the mind of the person who hears it[44]. Abelard questions this view in the gloss on the *Periermeneias* and abandons it in the *Glossule*. When discussing the nature of an *oratio* in the gloss, he opposes the opinion of certain Platonists that all *voces significativas ad placitum* signified naturally as the intellect was an instrument of nature, on the grounds that all signification was the result of human imposition[45]. In the gloss on the *De differentiis topicis* he is even more insistent that a *vox* did not signify unless a listener could grasp the sense of its imposition. Although written after the gloss on the *Periermeneias* this commentary on the topics must be earlier than the *Glossule* as he still defines a universal as a *vox* rather than as a *sermo*[46].

The meaning of words and statements.

A related shift of emphasis can be seen in Abelard's discussion of a number of different aspects of language, such as of *dictiones indefinite*. In the *Dialectica* he asserts that conjunctions and prepositions had to have a meaning in themselves if they were to be distinguished from letters and syllables, although their significance was uncertain. Abelard describes this position in the gloss as one currently held, but refuses to accept it, arguing instead that indefinite words had no intrinsic meaning except within the context of a phrase[47]. While in the *Dialectica* Abelard

(43) *sup. Pred.* 121, 3-37; *sup. Per.* 336, 15-27; 350, 7; 364, 33; *TSum* I, 5, 19 (pp. 4, 7); II, 70-78 (pp. 50-53); III, 36, 62-64 (pp. 81, 90-92). Cf. *TChr* I, 7, 16, 23, 37, 124-125; III, 134; IV, 44-46.

(44) *Ed. sup. Per.* 76, 12-19.

(45) *sup. Per.* 363, 30-34; 372, 1-27.

(46) *sup. Top.* 294, 24; 305, 1; cf. 27, 1-2: *quia solas voces universales, id est de multis predicabiles concedimus esse.* This contradicts *Glossule* 523, 5-8: *Vox vero illud non habet ... predicabilitatem de pluribus, sed est illud quod predicatur, quia est sermo predicabilis.* Jolivet suggests that the gloss on the *Periermeneias* might have been written after the *Glossule* because it includes mention of the *Sophistici Elenchi*, not mentioned in the gloss on Porphyry (see below, p. 103, n. 43) and that *sermo* might not be used in *sup. Per.* because it concerned propositions rather than universals. The care with which Abelard changed *vox* to *sermo* or *vocabulum* in the *Glossule* and *TChr*, however (see above, nn. 33, 38), suggests that Abelard would not have gone back to an earlier position in *sup. Per.* or *sup. Top.* Cf. 'Abélard et Ockham, lecteurs de Porphyre', *Abélard*, *Neuchâtel*, p. 33.

(47) *D.* I, 118-120; 120, 5: *quasdam proprietates circa res eorum vocabulorum quibus apponuntur prepositiones, quodammodo determinent.* Cf. I. DAMBSKA, 'La sémiotique

agrees with a grammatical explanation *(ut grammaticis consentientes qui etiam logice deserviunt)*, he emphasises much more the psychological function of indefinite words in the gloss, and formulates as a criterion of meaning that a word must form an intellection *(intellectus)* in the mind[48].

There is a similar contrast in his discussions of a phrase. Abelard follows Priscian in the *Dialectica* in distinguishing the complete or perfect sense of a complete construction *(homo currit)* and the incomplete sense of one grammatically unfinished *(homo currens)*. In the gloss he asserts that both phrases have an identical meaning because one creates the same intellection as the other *(idem penitus significant... per se etiam dicta eandem conceptionem facit)*[49]. Although commenting in the *Dialectica* that the same phrase might be used according to different states of mind, he does not mention the idea formulated in the gloss that different types of phrase could form the same intellection[50].

One difference which has often been noted between the *Dialectica* and the gloss lies in the analysis of the substantive verb. In both works Abelard places his discussion of the copula within criticism of those who, following Priscian, asserted that every verb principally signified an action or experience *(actionem vel passionem)*[51]. He could not accept their claim that there was no difference between nuncupative and substantive verbs *(ego nuncupor Petrus* and *ego sum Petrus)*[52]. Abelard's argument in the *Dialectica* is that in 'I am Peter' the copula linked the essences of things, *quaslibet rerum essentias eque secundum inherentiam copulare potest*. This was an inherent ambiguity within what he admitted was inappropriately defined by Priscian as a substantive verb[53].

The problem which Abelard admitted with this explanation was how to explain figurative statements like 'Homer is a poet'. He places his discussion in the *Dialectica* within the context of commentary on the position held by his teacher *(magister noster)* that accidental predication came about, not through the verb, but through the figurative and non-literal expression as a whole. Similar criticism of the idea (attributed to William of Champeaux) that two different senses could co-exist in a proposition, one grammatical, the other dialectical, is voiced in Abelard's gloss on the topics[54]. He comments in the *Dialectica* that he used to defend

des "Dictiones Indefinite" dans la Dialectique d'Abélard', *Cahiers de l'Institut du moyen âge grec et latin* 21 (1977), 10-22.

   (48) *sup. Per.* 337-340.
   (49) *D.* II, 148, 17-149, 19; *sup. Per.* 373, 1-33.
   (50) *D.* II, 152, 17-26; *sup. Per.* 373, 21-30.
   (51) *D.* I, 130, 1-12; 132, 38-133, 28; cf. *sup. Per.* 346, 1-24.
   (52) *D.* I, 133, 29-134, 27; *sup. Per.* 360, 3-18.
   (53) *D.* I, 131, 6-7; 133, 14-15.
   (54) *D.* I, 135, 28-136, 36; *magister noster* is clearly the same teacher as *magister noster V.* in *D.* II, 168, 11-169, 28. De Rijk (pp. xx-xxi) argues that the former is

the position of his teacher by arguing that 'Homer' and 'poet' both designated Homer without respect to his existence and that the construction of the phrase was improper in so far as its meaning came from the phrase as a whole rather than from individual words[55]. As if to insist that he was no longer subservient to the opinion of his teacher, Abelard then tentatively advanced the hypothesis that 'is a poet' should be taken as equivalent to a single verb *(pro uno verbo)* and thus a single predicate[56]. This meant that *est opinabile* could legitimately be predicated of a *chimera* without invoking its existence. A figurative expression was not improper, but presented a new ambiguity of *vox (nova vocis equivocatio)*[57].

The position which Abelard adopts in the gloss on the *Periermeneias* is different from that in the *Dialectica*, but is it more or less developed? In the latter work he arrives at his conclusion that the copula and predicate should be considered as equivalent to one word *(pro uno verbo)* only at the end of his discussion of the substantive verb. He presents a similar, though subtly modified solution at the beginning of the equivalent section in the gloss as if it has already been worked out: namely that any verb could also have the sense of a noun (differing only in its signification of time) and that the meaning of a substantive verb, when joined to another word, lay in the force of that combination as a single verb or word *(in vi unius verbi vel dictionis)*[58]. While retaining the idea of the *Dialectica* that a copula had significance, not in itself, but as part of a single predicate, Abelard included in the gloss a new element, not found in that work — that the sense of such a predicate, involving a copulative verb, lay in its having the force of a single word[59].

William of Champeaux, the latter Ulger, a teacher whom Abelard never mentions in the *Historia Calamitatum*. Following Prantl, *Geschichte der Logik im Abendlande* II(Leipzig, 1861), p. 124 n. 83, he argues that the argument attributed to *magister noster V.* in *D.* I, 112, 25-29 is inconsistent with that of William. But, as Jolivet points out (*Arts du langage*, p. 66 n. 22), there are 'realist' aspects to this argument that a *vox* could have multiple meanings, similar to that attributed to *magister noster W.* in *D.* V, 541, 32. His argument about figurative expressions is also similar to that attributed to *preceptor Willelmus (sup. Top.* 279, 39) — that there were two senses to a proposition, grammatical and dialectical. Ulger, first known to teach in Angers in 1107, died 16 Oct. 1149. Is it likely Abelard could have been so influenced by a teacher of his own generation? No initial is given to *magister noster* in *D.* I, 57, 59, 60, 64, 67, 82, 116; II, 195, while *V.* is added in I, 105, 123, 141. Could *V.* not be a misreading of an original *W.*, copied correctly only once, in *D.* V, 541?

(55) *D.* I, 136, 19-26 and II, 169, 4-24.
(56) *D.* I, 138, 11-17.
(57) *D.* I, 136, 17-18.
(58) *sup. Per.* 346-350. N. Kretzmann comments in a footnote that this passage might have implications for the chronology of Abelard's writings, but still maintains that the position of the *Dialectica* is more advanced than that of the gloss, 'The culmination of the Old Logic in Peter Abelard', *Renaissance and Renewal in the Twelfth Century*, ed. R. L. BENSON & G. CONSTABLE (Oxford, 1982), p. 509 n. 62 (488-511).
(59) *sup. Per.* 349, 1; 360, 23-27 etc.

His explanation in the *Dialectica* that a copula linked the essences of things posed the inevitable problem of how to explain its function in the case of a non-existent subject, a problem which he had inherited from his earlier defence of the argument of his teacher, William of Champeaux. This problem did not arise in the gloss on the *Periermeneias* because here he transferred his attention to what was intended to be predicated of a subject. In the case of 'Socrates is white', although both whiteness and 'a white thing' were joined, only whiteness was predicated, because this was what was intended to be joined:

> Duo itaque coniunguntur Socrati per album predicatum, albedo scilicet in adiacentia et album, id est ipsum affectum albedine, in essentia; sola tamen albedo predicatur, quia sola coniungi intenditur. Non enim quicquid coniungitur predicatur, sed id solum quod propositione coniungi intenditur[60].

This is not the 'inherence theory' of predication criticised in the *Dialectica*, but a further advance on the position of the latter work[61].

The one passage which Geyer cited as evidence that the argument of the *Dialectica* was 'more developed' than that of the gloss, occurred in its discussion of figurative statements:

> Similiter cum dicitur 'Homerus est poeta' figurative in sensu 'poema Homeri exsistit', 'poeta' quodammodo ad significationem poematis habet se, quia poetas vocamus ex poematibus que significant... Itaque 'est' verbum, gratia poeta quod ei supponitur, veram predicationem per figuram reddit. ... Possumus tamen hic et per 'Homerus' resolvendum in genetivum eum qui mortuus est, per translationem vel equivocationem significare et per poema dictamen, quippe hic est sensus 'poema ipsius exsistit', magis tamen tota significativa oratio, quasi ad unum sensum totaliter sit instituta, pensanda est, quam ut partes aliquid significent, de quo in oratione supra tractavimus[62].

Geyer thought that this was the position which Abelard says in the *Dialectica* that he used to hold in defence of the opinions of William of Champeaux, namely that in figurative constructions there was a sense of the phrase which was quite different from the significance of its individual parts[63]. While this argument finds some echo in the *Editio* on the *Perier-*

---

(60) *sup. Per.* 360, 23-27.

(61) De Rijk described the doctrine of the gloss as the 'inherence theory' in contrast to the 'identity theory' of the *Dialectica*, in the introduction to his edition (p. xxxviii), but retracted this view in 'Die Wirkung der neuplatonischen Semantik auf das mittelalterliche Denken über das Sein', *Sprache und Erkenntnis im Mittelalter. Akten des VI Internationalen Kongress für Mittelalterliche Philosophie. 29 August.-3 September, 1977 in Bonn, Miscellenea Medievalia* 13 (Berlin, 1981), p. 31 (19-35).

(62) *sup. Per.* 480, 22-25, 28-29, 32-37; cf. *Geyer*, p. 606.

(63) See above, n. 55.

meneias, it is not that put forward in the gloss either in the passage quoted above or in the discussion *in oratione* to which he refers[64]. His position in the latter is that in a figurative construction there was a transference *(translatio)* of meaning from one end to another. This notion of *translatio*, not found in the *Dialectica*, is discussed in the gloss on the *Categories* and developed further in that on the *Periermeneias* and in *TSum*[65]. For example in 'this corpse was a man' there was no contradiction between the terms because the predicate in this case had changed its meaning through conjunction with the copula[66]. Whereas in the *Dialectica* Abelard had only described this as *equivocatio*, in the gloss he introduces the idea of transference in order to emphasise that ambiguity was not an inherent quality of language, but stemmed from the use to which it was put.

The change is consistent with his desire in the gloss to emphasise that a word does not have multiple meaning in itself. While *est* had the force of a conjunction it did not have an inherent significative function[67]. He did not talk about copulating the essences of things, as he had in the *Dialectica*, but distinguished between verbal connection and true predication. Similarly in defining the meaning of a proposition in the gloss he avoids any definition invoking essences or things. In the *Dialectica* he defined its meaning by analogy with the way in which things existed *(quasi quidam rerum modus habendi se)* and used phrases like *essentias rerum* and *existentias rerum* to denote what was signified[68]. Abelard carried his argument much further in the gloss on the *Periermeneias*, by insisting that its meaning was no manner of essence and by introducing the concept of the *dictum propositionis* — what was said by a proposition[69]. This use of *dictum* does not occur either in the *Editio* on the *Periermeneias* or in the relevant section of the *Dialectica*.

Abelard's analysis of the *maxima propositio* in the gloss on the *De differentiis topicis* is an extension of his approach to the proposition in his

---

(64) *Ed. sup. Per.* 131, 27-133, 30; 132, 1-3: *Vere esse predicatur de Homero secundum accidens quia hoc modo, quoniam poete inest, id est coniungitur ei esse, a parte predicandi.* Cf. *sup. Per.* 364, 27-365, 3.

(65) See above, n. 43.

(66) *sup. Per.* 478, 29-479, 40. The concept of *translatio* is not mentioned in *D.* I, 63, 30 when the example of *homo mortuus* is given.

(67) *sup. Per.* 362, 32-33: *Unde interpositum tertium nil significationis in se tenet, quod intellectus copulet, sed tantum rem predicati supposuiti.*

(68) *D.* II, 160, 35; cf. II, 157, 14; 205, 25-27; III, 390, 11. On Abelard's doctrine of the proposition, see: BEONIO-BROCCHIERI, *La Logica*, pp. 64-70; JOLIVET, *Arts du langage*, pp. 78-85; de RIJK, 'La signification de la proposition (dictum propositionis), chez Abélard', *P. le Vén.-P. Abélard*, pp. 547-55; A. de LIBERA, 'Abélard et le dictisme', *Abélard, Neuchâtel*, pp. 59-92.

(69) *sup. Per.* 367, 12-13: *et dicta eorum, que sunt quasi res propositionis, cum tamen nulle penitus essentie sint.*

88

commentary on the *Periermeneias*. It is quite different from that given in the *Dialectica*, in which Abelard follows the view held by William of Champeaux — closer to that of Boethius — that the meaning of a maxim lay in the multitude of hypothetical consequences which it implied[70]. He insists quite firmly in the gloss on Boethius that a maxim had only a single meaning on the grounds that a maxim was formulated for the purpose of an argument and not for any of its multiple consequences. He justified this change of position by referring back to an argument already developed in an earlier discussion of hypothetical syllogisms (quite possibly to that of the *Dialectica*), that even in such a syllogism, the antecedent had always to be understood in any consequence[71]. The change of opinion, away from that held by William, is consistent with other changes which have been observed, away from the idea that any word or phrase contained a multiplicity of meanings in itself, focussing instead on the purpose for which any aspect of language was used. His argument about the *maxima propositio* continued that put forward in the gloss on the *Periermeneas*, that the plurality of *dicta* perhaps possible in a proposition did non stem *ex vi vocis*, but from the plurality of inter-pretations which might be made of a proposition[72].

The conclusion which we can draw from this study of Abelard's chang-ing views of signification is that the series of *Glosse* on Porphyry, Aristotle and Boethius *(Logica ' Ingredientibus ')*, present more developed ideas than those of the *Dialectica* and so are more likely to be an earlier rather than a later composition. The trend of Abelard's thought visible in his various glosses on the *Isagoge* is away from any argument that a *vox* signified in itself. His description of a universal as a *sermo* in the *Glossule* rather than as a *vox* as in the earlier glosses served to emphasise his theme that the capacity of a word to signify derived from the use to which it was put. In the gloss on the *Periermeneias*, Abelard had not yet intro-duced this *vox/sermo* distinction, but he had moved towards a greater emphasis on the meaning of language as dependent on the context within which it was used than he had formulated in the *Dialectica*, in which he still assumes that a *vox* has a significative function.

The clearest contrasts have been noted between the *Dialectica* and the glosses on the *Periermeneias* and *De differentiis topicis*. The gloss on the *Categories* would still be later than *Dialectica* as it introduces certain ideas, notably about *translatio*, developed in later writings, but not found in the *Dialectica*. It is harder to compare the latter text with the gloss on

---

(70) *D*. III, 309, 25-310, 19.

(71) *sup. Top*. 238, 35-239, 6. See GREEN-PEDERSEN, 'William of Champeaux on Boethius' Topics According to Orleans Bibl. mun. 266', *Cahiers de l'Institut* 13 (1974), 13-30 and 'The doctrine of the "maxima propositio"' (see above, n. 14).

(72) *sup. Per.*, ed. MINIO-PALUELLO, pp. 31, 30-32, 3.

Porphyry *(' Ingredientibus ')* because its opening section, which would
have covered similar subject matter, is missing from the manuscript.
However, because Abelard begins to develop some themes in this gloss
on the *Isagoge* and promises to explain them further in forthcoming
commentary on Aristotle, it would seem most likely also to have been
written after the *Dialectica*[73]. These glosses may themselves be a revision
of an earlier set of commentaries which have not survived, but of these
nothing can be said. There are some textual parallels between Abelard's
gloss and *Editio* on the *Categories* which suggest that this might be the
case, but in general the *Glosse* present a quite different, much more developed commentary[74].

The glosses and the Theologia ' Summi boni '.

It has already been seen that in *TSum* Abelard refers to his discussion
of the predication of composite names in the *Dialectica*, but what evidence
is there, if any, that he had also composed the glosses on Porphyry,
Aristotle and Boethius before his first treatise on the Trinity?

While his argument in the first part of book III is based on the difference
between predication of identity and of accident (for further discussion
of which he refers back to the *Dialectica*), he concludes his initial explanation of the generation of the Son from the Father by referring back to
an earlier exposition of how *voces* could be turned from meaning one thing
to meaning another, not through ambiguity, but through association
with other words:

> Sepe autem voces ex adiunctis a propria significatione evocantur
> ad aliam, sicut alias de translationibus tractantes ostendimus, et hic
> quoque pluribus confirmavimus exemplis quod nomen ex adiuncto
> significationem commutat[75].

Abelard had introduced this notion (not mentioned in the *Dialectica*), in
the gloss on the *Categories* in discussion of ambiguous words, in which
he gives two of the same examples as in the *Theologia ' Summi boni '*
(auriga navis, prata rident), but promises to discuss the subject more
fully in commentary on the *Periermeneias*[76]. In this subsequent gloss he
dwells at some length on all of the different kinds of *translatio* which he
mentions in *TSum*, including the change in meaning of verbs, adverbs
and prepositions when used in a different context[77]. The reference in

(73) See above, n. 15.
(74) DAL PRA, pp. XXIII-XXVI.
(75) *TSum* III, 62-63 (pp. 90-91).
(76) *sup. Pred.* 121, 3-37.
(77) *TSum* III, 63-64 (pp. 91-92); cf. *sup. Per.* 478, 20-479, 40; 336, 20-27; 338, 21-40;
327, 28-35 (following the sequence of examples in *TSum*).

90

TSum might equally apply either to the gloss on the *Perier-meneias* or to that on the *Categories*, while it cannot apply to the *Dialectica*. This concept of *translatio* or metaphor allowed Abelard to interpret phrases like 'God from God, light from light' in a way which did not conflict with his own understanding of the Father as God's omnipotence and the Son as his wisdom, as well as to interpret Platonic teaching about the mind of God as concordant with Christian doctrine[78].

Abelard also comments in *TSum* on the usefulness of dialectic to combat heretical opinions about providence and free will, but reserves discussion to elsewhere, *De libero autem arbitrio convenientius alibi disserendum nobis reservamus*, a statement repeated in identical form in *TChr*[79]. This subject is touched on in the *Dialectica*, but he devotes more attention to it in the gloss on the *Periermeneias*, in which he counters the same heresy as he mentions in *TSum*, that because all things were foreseen by God, they had to exist by necessity. He would also come back to this question in the *Theologia 'Scholarium'*[80]. It is not clear from the reference in *TSum* to what work Abelard is referring.

In his gloss on the *Periermeneias* Abelard demonstrates a greater familiarity with patristic argument (notably Augustine, Boethius and Gregory the Great) on providence and free will than in the *Dialectica*, or in his commentary on the *Isagoge* and *Categories*[81]. Of particular interest is a discussion, again not found in other logical writings, of how names were applied to God to denote different properties of an undivided essence:

> Nec ulle sunt proprietates quas in Deo intelligamus, dum eum providentes vel fatalem dicimus vel scientem vel intelligentem vel bene agentem, sed more humano loquentes simplicem eius essentiam et in se omnino invariabilem pro his que per eum invariabilem varie fieri contingunt et varie a nobis excogitantur, variis designamus nominibus, ut sapientia dicatur secundum hoc quod recte per eum omnia disposita, providentia secundum hoc quod omnia que futura erant, ipso faciente vel permittente ipsum nec tunc quando non erant, latebant[82].

This idea that the various aspects of his nature *(proprietates)* were not separate from God was a fundamental theme of the *Theologia 'Summi boni'*.

The gloss on Porphyry *('Ingredientibus')* was certainly written before *TSum*, as comparison of Abelard's analysis of identity and differ-

---

(78) *TSum* III, 65-66 (p. 92).
(79) *TSum* II, 6; *TChr* III, 5.
(80) *D.* II, 215, 15-216, 19; *sup. Per.* 426, 22-431, 12; *TChr* V, 57-58; *TSch* III, 83-111 (ed. COUSIN, pp. 138-46).
(81) *sup. Per.* 427, 10-19; 428, 25-32; 429, 29.
(82) *sup. Per.* 428, 9-17.

VII

ence in the two works makes clear[83]. Because the discussion of this subject in the *Gl. sec. voc.* is so close to that of *TSum*, this revision of the gloss on Porphyry may have been produced during the same general period. The *Gl. sec. voc.* include a discussion of the constituent parts of logic which is more developed than that in the other glosses on Porphyry and Aristotle, but less so than that in the gloss on Boethius and in the *Glossule* on Porphyry[84]. This would suggest that Abelard revised his gloss on Porphyry after completing that on the *Periermeneias*, but before these other glosses.

There is no clear indication as to whether Abelard composed his gloss *super Topica* before or after *TSum*, but he must have done so before turning the *Gl. sec. voc.* into the *Glossule*, as he still defines a universal as a *vox* rather than as a *sermo* in commenting on Boethius[85]. Because he promises in the gloss on the *Periermeneias* to deal with some subjects *in topicis* and refers in the latter back to his earlier commentary on Aristotle, it seems unlikely that the two glosses would have been separated by too great a period of time[86]. Whereas in the *Glossule* Abelard incorporates some passages directly aimed at Roscelin of Compiègne, the only teacher whom he singles out for criticism in commenting on Boethius is William of Champeaux: *Et profecto preceptor noster Willelmus eiusque sequaces duos sensus tam in propositionibus quam in questionibus assignabant*[87]. There is little trace in the gloss *super Topica* of any controversy with Roscelin over his doctrine of the Trinity or over the definition of a universal.

Apart from the *Timaeus* of Plato, the *De differentiis topicis* is the text which Abelard cites the most frequently in *TSum* (eleven times). In particular it provided important justification for his argument that difference of definition was not the same as difference of identity[88]. When extending *TSum* into the *Theologia Christiana* — probably a gradual process — he incorporated only two new references to the *De differentiis topicis*, quite insignificant in number when compared to the large amount of new patristic quotation, from Augustine and Jerome in particular[89]. When he first composed the *Theologia ' Summi boni '* Abelard had complete familiarity with the texts of Porphyry, Aristotle and Boethius.

(83) See above, p. 77-78.
(84) Gl. sec. voc., ed. GEYER, 584; cf. *sup. Por.* 3-4, *sup. Pred.* 114, *sup. Per.* 310, *sup. Top.* 209-210, *Glossule* 506; cf. JOLIVET, *Arts du langage*, p. 131 n. 55.
(85) *sup. Top.* 271, 1.
(86) See above, n. 15.
(87) *sup. Top.* 217, 38-40.
(88) In particular, *TSum* II, 84, 96, 110 (pp. 55, 59, 64). This compares with nine references to the *Categories*, six to the *Periermeneias*, nine to the *Isagoge* and eight to Augustine's *De Trinitate*, the patristic text most cited in *TSum*.
(89) *TChr* III, 49; V, 33.

This was the only version of the *Theologia* in which he gave more classical than patristic quotation[90].

Other writings on the trivium.

Although Abelard did not add much new quotation from the ancient logicians in *TChr*, he did incorporate a number of new references to his own writings on logic. One of these is to the gloss on the *Periermeneias*, said to have been written a long time previously *(sicut iamdudum ex II Periermeneias didicimus)*, a reference inserted into a passage not otherwise modified in *TChr*[91]. Two other references are to previous commentary on Porphyry, perhaps to the *Glossule* as this contained his most recent reflections on the text[92].

The most important new reference is to a *Grammatica*, which he says contains a new discussion of *predicamenta*, in particular of the distinction between a property and its subject (like *paternitas* and *pater*): *de hoc tractatum in retractatione predicamentorum nostra continet Grammatica*[93]. He attempts to rectify any inadequacy a reader might find in that treatise:

> Si quis vero graviter accipiat quod hoc loco lectorem ad retractationem predicamentorum invitaverimus, atque hunc sibi tractatum sufficere non posse dicat, et ob hoc eum quasi imperfectum arguat, breviter de predicatione patris et paternitatis instrui poterit, quare videlicet, cum diversam rem paternitatem a patre nolimus esse, ea tamen sibi invicem per predicationem non iungamus, ut videlicet dicamus patrem esse paternitatem vel e converso[94].

The *Grammatica* is also the only one of his writings to which Abelard added a reference in the *TSch*, according to which it included a discussion of how spirit could not be defined by space, unlike material entities[95]. Given the theological implications of such subject matter, the *Grammatica* is more likely to have been written after, rather than before *TSum*[96].

---

(90) On a rough count, excluding repeated quotation and treating the logical works of Boethius as 'classical', *TSum* has 45 different patristic texts against 68 classical quotations; *TChr* (excluding the recension *CT*), has a ratio of 199 patristic to 101 classical text. In *TSch* this ratio is 164 to 55 (177 to 59 in its final recension).

(91) *TChr* IV, 9, referring to *sup. Per.* 475-478.

(92) *TChr* III, 82 and IV, 92 referring to *Glossule* 576-577 and 564-565 (or *Gl. sec. voc.*, ed. OTTAVIANO, pp. 202-3 and, 190-2; the latter could also apply to *sup. Por.* 74-80).

(93) *TChr* IV, 155.

(94) *TChr* IV, 158.

(95) *TSch* III, 70 (ed. COUSIN, p. 135): *Quod autem nec loco moveri possit qui spiritus est, tam philosophorum quam sanctorum assertione docemur, sicut de quantitate tractantes ostendimus, cum Grammaticam scriberemus.* Quantity was the second of the *predicamenta* which Abelard studied in the *Dialectica* I, 56-76, but he does not deal here with the question of spirit.

(96) So concluded VAN DEN EYNDE, 'Les écrits perdus d'Abélard', 475.

Because the description of the argument of the *Grammatica* is textually very similar to part of the *Glossule*, Geyer concluded that Abelard was really referring to a gloss on the *Categories* which he thought might have followed the Lunel *Glossule* (in other words, part of his *Logica* ' *Nostrorum petitioni sociorum* ')[97]. This hypothesis assumes that Abelard made a bad mistake in identifying his own work. Could not the *Grammatica* simply have had an argument in common with the *Glossule*? Both works seem have been written between *TSum* and *TChr*. Another reference in *TChr* to discussion of the category of substance also corresponds to part of the *Glossule*, but not at all to the gloss on the *Categories*, as Geyer noted: *de quo quidem latius in predicamento substantie alibi nobis agendum fuit*[98]. There are two other references to an existing analysis *de discretione predicamentorum* which cannot apply to any passage in the gloss on the *Categories*, concerning the identity of and distinction between forms and that in which a form existed — the subject matter of the *Grammatica*[99]. One can thus venture to conclude that all the new references to discussion of categories incorporated into *TChr* are to the *Grammatica*, a treatise which, if it had survived in manuscript, might throw quite new light on the evolution of Abelard's thinking about language[1].

Besides the *Grammatica*, definitely written after the *Dialectica* and probably after the glosses on Aristotle, Abelard also conceived of a *Rethorica*, but it is not known if he ever completed this work as no manuscript survives. He mentions this projected *Rethorica* twice within his commentary on the topics, in a section which is heavily indebted to the *De inventione rhetorica* of Cicero[2]. Having already demonstrated his competence within the study of dialectic, through both a treatise and commentaries on the subject, it was only normal for Abelard to extend his analysis of language into the fields of grammar and rhetoric. Another important treatise is the *Tractatus de intellectibus* (found in MS Avranches, Bibl. mun. 232, ff. 64-68v; s. xii), the authenticity of which is no longer in doubt[3]. In this work he examines the nature of intellections or thoughts,

---

(97) Geyer, pp. 618-19; cf. *Glossule* 549, 12-22.

(98) *TChr* III, 153; cf. *Glossule* 535, 40-536, 10.

(99) *TChr* IV, 46 and 48 (about forms and their subject), *cum de discretione predicamentorum disseremus*, the same subject matter as contained in the *Grammatica* *(tractatum in retractatione predicamentorum)*, according to *TChr* IV, 155.

(1) For further discussion of the *Grammatica* and its contents, see MEWS, 'Aspects of the evolution of Peter Abaelard's thought on signification and predication', to appear in the *Actes du septième symposium européen de logique médiévale, Poitiers 17-22 juin 1985 : Gilbert de Poitiers et ses contemporains.*

(2) *sup. Top.* 263, 25; 267, 14; it may also be referred to in *sup. Top.* 242, 28: *de quo plenius in tractatu argumenti disputabimus.*

(3) L. URBANI ULIVI, *La psicologia di Abelardo e il "Tractatus de intellectibus"* (Rome, 1976), with an edition on pp. 103-27. The *Tractatus* is attributed to Abelard in the manuscript. Geyer thought that it was the work of a pupil developing the thought of his master.

generated through reason, rather than through sensory perception, imagination or estimation *(existimatio)*. After outlining the relation between these various aspects of the human psyche, he analyses the different kinds of intellection mediated through *sermones*. In using the term *sermo* to denote a word which signified both a thought and a thing, Abelard took his argument a stage closer to that formulated in the *Glossule*[4]. While there are a number of passages textually identical in the *Tractatus* and *Glossule (L)*, one sentence is subtly different in the latter:

Solet frequenter < *enim L* > queri de significatione atque intellectu universalium vocum < *nominum L* >, quas res videlicet < *scilicet L* > significare habeant, aut que res in eis intelligantur < aut... intelligantur *om. L* >[5].

The change from *vox* to *nomen* parallels the replacement of *vox* with *sermo* or *vocabulum* already noticed elsewhere in the *Glossule* and in *TChr*[6]. Abelard was not particularly concerned with universals as such in the *Tractatus* and so described them as *voces* as he had done in all previous glosses. It seems most logical to assume that Abelard redefined a universal as a *sermo* in the *Glossule* only after he had written the *Tractatus*, perhaps as a result of using *sermo* to mean a significative word in the latter work. Although he had mentioned intellections in passing a number of times in the *Dialectica*, he never devoted a whole section to the subject. This may have motivated him to produce an independent treatise *de intellectibus*, to supplement the arguments put forward in his gloss on the *Periermeneias*.

From this study of the evolution of Abelard's terminology and thinking about language, we can suggest the following chronological sequence for his writings: *Ed. sup. Por.*; *sup. Cat.*; *sup. Per.*; *de divisionibus*; *Introductiones parvulorum*; *liber fantasiarum*.

Dialectica.

Glosse sup. Por.; *sup. Pred.*; *sup. Per.*; *Gl. sec. voc.*; *sup. Top.*

TSum (perhaps before *sup. Per.* and *sup. Top.*).

Rhetorica (?); *Grammatica*; *Tract. de int.*

Glossule.

TChr.

The sequence proposed here is only tentative, as the evidence is often inconclusive. The exact sequence of the writings prior to the *Dialectica* is

---

(4) *Tr. de int.* 123, 19-21: *Alioquin cum singuli sermones intellectus quoque sicut et res significare dicuntur, non tamen ideo de intellectibus rursum alios intellectus constituunt.*

(5) *Tr. de int.*, pp. 123, 22-24; cf. *Glossule* 530, 24-531, 19. This passage of the *Glossule* is also related textually to the *Gl. sec. voc.*, ed. OTTAVIANO, pp. 134-5.

(6) See above, n. 33.

not known, while the relationship of the glosses on the *Periermeneias* and *Topica* to *TSum* deserves further scrutiny. Similarly the exact date of the *Grammatica* and *Rethorica* (if written) is not certain. Abelard may well have transformed the *Theologia ' Summi boni '* into the *Theologia Christiana* over a long period of time, while producing some of these works on the *trivium*. The manuscripts of the *Glossule* and *TChr* present copies of texts undergoing a process of continuous revision.

The date of the Dialectica.

Now that a possible sequence of writings has been proposed, it remains to establish a more precise date for the *Dialectica*. The most specific references to the author's personal situation occur in the prologues to its second and fourth treatises. Both prologues form an integral part of the text and do not seem to have been added at a later date.

He mentions at the beginning of the second treatise that attempts were being made by jealous rivals to obstruct his writing and study, but that he refused to be pressured into abandoning the *Dialectica*:

Etsi enim invidia nostre tempore vite scriptis nostris doctrine viam obstruat studiique exercitium apud nos non permittat, tum saltem eis habenas remitti non despero, cum invidiam una cum vita nostra supremus dies terminaverit, et in his quisque quod doctrine necessarium sit, inveniet[7].

This passage was interpreted as a reference to the council of Sens (1140) by Cousin and the council of Soissons (1121) by Cottiaux, Nicolau d'Olwer and de Rijk, but to the period prior to this latter council by Robert[8]. Geyer did not read a specific date into the passage, but thought that the reference to the Last Day and another comment of Abelard expressing hope that God would give him time to complete the *Dialectica*, implied that he must have written the work towards the end of his life[9]. As Nicolau d'Olwer commented, this argument lacks foundation as Abelard is using conventional pieties which he could have used at any time. It is not clear from this prologue whether the difficulties which he was facing applied to his writing on logic or on theology.

He gives more detail at the beginning of the fourth treatise and specifies that the accusations were against his writing on dialectic:

Novam accusationis calumniam adversus me de arte dialectica scriptitantem emuli mei novissime excogitaverunt, affirmantes qiudem de

---

(7) *D.* II, 145, 18-22.
(8) Cottiaux, 265; Nicolau d'Olwer, 377 ; de Rijk, p. xxii; Robert, pp. 188-90; cf. *D.* II, 145, 19; 146, 20.
(9) Geyer, p. 607.

his que ad fidem non attinent, christiano tractare non licere. Hanc autem scientiam non solum nos ad fidem non instruere dicunt, verum fidem ipsam suarum implicamentis argumentationum destruere[10].

As Robert rightly observed, the accusation which Abelard claims in the *Dialectica* as having recently *(novissime)* made, corresponds to that mentioned in the *Historia Calamitatum*, that a monk should not study secular literature[11]. At no other time was he ever criticised specifically for writing on dialectic, as after he produced *T Sum*, hostility was focussed on his theological writing. In the *Dialectica* Abelard counters the charge that dialectical argument could weaken the Christian faith by asserting that dialectic was necessary to counter the sophistical reasoning of schismatics, by whom he could have had Roscelin in mind. He did not defend his use of pagan wisdom within his theology as he did in the *Theologia Christiana*[12]. From the example which he gives of faulty reasoning about the Trinity in the *Dialectica*, it would seem that he was beginning to develop his ideas on the subject, but that his critics had not yet seized on this, only on his writing on logic.

Nicolau d'Olwer thought that these two prologues could have been part of an original or even second recension, left unrevised in the recension found in the Paris MS. However, just as it would be quite inconsistent of Abelard not to have revised his discussion of *vox* in the *Dialectica*, so it would be quite out of character for him not to have revised these prologues. In the *Theologia ' Scholarium '* he took care to modify the introduction to its second book, eliminating those passages critical of dialecticians, because the arguments which he had been using against Roscelin were being turned against himself[13]. It seems unthinkable that he should not have done the same in the *Dialectica*.

Arguments for a date before his entry into St Denis.

The arguments which Nicolau d'Olwer used to justify identifying an initial recension of the *Dialectica* to the period before Abelard became a monk at St Denis are slight in the extreme[14]. One is that in its fourth treatise Abelard reports his critics as saying that a Christian should not involve himself with dialectic, so this must have been before he became a monk[15]. There is no record of any such accusation before his entry into St Denis. Another is that because Abelard mentions the city of Paris in

---

(10) *D.* IV, 469, 5-9.

(11) *Hist. Cal.* 663-89.

(12) *D.* IV, 470, 3-471, 10; cf. *TChr* II, 1.

(13) See Mews, 'Peter Abelard's *Theologia* ... re-examined', 134.

(14) De Rijk (p. xxii n. 9) comments that most of Nicolau d'Olwer's arguments are inconclusive.

(15) Nicolau d'Olwer, 378.

a logical example he had to have written the *Dialectica* when he was living there. Geyer used the same argument as evidence of a date after 1133[16]. Nicolau d'Olwer's argument that Abelard could not have coined logical examples such as *osculetur me amica, festinet amica, Petrum diligit sua puella* and *Petrus diligit suam puellam* because not only was he a monk, but he had been castrated, relies on a similar assumption that a logical example describes one's personal state[17]. While there might be a psychological significance to such examples, they cannot be used as evidence of Abelard's situation at the time.

The date of Abelard's entry into St Denis.

One objection to dating the *Dialectica* to after his becoming a monk could be that he would not have had the time or the means to write this work, the various glosses on Porphyry, Aristotle and Boethius and the *Theologia ' Summi boni '* before the council of Soissons in April 1121. The exact date of his entry into St Denis is not known, but it must have been after 1115 (to allow time for the birth of Astralabe), but before July 1118[18]. Because Héloise's uncle, Fulbert, does not appear in a list of canons of Notre-Dame signatory to a charter of 1117 (although he reappears in 1119), he may have fallen into disgrace because of his involvement in Abelard's castration by this date[19]. Abelard would thus have had at least four, if not five years in which compose these various works, mostly of logic. He mentions that at the time he was physically involved with Héloise, he had lost interest in his work, his lectures had become repetitive and his only inspiration was for writing love songs rather than

---

(16) *Ibid.*, 378-79; GEYER, pp. 608-9.

(17) *D.* II, 151, 15; 152, 21; 319, 1-6. One could add the example of an argument based on probability rather than true inference, given in *D.* III, 277, 30-278, 2, the assumption that because a girl was found by surprise talking at night to a young man, there existed an amorous relationship between them. This is only a variation, however, of an example given by Boethius in the *De differentiis topicis* (*PL* 64, 1211A) about a lady who went into a brothel. The example *Petrus diligit puellam suam* has the same status as *Pompeius diligit uxorem suam*, given in *sup. Top.* 233, 13-19. Bernard of Chartres used an example about the differing states of a virgin to illustrate a grammatical point, presumably so that it would be remembered by his students, *Metalogicon* III, 2 (ed. WEBB, pp. 124-25). For a similar end Abelard used very secular examples in *TSum* III, 79 (pp. 98-99) about *concumbere* having the same meaning as *cognoscere* and *digerere* as *exire (purgare ventrem)*, comments not repeated in later versions of the *Theologia*.

(18) Van den Eynde demonstrated that the letter of Fulco to Abelard must have been written before July 1118, 'Détails biographiques', 217-20.

(19) Fulbert is mentioned in charters 130 (1102), 143, 145 (1107), 148 (1108), 182 (1 April 1119), 194 (1122), 203 and 207 (1126), of Notre-Dame, *Cartulaire général de Paris* I, ed. R. DE LASTEYRIE (Paris 1887), pp. 154, 163, 165, 168, 204, 215, 223, 227. See BAUTIER, 'Paris au temps d'Abélard', p. 56 n. 1 (not mentioning the charter of 1119).

philosophy[20]. Entering the monastery enabled him to devote himself much more fully to his study, for economic as well as personal reasons. After a period of initial difficulty at St Denis he obtained permission to live and teach at a *cella* or church dependent on the abbey, in the vicinity[21]. The period which followed he described as very successful, marred only by the hostility of jealous rivals who tried to stop him from teaching. Judging from the comments made by Roscelin of Compiègne in a vitriolic letter to his former pupil *c.* 1120-21, they were not successful, until the judgement of the council of Soissons. In any case his critics could not prevent Abelard from writing on logic or beginning to develop his ideas about the Trinity.

Arguments for a date after 1121.

One argument which Geyer used to justify a later date for the *Dialectica* was that Abelard would not have made the frequent, sometimes critical references to William of Champeaux before his death in January 1121[22]. Yet Abelard did not hesitate to disagree with his former teacher while he was alive. None of the references to *magister noster* is explicit enough to assert that William had since died[23]. They could have been made any time after William had given up teaching at St Victor, in June/July 1113. Almost all the references to William occur in the first two treatises of the *Dialectica*, as if Abelard then grew tired of contrasting his opinions with those of his teacher. He made no explicit mention of his former teacher in his glosses, apart from once in that on Boethius.

The major argument which has been used in favour of a late date for the *Dialectica* is that because in its fifth treatise Abelard criticised those Platonists who identified literally the Platonic world soul with the Holy Spirit, he was withdrawing a position he had once held:

> Sunt autem et qui hanc divisionem virtualis totius non de anima generali sed singulari, quam animam mundi Plato vocavit, accipiunt ; ... Sunt autem nonnulli catholicorum qui allegorie nimis adherentes sancte trinitatis fidem in hac consideratione Platoni conantur ascribere, cum videlicet ex summo deo, quem tagaton appellant, noy naturam intellexerunt quasi filium ex patre genitum ; ex noy vero animam mundi esse quasi ex filio spiritum sanctum procedere. Qui quidem

---

(20) *Hist. Cal.* 351-4: *Quem etiam ita negligentem et tepidum lectio tunc habebat, ut iam nisi recitator pristinorum essem inventorem, et si qua invenire liceret, carmina amatoria, non philosophie secreta.*

(21) *Ibid.* 666-79; *Epist. ad Abaelardum*, ed. J. Reiners, *Der Nominalismus in der Frühscholastik*, BGPTMA 8 (1910), 79, 12-29.

(22) *Geyer*, p. 606.

(23) See above, n. 54.

spiritus, cum totus ubique diffusus omnia contineat, quorumdam tamen
fidelium cordibus per inhabitantem gratiam sua largitur charismata,
que vivificare dicitur suscitando in eas virtutes ; ...sed hec quidem fides
Platonica ex eo erronea esse convincitur quod illam quam mundi animam vocat, non coeternam deo, sed a deo more creaturarum originem
habere concedit... Unde nullo modo tenori catholice fidei ascribendum
est quod de anima mundi Platoni visum est constare, sed ab omni
veritate figmentum huiusmodi alienissimum recte videtur, secundum
quod duas in singulis hominibus animas esse contingit[24].

Working on the assumption that Abelard identified the world soul with
the Holy Spirit in the *Theologia*, Cousin thought that in this passage
Abelard might have been retracting an opinion which he had once held, in
response to one of the accusations made against his teaching in 1140[25].
Believing that the *Theologia* ' *Scholarium* ' might have been written by
as early as 1125-26, Geyer, Cottiaux and Nicolau d'Olwer thought that
Abelard might have been able to 'withdraw' his earlier position any time
after 1133 — an opinion invalidated by the research of Ostlender, who
showed that two recensions of the *Theologia* ' *Scholarium* ' were produced
in reaction to the criticisms of William of St Thierry and Bernard of
Clairvaux in 1140[26]. In neither of these recensions is there any indication
that he was reconsidering his ideas about the world soul.

In this passage of the *Dialectica* Abelard was criticising those who
adopted Platonic doctrine uncritically, because they interpreted a general
concept — the world soul — in a particular sense, so leading to the
erroneous conclusion that a man had two souls, physical and spiritual.
He describes the world soul as a veiled analogy *(figmentum)*, not to be
interpreted literally. He insists similarly in the *Theologia* that a world
soul cannot mean any specific thing, but adds the notion of *involucrum*
to that of *figmentum*[27]. The basic caution against literal interpretation of
Plato is thus retained, but there is a deeper investigation into the true
significance of the *anima mundi*. The argument of this part of the *Dialectica* is quite consistent with comments he makes about Plato elsewhere
in this work and in the glosses, and provides no evidence in favour of
a date after 1133. This passage makes more sense, in fact, if it was written
before *TSum*, when his theological ideas were still in embryo.

---

(24) *D.* V, 558, 18-559, 8.

(25) Cousin, *Ouvrages inédits*, p. xxxv ; Geyer, p. 608; Cottiaux, 266; Nicolau
d'Olwer, 381.

(26) Ostlender, 'Die Theologia "Scholarium" des Peter Abelards', 276-80.

(27) *TSum* I, 37 (p. 13, 17-20); cf. *TSum* I, 56 (p. 20, 25); *TChr* I, 123; *TSch* I, 186
(p. 55). The consistency of Abelard's thought on the world soul was pointed out by
Robert, p. 190, and more recently by T. Gregory, 'Abélard et Platon', *P. Abelard,
Louvain*, p. 63 (38-64). See too, Mews, 'The development of the *Theologia*', p. 185.

Abelard, William of Conches and Thierry of Chartres.

To whom is Abelard referring in this passage of the *Dialectica*? Two writers who come to mind are William of Conches and Thierry of Chartres. William identifies the world soul with the Holy Spirit without qualification in his earliest writings (glosses on the *Consolatio Philosophiae* and *Timaeus*) while in later works (glosses on Macrobius and Plato, the *Philosophia mundi*) he reports this opinion without committing himself[28]. He does not mention it all in the *Dragmaticon*, composed c. 1144-49[29]. The chronology of William's career is little known, but he says in the latter work that he had been teaching for more than twenty years, which would lead us to a date some time before 1124-25. If a reference to a *magister G.* in the Chartres letter book is to William of Conches, then he may have been teaching there as early as 1116[30]. It is thus chronologically possible that Abelard could have been referring to the opinions held, among others, by William, who might have modified his comments in reaction to Abelard's teaching. A number of his arguments about the Trinity in the *Philosophia mundi* echo those of Abelard, but it is difficult

(28) *Comm. in Boetium*, ed. C. JOURDAIN, 'Des commentaires inédits de Guillaume de Conches et de Nicolas Triveth sur la Consolation de Boèce', *Notices et extraits des MSS de la bibliothèque impériale* XX, 2 (Paris 1862), pp. 60-61, 75-76, almost identical to the *Glosae in Timaeum*, ed. T. SCHMID, 'Ein Timaioskommentar in Sigtuna', *Classica et Medievalia* 10 (1949), 239 (220-66). William's authorship of the latter is defended by GREGORY, *Anima mundi. La filosofia di Guglielmo di Conches e la scuola di Chartres* (Florence, 1955), pp. 15-16, but doubted by E. JEAUNEAU, *Glosae super Platonem* (Paris, 1965), p. 14. A neutral position is given by William in the latter *Glosae*, p. 145 and in a gloss on Macrobius (cited by Jeauneau, p. 145 n.(c). See also his *Philosophia mundi* 13, ed. G. MAURACH (Pretoria, 1980), pp. 22-23.
(29) *Dragmaticon (Dialogus de substantiis physicis)*, ed. G. GRATAROLUS (Strasbourg, 1567), pp. 5-6.
(30) *Ibid.*, p. 210; ed. A. WILMART, *Analectica Reginensia* (edition of prologue to Book VI), Studi et testi 5 (Vatican City, 1933), p. 264. There is no positive proof as to the identity of *magister G.*, cited by L. MERLET, 'Lettres d'Yves de Chartres et d'autres personnages de son temps 1081-1130', *Bibl. de l' École des Chartes* 16 (1855), 463 (443-71), although J. O. WARD suggests that it is William of Conches, 'The date of the commentaries on Cicero's *De inventione* and the Cornifician attack on the liberal arts', *Viator* 3 (1972), 226 (219-73). R. W. SOUTHERN supports a date as early as 1115 for William's teaching career, though emphasises that it is not known where he taught: 'Medieval Humanism and the School of Chartres', *Medieval Humanism and Other Studies* (Oxford, 1970), pp. 71-73 (61-85); *Platonism, Scholastic Method and the School of Chartres*, Stenton Lecture (Reading University Press, 1979); 'The Schools of Paris and the School of Chartres', *Renaissance and Renewal in the Twelfth Century*, pp. 129-30 (113-37). William does seem to have studied under Bernard of Chartres, as reported by John of Salisbury, *Metalogicon* I, 24 (p. 57). He also mentions Chartres and its cathedral in his writing; see JEAUNEAU, 'Deux rédactions des gloses de Guillaume de Conches sur Priscien', *RTAM* 27 (1960), 235 (212-47).

to be sure of direct influence[31]. Both he and William make extensive use of the notion of *involucrum* in their interpretation of classical texts, although William was more concerned to elucidate cosmological than theological elements in his reading of Plato[32].

Abelard's relationship to Thierry of Chartres is rather more enigmatic. Thierry comments in his commentary on the *Hexaemeron* that Christians call the world soul the Holy Spirit, but when he wrote this text is not known[33]. He had become a master at Chartres by 1119, the year Bernard, perhaps his brother, became chancellor, so he could have been one of those Platonists referred to in the *Dialectica*[34]. Thierry seems to be the teacher criticised by Abelard in *TChr* for reputedly believing in the eternity of the world as was Bernard, for teaching that the words of the eucharistic formula possessed an efficacy independent of the merit of the person who uttered them[35]. The accusation against Thierry, even if inaccurate, reflects the same suspicion of a literal interpretation of Plato as voiced in the *Dialectica*.

Although Thierry was present at the council of Soissons and was even reprimanded by his bishop for a comment he made in the face of the papal legate, this does not mean that he was necessarily a faithful supporter of Abelard[36]. According to an anonymous biographical note, Abelard had tried to study arithmetic under Thierry, but had to give it up because he had no taste or ability in the subject. This corresponds to what Abelard says in the *Dialectica* about his having no aptitude for arith-

(31) So thought William of St Thierry, *De erroribus Guillelmi de Conchis*, ed. J. LECLERCQ, 'Les lettres de Guillaume de St Thierry à saint Bernard', *Rev. bén.* 79 (1969), 382-91 (275-91).

(32) See JEAUNEAU, 'L'usage de la notion d'integumentum à travers les gloses de Guillaume de Conches', *Archives d'histoire doctrinale et littéraire du moyen âge* 24 (1957), 35-100 and M.-D. CHENU, 'Involucrum : le mythe selon les théologiens médiévaux', *ibid.* 22 (1955), 75-79.

(33) *De sex dierum operibus*, ed. N. HÄRING, *Commentaries on Boethius by Thierry of Chartres and his School* (Toronto, 1971), p. 567.

(34) On the chronology of Thierry's career, see WARD, *art. cit.*, 239-40. Southern emphasises again the lack of firm evidence as to his teaching at Chartres, before becoming its chancellor in 1142 (although he was an archdeacon of Dreux in the 1130's), 'The Schools of Paris and the School of Chartres', p. 130.

(35) *TChr* IV, 80. These seem certain to be the two brothers, Bernard and Thierry, mentioned by Otto of Freising, *Gesta Frederici I*, 47, ed. G. WAITZ-B. DE SIMSON, *MGH.SS* (Hannover, 1912), p. 77. They were identified with the two teachers of Chartres by A. CLERVAL, *Les écoles de Chartres au Moyen Age* (Paris, 1895), p. 159; although this was doubted by Southern, 'Humanism and the School of Chartres', p. 70 n. 1, this was supported by Ward in a long discussion of their relationship, *art. cit.*, 263-66. A gloss on the *Timaeus* has been attributed to Bernard by P. E. DUTTON, 'The Uncovering of the Glosae super Platonem of Bernard of Chartres', *Medieval Studies* 46 (1984), 192-221, the edition of which is eagerly awaited.

(36) *Hist. Cal.* 878.

metic[37]. The anecdote illuminates both his relationship to Thierry and his attitude to the *quadrivium* as a whole. Unlike Thierry, who was equally at home in the *trivium* and *quadrivium*, Abelard had no major interest in purely scientific questions, being convinced in the primacy of dialectic as the basis of all knowledge[38]. He was nonetheless familiar with the approach of scholars like William and Thierry to the interpretation of classical texts. At the council of Soissons he enjoyed the support of Geoffrey of Lèves (bishop of Chartres 1115-49), perhaps an indication of earlier contact with Chartres and its academic community[39]. Abelard's approach was, however, different from that of both William of Conches and Thierry; the criticism of Platonists in the *Dialectica* illustrates that divergence.

Abelard and the new logic.

When listing in the *Dialectica* the texts of logic in current use in his day, Abelard does not name any of the new works of Aristotle which would become known to logicians in the 1130's. He quotes briefly from the *Prior Analytics*, but this work does not provide a major source of influence[40]. He does not quote at all from the *Topics* or *Sophistici Elenchi* of Aristotle, both of which were used extensively by Adam of Balsham *(Parvipontanus)* in his *Ars disserendi*, composed in 1132[41]. If Abelard revised the *Dialectica* in the mid-or late 1130's, it seems unusual that he should make so little mention of the new logic. He refers to the *Topics* and *Analytics* in a general sense in his glosses on Porphyry and Aristotle, citing the same definition of a syllogism taken from the *Prior Analytics*

---

(37) R. L. POOLE, *Illustrations of the History of Medieval Thought and Learning* (London, 1920²), pp. 314-7; a fuller text is edited by L. HÖDL, *Die Geschichte der scholastischen Literatur und der Theologie der Schlüsselgewalt*, BGPTMA 38, 4 (1960), pp. 79-86.

(38) *D.* II, 153, IV, 470, 4-471-10; see JOLIVET, *Arts du langage*, p. 19. On Thierry's approach, see JEAUNEAU, 'Mathematique et Trinité chez Thierry de Chartres', *Miscellenea Medievalia 2. Die Metaphysik im Mittelalter*, ed. P. WILPERT (Berlin, 1963), pp. 289-95.

(39) *Hist. Cal.* 789-867. On Geoffrey, see W. M. GRAUWEN, 'Gauffried, bisschop van Chartres (1116-1149), vriend van Norbert en van de "Wanderpredigen"', *Analecta praemonstratensia* 58 (1982), 161-209.

(40) *D.* II, 146, 10-17, although he comments (145, 24), that Aristotle wrote on forms of categorical syllogism *breviter quidem et obscure*. Abelard quotes from the *Prior Analytics* in *D.* II, 232, 4-12; 233, 35-234, 8; the reference in II, 245, 23-246, 2 is only general. Cf. MINIO-PALUELLO, *Aristoteles Latinus III*, 1-4, *Analytica Priora* (Bruges-Paris, 1962), pp. 433-36.

(41) MINIO-PALUELLO, 'The "Ars Disserendi" of Adam of Balsham "Parvipontanus"', *Medieval and Renaissance Studies* 3 (1954), 116-69 and *Twelfth Century Logic I. Adam Balsamiensis Parvipontani Ars Disserendi* (Rome, 1956).

as in the *Dialectica*[42]. Whereas in the latter work Abelard refers to the *Sophistici Elenchi* through a reference of Boethius, in the gloss on the *Periermeneias* he adds a comment that he had once read a manuscript claiming to contain the *Sophistici Elenchi*, but he was not sure of its authenticity because its contents did not seem to agree fully with the description of Boethius[43]. He includes one other brief reference to the *Sophistici Elenchi* in this gloss[44]. One gains the impression that Abelard was relying on notes taken from his reading, or simply on his memory, and that he did not have any complete text of these works to hand.

While James of Venice translated the three new works of Aristotle around 1128 (probably only an approximate date), there did exist a rare, older translation, which Thierry of Chartres used when copying these texts into his *Heptateuchon*, a source book of forty-five different works on the *trivium* and *quadrivium*, completed by 1141[45]. The translation of the *Prior Analytics* familiar to Abelard was that known to Thierry. Because the text of the *Categories* and of the *Periermeneias* is so close to that of the *Heptateuchon*, it may be assumed that the manuscript of the *Sophistici Elenchi* which Abelard mentions was also closely related, if not identical, to that used by Thierry of Chartres[46]. Unfortunately the fire at the library of Chartres during the last war has made it difficult to identify positively the forty-five books bequeathed by Thierry to the cathedral and which he may have copied into the *Heptateuchon*[47].

(42) Abelard speaks of the *Analytics* in general in *sup. Por.* 2, 8-15 and *sup. Pred.* 111, 5-12, but distinguishes between the *Prior* and *Posterior Analytics* (not very accurately), in *sup. Per.* 394, 10-26; *Gl. sec. voc.*, ed. GEYER, 586, 21-29 and *Glossule* 509, 2-9.

(43) Abelard was familiar with the *Sophistici Elenchi* from the gloss of Boethius on the *Periermeneias*, *D.* II, 181, 17, repeated in *sup. Per.* 399, 5; he quotes directly from this text in *sup. Per.* 400, 32-36. Jolivet suggests that *sup. Per.* might have been written after the *Glossule* because it is not mentioned in the latter glosses (see above, n. 46). Abelard's use of *vox* in *sup. Per.* would suggest rather that he knew of the work, but did not mention it when writing the *Glossule* (a revision of earlier glosses).

(44) *sup. Per.* 489, 3 (ed. MINIO-PALUELLO, p. 13, 17).

(45) On the date of the translations of James of Venice, see MINIO-PALUELLO, 'Iacobus Venetus Grecus, canonist and translator of Aristotle', *Traditio* 8 (1952), 271 n. 16 (265-304). Only the prologue of the *Heptateuchon* has been edited (from MSS Chartres 497-8, extant only in microfilm deposited at the IRHT, Paris and elsewhere), by JEAUNEAU, 'Le prologus in Eptateuchon de Thierry de Chartres'? *Medieval Studies* 16 (1954), 171-5, reprinted in 'Note sur l'École de Chartres', *Studi Medievali* N.S. 5 (1960), 853-5.

(46) MINIO-PALUELLO, 'I "Primi Analytici": la redazione carnutense usata da Abelardo e la 'vulgata' con scolii tradotti dal greco', *Rivista di filosofia neo-scolastica* 46 (1954), 211-23, and on Abelard's text of the *Periermeneias*, *Twelfth Century Logic* II, pp. XXXII-XXXIII. His observations apply equally to the text used in the literal gloss on the *Periermeneias*; cf. *Ed. sup. Per.* 76, 10; 85, 25; 89, 26 (*Aristoteles Latinus* II, 1-2, pp. 6, 4; 7, 20; 8, 14), etc.

(47) R. GIACONO, 'Masters, Books and the Library at Chartres according to the Cartularies of Notre-Dame and Saint-Pierre', *Vivarium* 5 (1974), 43 (30-51).

104

This textual evidence indirectly gives plausibility to the anecdote about Abelard's having studied briefly with Thierry — who had much greater knowledge of the new logic than Abelard and was to earn the reputation of having been the first to introduce the *Prior Analytics* and *Sophistici Elenchi* into the curriculum[48]. Thierry was only one of a number of scholars engaged in bringing previously unread texts of Aristotle into wider circulation. Abelard was aware that Aristotle had written much more than the *Categories* and *Periermeneias*, but he was not influenced by the new logic to anything like the extent of the logicians who would emerge in the 1130's. One of them, master Alberic, would criticise one of the few references which Abelard made to the *Sophistici Elenchi* for revealing a failure to understand that work[49]. Ironically this was the one text of Aristotle which Abelard would mention in a small tract written in defence of his use of dialectic to discuss matters of religious belief at about the same time as he was drafting the *Theologia ' Scholarium '*, namely the 1130's[50]. Yet he never mentions this or any of the other new works of Aristotle in his theological writings. In this respect, Abelard would be outpassed by a later generation.

II. The *Dialogus (Collationes)* and related texts

Like the *Dialectica*, Peter Abelard's *Dialogus inter philosophum, Iudaeum et Christianum* or *Collationes* is a difficult work to date[1]. The

---

(48) A. Vernet, 'Une épitaphe inédite de Thierry de Chartres', *Recueil de travaux offerts à M. Cl. Brunel* 2 (Paris, 1955), pp. 660-70.

(49) Alberic's comment *bene dixisti quod non invenisti, quia non intellexisti*, found on f. 92ra of the Berlin MS Preussischerkulturbesitz, lat. fol. 624, refers to Abelard's remark in the *sup. Per.* (see above, n. 146), found on ff. 97-164 of the same manuscript. Cf. de Rijk, *Logica Modernorum* I, p. 620.

(50) *Epist. 13*, ed. Smits, p. 273. On the date of this treatise, see Smits, *Letters IX-XIV*, pp. 174-88.

(1) The title *Dialogus Petri Baiolardi* is found in the MS Vienna, Nationalbibliothek cvp 819, ff. 1-61 (s. xii-xiii), but *collaciones Petri Abaelardi* in MS Oxford, Balliol College 296, ff. 169-189v (s. xiv). The MS London, British Library, Royal XI.A.5, ff. 73-98v (s. xii-xiii) is incomplete, but textually close to the Balliol MS, of which the following are transcriptions: Cambridge, Trinity College 0.5.14; London, British Library, Landsdowne 209, ff. 32-79v; Oxford, Corpus Christi College 312, ff. 192-208 and Queen's College 284, pp. 1-111 (all s. xvii). The title *Dialogus inter philosophum, Iudaeum et Christianum* was invented by F. H. Rheinwald for his edition from the Vienna MS, *Anecdota ad historiam ecclesiasticam pertinentia* 1 (Berlin 1831), reprinted by Migne, *PL* 178, 1609-84 and with only minor corrections by Cousin, *Petri Abaelardi Opera* 2, pp. 644-715. It was retained by R. Thomas for his edition (Stuttgart-Bad Cannstatt, 1970), which was criticised by G. Orlandi, 'Per una nuova edizione del Dialogus di Abelardo', *Rivista critica di storia della filosofia* 34 (1979), 474-94, for depending too much on the Vienna MS and ignoring the fact that the other MSS contain

traditional opinion, first put forward by Robert in 1909 and accepted by most scholars without question, is that Abelard wrote the *Dialogus* in the last years of his life, after he had entered the monastery of Cluny. in June 1140[2]. This view was challenged by Buytaert, who argued that it was written before the council of Sens, a hypothesis rejected by Thomas, who has defended the traditional date of 1140-1142[3]. The question is important for our understanding of the evolution of Abelard's thought. As with the *Dialectica*, the arguments of the *Dialogus* will be compared with those of his other writings in an attempt to situate the treatise within the context of his overall literary output. Before doing so, however, we shall review the arguments about its date which have so far been brought forward.

The state of the question.

Robert based his argument that the *Dialogus* was written after the council of Sens (2 June 1140) on a passage in the work which he thought was a reference to the condemnation of the *Theologia* at that council:

a later recension of the work. Buytaert thought that the title *Collationes* was more authentic because Abelard uses *collatio* to refer to the debate (*Exp. in Hex.*, PL 178, 768B) as do the participants (*Dial.* 31, 154, 169, 1156, 1260), who never use the term *dialogus*; 'Abelard's Collationes', *Antonianum* 44 (1969), 18 n. 1 (18-39). Although Buytaert may well be correct in this, the title *Dialogus* will be retained for convenience, references being to the line of Thomas's edition.

(2) ROBERT, *Les écoles*, p. 210; COTTIAUX, 'La conception de la théologie chez Abélard', 263; SIKES, *Peter Abailard*, pp. 267-8; D. VAN DEN EYNDE 'La chronologie des écrits d'Abélard à Héloïse', 348 (for full references, see part I, nn. 1-3). Robert's dating is accepted without any acknowledgement by: B. GEYER-F. UEBERWEG, *Grundriss der Geschichte der Philosophie II. Die Patristische und Scholastische Philosophie* (Berlin, 1922), p. 216; E. GILSON, *La philosophie au moyen âge* (Paris, 1934²), p. 292; R. OURSEL, *La dispute et la grâce* (Paris, 1959), p. 82; H. LIEBESCHÜTZ, 'The Significance of Judaism in Peter Abelard's Dialogus', *The Journal of Jewish Studies* 12 (1961), 1 (1-18); M. de GANDILLAC, 'Intention et loi dans l'éthique d'Abélard', *Pierre Abélard-Pierre le Vénérable ... Cluny 1972*, p. 585 (585-608) and 'Le "Dialogue" d'Abélard', *Cahiers de la revue de théologie et de philosophie* 6 (1981) 3 (3-17); J. JOLIVET, 'Abélard et le philosophe (Occident et Islam au XIIᵉ siècle)', *Revue de l'histoire des religions* 164 (1963) 182 (181-9) and 'Doctrines et figures de philosophes chez Abélard', *Petrus Abaelardus*, ed. THOMAS, p. 108 (103-20); (with more reserve) J. VERGER et J. JOLIVET, *Bernard-Abélard ou le cloître et l'école* (Paris, 1982), p. 107; R. THOMAS, *Der philosophische-theologische Erkenntnisweg Peter Abelards im Dialogus inter Philosophum, Iudaeum et Christianum* (Bonn, 1966), pp. 27-29.

(3) BUYTAERT, 'Abelard's Expositio in Hexaemeron', *Antonianum* 43 (1968), 184-6 and 'Abelard's Collationes', *ibid.* 44 (1969), 33-39, conclusions accepted by D. E. Luscombe, *Peter Abelard's Ethics*, p. XXVII and P. J. PAYER, *A Dialogue of a Philosopher with a Jew and a Christian*, Medieval Sources in Translation 20 (Toronto, 1979), pp. 6-8. Thomas expressed his disagreement in 'Die Persönlichkeit Peter Abaelards im "Dialogus inter Philosophum, Iudaeum et Christianum" und in den Epistulae des Petrus Venerabilis — Widerspruch oder Uebereinstimmung?', *Pierre Abélard-Pierre le Vénérable ... Cluny 1972*, pp. 256-61 (255-69).

Quod vero ingenii tui sit acumen, quantum philosophicis et divinis sententiis memorie tue thesaurus abundet, preter consueta scolarum tuarum studia, quibus in utraque doctrina pre omnibus magistris etiam tuis sive ipsis quoque repertarum scientiarum scriptoribus constat floruisse ; certum se nobis prebuit experimentum opus illud mirabile *Theologie*, quod nec invidia ferre potuit nec auferre prevaluit, sed gloriosius persequendo effecit[4].

This was the only evidence which Robert cited, although some scholars have claimed further arguments in favour of such a date: that its unfinished state indicates that Abelard must have died before completing the work; that its style suggests a 'calm resignation' belonging to the end of his life[5]; that Abelard's contact with Peter the Venerable at Cluny may have given him knowledge of an Islamic philosopher, on whom he may have based the philosopher in the *Dialogus*[6]. These arguments were seen as corroborating rather than proving a date of 1140-1142.

Buytaert was the first scholar to question the assumption that the persecution mentioned in the *Dialogus* referred to the council of Sens, on the grounds that Abelard would have been 'too deflated' after 1140 to have written 'such proud words'[7]. He argued for a date *c.* 1136 when Abelard's works were enjoying a new success. As Buytaert pointed out, Abelard did not have to be at Cluny in order to learn about Muslim philosophers, while the argument based on its unfinished state was invalid because a reference in the *Expositio in Hexaemeron* to an earlier *collatio* seemed to be to the *Dialogus*[8]. Thomas criticised these arguments, claiming that Abelard was only being ironic in allowing the philosopher to praise the fame of the *Theologia*, not really accepting such flattery; he also doubted that the *secunda collatio* referred to in the *Expositio in Hexaemeron* was the *Dialogus* and suggested that it could have been any form of monastic conference[9].

Reviewing the arguments of both Buytaert and Thomas, it is evident that no strong case has yet been made either for or against a date after 1140 for the *Dialogus*. The passage about persecution of the *Theologia* is too vague for any positive conclusion to be drawn from it. Buytaert's argument about Abelard being 'too deflated' is too subjective to be accorded confidence. Thomas, on the other hand, does not bring forward any major new evidence in favour of 1140-1142. To gain a more certain

---

(4) *Dial.* 45-62.
(5) SIKES, p. 268.
(6) JOLIVET, 'Abélard et le philosophe', 181-9.
(7) BUYTAERT, 'Abelard's Expositio in Hexaemeron', 185.
(8) See above, p. 104, n. 1.
(9) THOMAS, 'Die Persönlichkeit Peter Abaelards', pp. 256-61.

idea, we schall look at the evolution of Abelard's thought as a whole and at the themes of the *Dialogus* in particular.

Is the Dialogus unfinished?

One of the arguments which has been invoked in favour of a date 1140-42 is that the work is unfinished, and that Abelard must have died before being able to finish it[10]. In both recensions of the *Dialogus*, the second *collatio* concludes with an invitation of the Christian to the philosopher, if he had any further question, to add this or to hurry on to what remained:

> Quod quia ex inquisitione summi boni pendebat, si quid superest quod de ipso ulterius queri censeas, licet te subinferre vel ad reliqua festinare[11].

It is not entirely clear whether by *ad reliqua* the Christian is referring to other matters which he intended to discuss or to what the philosopher might have thought remained to be dealt with. The fact that Abelard, as judge in the debate between the philosopher and the Christian, does not intervene at the end of this second *collatio* has also been interpreted as indicating that the *Dialogus* in unfinished[12]. In order to answer the question of whether Abelard would have completed the work if he could have done so, it is necessary to look at the structure of the *Dialogus* as a whole.

Abelard exposes his theme in the preface which introduces the two *collationes*. A philosopher asks Abelard to preside as judge over the discussions which he has been having with a Jew and with a Christian about the relative value of their different approaches to the supreme good and human beatitude. Having long studied the writings and arguments of the philosophers in the schools, the philosopher had turned to moral philosophy and the study of the Jewish and Christian religions in his search for wisdom[13]. Abelard places himself in the role of the listener who has to weigh up the value of the arguments put forward, extracting what is important from everything that is said. These comments of Abelard are in fact advice to the reader as to how to evaluate the text which follows. He insists on the importance of listening and learning before making any judgement both in this preface and the short paragraph which serves to join the two *collationes*[14]. There is no indication that Abelard intended to give a final adjudication of the two debates, and

---

(10) See Sikes, Gilson, de Gandillac, Oursel (p. 105, n. 2 above).
(11) *Dial.* 3426-8.
(12) This opinion was first was put forward within a detailed study of its contents by S. M. Deutsch, *Peter Abaelard* (Leipzig, 1883), p. 445 (433-52).
(13) *Dial.* 18-27.
(14) *Dial.* 68-78, 1165-71.

indeed to have done so would have been alien to the literary tradition of philosophical dialogue which he was emulating. The function of the *Dialogus* was, like that of the *Sic et Non*, to allow the reader to weigh up different arguments which were put forward, in this case about the supreme good and the path to beatitude, and so come to a considered opinion.

In the first *collatio* Abelard uses the philosopher and the Jew to put forward different arguments about the relative value of natural law and the written Law of the Jews and the merit of observing the precepts of the latter, particularly circumcision. Abelard conveys his underlying message by attributing part of his argument to the Jew, that the Law is ultimately based on a command to love God and one's neighbour, and part to the philosopher, that although the Law was given to the Jews, a gentile was not obliged to follow precepts beyond those of natural law in his search for beatitude[15].

The second *collatio*, much longer than the first, centres around a comparison of the approach of the philosopher and the Christian to the nature of the supreme good and to how it can be attained. Abelard suggests that *ethica*, or moral philosophy, is in the final analysis the same as what the Christian calls *divinitas*, but while the discipline of the philosopher is so named after the path man takes to arrive at the supreme good, that of the Christian is named after the supreme good itself[16]. As in the earlier conference, Abelard's intention is to illustrate how the two approaches complement rather than confront each other. Both participants emphasise the importance of investigating all questions rationally, without accepting arguments simply on the grounds of authority, and agree that the supreme good of man must lie in the beatitude of a future life and that this could only be attained through the practice of virtue[17]. The philosopher's exposition of the supreme good and supreme evil, as well as of virtue, obtains the approval of the Christian, who then proceeds to give his interpretation of man's supreme good as consisting in the vision of God[18]. The Christian concludes with

(15) *Dial.* 831-52, 1154-62.

(16) *Dial.* 1265-69: *Quam quidem vos ethicam, id est moralem, nos divinitatem nominare consuevimus. Nos illam videlicet ex eo quod comprehendentum tenditur, id est Deum, sic nuncupantes vos ex illis per que illuc pervenitur, hoc est moribus bonis, quas virtutes vocatis.*

(17) *Dial.* 1478-1503, 1665-8.

(18) *Dial.* 2437-2757. The philosopher asks the Christian to explain the path to the supreme good, but only after further clarification of 'good' and 'evil', 3122-30: *Et hinc ... sermo est, ut iam summo bono nostro quam summo malo, ut tibi visum est, descriptis iuxta propositum nostrum, quibus ad ea pertingitur viis, non minus diligenter aperias, ut eo melius has tenere vel illas vitare possimus, quo amplius noverimus. Sed ... ut primo determinatum sit, quid bonum vel malum generaliter sit dicendum, id quoque, si vales, definire desidero.*

a long discussion of the definition of good and evil, but he does not dresent his own view of how man can attain beatitude beyond comments which he makes about the essence of virtue lying in charity.

In this respect the *Dialogus* is incomplete. The Christian's major argument concerns only the nature of the supreme good and does not deal with any more specific aspect of doctrine. There are certain stylistic features of the final speech of the Christian which suggest that Abelard did not intend to add further to the second *collatio* as it stood. At the end of both the *Historia Calamitatum* and the *Theologia ' Scholarium '* Abelard concludes, as in the final speech of the Christian, with a meditation on the goodness of God being more profound than any evil or misfortune. He emphasises the subjectivity of much of what people think is good compared with the goodness of God and in both the *Hist. Cal.* and the *Dialogus* he concludes by dwelling on the verse *Fiat voluntas tua*[19]. The similarity between the end of the Christian's last speech and the conclusion of these two other works would suggest that Abelard was deliberately bringing the *Dialogus* to a close.

While the argument of the Christian is incomplete in not dwelling on what he understood was the way in which man could attain final beatitude, it is not necessary to assume that Abelard died before finishing the work. Could he have decided simply not to continue the *Dialogus* any further? Were his ideas about the path of salvation not yet mature? To answer these questions we must look at the development of his thought as a whole.

The Dialogus and Abelard's writings on theology.

The one certain fact we have for the date of the *Dialogus* is that it was composed after the *Theologia Christiana*, to the second book of which the Christian makes specific reference:

> Inter nos, qui hec recipimus, habent ista locum et maxime rationibus nonnumquam fidem astruendam esse vel defendendam, de quibus quidem memini contra eos, qui fidem rationibus vestigandam esse denegant, secundus etiam *Theologie Christiane* liber tam virtute rationum quam auctoritate scriptorum plenius disserit et rebelles convincit[20].

The second book to which he refers is one which he added to the original text of his treatise on the Trinity, the *Theologia ' Summi boni '* in order to counter those who argued that philosophical reasoning should not be used to explain matters of faith. It seems unlikely that Abelard should be

---

(19) *Dial.* 3381-3421; *cf. Hist. Cal.* 1592-1609 and *TSch* III, 119-20 (ed. Cousin, p. 149).

(20) *Dial.* 1497-1503.

referring to the second book of the *Theologia ' Scholarium '*, the later, quite revised version of the *Theologia Christiana*, which was condemned at the council of Sens in 1140. Only the introduction to its second book of *TSch*, based on a summary of the second, third and fourth books of *TChr*, was concerned with defending the use of philosophical reasoning[21]. Abelard always refers to the final version of his treatise as the *Theologia*, both in its text and in references in other works, while the title of *Theologia Christiana* is only used to refer to *TChr*. In addition, we may note that Abelard quotes verbatim a number of passages which occur in *TChr*, but not in *TSch*.[22]

The nature of the passages which Abelard added to his original treatise in the *Theologia Christiana* indicates that they would have been added sometime after the council of Soissons, held in April 1121. In replying to accusations about both his method and his doctrine of the Trinity, notably about the attribution of power to the Father, which were made, at that council, Abelard could develop his ideas about a number of different points, all of which he incorporated into the text of the *Theologia Christiana*. The manuscripts of *TChr* which survive represent the state of Abelard's text only at a specific moment in time. He may have started to add individual passages or patristic quotations to the text of the *Theologia ' Summi boni '* even before the council of Soissons. In the period immediately after the council Abelard was engaged in extensive reading of the Fathers, as evidenced by the episode about his research into the identity of St Denis which he describes in the *Historia Calamitatum*[23]. He may have begun to add much of the new patristic quotation to the *Theologia Christiana* at the same time as compiling the *Sic et Non*. Comparison of the patristic texts quoted within the *Theologia ' Summi boni '* with those of the *Sic et Non* would suggest that Abelard began to draft the latter work only after *TSum*, but before *TChr*[24]. He was goaded

---

(21) *TSch* II, 1-61 (pp. 62-83).

(22) *Dial.* 1458-77 reproduces *TChr R* II, 117, but not the text as found in *TChr CT* II, 117, also found in *Epist. XIII* (*PL* 178, 353B-D, ed. Smits, p. 272). This indicates that the *Dialogus* was probably written before *TChr CT* and *Epist. XIII*. Other texts common to both works are *Dial.* 2065-87 (*TChr* II, 46-48) and 3309-11, 3349-58 (*TChr* I, 2).

(23) *Hist. Cal.* 941-61.

(24) Only *TSum* II, 24 and 39 (ed. Ostlender, pp. 35, 39) contain catenae also found in *SN* 18, 12-15 and *SN* 13, 3-4. Other single passages found in both texts include: *TSum* I, 35 (p. 12) (*SN* 15, 6); II, 62 (p. 47) (15, 1); II, 104 (p. 62) (9, 13); II, 106 (p. 63) (9, 4); III, 6 (p. 70) (8, 30); III, 23 (p. 77) (8, 31). Sometimes (as in *TSum* I, 35) a text is rewritten in *TChr* according to a more correct version found in *SN*, while very often *TChr* has extended catenae of *SN* texts, where there is only one in *TSum*, as if Abelard started the *Sic et Non* by taking a text he had used in *TSum*, then extending it with many others and modifying *TChr* accordingly. See Mews, 'Peter Abelard's *TChr* and *TSch* re-examined', nn. 25-28. and nn. 53 and 79 below.

into critical study of the arguments of the Fathers by accusations that he did not pay them sufficient attention[25].

The date of the *Theologia Christiana* cannot therefore be given with any precision, but it seems safe to assign the two very similar recensions which survive in manuscript *(TChr D* and *R)* to the period 1122-1126, when Abelard was installed at the site of the Paraclete and had resumed his teaching activity, having escaped from St Denis. In composing the *Theologia Christiana* he seems to have drawn on a number of different works: the *Sic et Non* for much, though not all of the patristic quotation; the *Glossule* on Porphyry for his discussion of identity and difference; the *Grammatica* for a new analysis of predicaments *(retractatio predicamentorum)*; quite possibly an *Exhortatio ad fratres et commonachos*, since lost, for the new second book of *TChr*[26]. All these texts were most likely written after *TSum*.

The major difference between *TSum* and *TChr* on the one hand and the *Theologia ' Scholarium '* on the other is that while the former were studies of the nature of the supreme good, as announced by their incipit *Summi boni perfectionem, quod Deus est, ipsa Dei sapientia incarnata... diligenter distinxit, TSch* placed the doctrine of the Trinity within the context of faith and the means by which man could be saved. It opened with the statement: *Tria sunt, ut arbitror, in quibus humane salutis summa consistit, fides videlicet, caritas et sacramenta*[27]. In the *Theologia ' Scholarium '* Abelard eliminated or greatly abbreviated the long digressions which he had incorporated in the *Theologia Christiana*, so as present a more homogenous treatise which served as a detailed study of his teaching on faith in God. A number of drafts of *TSch* survive *(tsch FH, TChr CT, tsch Z, T)* which allow the process of this revision to be studied in detail[28]. One of the reasons for giving a quite new introduction to the *Theologia* was that Abelard had developed a body of teaching about faith. the sacraments and charity, based on his reflection on the questions which he had raised in the *Sic et Non* and which has been recorded in a number of collections of his *sententie*[29]. Firm dates are difficult to obtain, but he probably began drafting *TSch* only after returning to teach in Paris in the early 1130's, perhaps as early as 1132/33, while it would most likely

---

(25) *Hist. Cal.* 751-81.

(26) On the *Glossule* and *Grammatica*, see above, pp. 92-3; on the *Exhortatio ad fratres et commonachos*, see below, pp. 116-17.

(27) *TSum* I, 1 (p. 2²⁴). *TChr* I, 1; *TSch* I, 1 (p. 2).

(28) MEWS, 'Abelard's *TChr* and *TSch* re-examined', 138-48.

(29) *Sententie Petri Abelardi (Sententie Hermanni)*, ed. S. BUZZETTI (Florence, 1984), also edited as *Epitome Theologiae Christianae, PL* 178, 1695-1758; *Sententie Florianenses*, ed. H. OSTLENDER, Florilegium Patristicum 19 (Bonn, 1929); *Sententie Parisienses*, ed. A. LANDGRAF, *Écrits théologiques de l'école d'Abélard* (Louvain, 1934), pp. 1-60.

VII

112

have been completed by 1137, when he left the Mont Ste Geneviève for an unknown period[30].

In assessing the date of the *Dialogus*, it is also necessary to look at the commentary on Romans, written before the third book of *TSch*, and at the *Ethica*, composed after this third book[31]. Comparisons will also be made with Abelard's various writings for Heloise and the nuns of the Paraclete, notably the sermons and *Expositio in Hexaemeron*, but their dating is less certain and will be discussed in due course.

The Dialogus, sermo 3 and the commentary on Romans.

The first *collatio*, between the philosopher and a Jew bears many points of comparison with *sermo* 3, a small tract on the circumcision of Christ, and with the commentary on Romans[32]. Abelard touches on circumcision and the insufficiency of the Jewish Law in the *Theologia Christiana*, but does not dwell on this and prefers to contemplate the virtuous example and teaching of the pagan philosophers. He comments that the injunction made to Abraham to circumcise his progeny referred only to the seed of Isaac, and so the Jewish race, and not to that of Ishmael and emphasises the importance of God's revelation through a natural law, inscribed in the hearts of some enlightened gentiles[33]. Much more developed arguments occur in the sermon, in which Abelard demonstrates that the patriarchs were justified without having been circumcised, arguments virtually identical to those of the philosopher in the *Dialogus*[34]. The Jew in the *Dialogus* dwells on another aspect of Abelard's argument, that the true purpose of circumcision was to distinguish the Jewish people from their neighbours so as to protect them

(30) MEWS, 'Abelard's *TChr* and *TSch* re-examined', 155-6.

(31) Abelard refers to *TSch* I, 29-32, 41-52 and 94-188 in *Comm. Rom.* (pp. 152-3, 69, 68) as having already be discussed, although he might conceivably be referring to *tsch* or *TChr*; he refers in *Comm. Rom.* (pp. 75-76, 225, 259-60 and 281-2) to subjects to be dealt with in the *Theologia*, which are touched on in *TSch* III, 96-120 (pp. 142-9). Buytaert in his introduction (CCCM 11, pp. 17-18, 24-26) concludes that the commentary must have been written after *TSch* II because *Comm. Rom.* (pp. 70-71) refers to philosophical analogies of the Trinity (cf. *TSch* II, 112-16; pp. 97-98), but the analogies mentioned in the commentary are not those of *TSch* about the seal of three properties, they are closer to those of *TChr* IV, 86-92, invoking an earlier image of a bronze substance and bronze statue as two properties in one entity. The *Ethica* (p. 96) refers to *TSch* III in the past tense. *TSch* I (last part), *TSch* II (first and last parts) and *TSch* III (beginning) were all based on the draft *TChr CT*; if *Comm. Rom.* is earlier than the revised middle part of *TSch* II, as indicated by comparison of the analogies, it would also precede the copying out of the complete *TSch* from *TChr CT*, though possibly come after the drafts *tsch Z* or *T*.

(32) *Sermo* 3 (*PL* 178, 398B-409A); *Comm. Rom.* (pp. 87-90, 93-96, 121-51).

(33) *TChr* II, 15-25.

(34) *Dial.* 331-87; cf. *Sermo* 3 (398C-400B).

from infidelity and to serve as a sign of interior holiness[35]. The difference between the two works is that in the sermon Abelard extends his discussion to cover baptism as well.

The discussion of the purpose and limitations of the Law, and in particular of circumcision, is much more developed in the commentary on Romans than in either the *Dialogus* or the sermon. The basic theme of the commentary had already been outlined in *TChr*, but it is given much greater scriptural support: that the gentiles received God's revelation without the benefit of the Law and that circumcision was only a sign of interior virtue, an observance enjoined only on the seed of Isaac and not that of Ishmael as well[36]. Whereas in both the sermon and the *Dialogus* Abelard describes circumcision indiscriminately as both *signum* and *signaculum* (echoing Romans 4, 11), in his commentary on Romans he distinguishes between the two concepts: *signum* he glosses as a reference to the physical descendants, *signaculum* to his spiritual, or gentile descendants[37]. This would indicate that the commentary was written after the sermon and the *Dialogus*. That the commentary is later than the sermon is also shown by the fact that whereas in the sermon he always follows the exegesis of Origen uncritically, in the commentary he has a more nuanced attitude and criticises Origen's interpretation of the 'second' circumcision effected by Joshua[38]. On this, as on other matters, the commentary seems to contain more mature reflection than either the sermon or the *Dialogus*.

The Dialogus, Theologia Christiana (Book II) and the Ethica.

Many of the ideas of the second *collatio*, between the philosopher and a Christian can be compared with the arguments of the second book of the *Theologia Christiana*. Abelard had added this book to his original treatise on the Trinity *(TSum)* in order to answer the criticisms which had been made of his use of pagan writers; he sought to demonstrate that the final goal of all philosophy was the supreme good, in other words God, and that their moral teaching was fully in accord with the true values of the Christian religion[39]. This is precisely the theme of the

---

(35) *Dial.* 560-624; cf. *Sermo* 3 (402A-403D).

(36) *Comm. Rom.* (pp. 87-90, 93-96, 135-6).

(37) *Ibid.* (pp. 127-9); cf. *Sermo* 3 (402BC) and *Dial.* 599-607.

(38) *Sermo* 3 (403B-409A); *Comm. Rom.* (pp. 142-3). Cf. BUYTAERT, CCCM 11, pp. 33-34.

(39) *TChr* II, 28: *Quod si minus videtur esse ad meritum salvationis quod dicitur 'amore virtutis' et non potius 'amore Dei', ac si virtutem vel aliquod bonum opus habere possimus quod non secundum ipsum Deum ac propter ipsum sit, — facile est et hoc apud philosophos reperiri, qui summum bonum quod Deus est, omnium tam principium, id est originem et causam efficientem, quam finem, id est finalem causam constituunt, ut omnia scilicet bona amore ipsius fiant, cuius ex dono proveniunt. TChr II, 44: Si enim diligenter*

114

second *collatio* of the *Dialogus*, but whereas in *TChr* Abelard simply presents ideas about the value of pagan ethical teaching, in the *Dialogus* he presents it in terms of a comparison between classical and Christian thought.

Before expounding what he understands by 'the supreme good' and 'virtue', the philosopher delivers a statement of his method which is reminiscent of the prologue to the *Sic et Non*. He insists that he will accept no argument from authority without first examining it rationally[40]. In defence of such an approach the philosopher cites passages from Augustine which occur in identical form in the second book of *TChr*, while the Christian refers to the *Theologia Christiana* by name, in a passage already discussed[41]. The parallelism between the two works can be studied further by comparing their expositions of the nature of virtue. In *TChr* Abelard describes the moral teaching of the philosophers rather haphazardly, dividing those virtues which were active, like justice, from those which were contemplative, like abstinence, fortitude and continence[42]. He refers to the fourfold division of virtues into those which were political, purifying, of the purified mind and exemplary, taken from Macrobius, but does not pursue this in detail[43]. He mentions this classification in the *Dialogus*, but follows through more systematically the traditional division of Cicero of the virtues into prudence (mother of all virtue), justice, fortitude and temperance. The philosopher provides much more precision than Abelard gives in *TChr* by analysing as well the component parts of these virtues[44]. Although given to the philosopher to deliver, this account meets with the Christian's approval and is clearly intended to represent Abelard's own commentary on the nature and classification of virtue[45]. He wanted to show that an account based on Cicero and other classical philosophers was not inconsistent with Christian doctrine.

Abelard's *Ethica* or *Scito teipsum* would have discussed virtue in its

---

moralia Evangelii precepta consideremus, nihil ea aliud quam reformationem legis naturalis invenimus, quam secutos esse philosophos constat, — cum lex magis figuralibus quam moralibus nitatur mandatis, et exteriori potius iustitia quam interiori abundet.

(40) *Dial.* 1341-2.

(41) See above, pp. 109-110, nn. 20, 22.

(42) *TChr* II, 45-51 (charity), 52-58 (justice), 59-73 (abstinence), 74-86 (fortitude or magnanimity), 87-108 (continence).

(43) *TChr* II, 64; *cf. Dial.* 1880-6.

(44) *Dial.* 2015-2291.

(45) Abelard's exposition, based on the *De inventione*, does not differ greatly from that of other contemporaries, notably Hugh of St Victor. See the numerous studies of P. Delhaye, including 'La place de l'éthique parmi les disciplines scientifiques au xiie siècle', *Miscellenea Mediaevalia in honorem Arthur Jansenn* (Louvain, 1948), pp. 29-44; 'L'enseignement de la philosophie morale au xiie siècle', *Medieval Studies* 11 (1949), 77-99; '"Grammatica" et "Ethica" au xiie siècle', *RTAM* 25 (1958), 59-110. One is curious to know whether there was any moral content in Abelard's *Grammatica*.

second book, but only an introductory fragment survives in the longest manuscript of the work[46]. The first book, on the nature of vice and sin, survives in complete form. Although it is impossible to compare the analysis of virtue in its second book with that of the *Dialogus*, there are a few references to sin in the latter which can be compared to the account given in the *Ethica*. At several places within the *Dialogus* Abelard refers to sin, not as an act or a deed, but as a bad will *(mala voluntas)*, the same definition as he gives in the commentary on Romans and in the *Theologia* ' *Scholarium* '[47]. This definition is refined quite considerably in the *Ethica*: a distinction is drawn between the will to sin, not in itself sinful, and consent to that *mala voluntas*, which constituted the true sin[48]. Abelard thus retained his emphasis on the interior, subjective nature of moral wrong, but deepened his analysis of man's general inclination to sin, which was not sinful in itself. That the *Dialogus* shares the same earlier definition as the commentary on Romans and *TSch* provides a strong argument that the *Dialogus* was written before the *Ethica*. It is also consistent with the earlier observation based on the different accounts of circumcision, that the *Dialogus* was written before the commentary on Romans, itself prior to Book III of *TSch*.

The Dialogus, Soliloquium and Exhortatio.

The *Dialogus* can also be compared to the so-called *Soliloquium*, a short tract written in the form of a dialogue between *Petrus* and *Abaelardus*[49]. Like the second *collatio*, it is concerned with the relationship between the vocation of the philosopher and that of the Christian, although the comparison is approached through the meaning of the words 'philo-

---

(46) *Ethica* (pp. 129-30).

(47) *Dial.* 1143-44: *Anime vero reatus sicut voluntate ipsius committitur ...;* 1870-72: *Sive enim peccatum in voluntate sive in operatione constituas, clarum est in malis hominibus alium alio nequiorem habere voluntatem et amplius nocere sive deterius agere. Cf. Comm. Rom.* (p. 206), *TSch* III, 107 (p. 107).

(48) *Ethica* (pp. 12-14): *Non itaque concupiscere mulierem sed concupiscentie consentire peccatum est, nec voluntas concubitus, sed voluntatis consensus dampnabilis est.* On this, see Luscombe's note (p. 14 n. 1) and in particular the study of R. BLOMME, *La doctrine du péché dans les écoles théologiques de la première moitié du XIIe siècle* (Louvain, 1958), pp. 222-58. The *Dialogus* also appear to predate the *Problemata Heloissae*, which introduce the idea of sin as consent *(PL* 178, 710CD): *Cogitationes, que inquinant, de corde exeunt, cum ad hoc perpetrandum consentimus quod cogitavimus. Ubi autem non est sensus, non potest esse consensus, sicut in parvulis aut stultis ... Sicut ergo cogitationes exeunt de corde, cum per consensum ad opera tendunt, ita homocidium et adulterium et cetera peccata de corde docet exire, nec aliter peccata esse, nisi per consensum prius fuerint in corde, quam exhibeantur in opere.* This would indicate that the *Probl. Hel.* were written after *TSch,* though perhaps before the *Ethica,* which has a more developed exposition.

(49) Found among the letters of Berengar *(PL* 178, 1876C-80A).

sopher' and 'Christian' rather than through their teaching. The crux of the argument is that *philosophi* and *christiani* are words which both refer to people who seek and live by the wisdom of God, which could be identified with Christ himself[50]. The debate of the second *collatio* expresses a much greater awareness of the differences which separate the philosopher from the Christian, but it develops the concern of the *Soliloquium* to establish the underlying identity of interest between the two vocations. From the thematic point of view, there can be no doubt that the *Dialogus* is a later work than the *Soliloquium*.

Abelard refers in this internal dialogue to an *Exhortatio* which he had written, addressed to his brothers and fellow monks:

> De fide autem philosophorum atque vita seu etiam disciplina morum in *Exhortatione* nostra ad fratres et commonachos nostros satis arbitror esse expositum. Quam quidem *Exhortationem* quisque legerit, videbit philosophos non tam nomine quam re ipsa christianis maxime sociatos[51].

The contents of this *Exhortatio*, known only through this reference, correspond very closely to those of the second book of *TChr*, also concerned with the faith of philosophers in the supreme good and their moral teaching. Van den Eynde's suggestion that part at least of the second book of *TChr* could have been copied from the *Exhortatio* is quite plausible, given that its tone is so different from that of the rest of *TChr*. He once addresses his audience as *fratres* and makes frequent assertions about the worldliness of contemporary monasticism and of abbots in particular[52]. Abelard eliminated all such references in *TSch*.

There are a few patristic quotations in the *Soliloquium* which also occur in the *Theologia Christiana*, but they are not sufficient to prove that one work is dependent on another[53]. More revealing is the statement in the *Soliloquium* that the philosophers expounded the doctrine of the

---

(50) *Sol.* (1878B): *Etsi hoc quidem modo sermonis usus non habeat — ut videlicet aut christianos nunc specialiter nominem philosophos, aut eorum de Christo scientiam aut a Christo traditam doctrinam appellemus logicam — profitemur tamen his quae dicis nominum ethimologias maxime consentire.*

(51) *Sol.* (1877D-78A).

(52) VAN DEN EYNDE, 'Les écrits perdus d'Abélard', 470-3; cf. *TChr* II, 46: *Numquid hoc, fratres, ad aliquam turpitudinem inclinandum est ...*; see also *TChr* II, 57 and 71 for critical comments on the religious life.

(53) *Sol.* (1877CD, 1878AB) — *TChr* I, 118-19, *CT* I, 16a, IV 66b). Because *TChr* I, 119 has been added to *TSum* I, 57 (p. 21), it is likely that the *Sol.*, containing the same sequence of quotations as *TChr* I, 118-19 would have been composed after *TSum*. Abelard's technique seems to have been to add a patristic text to the margin of *TSum* to reinforce a theme, extending this list of quotations over a period of time. *TChr R* I, 120-121 contains even further texts added at this point.

Trinity more thoroughly than the prophets of the Old Testament[54]. Abelard had twice made this claim in the *Theologia ' Summi boni '*, but he deliberately omitted all such reference to the philosophers having a superior religious insight in both *TChr* and *TSch*[55]. This was not so much a change of mind as a greater degree of caution, so that his argument would not seem to conflict too violently with what was said in the Christian creeds about God having spoken through the prophets. As both the *Exhortatio* and the *Soliloquium* mentioned the moral teaching of the philosophers, they would most likely have been written after *TSum*, which does not dwell on the subject.

A common thread runs through the *Exhortatio*, *Soliloquium* and second book of *TChr*, a desire to relate the faith and moral teaching of the philosophers to that of the Gospel. Abelard's message was that the ancient philosophers provided a valuable example to Christians, particularly so far as leading the monastic life was concerned. If the *Exhortatio* was as critical of contemporary monasticism as the second book of *TChr*, it would seem most likely to have been written after he had escaped from the abbey of St Denis either late in 1121 or early 1122, perhaps as a riposte to his fellow monks. After a period as a hermit on the banks of the Ardusson, Abelard established a community of disciples around an oratory which he built, dedicated initially to the Holy Trinity, but then re-dedicated to the Paraclete. According to his description in the *Historia Calamitatum* (based partly on a passage of Jerome also in *TChr*) Abelard sought to model his community on the example set by the ancient philosophers[56]. His belief that they were inspired by God is evident from the strong emphasis which he placed on the Holy Spirit in the *Soliloquium* and *TChr*[57]. The second *collatio* of the *Dialogus* contains a more detailed reflection than these other works on the same question of the relationship between the teaching of the philosophers on the supreme good and the nature of virtue to that of Christian doctrine. Abelard's sympathy for the philosopher is shown by the completeness of the exposition of his ideas. The Christian explains his view of man's final end, the vision of God, but does not deliver an opinion on the way in which man

---

(54) *Sol.* (1877C): *Adeo namque de fide Trinitatis aperte disseruerunt, ut mirabile sit eos quoque in plerisque diligentius quam prophetas ipsos totam huius fidei summam exposuisse.*

(55) The phrase in *TSum* I, 65 (pp. 24-25) about the deeper insight of Job, a gentile, than of the prophets into the resurrection seems to be deliberately omitted in *TChr* II, 26, while the discussion of the superior understanding of the philosophers in *TSum* III, 66 (p. 92) is not retained at all. On Abelard's general image of philosophers, see JOLIVET, 'Doctrines et figures de philosophes chez Abélard' (see above, p. 105, n. 2).

(56) *Hist. Cal.* 1038-1195; *cf. TChr* II, 61-63.

(57) *Sol.* (1878C); *TChr* I, 68-129.

can attain beatitude, concluding only with discussion of the meaning of 'good' and 'evil'.

The Dialogus and the Expositio in Hexaemeron.

This discussion of the meaning of 'good' and 'evil' is referred to specifically by Abelard within his *Expositio in Hexaemeron*:

Quid autem proprie bonum ac per se, scilicet sine adiectione vel quid malum sive indifferens dicatur, in secunda *collatione* nostra, quantum arbitror, satis est definitum[58].

Although Thomas suggested that *collatio* might refer to any monastic conference, the coincidence that Abelard should conclude the second *collatio* in the *Dialogus* with precisely this subject makes it hard to imagine that he should be thinking of some other text[59]. In no other work does he define at length the terms 'good' and 'evil'.

The questions remains, however, of when the *Expositio in Hexaemeron* was written. Its original editors, Martène and Durand, suggested that the *Expositio* must have been composed after the council of Sens because in a passage in which he discusses whether the stars and planets are living beings, Abelard does not mention his doctrine that the world soul was a prefiguration of the Holy Spirit[60]. The weakness of the argument that Abelard adopted a 'more orthodox' opinion after the council of Sens has already been commented upon in discussion of a passage in the *Dialectica* about the world soul[61]. The reverse argument put forward by Buytaert, that because the *Expositio* contains ideas about the Trinity which were condemned at Sens, it must have been composed before 1140 is equally weak as there is no evidence that the council forced Abelard to modify his thinking on any point[62].

As Buytaert correctly pointed out, the *Expositio* contains one passage which occurs in exactly the same form in the *Theologia Christiana*, recension *CT* — the major draft which Abelard prepared in planning the text of the *Theologia ' Scholarium '*[63]. There is a certain peculiarity about this passage: while Abelard always copied from *TChr CT* to *TSch* (and not the other way round, as Buytaert thought), the additional phrases in *TChr CT* and the *Expositio* about God's creative wisdom, which emphasise its providential as well as rational aspect, are not copied

---

(58) *Exp. in Hex.* (768B; ed. ROMIG, p. 88).

(59) VAN DEN EYNDE, 'Chronologie des écrits d'Abélard à Héloïse', 349; see above, p. 105, n. 3.

(60) MARTÈNE and DURAND, *PL* 178, 729-30, referring to *Exp. in Hex.* (752A-753D; ed. ROMIG, pp. 51-55).

(61) See above, part I, pp. 98-99.

(62) BUYTAERT, 'Abelard's Expositio in Hexaemeron', 187-8.

(63) *Ibid.*, 168-70, 186.

into *tsch ZT* (later drafts) or *TSch*[64]. The one simple explanation for this is that Abelard added these phrases to the text of his draft (of which the manuscripts *C* and *T* are independent copies) after he had copied this draft into a later one *(tsch Z)*. He could have added these phrases either before, or perhaps more likely, at the same time as he was copying out this particular passage into the *Expositio*. In any case this means that the *Expositio* waz probably written after *tsch Z*.

Further comparison of the *Expositio* with *tsch Z* and *T* provides more detail. In *tsch ZT* 45-46 Abelard discussed the verse of Genesis (1, 26) *Faciamus hominem ad imaginem et similitudinem nostram*, developing the idea that man was made in God's image, but woman in his similitude. This argument is expanded at some length in the *Expositio*, but is not found in any previous version of the *Theologia*[65]. Abelard also extended in *tsch T* 76-77 a comment which he had made briefly in *tsch Z* (itself copied from *TChr*) about *creavit* (Gen. 1, 1) as a singular verb, applied to a plural noun, *Heloim*. The argument of *tsch T* also occurs in his commentary on this verse in the *Expositio*[66]. This would suggest that it may have been composed at about the same time as *tsch T*.

There is no clear indication whether the commentary on Genesis was written before or after that on Romans, but we may observe that Abelard's remarks about the sin of Adam are much less detailed than those on the text of St Paul[67]. In commenting on the *Hexaemeron* he was concerned with God's self-revelation through the seven days of creation, while the Epistle gave him an opportunity to analyse sin and man's redemption in Christ. The commentary on Genesis breaks off at 2, 25, just before description of the Fall. A logical thematic continuity is evident if the commentary on Romans followed that on Genesis. That on Romans is also much longer and has far more citation of patristic authority. Abelard mentions in his commentary that he intended to cover a certain point in future discussion of the Epistle to the Galatians, as if he was envisaging

---

(64) *Exp. in Hex.* (737D; ed. ROMIG, p. 18), *TChr CT* I, 18. The additional phrases found in *Exp. in Hex.* and *TChr CT* are given in brackets: ... *hoc est in sapientia sua ostendit, id est (nihil temere) sed omnia rationabiliter (ac provide). De quo ... id est ratione (et providentia preeunte), cuncta condidit sive ordinavit.* These phrases are not found in *tsch* 69 or *TSch* I, 52 (p. 20). It must be emphasised that the manuscripts *C*, *T* and *Z* are only copies of the same draft at different stages in time; for clarity's sake only, these are distinguished as separate drafts.

(65) Lines 505-510 only of *tsch* 46 occur in *FH*, an earlier draft than *CT*, but as a note appended to the end of the text, misinterpreted as an error of the copyist by Buytaert who thought that *FH* was an abbreviation of *Z*; cf. *Exp. in Hex.* (760D; ed. ROMIG, p. 71).

(66) Cf. *Exp. in Hex.* (739C; ed. ROMIG, p. 22).

(67) *Exp. in Hex.* (ed. ROMIG, pp. 121-5, 134-5; ed. BUYTAERT, 'Abelard's Expositio in Hexaemeron', 175-6) contain the only references to sin; the final section is not found in *PL* 178.

a series of commentaries on the Pauline Epistles[68]. That Abelard did lecture on this part of scripture is evidenced by the *Commentarius Cantabrigiensis*, a *reportatio* of the master's teaching on St Paul[69]. If the commentary on Romans was written before the completion of *TSch*, then the *Expositio in Hexaemeron* would most likely also have been composed during the planning of *TSch*, after *TChr CT*.

There is a close relationship between the comments of Abelard on each of the six days of creation and the hymns which he wrote for each day of the week for the nuns of the Paraclete[70]. No exact date can be given for the book of hymns, but it would probably have been produced at a relatively early stage in the life of the community, founded in 1129 and accorded a papal privilege 28 November 1131. The hymns preceeded Abelard's sending of the collection of sermons to the Paraclete, although individual sermons may belong to an earlier date[71]. Like the *Expositio in Hexaemeron*, the hymns are the result of a close meditation on the opening chapters of Genesis. Although the evidence is circumstantial, the most likely date for the *Expositio* is in the early 1130's, perhaps soon after 1132/33, when Abelard could resume teaching on the Mont Ste Geneviève while continuing to occupy himself with the community of the Paraclete. The *Dialogus*, referred to in the *Expositio in Hexaemeron*, must have been written some time before this date.

The Dialogus and the Theologia ' Scholarium '.

The biggest contrast between the *Dialogus* and the *Theologia ' Scholarium '* lies in the failure of the Christian in the second *collatio* to explain the way in which man could attain final beatitude. While Abelard does not concern himself with this in the *Theologia ' Summi boni '* or *Theologia Christiana*, he opens the *Theologia ' Scholarium '* with the assertion that the path to salvation lay through faith, charity and the sacraments[72]. In *TSch* the lengthy analysis of the logic of statements about God as three persons is much simplified, criticism of false dialecticians turned into a defence of the use of pagan wisdom through quotation of the Fathers, and the account of the example and moral teaching of the ancient philo-

---

(68) *Comm. Rom.* (p. 307).

(69) *Commentarius Cantabrigiensis in Epistolas Pauli e Schola Petri Abaelardi*, ed. A. LANDGRAF, Notre-Dame University Publications in Medieval Studies 2, 4 pts (Notre-Dame, Indiana, 1937-45). The discussion on Galatians (2, p. 351) corresponds to Abelard's reference in *Comm. Rom.*

(70) J. SZÖVÉRFFY, *Peter Abelard's Hymnarius Paraclitensis* 2 vols. (Albany, New York-Brookline, Mass. 1975), 1, p. 108; E. KEARNEY, 'Peter Abelard as Biblical Commentator: A Study of the Expositio in Hexaemeron', *Petrus Abaelardus*, ed. THOMAS, p. 200 (199-210).

(71) *PL* 178, 379-80.

(72) See above, p. 111 n. 27.

sophers in book II of *TChr* eliminated[73]. The result was a monograph, much more tightly argued than *TChr*, which provided a detailed study of his teaching on faith in God. An introduction to the subject, as well as to Abelard's teaching on Christ, the sacraments and charity, was given in the various collections of *sententie* which circulated among his students[74]. The structure of this course of teaching was provided by the *Sic et Non*.

One passage in the *Dialogus* is more similar to part of *TSch* than *TChr*, namely Abelard's commentary on the quotation of Gregory which opened the *Sic et Non*: *Fides non habet meritum, cui ratio humana prebet experimentum*[75]. He had used this text in *TSum* to attack the excesses of dialectical reasoning which Roscelin applied to the Trinity, copying his comments without alteration into *TChr*[76]. In the *Theologia ' Scholarium '*, however, he accused those who used this text of Gregory to justify forbidding all rational discussion of matters of faith, of seeking to find comfort for their own ignorance, *sue solatium imperitie*. The philosopher uses exactly the same phrase in the *Dialogus*[77]. Similar arguments in defence of the use of dialectic occur in *Epist. XIII*, a small tract written to counter his critics, probably at about the same time as he was drafting *TSch* namely the early 1130's[78]. This tract develops some of the arguments, of the philosopher in the second *collatio* about the importance of subjecting statements about belief to the rules of dialectic. The difference is that whereas in the *Dialogus* Abelard, speaking through the voice of the philosopher, justified his method by direct reference to the example of the ancient philosophers, in *Epist. XIII* and *TSch* he laid greater emphasis on patristic authority to sanction the same approach.

The Dialogus and the Sic et Non.

Although in range of subject matter the *Dialogus* is rather different from the *Sic et Non*, the prologue of the latter shares in common with the *Dialogus* an emphasis on the importance of submitting all arguments to the scrutiny of reason. The didactic value of both works lay in the fact that the student was required to elicit his own conclusion from the apparently contradictory arguments with which he was presented. It may be no coincidence that the two works should occur together in one of the three surviving medieval manuscripts of the *Dialogus* (London,

(73) MEWS, 'Abelard's *TChr* and *TSch* re-examined'.
(74) See above, p. 111 n. 29.
(75) *Dial.* 1372-94; *SN* 1, 1.
(76) *TSum* II, 24 (p. 35), *TChr* III, 50 and in a different context, *TSch* II, 45 (p. 77).
(77) *Dial.* 1376; cf. *TChr CT* III, 8b.
(78) *Epist. XIII* (ed. SMITS, pp. 272) has some of the same quotations as in *Dial.* 1455-77, but parallels the text of *TChr CT* II, 117 rather than that of *R* at this point (see above p. 110 n. 22).

122

Brit. Lib. Royal XI. A. 5; s. xii-xiii = L). The particular recension of the *Sic et Non* in this manuscript records the state of its text at about the same time as the recension R of *TChr*. The *Dialogus* was written some time after *TChr*, and therefore probably after the bulk of the *Sic et Non*, though not necessarily after the final recension *(MKA)* of the latter. This latter recension may in turn predate some of the sermons delivered at St Gildas[79].

The date of the Dialogus.

From the arguments so far presented, it appears that the *Dialogus* must be dated to some time between the *Theologia Christiana* and the initial drafts of the *Theologia ' Scholarium '*. It must have been written before the *Expositio in Hexaemeron* and probably before the sermons delivered at St Gildas and the Paraclete. Can any more precise date be obtained?

The passage in the preface to the *Dialogus*, in which the philosopher praises Abelard's *Theologia* as having been made more famous by the jealousy and persecution which it generated must refer, not to the council of Sens, but to the council of Soissons in 1121. Public censure of the *Theologia ' Summi boni '* had only driven Abelard to enlarge the work into the *Theologia Christiana*. The praise of the philosopher would make less sense if it was written in the early 1130's, after a period of exile in Brittany, but before the drafting of a new, much revised *Theologia*. Abelard makes no attempt to emphasise his own orthodoxy in the *Dialogus*, as he does in the preface to *TSch*. He never lost his belief in the capacity of dialectic to investigate statements of religious doctrine, but in the 1130's his tone is more defensive; he insists on his orthodoxy with greater vehemence and has greater recourse to patristic authorities to justify his method than he had in the past.

The emphasis which Abelard accords to the role of the philosopher in the *Dialogus* corresponds more closely to that of the *Soliloquium* and above all of the *Theologia Christiana*. The exact date of *TChr* is not known, because it was a work to which Abelard continued to make additions

---

(79) *TChr* V, 23 and 38-40 contain texts found in identical order only in *SN DL* 32, 6-7 and 35-15 and which were probably added to the margin of the exemplar of *R* (evident from irregularities in *R*). In the *Dial.* 3089-3102 Abelard attributes a discussion of the bodily assumption of the apostle John to Jerome, while in his sermon 25 (538CD) he quotes from a text of Ambrose (incorrectly Augustine in the printed edition, but correct in sermon 26, 543D) on the subject. This in turn seems to be an excerpt from *SN* 87, 10, found only in *SN MKA*; cf. VAN DEN EYNDE, 'Le recueil des sermons', 39-40. Similarly in sermon 32 (580AB) he quotes and discusses the same combination of texts as found in *SN MKA* 102, 1-4. Although one can never be certain from where Abelard takes his text, one could suggest that *SN MKA* postdates the *Dialogus*, but is, at least in part, prior to these sermons. He might thus have completed the *Sic et Non* while at St Gildas.

— probably in the margin of his text — over a long period of time. The surviving manuscripts simply record its state at a given moment. One can hasard a guess that it might have reached the form reflected in *R* (the earliest complete manuscript) by about 1124. Time must be allowed for the *Grammatica, Glossule super Porphyrium, Exhortatio ad fratres et commonachos* and part at least of the *Sic et Non* to have been composed after *TSum*. One should not forget the *Tractatus de intellectibus*, composed perhaps about the same time as, or a little before the *Glossule*. As is clear from the description in the *Historia Calamitatum*, Abelard's students undertook the economic responsibility for the life of the community around the Paraclete, leaving the master free to devote himself to study[80]. Given that the circumstances of his situation as abbot of St Gildas would make it unlikely that Abelard could have composed the *Dialogus* while in Brittany, the only other possible date for the work would be while he was studying and teaching at the Paraclete.

An insight into Abelard's state of mind in this period is provided by his comment that the attacks which were made on his teaching led him to think about going to live in a Muslim country, where he believed there might be a greater degree of tolerance and where people might even doubt that he was a Christian because of the accusations made against him[81]. This sympathy for the tolerance which he thought he could find in Islam is echoed in the image of the philosopher as presented in the *Dialogus*. As Jolivet has shown, Abelard's philosopher is a monotheist, whose Islamic connections are indicated by a reference to his having been circumcised as a descendant of Ishmael[82]. Although he may have heard reports about some Islamic philosophers, Abelard does not seem to base his portrait on any one individual, but rather projects onto the philosopher his image of someone who questioned the validity of both the Jewish and Christian faiths. The circumstances of Abelard's situation at the Paraclete, in particular his sense of alienation from ecclesiastical authority and sympathy for a tolerant Islam, illuminate some of the pre-occupations of the *Dialogus*.

For how long was Abelard teaching at the Paraclete? The exact date of his appointment to St Gildas-de-Ruys is not known. The anonymous Maurist author of a history of the monastery, who had access to all its surviving records, gave a date of around 1128[83]. Following an erroneous date given by Duchesne to the expulsion of the nuns from the Argenteuil

---

(80) *Hist. Cal.* 1111-19.

(81) *Ibid.* 1221-28.

(82) *Dial.* 5-6, 727-32; cf. JOLIVET 'Abélard et le philosophe', 181.

(83) MS Paris, Bibl. nat. franç. 16822, pp. 538 and 886. The author, a monk of St Gildas, used a history of the monastery compiled by Dom Noël Mars c. 1653 and incorporated it into his text.

124

(which he attributed to 1127 rather than to 1129), various authors have given 1126 or even 1125 as the date of Abelard's appointment to St Gildas[84]. Two separate clues, however, suggest that the date is more likely to be around 1127:

His sermon on John the Baptist, much longer than any of the other sermons and an important exposition of the true monastic life, seems to have been delivered at a relatively early date in his abbacy because in it he fulminates against the widespread practice of monks living in obedientiaries, leading neither a coenobitic or an eremitic life. This must have written before he himself was obliged to live apart from the community[85]. He attacks other corrupt practices at St Gildas and proposes the example of the desert fathers and of the ancient philosophers a guide for monastic example. The sermon reads as if it were a statement of intent to reform the community of the religious life, notably Norbert of Xanten, whom he derided for having recently tried to accomplish a miracle and blaming the spectators when it did not work[86]. He probably also had Norbert in mind in criticising religious who accepted promotion to the episcopate[87]. Norbert left France in 1126, being consecrated archbishop of Magdeburg on 25 July of that year[88]. The sermon would thus be likely to date from the feast of John the Baptist (24 June) 1126 or, more likely, 1127.

Abelard may have left the Paraclete because his old patron, Stephen Garland, who had helped him obtain permission from the king to be freed from his obligations to St Denis in March 1122, was ousted from his position of chancellor and seneschal of France by Suger sometime after 3 August 1127[89]. It is no coincidence that Bernard of Clairvaux should have played a significant part in the campaign against Stephen Garland, as evident from his *Epist.* 78 to Suger, and that this letter should follow *Epist.* 77, to Hugh of St Victor, a reply to questions of Hugh about theological doctrines very close to those of Abelard. Both letters date to 1127[90]. Although Abelard does not identify by name the two *novi*

---

(84) Duchesne's date of the expulsion to 1127 (*PL* 178, 169A), is corrected to early 1129 (confirmed by royal assent 14 April), by A. LUCHAIRE, *Actes du Louis VI le Gros* (Paris, 1890), no. 431, pp. 199-200.

(85) *Sermo* 33 (589BC, 589D-90A).

(86) *Ibid.* (605BD); similar criticism is expressed in a sermon edited by L. J. Engels, 'Adtendite a falsis prophetis (Ms. Colmar, ff. 152v/153v). Un texte de Pierre Abélard contre les Cisterciens retrouvé?', *Corona Gratiarum. Miscellenea patristica, historica et liturgica Eligio Dekkers ... oblata* 2 vols. (Bruges, 1975), 2, pp. 195-210.

(87) *Sermo* 33 (599A-605B).

(88) This is argued by Van den Eynde, 'Le recueil des sermons', 50 and the date of 1127 advocated by J. Miethke, 'Abaelards Stellung zur Kirchenreform. Eine biographische Studie', *Francia* 1 (1973), nn. 72 and 114 (158-92).

(89) LUCHAIRE, *Actes de Louis VI*, no. 399, 410, pp. 185, 190-1.

(90) *Epist.* 77, 78, *S. Bernardi Opera*, ed. J. LECLERCQ 8 vols. (Rome, 1955-77), 7, pp. 184-210.

apostoli who campaigned against him at this time, it seems likely that he was referring to Norbert and Bernard of Clairvaux[91].

If a date of around 1127 is accepted for his appointment to St Gildas, Abelard would have been teaching at the Paraclete for upto five years, time for him to have written not just the *Theologia Christiana* and those works which immediately preceeded it, but also the *Dialogus*. We can suggest a tentative date of around 1125-1126.

The one other period which might be considered for the *Dialogus* is the early 1130's, prior to the drafting of the *Theologia ' Scholarium '*, but as already mentioned, the difference in emphasis between the two works makes this much less likely. Again the date of Abelard's return to Paris is not known for certain, but it was probably linked to the return to influence of Stephen Garland, who re-obtained the position of chancellor late in 1132[92]. As dean of the abbey of Ste Geneviève from 1111 until his death in 1140, Stephen would have been crucial in allowing Abelard to return to Paris and to teach in the school of that abbey. The *Theologia ' Scholarium '* would have been planned and drafted over the period 1132/ 33-1137 simultaneously with the redaction of the *Expositio in Hexaemeron* and then the commentary on Romans. The other writings for the Paraclete would also date to these years. Exactly when he composed the *Ethica* is not known, apart from the fact that it was written after *TSch*. It may have been preceded by the *Problemata Heloisse*, because in some replies to Heloise Abelard anticipates the definition of sin in the *Ethica* as consent to an evil will rather than as an evil will itself[93].

Abelard left the Mont Ste Geneviève sometime in 1137, perhaps prompted by the fall from influence of Stephen Garland after the death of Louis VI (1 August 1137) and the return to power of Suger of St Denis[94]. He returned to the Mount at an unknown date, where he was joined by Arnold of Brescia c. 1139/40[95]. In response to the accusations which were made against his teaching by William of St Thierry and Bernard of Clairvaux Abelard wrote his *Confessio fidei ' Universis '* and much fuller *Apologia contra Bernardum*. These works, like the revisions which he made to the *Theologia ' Scholarium '* (recensions *AP* and *O*) date to 1140, probably before the council of Sens, of which they make no mention[96].

---

(91) *Hist. Cal.* 1196-1212; cf. VAN DEN EYNDE, 'Détails biographiques sur Pierre Abélard', 217-23 and MIETHKE, *art. cit.*, 167-70.

(92) LUCHAIRE, *Actes du Louis VI*, no. 498, p. 229; see BAUTIER, 'Paris au temps d'Abélard', pp. 68-71.

(93) See above, p. 115 n. 48.

(94) JOHN OF SALISBURY, *Metalogicon* II, 10 (p. 78); BAUTIER, *art. cit.*, p. 77.

(95) JOHN OF SALISBURY, *Historia Pontificalis*, ed. M. CHIBNALL (Edinburgh, 1956), p. 63. He might have gone to the Paraclete in the interim, if the redaction of the *Problemata Heloissae* in the late 1130's is an indication.

(96) On these texts, see MEWS, 'The lists of heresies imputed to Peter Abelard', *Revue bénédictine* 95 (1985), 73-110.

126

There is no evidence that Abelard undertook any major new writing while he was a monk at Cluny. According to Peter the Venerable he was a sick man when he arrived at the monastery; for reasons of health he was later moved to the priory of St Marcel-sur-Saône, where he died 21 April 1142.

III. Conclusions

The *Dialectica* and the *Dialogus inter philosophum, Iudaeum et Christianum (Collationes)* are not works which belong to the last years of Abelard's life. If they are dated — very approximately — to around 1117 and 1125-26 respectively, a continuity to the evolution of his writings on both logic and theology becomes apparent.

From comparison of individual arguments of the *Dialectica* with those in the glosses on Porphyry, Aristotle and Boethius, commonly called the *Logica ' Ingredientibus '*, it would seem that the independent treatise is the earlier work, which may tentatively be dated to some time after he had become a monk at St Denis (*c.* 1116-1117). The *Dialectica* may well resume and synthesise the arguments of earlier works, such as the *Introductiones parvulorum* (probably a treatise different from his 'literal' glosses) and *liber fantasiarum* to which he makes reference. There is no conclusive evidence in the single surviving manuscript of the *Dialectica*, however, that any passages have been interpolated into its text as part of an imagined second or third recension, as suggested by Nicolau d'Olwer. The *Dialectica* seems to belong to a period in which Abelard, as a monk of St Denis, could devote himself to the study of logic with a new energy. Prior to these years, while he had a physical relationship with Heloise, he was, by his own admission, more interested in writing about love than about philosophy.

The composition of an independent text on dialectic was not in itself an original achievement. The *Introductiones parvulorum*, unfortunately no longer extant, may have been modelled on the *Introductiones* of William of Champeaux. Abelard may also have wished to emulate the *Dialectica* (also lost or unidentified) of his other major teacher, Roscelin of Compiègne[97]. Abelard gave equal importance to independent exposition and commentary on the ancients. For this reason he followed the *Dialectica* with new glosses on Porphyry *(Isagoge)*, Aristotle *(Categories, Periermeneias)* and Boethius *(De differentiis topicis)*. In writing these glosses he could continue to refine his ideas on individual aspects of logic, in parti-

---

(97) *Epist. XIV* (ed. Smits, p. 280): *Hic sicut pseudo-dialecticus ita et pseudo-christianus cum in Dialectica sua nullam rem, sed solam vocem partes habere astruat, ita et divinam paginam impudenter pervertit ...*; on the *Introductiones* of William, see above, p. 75, n. 11.

cular seeking to clarify the distinction between a word as a physical sound and its capacity to signify, which was dependent on the context within which it was used.

At the same time as he was teaching dialectic, Abelard was beginning to develop his ideas about the trinity of persons in God. Just as people with different linguistic backgrounds might express the same underlying intellection, so the ancient philosophers could grasp some of the same basic insights into the nature of God as did the prophets of the Old Testament. While the precedent of seeking logical analogies for the doctrine of the Trinity had already been set, among others, by Roscelin, Abelard refused to accept his teacher's argument that the three persons could be likened to three *res*. In order to refute his former teacher he drew on a great number of philosophical texts, but although he may have been influenced by the study of Plato and Macrobius as undertaken at Chartres, he was suspicious of adopting too literal an interpretation of Platonic concepts. He preferred to take Aristotle as his final authority. The first version of his treatise on the Trinity, the *Theologia ' Summi boni '*, contained the extension of his thinking about language into an analysis of statements of belief.

After completing *TSum* Abelard continued to write on secular subjects: he sought to complement the *Dialectica* by producing a *Grammatica* (also referred to as a *retractatio predicamentorum*, perhaps a reworking of the first part of the *Dialectica*, the *liber partium*) and a *Rethorica* (at least planned, if not written). He also composed a *Tractatus de intellectibus*, in which he developed further his ideas about signification, and revised yet again his comments on Porphyry *(Glossule* or *Logica ' Nostrorum petitioni sociorum '*, a revision of the *Glosse secundum vocales)*. Exactly when he produced these works is not known for certain, but it seems more likely time-wise that he would have composed them after he had escaped from St Denis and had begun to teach on the site of the Paraclete.

The accusations which were made against Abelard's treatise on the Trinity, in particular that he paid too much attention to *ratio* and not enough to *auctoritas*, prompted him to compile a collection of contradictory patristic quotations, initially about the Trinity and the person of Christ, but then about other subjects as well (the sacraments and charity) under the title of *Sic et Non*. The result was a portable library of quotation with which Abelard could supplement his theological writing and teaching. He probably started to develop the *Sic et Non* soon after the council of Soissons, but continued to add to the work over a long period of time. Similarly his expansion of the *Theologia ' Summi boni '* into the *Theologia Christiana* may have been a gradual process. Into this revision of the *Theologia* Abelard incorporated much of his patristic reading as well as new ideas of logic, as formulated in his *Grammatica* and *Glossule* on Porphyry. In the second book of *TChr* he may have drawn on a polemical

128

Exhortatio which he had written probably soon after his escape, addressed to the monks of St Denis.

His desire to establish the common ground between the moral teaching of philosophy and the Gospel led Abelard to write his *Dialogus* or *Collationes*, in which he compared the opinions of a philosopher with those of a Jew and of a Christian. The reader was left to establish for himself the fundamental identity of interest which united the three participants. In composing this treatise Abelard could bring together both the secular and religious aspects of his teaching. Having written a *Dialectica, Grammatica* and (perhaps) *Rethorica*, he wished to move to another branch of philosophy, that of ethics; but rather than produce an independent treatise on the subject, he sought to relate classical ethical doctrine to the teaching of the Jewish and Christian faiths. The idea of producing such a dialogue was not entirely original. Gilbert Crispin, a generation earlier, had produced a very popular dialogue of a Christian with a Jew, while another of a Christian with a gentile, but these were fundamentally dogmatic works, closely dependent on the writing of Anselm of Canterbury[98]. Abelard would give much greater importance to the role of the philosopher, who was engaged in a quest into the nature of the supreme good and into how man could achieve beatitude. In the first of the two debates Abelard advanced his theme that the philosopher was not obliged to add the precepts of the Jewish Law to those of natural law, while in the second that which the philosopher knew as ethics was fundamentally the same as the *divinitas* of the Christian. His idealised presentation of the philosopher may have been influenced by his feeling at the time that there might be more tolerance in a Muslim than in a Christian country. The Christian in the *Dialogus* presents a less rounded exposition of his beliefs, and while explaining in philosophical terms his conception of man's final end as the vision of God and the meaning of 'good' and 'evil', does not enuntiate the Christian doctrine of the path to salvation.

The experience of being abbot at St Gildas and then of establishing a religious community at the Paraclete under the authority of Heloise obliged Abelard to develop his thinking in a new direction, in which his ideas were framed more within a scriptural than within a purely philosophical context. From the outset in his writings for the Paraclete he laid

---

(98) Gilbert Crispin, *Disputatio Iudaei et Christiani*, ed. B. Blumenkranz, *Stromata patristica et mediaevalia* 3 (Utrecht 1956) and *Disputatio Christiani cum gentili de fide Christi*, ed. C. C. J. Webb, 'Gilbert Crispin's Dispute of a Christian with a Heathen, *Medieval and Renaissance Studies* 3 (1954), 55-77. See too the studies of Blumenkranz, 'La Disputatio cum Iudaei cum Christiano de Gilbert Crispin, abbé de Westminster', *Revue du moyen âge latin* 4 (1948), 237-52 and *Les auteurs chrétiens latins du moyen âge sur les Juifs et le Judaïsme* (Paris-The Hague, 1963), and R. W. Southern, 'St Anselm and Gilbert Crispin, Abbot of Westminster', *Medieval and Renaissance Studies* 3 (1954), 78-115.

great emphasis on the study of scripture. When he returned to Paris in the early 1130's he continued to teach both *lectio philosophica* and *lectio sacra*, as he had done since 1114, but his literary effort was now directed to a programme of scriptural commentary, notably the *Expositio in Hexaemeron* at the request of Heloise and a much longer commentary on Romans. These works were composed at the same time as he was drafting a major new revision of the *Theologia (' Scholarium ')*, which, as he stated in its preface, was intended to provide an introduction to the study of scripture. In the commentary on Romans he developed a number of themes outlined in the first *collatio* of the *Dialogus*, but went further in examining the redemption. The *Ethica* was to develop the ideas of the second *collatio* about vice and virtue. He also planned an *Anthropologia* about the incarnation, but it is not known if the project ever came to fruition[99].

Abelard's original passion for the study of dialectic developed into an ambition to apply its principles to the range of sacred as well as of secular learning. He gradually envisaged a series of works, each related to the other, which would reflect his conception of the underlying unity of all wisdom: *Dialectica, Grammatica, Rethorica, Theologia, Anthropologia* and *Ethica*. They were intended to complement a series of commentaries on those texts which formed the basis of his teaching. The common thread running through these works was a conviction in the importance of philosophical endeavour. Among his students he was always known as 'the Peripatetic of Le Pallet' or simply 'the Philosopher'. The irony was that in the 1130's Abelard was no longer at the forefront in the teaching of logic, having written his major works on the subject well over ten years earlier, before the new texts of Aristotle had become widely known. To his critics, generally quite ignorant of the new developments taking place in logic, he was an arrogant dialectician who made blasphemous statements about the Trinity, the redemption, the power of the Church and the nature of sin. In his own mind, Abelard was simply trying to extend the insights which he had gained in the study of philosophy into a coherent body of doctrine which expressed his understanding of Christian belief and morality.*

---

(99) *Comm. Rom.* (p. 215); in subject matter this seems identical to the *Tropologia* mentioned earlier (p. 118); the latter may be an error incurred through the mistake of a scribe.

(*) I would like to express my gratitude to M. Jean Jolivet both for prompting this study and for the attention which he has given to its arguments.

Summary of the career and writings of Peter Abelard

This list brings together those chronological details about Abelard's life and writings discussed either in the preceding study or in the articles listed in its opening footnote. For further detail of the editions referred to, see the list of abbreviations. Recensions are indicated by the sigla of the MSS in which they occur, as cited in these editions. Round brackets indicate that a work is no longer extant. The exact sequence of certain texts is not known, while the dates are only approximate. Further research may clarify points of detail.

1079   Born at Le Pallet.

c. 1095-1102   Studies dialectic with different teachers, including Roscelin of Compiègne at Loches and finally William of Champeaux in Paris.

c. 1102-5   Teaching at Corbeil and then Melun.

1102-8   *Editio super Porphyrium*; *Editio super Predicamenta Aristotelis*; *Editio super Periermeneias Aristotelis*; *de divisionibus Boethii* ('literal' glosses).

c. 1105-8   Returns to Brittany; further study of dialectic.

1108-9   Returns to Paris to study rhetoric; debate with William of Champeaux about universals.

1109-12   Teaching at Melun and then on the Mont Ste Geneviève.

1109-16   *(Introductiones parvulorum; liber fantasiarum)*; *sententie secundum magistrum Petrum (?)*.

1113   Short stay at Laon to study divinity.

1113-14   *(Expositio in Ezechielem)*.

1114-16   Teaching at Notre-Dame, Paris; affair with Heloise, birth of Astralabe, followed by secret marriage; *(carmina amatoria)*.

1116/17-21   Castration, followed by entry into St Denis; subsequently moves to a church dependent on St Denis to continue his former teaching activity.

c. 1117-21   *Dialectica.*
              Glosse super Porphyrium, super Predicamenta, super Periermeneias, sup. Topica (Logica ' Ingedientibus ') [*sup. Per.* and *sup. Topica* perhaps after *TSum*].
              Glosse super Porphyrium secundum vocales.

c. 1120	*(Epist. ad canonicos Turonensis S. Martini)*; *Theologia ' Summi boni' (EL)*. *Epist. XIV*; *TSum (B)*.
April 1121	Council of Soissons, followed by short stay at St Medard and then return to St Denis.
1121	First recension of *Sic et Non (Z)*; (possibly) begins to extend *TSum* into *TChr*; *Epist. XI*.
late 1121	Escapes from St Denis; stays at St Ayoul, Provins; *(Exhortatio ad fratres et commonachos)*.
March 1122	Negociates his release from obligation to St Denis and obtains permission to establish an oratory dedicated to the Holy Trinity near Quincy.
1122-27	Resumes teaching activity on the site of his oratory, re-dedicated to the Paraclete.
1120-24(?)	*(Rethorica* planned, if not written; *Grammatica)*. *Tractatus de intellectibus*; *Glossule super Porphyrium*.
c. 1122	*Soliloquium*.
1121-26	*Sic et Non* (recension *TCEB*); *Theologia Christiana (D)*; *Sic et Non (DL)*; *TChr (R)*.
c. 1125-26	*Dialogus inter philosophum, Iudaeum et Christianum* (collationes).
1127	Collapse of community around Paraclete; appointment as abbot of St Gildas-de-Ruys.
1127-28	*Sermo 33*; *Sermo ' Adtentite a falsis prophetis '* (?).
1127-32	*Epist. XII* (?); sermons to monks of St Gildas; *Sic et Non (MKA)*.
1129	Expulsion of nuns from Argenteuil; Abelard invites Heloise to establish a monastic community at the Paraclete.
Jan. 1131	Abelard present at consecration of new altar at Morigny.
28 Nov. 1131	Obtains a papal charter for the Paraclete.
1132-33	*Historia Calamitatum*.
1132-37(?)	*Epist. II-X*; *(Psalterium* prior to *Epist. IV)*; *Hymnarius Paraclitensis*; sends sermons to the Paraclete.
1132-33	Returns to Paris, attached to the school of Ste Geneviève, probably through the intervention of its dean, Stephen Garland.

132

1133-37(?)	Early drafts of the *Theologia* ' *Scholarium* ' *(tsch FH, TChr CT; tsch Z* based on *FH* and *CT)*. *Expositio in Hexaemeron*; *Epist. XIII*; *tsch T*. *Comm. in Ep. ad Romanos* [plans to write *Anthropologia* and *Comm. in Ep ad Galatas*]. *Theologia* ' *Scholarium* ' (complete text *BDKM* based on *tsch T* and *TChr T*, with new material). Also in this period formulation of collections of his *sententie* : *Sententie Florianenses* (before *tsch T*); *Sententie Abaelardi* (recensions *G, C, P* contemporary with *tsch Z, T*; recensions *AMN* after *TSch* I); *Sententie Parisienses*; *Commentarius Cantabrigiensis* (on the Pauline Epistles).
late 1137	Leaves the Mont Ste Geneviève (possibly related to the loss of influence of Stephen Garland after the death of Louis VI, 1 August 1137); returns to the Mount at an unknown date.
c. 1137-38	*Problemata Heloissae.*
1138-39	*Ethica.* *(liber sententiarum magistri Petri)* (summary of the teaching of Abelard, seen by William of St Thierry).
1140	*Theologia* ' *Scholarium* ' (recensions *AP* and *O*); *Confessio fidei* ' *Universis* '; *Confessio fidei ad Heloissam*; *Apologia contra Bernardum.*
2 June 1140	Council of Sens; later enters the monastery of Cluny.
21 Apr. 1142	Death at St-Marcel-sur-Saône.

Abbreviations: texts of Abelard

Comm. Rom.   *Commentaria in Epistolam Pauli ad Romanos*, ed. E. M. BUYTAERT, Petri Abaelardi Opera Theologica I, Corpus Christianorum. Continuatio Mediaevalis 11 (Turnhout, 1969).

D.   *Dialectica*, ed. L. M. de RIJK, Wijsgerige teksten en studies (Assen, 1956, 1970²).

Dial.   *Dialogus inter philosophum, Iudaeum et Christianum*, ed. R. THOMAS (Stuttgart-Bad Cannstatt, 1970).

Ed.   *Editio super Porphyrium, super Categorias, super Periermeneias Aristotelis, De divisionibus* (literal glosses), ed. M. DAL PRA, *Pietro Abelardo. Scritti filosofici* (Rome-Milan, 1954 ; *Scritti di logica*, 1969²), pp. 3-203.

Epist. II-V   'The Personal Letters between Abelard and Heloise', ed. J. T. MUCKLE, *Medieval Studies* 15 (1953), 47-84.

Epist. VI-VII   'The Letter of Heloise on Religious Life and Abelard's First Reply', ed. MUCKLE, *ibid.* 17 (1955), 240-81.

Epist. VIII   'Abelard's Rule for Religious Women', ed. T. P. McLAUGHLIN, *ibid.* 18 (1956), 241-92.

Epist. IX-XIV *Peter Abelard. Letters IX-XIV*, ed. E. R. SMITS (Groningen, 1983).

Ethica   *Peter Abelard's Ethics*, ed. D. E. LUSCOMBE (Oxford, 1971).

Exp. in Hex.   *Expositio in Hexaemeron*, PL 178, 731-841; ed. M. F. ROMIG, *A Critical Edition of Peter Abelard's Expositio in Hexaemeron* (Unpublished Ph. D. dissertation, University of Southern California, Los Angeles, 1981).

Gl. sec. voc.   *Glossae super Porphyrium secundum vocales*, ed. B. GEYER (fragments only), *Peter Abaelards Philosophische Schriften III*, Beiträge zur Geschichte der Philosophie und Theologie des Mittelalters 21, 4 (1933, 1973²), pp. 583-8; 'Un opusculo inedito di Abelardo', ed. C. OTTAVIANO, *Fontes Ambrosiani* 3 (Florence, 1933), pp. 95-207.

Glossule   *Glossulae super Porphyrium*, ed. GEYER, *Philosophische Schriften II· Die Logica 'Nostrorum petitioni sociorum'*, BGPTMA 21, 4 (1933, 1973²), 505-80.

Hist. Cal.   *Abélard. Historia Calamitatum*, ed. J. MONFRIN (Paris, 1959, 1979⁴).

Probl. Hel.   *Problemata Heloissae*, PL 178, 677-730.

Sermo 1-33   *Sermones*, PL 178, 379-610.

SN   *Peter Abailard. Sic et Non*, ed. B. BOYER & R. McKEON (Chicago-London, 1976, 1977).

Sol.   *Soliloquium*, PL 178, 1876C-1880A (among the letters of Berengar); ed. C. S. F. BURNETT, 'Peter Abelard, Soliloquium', *Studi Medievali* N.S. 26 (1985).

sup. Per.   *Glossae super Periermeneias*, ed. GEYER, *Philosophische Schriften I. Die Logica 'Ingredientibus'*, BGPTMA 21, 3 (1927), 303-503; ed. L. MINIO-PALUELLO, *Twelfth Century Logic. Texts and Studies II. Abaelardiana Inedita* (Rome, 1958), pp. 3-108.

sup. Por	*Glossae super Porphyrium ('Ingredientibus')*, ed. GEYER, *ibid.* 21, 1 (1919), pp. 1-109.
sup. Pred.	*Glossae super Praedicamenta*, ed. GEYER, *ibid.* 21, 2 (1921), pp. 111-305.
sup. Top.	*Super Topica Glossae*, ed. DAL PRA, *Scritti filosofici*, pp. 205-330.
TChr	*Theologia Christiana*, ed. BUYTAERT, CCCM 12 (Turnhout, 1969), pp. 1-372.
tsch	*Theologia 'Scholarium'* (shorter recensions or drafts), ed. BUYTAERT, CCCM 12 (Turnhout, 1969), pp. 373-451.
TSch	*Theologia 'Scholarium'* (longer recensions; full version), ed. V. COUSIN *(Introductio ad theologiam)*, *Petri Abaelardi Opera* 2 vols. (Paris, 1849, 1859), 2, pp. 2-149.
TSum	*Theologia 'Summi boni'*, ed. H. OSTLENDER, BGPTMA 35, 2-3 (1939).

Abbreviations: secondary literature

Abélard en son temps	*Abélard en son temps. Actes du colloque international organisé à l'occasion du 9e centenaire de la naissance de Pierre Abélard (14-19 mai 1979)*, ed. J. JOLIVET (Paris, 1981).
Abélard, Neuchâtel	M. DE GANDILLAC, J. JOLIVET, G. KUNG, S. VANNI ROVIGHI, *Abélard; le «Dialogue»; la philosophie de la logique. Actes du colloque de Neuchâtel 16-17 novembre 1979*, Cahiers de la Revue de théologie et philosophie 6 (Genève-Lausanne-Neuchâtel, 1981).
BUYTAERT, CCCM 11	E. M. BUYTAERT, General Introduction (see above *Comm. Rom.*).
COTTIAUX	J. COTTIAUX, 'La Conception de la théologie chez Abélard', *Revue d'histoire ecclésiastique* 28 (1932), 247-95, 533-51, 788-828.
De RIJK	L. M. de RIJK, Introduction (see above *D.*).
GEYER	B. GEYER, Untersuchungen (see above *Gl. sec. voc.* and *Glossule*).
P. Abelard, Louvain	*Peter Abelard. Proceedings of the International Conference, Louvain May 10-12, 1971*, Mediaevalia Lovaniensia Series I, Studia II, ed. E. M. BUYTAERT (Louvain-The Hague, 1974).
P. Abaelardus, Trier	*Petrus Abaelardus (1079-1142). Person, Werk und Wirkung*, Trierer Theologische Studien 38, ed. R. THOMAS (Trier, 1980).
P. Abélard-P. le Vén.	*Pierre Abélard-Pierre le Vénérable; les courants philosophiques, littéraires et artistiques en occident au milieu du XIIe siècle. Abbaye de Cluny 2 au 9 juillet 1972*, Colloques internationaux du Centre national de la recherche scientifique 546 (Paris, 1975).
ROBERT	G. ROBERT, *Les écoles et l'enseignement pendant la première moitié du XIIe siècle* (Paris, 1909).
SIKES	J. G. SIKES, *Peter Abailard* (London, 1932).

References are normally to the page or column and line of the editions cited above, to the line only of *Dial.* and *Hist. Cal.*; *TSum* and *TSch* are also cited by the book and paragraph of forthcoming editions, consistent with the system adopted by Buytaert in his edition of *TChr*, followed here. The orthography of quoted extracts has been standardised for the sake of consistency.

VIII

ASPECTS OF THE EVOLUTION OF PETER ABAELARD'S THOUGHT ON SIGNIFICATION AND PREDICATION

One of the most distinctive characteristics of Peter Abaelard's thinking about logic, as about theology, is that it was in a state of continuous movement. His arguments on specific subjects, such as signification and predication, vary considerably from one work to another. Are the differences in his argument significant or do they simply reflect the varying demands of diverse audiences and literary genres? If different versions of the same work are compared, notably of his *Theologia* and of his glosses on Porphyry, it becomes apparent that Abaelard paid much attention to modifying the detail of an exposition. He seems never to be fully satisfied with what he has written [1]. Far from revealing an *insouciance* with regard to vocabulary

[1] The major versions of the *Theologia* in chronological sequence are: *Theologia 'Summi boni'* (*TSum*), ed H. OSTLENDER, BGPTMA 35, 2-3 (1939); *Theologia Christiana* (*TChr*), ed. E. M. BUYTAERT, CCCM 12 (Turnhout, 1969) pp. 1-372; *Theologia ' Scholarium '* (*TSch* — shorter recensions or drafts), ed. BUYTAERT, CCCM 12 (Turnhout, 1969) pp. 373-451; *Theologia 'Scholarium'* (*TSch* — full version '*Introductio ad theologiam* '), PL 178, 979-1114. References to *TSum* and *TSch* will be to forthcoming editions, as well as to those of Ostlender and PL 178. On their interrelationship, see C. J. MEWS, « The development of the *Theologia* of Peter Abelard », *Petrus Abaelardus (1079-1142). Person, Werk und Wirkung*, ed. R. THOMAS (Trier, 1980) pp. 183-98; « Peter Abelard's *Theologia Christiana* and *Theologia 'Scholarium'* re-examined », *RTAM* 52 (1985), pp. 109-58. The earliest glosses on the *logica vetus* are edited by M. DAL PRA, *Pietro Abelardo. Scritti di Logica*, Firenze, 1969², followed by the *Glossae super Porphyrium, super Praedicamenta Aristotelis* and *super Periermeneias Aristotelis* (cited as *sup. Por., sup. Pred., sup. Per.*) ed. B. GEYER, *Peter Abaelards Philosophische Schriften I. Die Logica 'Ingredientibus'*, BGPTMA 21, 1-3 (1919-27); the final part of the gloss on the *Periermeneias* is edited by L. MINIO-PALUELLO,

or to the structure of an argument, the differences in his treatment of given topics suggest that he would constantly refine his argument without ever arriving at a set and final solution. In another study, I have advanced the hypothesis that some arguments of the *Dialectica* may not only be less sophisticated than those of the glosses on Porphyry, Aristotle and Boethius, but may pre-date those of the *Logica 'Ingredientibus'* [2]. The intention of this paper is to look in a little more detail at the evolution of Abaelard's thought on signification and predication through comparison of arguments in the *Theologia 'Summi boni'* and *Theologia Christiana* with those in the *Dialectica* and glosses. We shall also examine references Abaelard makes in *TChr* to his *Grammatica* (either no longer extant or not yet identified), enigmatically described as a *retractatio predicamentorum*, and suggest that this work contained some important new ideas of the peripatetic philosopher.

Perhaps the most well-known example of evolution in Abaelard's terminology is the change in his definition of a universal from that of a *vox* in the *Glosse* on Porphyry to that of *sermo* in the *Glossule* on Porphyry (*Logica 'Nostrorum petitioni sociorum'*) [3]. The change

---

Twelfth Century Logic. Texts and Studies II. Abaelardiana Inedita, Roma, 1958, pp. 3-108. Later still are the *Glossule super Porphyrium,* ed. GEYER, *Phil. Schr. II. Die Logica 'Nostrorum petitioni sociorum',* BGPTMA 21, 4 (1973²). The orthography of quoted extracts has been standardised for the sake of consistency to conform as close as possible with that of the MSS, against which extracts have been checked.

[2] Geyer judged the *Dialectica,* ed. L. M. DE RIJK (Assen, 1970²) to be his most mature work, dating it to 1133-37; L. N. D'OLWER, followed in broad outline by de Rijk (*Dialectica,* pp. XXI-XXIII), dates the single surviving version to the mid-1130s, although claims to detect evidence within its text for two earlier recensions, dating to both before and after 1121, « Sur la date de la Dialectica d'Abélard », *Revue du moyen âge latin* 1 (1945) pp. 375-90. M.-T. BEONIO-BROCCHIERI argues that some passages of the *Dialectica* contain ideas less developed than those in the glosses, *La logica di Abelardo,* Firenze, 1969², pp. 9-11, 68-99. Doubts about the hypothesis of Nicolau d'Olwer are expressed by the author in « The development of the *Theologia* of Peter Abelard », *Petrus Abaelardus,* ed. THOMAS, pp. 185-186; for a detailed study, see MEWS, « On dating works of Peter Abelard », *Archives d'histoire doctrinale et littéraire du moyen âge* 52 (1985) pp. 73-134.

[3] *Sup. Por.* 16, 20-21: « ... restat ut huiusmodi universalitatem solis vocibus ascribamus »; *Glossule* 522, 28-31: « Sic ergo universales esse dicimus, cum ex nativitate, id est ex hominum institutione, predicari de pluribus habeant; voces vero sive res nullatenus universales esse, etsi omnes sermones voces esse constat ».

in terminology, while not a major shift in his understanding of a universal, allowed Abaelard to clarify the distinction between a word as a physical sound and as a signifying agent. In the *Logica 'Ingredientibus'* as in the earlier literal glosses, *vox* is used in both senses [4]. *Vox* is also used of a universal in the anonymous *Glosse super Porphyrium secundum vocales,* a revised version of the gloss on Porphyry *'Ingredientibus',* of which the *Glossule* (*'Nostrorum petitioni sociorum'*) seems to be a further revision [5]. In the discussion of modes of identity and difference in the *Theologia 'Summi boni',* textually very close to that occurring in the *Glosse secundum vocales,* Abaelard gives the example of *voces* as the same if they had the effect of revealing the same intellection, to illustrate identity by effect. He makes a virtually identical comment in the *Glossule,* but with respect to *sermones* rather than *voces* [6].

This particular sentence is not reproduced in *TChr,* but in another passage of *TSum,* within the same discussion of identity and difference, Abaelard replaced *vox* with *sermo,* when he wanted to mean a signifying word [7]. He thus clarified his discussion of the multiple

---

[4] On the significance of the change, see for example, J. JOLIVET, *Arts du langage et théologie chez Abélard,* Paris, 1969, pp. 69-71; BEONIO-BROCCHIERI, *La Logica di Abelardo,* pp. 44-60.

[5] Fragments of the *Glosse super Porphyrium secundum vocales* are edited by GEYER, *Phil. Schr. III,* BGPTMA 21, 4 (1973²), pp. 583-588; a complete, though inaccurate edition is given by C. OTTAVIANO, « Un opuscolo inedito di Abelardo », *Fontes Ambrosiani* 3 (Firenze, 1933) pp. 95-207. See MEWS, « A neglected gloss on the 'Isagoge' by Peter Abelard », *Freiburger Zeitschrift für Philosophie und Theologie* 31 (1984) pp. 35-55. On universal words, cf. *Gl. sec. voc.* III 3: « Eadem persona enim appellatur ab universali nomine et a singulari; et nota 'subsistant' transferri de rebus ad voces pro 'appellantur subsistentia' ex adiunctione horum vocabulorum 'genus' et 'species', que vocibus data sunt ex significatione »; *ibid.* III 9: « Inventa est itaque vox singularis ut Socrates, vox universalis ut homo. Utraque autem Socrates appellat, id est personaliter significat: Socrates enim talis est, per quem ista vel inter se vel cum aliis ad eandem personam coniungi possunt ».

[6] *Gl. sec. voc.,* ed. GEYER, 588, 30-32; *TSum* II 88 (p. 57, 1-4); *Glossule* 560, 6-8. On this passage and on some of the examples which follow, see MEWS, « On dating the works of Peter Abelard », pp. 80-83.

[7] *TSum* II 102 (p. 61, 4-13), modified in *TChr* III 162 (variant passages in *TChr* given in italics): « Sed cum Aristotiles vester dicit in I Periermeneias voces [*sermones sicut*] et litteras non easdem [*eosdem*] omnibus esse, sed diversas [*diversos*] diversis, secundum officium significandi id dixit [*add. TChr: quod est sermonum et litterarum*], non secundum [*ipsam vocum*] prolationem, quia cum sit prolatio vocum naturalis omnibus, significandi officium apud omnes

18

sense of words as opposed to their single physical form at the expense of modifying the Boethian translation (*nec litterae omnibus eaedem, nec eaedem voces*) of a text of Aristotle[8]. This enabled him to accentuate the distinction between *prolatio vocum naturalis,* common to all, and the *officium significandi* of *voces,* evident only to those who grasped their imposition. He also added a comment on statements of Aristotle (quoted rather inaccurately) that there could be one *vox,* but many affirmations, and of Priscian, that many names could fall under one *vox,* so as to emphasise that a *vox* was single in its physical form as an uttered sound[9]. The name *vox* was applied from its acoustic quality, not from any signifying role[10]. The change in terminology reinforced a point which he makes more explicitly in *TChr* than *TSum,* that *idem* and *diversum* could assume other meanings from adjoining words[11]. He distinguished, as he had not done in

non tenetur, sed apud eos solummodo qui earum impositionem non ignorant. Qui etiam postmodum cum in II Periermeneias ait vocem esse unam et affirmationes multas, aut cum Priscianus dixit multa nomina incidere in unam vocem, 'multa' seu 'diversa' accipiuntur secundum hoc quod diversos intellectus efficere valent [hoc quod ... valent: *ipsum significandi officium ad diversos intellectus constituendos unde affirmationes vel nomina dicuntur. Vocem vero unam dixit ex ipsa prolationis et soni forma, non ex officio, cum videlicet 'vox' hoc nomen ex qualitate soni, non ex officio significandi datum sit*]». P. O. KING cites this passage from *TChr* to argue that Abaelard identified universals as *sermones* in his important thesis, *Peter Abailard and the Problem of Universals,* Princeton University Ph.D. 1982, University Microfilms International, p. 300, but does not record here that it contains significant revisions of *TSum.* The change from *vox* to *sermo* reveals Abaelard's sensitivity in speaking of 'signifying words'. *Sermo* is also introduced in this sense in *TChr* I 23: « Licet etiam ipsum nostre mentis conceptum ipsius sermonis tam effectum quam causam ponere, in proferente quidem causam, in audiente effectum, quia et sermo ipse loquentis ab eius intellectu proficiscens generatur, ut eundem rursus in auditore generet intellectum. Pro hac itaque maxima sermonum et intellectuum cognatione non indecenter in eorum nominibus mutuas fieri licet translationes. Quod in rebus quoque et nominibus propter adiunctionem significationis frequenter contingit ».

[8] *Periermeneias* I 16a, *transl. Boethii,* ed. MINIO-PALUELLO, *Aristoteles Latinus* II 1-2, Bruges-Paris, 1965, p. 5.

[9] *Ibid.* I 18a, *ed. cit.,* II p. 13; PRISCIAN, *Institutiones grammaticarum* II 5, *Grammatici Latini* II, ed. KEIL, Leipzig 1855, pp. 74-75.

[10] Cf. *Glossule* 522, 19-21.

[11] *TChr* III 161: « Hec quidem dicta sunt ad ostendendum quot modis 'idem' et 'diversum' accipiantur ex propria vi per se etiam dicta, cum frequenter ex adiunctis et alias assumant significationes vel istas deponant ». *TChr* III 163: « Sic itaque ex adiunctione subiectorum 'idem' et 'diversum' frequenter suas

T Sum, between the force which was proper to a word (*ex propria vi per se etiam dicta*) and the *significationes* which derived from its association with other words. Abaelard was concerned to show that a *vox* like *idem* or *diversum* could not signify in itself, in the way that the language of Priscian might suggest.

Such use of *sermo* in the *Glossule* and *TChr* to denote a signifying term, distinct from *vox* as a natural sound stands in contrast to the position adopted in the *Dialectica,* in which Abaelard, although acknowledging that not all *voces* were significative, says that *vox* took its name from *vocando, id est significando*[12]. Nowhere in the *Dialectica* or in the gloss on the *Periermeneias* does he use *sermo* when quoting or referring to the phrase of Aristotle *nec voces nec litterae* or make such a distinction between *vox* and *sermo*[13]. Given the care with which he altered this text in the *TChr,* it seems hard to believe that he should have reverted to an earlier position or have left such a statement uncorrected in the *Dialectica*[14].

This is not to say that he accepted the idea, which he attributes to *magister noster V.,* that a *vox* signified everything to which it applied. His teacher's argument was based on the definition of Priscian that a name signified substance and quality, so that *album* always signified the subject body as well as the quality of whiteness[15].

---

significationes commutant, sicut et cetere sepe dictiones, ut si dicam 'citharedus bonus' et 'homo bonus' etc.».

[12] *Dial.* I 128, 4-5.

[13] Cf. *Dial.* I 111, 13-21; *sup. Per.* 319, 35-321, 16.

[14] *Dial.* I 111, 27-115, 9.

[15] *Dial.* I 112, 24-31; cf. 113, 15-20: « Hi vero qui omnem vocum impositionem in significationem deducunt, auctoritatem pretendunt ut ea quoque significari dicant a voce quibuscumque ipsa est imposita, ut ipsum quoque hominem ab '*animali*', vel Socratem ab '*homine*', vel subiectum corpus ab '*albo*' vel '*colorato*'; nec solum ex arte, verum etiam ex auctoritate grammatice id conantur ostendere ». The position of *magister noster V.* is described as nominalist by DE RIJK (*Dialectica,* pp. xx-xxi), following C. PRANTL, *Geschichte der Logik im Abendlande,* II, Leipzig, 1861, p. 124 n. 83, and judged inconsistent with the realist opinions held by William of Champeaux. In *Logica Modernorum,* II 1, p. 191, he argues that Abaelard follows this magister, but adds that *significatio* is taken for *impositio.* De Rijk suggests that *magister noster V.* may be Ulger of Angers, a contemporary of Abaelard (*scholasticus* in Angers in 1107, died 16 Oct. 1149), perhaps referred to in *TChr* IV 77. This view is questioned by JOLIVET, *Arts du langage,* p. 66 n. 22, and by K. M. FREDBORG, who shows that the opinions attributed to *magister noster V.* by Abaelard correspond exactly to those attributed to *mag. W.* (William of Champeaux) in an anonymous report

He opposed this view to that of Garmundus, which he thought more rational, that a *vox* signified only what was contained in its *sententia*. He was critical of too wide a use of the word «signification», but while asking how a *vox* signified, does not question that a *vox* signifies [16]. His emphasis in the gloss on the *Periermeneias* is subtly different. Whereas in the *Dialectica* Abaelard comments *Est autem significare non solum vocum, sed etiam rerum*, in the gloss he asserts: *Non enim significare vocum tantum est* [est *om*. Geyer], *verum etiam rerum* [17]. He avoids saying that some *voces*, such as the barking of a dog, signified naturally, preferring to say that barking represented the dog's anger [18]. Absent from the *Dialectica* is the distinction between *significantia* and *voces significativa*, the latter reserved for those *voces* which were instituted to signify [19]. Abaelard also develops the idea that in the case of a word simply meaning a word, *vox* signified through a process of *translatio*, not through any intrinsic property. This concept of transference of meaning, not discussed in the *Dialectica*, has an important place in the glosses on the *Categories* and *Periermeneias*, as well as in every version of the *Theologia* [20].

The change from *vox* to *sermo* in the *Glossule* on Porphyry and in the *TChr* reflects a more general trend in the evolution of Abaelard's thought, towards distinguishing the physical component of language from its capacity to signify. This is evident from comparison of his

of various *sententie*, « Tractatus Glosarum Prisciani in MS Vat. lat. 1486 », *Cahiers de l'Institut du Moyen Age Grec et Latin* 21 (1977) p. 34 n. 77, pp. 43-44 (21-44). Because the argument attributed to *magister noster* in *Dial*. I 135, 28-136, 36 is imputed to *magister noster V*. in *Dial*. II 168, 11-169, 28, it would seem that the same teacher is referred to with or without an initial. For fuller references, see MEWS, « On dating the works of Peter Abelard », p. 87 n. 54.

[16] *Dial*. I 114, 14-15. De Rijk interprets Abaelard's theory of signification in terms of « liberating the noun from the domain of the *res* » and freeing logic from an ontological point of view, but points out apparent « inconsistencies » in his argument, *Logica Modernorum*, II 1, pp. 190-203.

[17] *Dial*. I 111, 13; cf. *sup. Per*. 335, 35-36.

[18] *Sup. Per*. 335, 32-35, 39-336, 3: « Nam latratus natura artifex, id est deus, ea intentione cani contulit, ut iram eius representaret; [...] Nam licet unaqueque vox certificare possit suum prolatorem animal esse, sicut latratus canis ipsum esse iratum, non tamen omnes ad hoc institute sunt ostendendum, sicut latratus est ad significationem ire institutus »; cf. *sup. Per*. 340, 19-29.

[19] *Ibid*. 336, 9-12.

[20] *Ibid*. 336, 12-26; cf. *sup. Pred*. 121, 3-37; 350; 7; 364; 33; *TSum* I 5, 19 (pp. 4, 7-9; 7, 19-28); II 70-78 (pp. 50, 16-53, 10); III 36, 62-64 (pp. 81, 17; 90, 34-92, 5). Cf. *TChr* I 7, 16, 23, 37, 124-125; III, 134; IV 44-46.

two major discussions of indefinite words. In the *Dialectica* Abaelard begins his argument by asserting that conjunctions and prepositions had to have some meaning as indefinite words, if they were to be distinguished from letters and syllables. *Dictio* was derived from *dicendo, hoc est a significando* [21]. While he comments that dialecticians had a stronger argument than grammarians in separating them from names and verbs, he accepted the view of those grammarians sympathetic to dialectic who argued that the meaning of indefinite words was uncertain as they determined some property of the *res* of the words to which they were applied [22]. In the gloss, however, he questions the assumption that indefinite words had to have any intrinsic meaning, and argues that they could only consignify when used with another word. He concludes by commenting that Priscian used « signify » in a wider sense than dialecticians [23].

The discussions of the substantive verb in both the *Dialectica* and the gloss on the *Periermeneias* are built around a critique of the definition of Priscian that every verb signified either an action or a passion [24]. The substantive, he argued in the *Dialectica,* was imposed *secundum essentiam* and not *secundum alicuius adiacentiam.* When used as *tertium interpositum,* it did not have the meaning of essence in itself, but served the function of copulating the essences of things [25]. Whereas grammarians interpreted the verb in *Petrus est albus* to mean that Peter was informed with whiteness, he insisted that *proprie* it expressed a predication of essence; the attribution of adjacence was only implied (*innuitur*) [26]. Abaelard rejects the grammarians' view (held among others by the author of the *Glosule in Priscianum*) that

---

[21] *Dial.* I 118, 4-7.

[22] *Dial.* I 120, 4: « Illa ergo mihi sententia prelucere videtur, ut grammaticis consentientes qui etiam logice deserviunt, has quoque per se significativas esse confiteamur, sed in eo significationem earum esse dicamus, quod quasdam proprietates circa res eorum vocabulorum, quibus apponuntur prepositiones, quodammodo determinent ».

[23] *Sup. Per.* 337, 11-338, 20; 340, 7-13.

[24] *Dial.* I 130, 1-133, 29; cf. *sup. Per.* 346, 1-24. For perceptive comments on Abaelard's ideas on predication, see K. JACOBI, « Diskussionen über Prädikationstheorie in den logischen Schriften des Petrus Abailardus », *Petrus Abaelardus,* ed. THOMAS, pp. 165-179; see also his « Die Semantik sprachlicher Ausdrücke, Ausdrucksfolgen und Aussagen im Abailards Kommentar zu Peri hermeneias », *Medioevo* 7 (1981) pp. 41-89.

[25] *Dial.* I 131, 3-8.

[26] *Dial.* I 132, 3-6.

est could ambiguously have the force of a verb, signifying an action or a passion or be a substantive, signifying all things *in essentia*[27]. By contrast, his argument in the *Dialectica* that *est* links different essences echoes the position held in the *Glosule* and reported in the *Note Dunelmenses* about *est* when used as a substantive: *Nam illud positum in propositione diversas essentias convenienter ad se invicem iungere affirmamus*[28].

The difficulty with such an explanation was how to explain the function of a substantive when it linked non-existent terms, as in *Homerus est poeta*. According to his teacher (referred to both as *magister noster* and as *magister noster V.*), the accidental predication did not occur through the verb, which retained its literal sense, but through the figurative and non-literal nature of the construction as a whole[29]. This implied a distinction between the grammatical and dialectical levels of meaning, such as he attributes to William of Champeaux in the gloss on the *Topica*[30].

Abaelard's solution in the *Dialectica*, put forward towards the end of his discussion, was to argue that *est album*, like *est opinabile*, was one verb: *esse album, esse opinabile*[31]. While recognising that this seemed to go against the rules of grammarians, he commented that those who occupied the «first grade» of learning left many questions for dialecticians to answer[32]. In glossing the *Periermeneias* he avoids

---

[27] Cf. *Dial.* I 132, 35-133, 15; cf. *Glosule in Priscianum*, ed. R. W. HUNT, « Studies in Priscian I », *Medieval and Renaissance Studies* 1 (1943) pp. 226, 28-227, 36. Similar views are put forward in a text studied by K. M. FREDBORG, « Tractatus Glosarum Prisciani in MS Vat. lat. 1486 », pp. 24-27 (see above n. 15), and by Master Guido, a contemporary of Abaelard, in glosses on Priscian; cf. C. H. KNEEPKENS, « Master Guido and his Views on Government: On Twelfth-Century Linguistic Thought », *Vivarium* 16 (1978) pp. 119-21 (108-41). I am indebted to I. Rosier for discussion of twelfth-century glosses on Priscian.

[28] *Glosule*, ed. HUNT, 227, 2-3; *Note Dunelmenses*, ed. HUNT, 228, 32-229, 4: « Cum enim cetera verba inventa prius essent, nullum erat per quod diverse essentie ut essentie copulari possent, quod nullum adhuc erat quod essentias ut essentias significaret. Et ideo necessarium fuit invenire tale copulativum vocabulum quod omnes essentias ut essentias significaret ut easdem copulare posset ». Abaelard denies, however, that *est* signifies any essence in itself, *Dial.* I 135, 11-13: « Nec mirum, cum interpositum significationem essentie non habeat, sed tantum copulationis officium, ut dictum est, teneat ».

[29] *Dial.* I 135, 28-32; also reported II 168, 11-169, 28.

[30] Cf. *sup. Top.* 271, 38-274, 10.

[31] *Dial.* I 138, 11-17.

[32] *Dial.* I 140, 23-29: « Quod autem grammaticorum regulis contrarii videmur,

VIII

direct criticism of the views of *grammatici* or of his teacher, and frames his argument about the substantive within commentary on the views of Priscian[33]. He begins his account with a modified version of the thesis which he presents only at the end of his discussion in the *Dialectica*, that the substantive verb was often combined with the noun, for want of an appropriate verb, to have the force of a single verb or word (*in vi unius verbi vel dictionis*)[34]. Not mentioned in the other work is the idea of *translation* to explain how a word could change its meaning in such a composite expression[35]. He acknowledges that the substantive always involved a *copulatio essentie*, but distinguished between what was intended to be copulated and what was conjoined[36]. His argument is that in *Socrates est albus*, only *albedo* was intended to be copulated to the subject; *album,* or what was affected by whiteness, was conjoined to the subjects through the substantive verb, used for want of a more appropriate verb[37]. While

quod multa componimus verba vel substantiva, ut 'esse hominem' vel ab aliis quam ab actionibus vel passionibus sumpta, ut 'esse album', propter rectam enuntiationum sententiam aperiendam, non abhorreas. Illi enim qui primum discipline gradum tenent, pro capacitate tenerorum multa provectis inquirere aut corrigenda reliquerunt in quibus dialectice subtilitatem oportet laborare».

[33] *Sup. Per.* 346, 2-4; 348, 33-37; 351, 3-8; 358, 24-26; 360, 2-9; 363, 12-24.
[34] *Ibid.* 348, 15-350, 39. N. KRETZMANN attempts to interpret the evolution of Abaelard's theory of the copula on the assumption that the gloss is earlier than the *Dialectica,* « The Culmination of the Old Logic in Peter Abaelard », *Renaissance and Renewal in the Twelfth Century,* ed. R. L. BENSON & G. CONSTABLE, Oxford, 1982, pp. 488-511; he comments on the significance of this passage for assessing the relative chronology of the two works only in an additional note, p. 509 n. 62. K. JACOBI does not accept Kretzmann's hypothesis of an evolution from an « *Ingredientibus* theory» to a *Dialectica* «revision theory» and « suggestion». He posits that Abaelard could have put forward a variety of suggestions, « Peter Abelard on the Speech Sign 'Est' », *The Logic of Being,* ed. S. KNUUTTILA and J. HINTIKKA, Dordrecht, 1985, p. 171 (145-180). In his stimulating study, Jacobi emphasises the originality of Abaelard's two-piece (as distinct from a more traditional three-piece) theory of predication. He argues that Abaelard was trying to remove the word *'est'* from the limelight of linguistic debate, as it did not constitute the central problem at the foundation of a theory of the proposition. I am grateful to Jacobi for allowing me to see a copy of his article in proof, as well as a draft of his forthcoming edition of *sup. Per.*
[35] *Ibid.* 350, 5-18.
[36] *Ibid.* 360, 13-22.
[37] *Ibid.* 360, 23-33: « Duo itaque coniunguntur Socrati per album predicatum, albedo scilicet in adiacentia et album, id est ipsum affectum albedine, in

there might be a *coniunctio essentie* denoted through the verb, he makes no mention of any *predicatio essentie* as in the *Dialectica*[38]. He thus did not have the same difficulty in explaining the role of *est* copulated to a non-existent entity. In *chimera est opinabilis* the verb

essentia, sola tamen albedo predicatur, quia sola coniungi intenditur. Non enim quicquid coniungitur, predicatur, sed id solum quod proposition [per propositionem *B*] coniungi intenditur. Qui enim propositionem facit 'Socrates est albus', solam albedinem inesse Socrati ostendit, et si haberet verbum per quod posset simpliciter album copulare Socrati, ita quod nil substantivi attingeret, profecto sic faceret, sed quia non est verbum per quod id fiat, venit ad substantivum, quod quia essentie tantum significationem habet, non potest ipsum proferri sine coniunctione essentie; in essentia vero non potest albedo [album Geyer] Socrati copulari, ut scilicet dicatur Socrates est albedo». This was used as evidence that Abaelard held an « inherence » theory of predication by DE RIJK, in contrast with the so-called « identity theory », *Dialectica*, pp. XL-XLIV, and *Logica Modernorum*, II 1, p. 105, a view which he withdrew in « Die Wirkung der neuplatonischen Semantik auf des mittelalterliche Denken über das Sein », *Sprache und Erkenntnis im Mittelalter. Akten des VI Internationalen Kongress für Mittelalterliche Philosophie, 29 August - 3 September, 1977 in Bonn, Miscellanea Medievalia,* 13, Berlin, 1981, p. 31 (19-35). The distinction, drawn from E. MOODY's interpretation of the achievement of fourteenth-century logic, *Truth and Consequence in Medieval Logic,* Amsterdam, 1953, pp. 33-37, is developed by J. PINBORG, *Logik und Semantik im Mittelalter. Ein Ueberblick,* Stuttgart-Bad Cannstatt, 1972, p. 53. Its usefulness has been questioned, not only by de Rijk, but also by M. TWEEDALE, *Peter Abailard and Universals,* Amsterdam-New York-Oxford, 1976, pp. 229-231 and in more general form by J. MALCOLM, « A reconsideration of the identity and inherence theories of the copula », *Journal of the History of Philosophy* 17 (1979) pp. 383-400. Further criticism of applying too rigid « theories » to Abaelard is made by K. JACOBI, « Diskussionen über Prädikationstheorie in den logischen Schriften des Petrus Abailardus », p. 167. William of Conches and Peter Helias criticised theories of the inherence of the predicate in the subject, according to DE RIJK under Abaelard's influence, *Logica Modernorum,* II 1, p. 106-7.

[38] *Ibid.* 360, 34-361, 3: « Unde ut et albedo [album *B*, Geyer] copuletur in adiacentia et secundum predicationem albedinis [secundum substantivum album *A*, Geyer] coniunctio essentie vere ponatur, adiectivum quod est *album*, coniungitur verbo, quod et formam quam significat, adiacentem predicat, et fundamentum quod nominat, essentialiter coniungat [coniungat *om. A*, Geyer], secundum albedinem tantum predicatur [praedicet *A*, Geyer], quia [quod *A*, Geyer] in ea tantum vi, ut dictum est, poni intenditur». Cf. *Dial.* I 132, 3-18. DE RIJK quotes this passage (360, 23-361, 3) in his important study, « Die Wirkung der neuplatonischen Semantik », p. 22 n. 6. Some, though not of all of his suggested emendations have been followed here, for which the Berlin and Milan MSS (*B* Preussischerkulturbesitz lat. fol. 624; *A* Bibl. Ambr. M 63 sup.) have been used to correct Geyer's text.

was transferred to a nuncupative sense, which, as he had already demonstrated, did not depend on any existence [39].

The distinction between conjunction and predication is developed at even greater length in his gloss on the *De differentiis topicis,* written after that on the *Periermeneias* [40]. He criticises the doctrine of his teacher William (of Champeaux) that there were always two senses to a statement, one grammatical, which was the level on which it was judged true or false, the other dialectical, concerned with predication [41]. According to William, grammatically, in *Socrates est albus* there was a copulation of essence between what was affected by whiteness and Socrates; for a dialectician, *Socrates est albedo* was the same as *Socrates est album,* because both implied that *albedo* inhered in Socrates. The same distinction is found in the *Glosule in Priscianum* [42]. Abaelard refused to accept that there could be two such senses to a construction [43]. The sense of *Socrates est albus* was determined by the intention behind the statement, namely that of predicating *albedo* of Socrates [44]. Although *albedo* could only be copulated *in adiacentia,* not *in essentia, albedo* and not *album* was predicated of the subject [45].

---

[39] *Ibid.* 361, 19-25.

[40] The glosses on the topics are not part of the *Introductiones parvulorum,* as shown by DAL PRA, *Scritti di Logica,* pp. XXXII-XXXVI. Valuable comments on the distinction between predication and conjunction in the glosses are made by DE RIJK in « Die Wirkung der neuplatonischen Semantik », pp. 19-35 (see above n. 37).

[41] *Sup. Top.,* ed. DAL PRA, 271, 38-273, 18.

[42] *Ibid.* 272, 6-38. Cf. *Glosule,* ed. HUNT, 227, 25-28: « Sed nota alium sensum esse huius propositionis 'Socrates est albus' ex vi predicationis, alium ex vi substantivi verbi. Ex vi enim predicationis hoc solum intendit hec propositio quod albedo inhereat Socrati, ex vi vero substantivi hoc dicit, quod illa res que est Socrates est album corpus, quia hoc dicit hec propositio in sensu quantum ad vim substantivi 'Socrates est alba res' ».

[43] *Sup. Top.* 273, 37-274, 10.

[44] *Ibid.* 275, 16-18: « Quippe cum audimus 'Socrates est albus' vel 'Socrates albus', per '*albus*' solum albedinem, non affectum albedine Socrati in animo nostro copulamus ».

[45] *Ibid.* 274, 39-275, 7: « At vero albedo in essentia vere copulari non potest. Unde ad fundamentum ipsius venimus, quod non in essentia substantivi [subiecti Dal Pra] verbi copulamus; albedinis similiter adiacentiam quam intendimus indicamus, dum videlicet proponimus ipsum Socratem esse ipsum subiectum albedinis, et licet duo copulentur, fundamentum scilicet in essentia et albedo in adiacentia, sola tamen predicari dicitur quia sola copulari intenditur, et propter copulationem eius tantum propositio fit et predicatum vocabulum maxime in

The contrast between his treatment of predication in the *Dialectica* and in the glosses on the *Periermeneias* and *De differentiis topicis* has a parallel in the change which Abaelard made in *TChr* to the discussion of identity and difference in *TSum*. As Geyer noted, his argument in *TSum* is almost identical to that occurring in the *Glosse super Porphyrium secundum vocales,* in particular their common statement that those things were said to be the same essentially which could be joined by a predication of essence, which was equivalent to saying «the same by predication» [46]. Yet in the *Glossule* on Porphyry Abaelard describes this opinion as erroneous because many things were essentially the same, such as a noun and a verb, but were not the same by predication [47]. Within the long discussion of identity and difference in *TChr*, even more developed than that in the *Glossule,* he omits the statement of *TSum* about identity of essence as the same as that by predication and develops the idea that things could be essentially the same, but different in property. He gives the example of the substance (*materia*) of a wax image as separate in property from what was made of wax (*materiatum*) [48]. *Materia* and *materiatum* could not be joined through predication, even though they were not separate in essence. The relevant passages can be compared (key phrases italicised), although the full text of *TChr*, too long to be quoted here, deserves to be read in its entirety:

(*TSum* II 82; pp. 54, 22-55, 13) Sex autem modis ac pluribus fortassis utrumque dicitur. Idem nam-	(*TChr* III 138) Quinque autem modis ac pluribus fortassis utrumque per se etiam acceptum dici

significationem eius subiecto copulatur, quia tantum ad subiectionem albedinis ostendendam subiecto coniungitur».

[46] *TSum* II 83 (p. 55, 2-5), quoted below; *Gl. sec. voc.,* ed GEYER, 588, 10-11: « Qui etiam modus [*scil.* secundum essentiam] idem est ille qui est idem predicatione ».

[47] *Glossule* 558, 17-21: « Nam idem dicitur in essentia, quorumcumque [quorum unumquodque Geyer] est eadem essentia, ita scilicet, ut hec essentia non sit illa, sicut hic homo et Socrates. Que identitas idem videtur esse cum identitate predicationis quibusdam, quod falsum est, cum multa sint eadem essentialiter et non predicatione, sicut nomen et verbum et cetera huiusmodi ». Geyer notes the difference (*Untersuchungen,* p. 601), but does not comment on its significance.

[48] Cf. *TChr* III 138. New discussion of property occurs in *TChr* III 140-141. Key passages on disjunction through predication occur in *TChr* III 173-174, 176, 186; IV 39-40, 46, 48-51, 154-158.

que sive unum aliquid cum aliquo dicitur secundum essentiam sive secundum numerum, idem diffinitione, idem similitudine, idem pro incommutato, idem effectu. Totidem modis e contrario dicimus diversum ac fortassis pluribus modis. [83] *Idem esse secundum essentiam dicimus, quorumcumque eadem est essentia,* ita scilicet, ut hoc sit illud, sicut idem est ensis quod mucro, vel substantia quod corpus sive animal sive homo sive etiam Socrates, et album quod durum; et *omnia eadem essentialiter dicuntur quecumque predicatione essentie invicem coniungi possunt, quod tale est ac si diceremus idem predicatione.* Verum est enim substantiam esse corpus sive animal, licet non omnem. Et hec quidem omnia que videlicet eadem sunt essentialiter, eadem numero necesse est, sed non convertitur. Nam fortassis hec manus idem est numero cum homine isto cuius est pars, et nulla pars a suo toto diversa est numero, nec tamen essentialiter idem est pars quod totum, cum ipsa essentia partis non sit essentia totius, nec sibi invicem predicatione coniungi queant. ... [91 (p. 57, 10-19)] Dicimus enim diversa aliqua secundum essentiam, quotiens videlicet essentia unius non est essentia alterius. ... *Omnia ergo essentialiter diversa dicimus que ita in propriis essentiis sunt ab invicem disparata,* ut hoc non sit illud; quod est dicere diversa oppositione sive *diversa predicatione.*

videtur. Idem namque sive unum aliquid cum aliquo dicitur secundum essentiam sive secundum numerum, *idem proprietate,* idem diffinitione, idem similitudine, idem pro incommutato. Totidem modis e contrario dicimus diversum ac fortassis pluribus. [139] *Idem aliquid cum aliquo essentialiter dicimus quorum eadem numero est essentia,* ita scilicet ut hoc et illud sint eadem numero essentia, sicut eadem numero essentia est ensis et mucro, vel substantia et corpus sive animal sive homo sive etiam Socrates, et album idem numero quod durum. Verum est enim substantiam esse hoc corpus sive hoc animal, licet non omnem. ... [140] Idem vero proprietate aliquid cum aliquo dicitur, quando hoc illius proprietate participat, ut album duri vel durum albi. Nam et album duritia participat que est proprietas duri, quod est dicere durum esse album, vel e converso durum albi. Nonnulla autem essentialiter eadem sunt que tamen proprietatibus suis distinguuntur, cum eorum scilicet proprietates ita penitus impermixte maneant, ut proprietas alterius ab altero minime participetur, etiam si sit eadem numero penitus utriusque **substantia.** ... [141] *Proprietates itaque ipse impermixte sunt per predicationem,* licet ipsa propriata, ut ita dicam, permixtim de eodem predicentur. Aliud quippe est predicare formam, aliud formatum ipsum, hoc est rem ipsam forme subiectam. ... [148] Dicimus autem ea ab invicem essentialiter diversa quecumque ita

28

ab invicem dissident, ut hoc non
sit illud, aut Socrates non est Plato
nec manus Socratis Socrates. ...
[153] Et notandum quod cum
*omne idem essentialiter cum aliquo
sit idem numero cum ipso, et e
converso*, non tamen omnes diversum essentialiter ab aliquo diversum in numero est ab ipso, ut
supra docuimus.

As evident from the above texts, in *TSum* Abaelard defined things
as essentially the same as those whose essence was the same, or
which could be joined by a predication of essence. Conversely things
were essentially different whose essences were disparate, and thus
different by predication. A part was not essentially the same as a
whole and could not be joined to it through predication even though
it was the same in number. In *TChr*, however, he defines things as
essentially the same as those whose essence was the same in number,
while avoiding any mention of an essence being predicated of essence.
He states that identity of essence was convertible with identity of
number (a point denied in *TSum*), referring his reader to more
extensive discussion elsewhere « on the predicament of substance » [49]
Rather than implying that an essence was predicated of an essence,
as in *TSum*, he argues that things could be essentially the same, but
distinct in property or predication.

This idea that things could be discrete by property, as distinct
from definition alone, is an important new argument in *TChr*, as
apparent from the changes which he made to the following text:

(*TSum* II 107; p. 63, 15-26)	(*TChr* IV 172). Quod si expres-
Quod si expressius prosequi veli-	sius prosequi velimus, quid sonet
mus, quid sonet persona in deo,	persona in deo, tantumdem valet
tantumdem valet quantum si dica-	quantum si dicamus eum esse vel

---

[49] *TChr* III 153: « De quo quidem latius in predicamento substantie alibi
nobis agendum fuit ». In the *Glossule* (558, 21-27) identity of essence is separated
from identity by number as in *TSum*, even though it has a different view of
identity by predication. This would suggest that the *Glossule* precede *TChr*, a
hypothesis corroborated by the absence of mention of *proprietas* and inclusion
of identity by effect as in *TSum*.

mus eum esse vel patrem, hoc est potentem, vel filium, hoc est sapientem, vel spiritum sanctum, hoc est benignum. [...] Tale est etiam patrem et filium et spiritum sanctum esse tres personas ab invicem discretas, tamquam si dicamus nullas harum mutuo sese exigere, ita scilicet, ut vel ex eo quod pater est, id est potens, sit filius, hoc est discretus, et e converso, vel ex eo quod pater est, spiritus sanctus sit, id est benignus, et e converso, vel ex eo quod est filius, sit spiritus sanctus, et e converso.

patrem, hoc est divinam potentiam generantem, vel filium, hoc est divinam sapientiam genitam, vel spiritum sanctum, hoc est divine benignitatis processum. [...] Tale est etiam patrem et filium et spiritum sanctum esse tres personas ab invicem discretas, tamquam si dicamus, tres personas ex diversitate proprietatum suarum ita ab invicem per predicationem disiunctas, ut nulla earum sit altera, neque scilicet pater sit filius aut spiritus sanctus, neque filius sit spiritus. De qua quidem predicationis oratione plene nobis disserendum in sequentibus erit.

In this text of *TSum*, as in many others, the difference between the persons is given as one of definition: «that he is the father» being identified with «that he is powerful» etc. One could construe, however, that the essence of *potens* was being predicated of the essence of *pater*, which did not explain why it could not be predicated of the other persons. The change which he introduced in *TChr* was to say that they differed by property and so could not be joined by predication. The notion of disjunction is an important innovation because it evoked the impossibility of linguistic coupling between terms, not a diversity on the level of essence [50]. He adds a statement in *TChr* which marks

[50] A very similar sentence in *TSum* II 103 using *ex eo quod potens est* etc. is omitted in *TChr* III 164. A similar, consistent change is evident in the following passages: 1. *TSum* I 2 (p. 3, 13-16): «Tale est ergo deum esse tres personas, hoc est patrem ed filium et spiritum sanctum, ac si dicamus divinam substantiam esse potentem, sapientem, benignam, immo etiam esse ipsam potentiam, ipsam sapientiam, ipsam benignitatem. [*TChr* I 4: Tale est ergo tres personas, hoc est patrem et filium et spiritum sanctum, in divinitate confiteri, ac si commemoraremus divinam potentiam generantem, divinam sapientiam genitam, divinam benignitatem procedentem, ut his videlicet tribus commemoratis summi boni perfectio predicetur, cum videlicet ipse deus et summe potens, id est omnipotens, et summe sapiens et summe benignus ostenditur] ». 2. *TSum* III 100 (p. 107, 17-20): «Cum enim deum esse patrem et filium et spiritum sanctum tale sit, ut diximus, deum esse potentem et sapientem et benignum

30

the evolution of his argument from that in *TSum*, in which he had only spoken of diversity of definition:

> Et fortasse cum dicimus in deo personas diversas, ita scilicet ut non solum sint diffinitione diverse, verum etiam predicatione ab invicem disiuncte, cum hec non sit illa, non est necesse ut hoc nomen 'diversum' per se hanc significationem gerat, sed ex adiuncto, quod est persona, id contrahat [51].

[potentem ... benignum: *potentiam, ut dictum est, generantem et sapientiam genitam et benignitatem procedentem* TChr I 23], cum istud nemo discretus ambigat, sive iudeus sive gentilis, nemini hec fides deesse videtur ». 3. *TSum* III 29 (p. 79, 1-9): « Cum autem in personis nulla sit discretio essentie ab invicem, non tamen oportet, dici: pater est filius vel spiritus sanctus est, vel filius est spiritus sanctus, quia et si quis sanum sensum in his verbis habere queat, eo scilicet quod eadem essentia que pater est, sit et filius et spiritus sanctus, sensus omnino falsus est secundum patrum acceptionem, que est huismodi ac si dicamus idem esse proprium patris et filii in eo scilicet quod pater est et quod filius est, hoc est idem esse diffinitione patrem quod filium [idem esse proprium ... quod filium: *personam generantem esse personam genitam vel esse personam ab utrisque procedentem. Quod et dicere eandem esse proprietatem utriusque persone, ita videlicet ut utreque persone eadem sint diffinitione terminande atque exprimende, quod omnino falsum est* TChr IV 34] ». 4. *TSum* II 31 (p. 38, 10-15): « Sed alius est in persona, alter ab altero ita scilicet discretus personaliter, pater a filio vel spiritu sancto, ut neque pater sit filius neque spiritus sanctus, quia licet alter sit hoc idem quod alter est secundum naturam eiusdem divine substantie, tamen alius est hic quam ille, cum sit ab eo personaliter discretus. [TChr III 71: Sed alius est in persona alter ab altero, id est in proprietate sue diversus ab illo, cum hic non sit hic qui ille sed hoc ipsum quod ille; nec alter alterius proprietatem communicet, ut supra meminimus. Alioquin personas sibi permiscendo confunderemus] ». 5. *TSum* III 1: « Sicut ergo dicimus hanc animam esse diversam diffinitionibus, secundum hoc scilicet quod est sapiens et iusta, ita deum concedimus esse diversas diffinitionibus personas, secundum hoc scilicet quod est potens et sapiens et benignus, ut supra determinavimus [potens ... determinavimus: *deus pater et filius et spiritus sanctus* TChr IV 1] ». 6. *TSum* III 27 (p. 78, 12-16): « Quippe diversitas illa personarum non in discretione essentie constat, sed magis in diversitate propriorum [propriorum: *proprietatum vel diffinitionum* TChr IV 32], ut diximus, sicut et diversitas personarum secundum grammaticos, que scilicet persone insunt Socrati, propter quas tamen non minus hoc nomen 'Socrates' singulare est ».
[51] TChr III 173. Cf. TChr III 176: « Quod si hoc loco diversas personas dicere non abhorres propter diversitatem proprietatum [...] multo magis in deo diversas esse personas concedi oportet, quas predicatione quoque a se disiunctas [disiuncte Buytaert] cognoscimus ». Cf. TChr III 176.

Although the kernel of his argument was implicit in *TSum*, he had concentrated on what was *proprium* or particular to each of the three persons. In *TChr* he retains his original analogy, drawn from Priscian, that the same man could be three persons in definition (who talks, who is talked to and who is talked about), but then adds that one person could not be predicated of another because of the diversity of properties expressed by each definition [52].

Abaelard puts his case about words which signified the same essence, but were disjoined through predication, in terms of an extension of, not of an exception to the rules of language. The basis of his argument, he says, was to be found in a *Grammatica* which he had written, apparently a reconsideration (*retractatio*) of predicaments:

> Non itaque fortassis incongruum est, ut, quemadmodum in ceteris rebus relationes a subiectis suis res diversas non ponimus; nec tamen ideo earum nomine per predicationem sibi coniungimus, ita etiam hic observemus, ut videlicet paternitatem dei vel relationem quam habet ad filium, nullo modo deum patrem vel etiam deum esse annuamus; sed omnino substantiam divinam sive personas singulas ab his [ad hic Buytaert] quas habent proprietatibus relativis per predicationem disiungamus, sicut hominem vel Socratem a paternitate quam habet, cum tamen ipsa paternitas non sit res alia ab ipsis, nec fortassis eadem cum res omnino recte dici non possit que in se veram non habet essentiam, ut sit in se una res numero a ceteris omnibus que ipsa non sunt rebus essentialiter discreta. — Sed de hoc diligentem, ut arbitror, tractatum in retractatione predicamentorum nostra continet *Grammatica* [53].

The argument hinges on the difference between a property and its subject, to which it could not be joined through predication, although not a separate entity (*res*). Abaelard was here countering a contemporary doctrine, which he says was held by many well-established teachers, that divine properties were different *res* from the divine substance — an exaggerated way of describing the distinction drawn by Gilbert of Poitiers among others, between a subject and its quality, as for example *deus* and *deitas* [54]. Abaelard singles out for

---

[52] Cf. *TSum* II 106 (p. 63, 1-9), copied into *TChr* III 171 with the additional sentence: « Que quidem propria superius sunt distincta ».
[53] *TChr* IV 155.
[54] *TChr* III 167: « Hoc enim ideo plurimum faciendum esse decrevi quod

particular criticism a teacher of Angers (probably Ulger, *scholasticus* and later bishop) who argued that a quality, like justice, was essentially different from its subject, both in man and in God, on the authority of Priscian's definition that a name signified a substance and a quality [55].

temporibus nostris nonnulli, inter vere catholicos computati atque etiam per assiduitatem studii divinorum librorum cathedram magisterii adepti, in tantam prorumpere ausi sunt insaniam, ut proprietates ipsas personarum alias res esse ab ipso deo vel ab ipsis personis profiteantur, hoc est paternitatem ipsam et filiationem et processionem spiritus, quas quidem ipsa etiam sanctorum patrum auctoritas 'relationes' appellat ». According to John of Salisbury, Robert de Bosco criticised the identification of a person with his property, citing Anselm of Laon, Gilbert the Universal, Alberic of Rheims and other masters in support of a distinction between the two terms. Cf. *Liber pontificalis*, ed. M. CHIBNALL, Edinburgh, 1956, pp. 17-19. H. C. VAN ELSWIJK examines the criticisms of Abaelard, and while acknowledging their closeness to the doctrine of Gilbert, concludes (on the questionable assumption that *TSch* was composed before 1126) that they were directed against a doctrine formulated prior to Gilbert. Elswijk rightly emphasises the importance of grammatical doctrine in Gilbert's theology. Cf. « Gilbert Porreta, sa vie, son œuvre, sa pensée », *Spicilegium Sacrum Lovaniense* 33 (Louvain, 1966) pp. 328-335.

[55] *TChr* IV 77: « Sunt enim, ut supra meminimus, qui ad assignandam [assignandas Buytaert] trium personarum diversitatem tres proprietates in eo intelligunt, tamquam tres res diversas essentialiter ab ipso deo. Quorum etiam unus, qui in Andegavensi pago magni nominis magister viget, in tantum prorumpere ausus est insaniam, ut omnia creaturarum nomina, ad deum translata, ipsi quoque deo convenire velit, ex quibusdam formis diversis essentialiter ab ipso deo sicut et in creaturis, veluti cum dicitur 'deus iustus' sicut et 'homo iustus', ita iustitiam ab ipso deo essentialiter diversam intelligit sicut ab homine, et similiter cum dicitur 'deus sapiens' et 'deus fortis'; necnon et propria ipsius dei nomina vult in ipso deo ita qualitates aut formas ponere sicut et in creaturis, ut est hoc nomen 'eternus' sive etiam 'deus' vel 'creator'. Quod maxime ex eo astruere nititur quod ait Priscianus: 'Proprium nominis est substantiam et qualitatem significare', et ex ipsa nominis diffinitione qua asserit unumquodque nomen subiectis corporibus vel rebus proprias vel communes distribuere qualitates ». The same teacher is referred to in *TSch* II 66 (1057B): *Tertius vero predictorum* [*scil.* in pago Andegavensi] *non solum predictas personarum proprietates res diversas ab eo constituit, verum etiam potentiam dei, iustitiam, misericordiam, iram et cetera huiusmodi, que iuxta humano sermonis consuetudinem in deo significantur, res quasdam et qualitates ab ipso diversas sicut et in nobis concedit, ut quot fere de deo vocabula dicuntur, tot in deo res diversas constituat.* A similar doctrine is attributed to a teacher in Burgundy (Gilbert the Universal?); cf. *TSch* II 63 (1056D): *Alter quidem totidem erroribus involutus, tres in deo proprietates, secundum quas tres distinguuntur persone, tres essentias diversas ab ipsis personis et ab ipsa divinitatis substantia constituit, ut videlicet paternitas Dei vel filiatio sive processio res quedam sint tam ab ipsis personis quam ab ipso deo diverse.* These doctrines are answered in part in *TChr* IV 154-158.

Abaelard was criticising a grammatical distinction between a property and its subject, transposed onto a theological plane. To the objection that if a property was not a *res*, it could not exist, he answered that *est* was ambiguous, its meaning being different for a substance or a property [56]. *Paternitatem esse* did not evoke its own essence. *Pater* could not be identified with *paternitas* because this would mean *pater* was so designated *ex participatione patris*, which was impossible. He referred again to his reconsideration of the predicaments, continuing its argument for those who felt the treatise insufficient:

> Si quis vero graviter accipiat quod hoc loco lectorem *ad retracta-tionem predicamentorum invitaverimus, atque hunc sibi tractatum sufficere non posse dicat, et ob hoc eum quasi imperfectum arguat,* breviter de predicatione patris et paternitatis instrui poterit, quare videlicet, cum diversam rem paternitatem a patre nolimus esse, ea tamen sibi invicem per predicationem non iungamus, ut videlicet dicamus patrem esse paternitatem vel e converso. [...] Sed neque e converso paternitas est pater, hoc est habens paternitatem respectu filii sui, cum ipsa omnino substantia non sit, ut ex se ipsa filium gignere possit, sed magis proprietas vel relatio substantie est quam substantia [57].

The same question of the disjunction between subject and property occurs earlier in the fourth book of *TChr*, in which he twice refers to discussion elsewhere on the distinction between predicaments. He draws a distinction between the identity of meaning of *unum* and *unitas* and the difference in their construction to demonstrate that such *voces* applied to God indicated an identity of essence, as if unity was the same as God, which would be impossible when applied to other substances.

> Quid etiam mirum si voces, cum a creaturis ad deum transferuntur, significationem varient, utpote hoc nomen 'pater' vel 'filius', con-structionis quoque vim commutent, cum ille etiam id faciant que significationem nullatenus mutare videntur? Nemo quippe recte intelligens unitatem aut plerasque alias formas ita a subiectis sub-stantiis dividit, ut eas ab eis numero vel essentialiter diversas existimet. Nec quis, cum dicit unitatem dei vel unum deum aut

---

[56] *TChr* IV 157.
[57] *TChr* IV 158.

34

simplicitatem dei et simplicem deum, sicut unitatem anime vel
unam animam aut simplicitatem anime vel simplicem animam ad
alium sensum hec nomina in deo accipit quam in anima. Non
tamen ita dicimus unitatem vel simplicitatem esse animam sicut
esse deum. Sed quelibet formarum nomina deo copulata solam
identitatem essentie monstrant, ac si dicamus idem esse unitatem
quod deum, quod minime in ceteris contingit substantiis, sicut
alibi, cum de discretione predicamentorum dissereremus, ostendimus. Quid itaque mirum, si 'pater' et 'filius' hec nomina a creaturis
ad deum translata, in creaturis sibi copulata solam identitatem essentie monstrent, in deo autem id solum non faciant, sed etiam
super identitatem proprietatis cum e contrario nomina [nomine
Buytaert] formarum, deo copulata, solam identitatem essentie monstrent quo [quae Buytaert] in creaturis contenta non sunt [58]? [...]
Unitas quoque et unum, et sessio et sedens eadem penitus fortasse
sunt in significatione, non in constructione, sicut *alibi* docuimus
cum de discretione predicamentorum nobis esset tractandum. Quid
igitur mirum est, si ponamus hec nomina 'pater' et 'deus omnipotens' eiusdem penitus esse significationis in deo, non tamen eiusdem
constructionis esse concedamus; nec ea in contextu orationis eundem penitus custodire sensum [59]?

This account of the distinction between predicaments would seem
to be the same as the *retractatio predicamentorum* or *Grammatica*
referred to later in *TChr*. An identical issue is involved, the relationship
between subject and property or form. It may also have contained
the discussion about diversity of essence and number, alluded to in
the third book of *TChr* [60]. The *Grammatica* certainly included a section
on the category of quantity, in which the physically circumscribed
nature of *corpus* was compared with the incorporeal nature of *albedo,*
according to a passage in the *Theologia 'Scholarium'*:

> Quod autem nec loco moveri possit qui spiritus est, tam philoso-
> phorum quam sanctorum assertione docemur, sicut de quantitate
> tractantes ostendimus, cum *Grammaticam* scriberemus. Id quippe
> solum quod locale est, localiter alicubi teneri, sicut est corpus.
> Nichil enim locale est vel localiter contineri potest nisi quod sui

[58] *TChr* IV 46.
[59] *TChr* IV 48.
[60] See above, n. 49. A similar question is discussed with reference to *genus,*
in *Glossule* 535, 40-536, 40.

interpositione circumstantium rerum distantiam intervalli potest facere, veluti si alicui continuo corpori stilus vel corpusculum aliquod inseratur, statim per eius interpositionem necesse est aliquam intervalli distantiam fieri inter particulas circumstantes, que post ad invicem continuate fuerant. Si vero albedo vel aliquid incorporeum illis inesset particulis, nulla eorum continuatio ideo deperiret [61].

Although they concern place rather than substance, these remarks on the non-physical nature of *albedo* parallel the comments made in the *Grammatica* (according to *TChr*) that a property was not a *res*. Geyer noticed that a similar discussion of place occurred in the *Glossule* on Porphyry, but not within a section on quantity. As no parallel passage is found in any of his other known writings on logic, he suggested that Abaelard must have been referring to another gloss on the *Categories*, now lost, but which would have been a continuation of the *Glossule* on Porphyry. He thought that the other references in *TChr* to a treatise *de discretione predicamentorum* also applied to this supposed gloss on the *Categories* [62].

---

[61] *TSch* III 70 (1105C); the passage is similar to the *Glossule* 549, 12-22, in a section *de specie*.

[62] GEYER, *Untersuchungen*, pp. 616-618. His hypothesis involves considerable forcing of the text of *TSch*, the reading of *Grammaticam* being attested by all manuscripts. The *Glossule* may well have arguments in common with the *Grammatica* as both were written between *TSum* and *TChr*. There is considerable discussion of grammatical subjects in these *Glossule*, which may also have occurred in the *Grammatica*, such as that introduced (537, 11-539, 22): *Unde questio alia de substantia nominis, alia de qualitate; alia de substantia verbi, alia de qualitate.* In this discussion, Abaelard tends to minimise the distinction between a noun and a verb, although commenting that they could not be predicated of each other (*Glossule* 539, 12-22; cf. 558, 20). This passage follows that about difference by number mentioned above (nn. 49 and 60). D. VAN DEN EYNDE argues that Abaelard did write the *Grammatica*, but does not identify other references to the work, « Les écrits perdus d'Abélard », *Antonianum* 37 (1962) pp. 473-476. A grammatical work based on discussion of the predicaments (attributed to Petrus Helias, but whose authorship has not been investigated) occurs in the Erfurt MS, Amplon. Q 29, ff. 22-30v (s. XIII[in]), *Tractatus Petri Helie de decem predicamentis gramatice inquisicionis,* Incipit: *Propositum quidem negotii nostri est grammaticas questiones sub brevitate perstringere. Erunt ergo X predicamenta ...* Explicit: (IV Pred.) *Queritur ergo utrum dividatur per suas partes vel non;* cf. M. MANITIUS, *Geschichte der Lateinischen Literatur des Mittelalters.* München, 1936, III, p. 186.

Why should Abaelard twice describe this work on predicaments as a *Grammatica*, if it was, as Geyer postulated, in reality a gloss on the *Categories?* Is it necessary to assume that either the entire manuscript tradition of both *TChr* and *TSch* is corrupt or that Abaelard erred twice in referring to his own writings? A simpler explanation would be to accept what Abaelard says at face value, namely that his *Grammatica* contained a reconsideration or second treatment (*retractatio*) of predicaments. Why, though, should he give the title *Grammatica* to a work which, from the references in *TChr* and *TSch* concerned the categories of substance, quality of quantity and not the traditional subject of matter of grammar — the letter, the syllable, the noun and verb and so on — as dealt with by Hugh of St Victor, for example, in his *De Grammatica* [63] ? Is there not a confusion of disciplines here?

For Abaelard, the grammatical sense of a proposition could not be different from its logical or dialectical sense, as he makes clear in his gloss on the Topics [64]. While there might be two ways of explaining its meaning, it could not contain two independent meanings. This was not the position of William of Champeaux and his followers, who maintained that there was a clear difference between the analyses of grammar and of dialectic. Much of Abaelard's criticism of the approach of *grammatici* was based on their assumption that each word had a *significatio*. In the *Dialectica*, while often critical of grammatical theory, there are still traces of its influence (as for example in discussion of indefinite words). In the gloss on the *Periermeneias* Abaelard has moved further away from such assumptions. Abaelard's understanding of what words mean is based on their function within a proposition or chain of words, in which one term is predicated by another. While not so concerned with analysing language in terms of the constituent parts defined by Priscian (letter, syllable etc.), he is still very interested in the nature of the differences between various parts of speech. In the first treatise of the *Dialectica*, which he refers to as the *Liber partium,* Abaelard examines the constituent elements of an *oratio* in terms of *antepredicamenta, predicamenta* and *postpredicamenta.* The first of these three sections is unfortunately missing from the manuscript; in the second he deals with substance, quantity and the other categories,

---

[63] Cf. *De Grammatica*, ed. R. BARON, *Hugonis de sancto Victore. Opera Propaedeutica*, Notre-Dame, 1966, pp. 75-163.
[64] *Sup. Top.*, ed. DAL PRA, pp. 271, 38-275, 33.

in particular quality; in the third he considers *voces significative,* divided into indefinite and definite words, the latter classed into nouns and verbs [65]. Inevitably he had to deal with many questions also treated by grammarians, but Aristotle, rather than Priscian, was his authority in dealing with the science of language [66]. In this first part of the *Dialectica* he considered the grammatical distinction between a noun and a verb as a legitimate question of logic, but treated it as subordinate to that between the predicaments of substance, quantity and quality etc.

From his references in *TChr,* it is most unlikely that the *Grammatica* was a gloss on Priscian or a treatise based on the linguistic categories of traditional grammar.

Could it have been a reconsideration (*retractatio*) of ideas put forward in the *Liber partium* of the *Dialectica?* The *Grammatica* contained discussion *de discretione predicamentorum,* in other words of the nature of the distinction between the predicaments of substance, quantity, quality and perhaps others. Predicaments, as he explains in the gloss on the *Categories,* were not things, but names under which all other names could be grouped [67]. Abaelard says that the

---

[65] De Rijk analyses the contents of this first treatise, and suggests that the *antepredicamenta* referred to the categories discussed by Porphyry, in the introduction to the *Dialectica,* pp. XXVIII-XXX.

[66] See above, n. 32. Abaelard's attitude towards grammarians may be explained in part by the rivalry between himself and an unnamed teacher who gave lectures on Priscian. This teacher, a protégé of William of Champeaux, had taken Abaelard's position at Notre-Dame, but lost influence once William came back to teach; cf. *Historia Calamitatum,* ed. J. MONFRIN, Paris, 1979⁴, pp. 66-67, 11. 112-116, 133-141. J. JOLIVET makes some pertinent comments about the close relationship between dialectic and a speculative grammar in Abaelard's writing, *Arts du langage,* pp. 28-62. He points out that Abaelard does not detach himself completely from a platonist tradition mediated through Priscian, but interprets it in his own way, « Non-réalisme et platonisme chez Abélard », *Abélard en son temps. Actes du colloque international organisé à l'occasion du 9ᵉ centenaire de la naissance de Pierre Abélard (14-19 mai 1979),* ed. J. JOLIVET, Paris, 1981, pp. 175-195.

[67] *Sup. Pred.* 116, 34-117, 7: « Arbitror autem hanc disiunctionem predicamentorum magis consideratam secundum significationem vocum quam secundum naturas rerum. Si enim rerum naturas attenderet, nulla apparet ratio, quare non plura aut pauciora predicamenta disponeret. Sed profecto secundum nominum significationem hec ratio visa est, quod decem consideravit nomina, in quibus omnium aliorum nominum tam generalium quam specialium significatio inciperet,

38

Grammatica dealt with the relationship between substance and quality, not predicable of each other (*disiuncte predicatione*), but not different in essence. The distinction between *white* and *whiteness* was for him as much grammatical as logical in that the impossibility of predicating one of the other did not make a statement about any ontological distinction. The theological doctrine which he was anxious to refute in *TChr* through an appeal to logic — that the properties of God were forms or *res* separate from the divine substance — was based on the definition of Priscian that a name signified both a substance and a quality. He was concerned to show that although different parts of speech, like *pater* and *paternitas* or *unitas* and *unum* could not be predicated of each other, they did not signify different entities. The essential to his argument was the idea that signification was not intrinsic to a *vox*, but depended on the context in which the *vox* occurred.

Abaelard's use of *Grammatica* as a title for such a work, so different from a treatise in the line of Priscian, may seem a remarkably bold move. It makes sense in that he was concerned with many of the same problems as grammarians, notably about the meaning of nouns and verbs, but preferred to analyse words from the standpoint of their predicative function within a phrase or proposition as a whole. His primary linguistic categories were thus based on the predicaments of Aristotle. While he might have accepted the conventional definition of grammar as *scientia recti loquendi*, he did not accept the linguistic assumptions on which much contemporary grammar was based.

A clue as to why Abaelard should want to re-think his arguments can be found by comparing the comments of *TSum* and *TChr* about predication with those of the *Dialectica* and of the glosses on the *Periermeneias* and the *De differentiis topicis*. As has already been seen, Abaelard argues in the *Dialectica* that *est*, when the *tertium adiacens*, linked essences without having a meaning in itself. In both the *Dialectica* and *TSum*, he argues that identity of essence involved a predication of essence. However, while anxious to divest the substantive verb of an intrinsic signification, Abaelard was still faced by the problem of what essence was signified by the terms copulated. He advanced a solution towards the end of his discussion in the *Dialectica*,

ideoque ea superposuit ceteris quasi prima naturaliter et digniora rerum continentia, cum videlicet ceteris universaliora sint ».

that *est albus* should be treated as one verb (*pro uno verbo*), namely *esse album*. In the gloss on the *Periermeneias* he makes less of a distinction between a name and a verb and suggests that the substantive and name together have the force of one verb or word (*in vi unius verbi vel dictionis*) at the outset of his discussion. The true predicate is not what was conjoined in essence, but what was intended to be predicated: *albedo* rather than *album*. The difference in approach parallels that between *TSum* and *TChr*. While in the first version of his *Theologia* Abaelard defined the difference between the persons in terms of definition (*esse potentem* etc.), in the second (*Theologia Christiana*) he introduces the notion of difference by property (*potentia* etc.), that which was demonstrated by the definition. He insists that such properties did not have any separate existence from their subject, even though they could not be joined in predication to their subject. He avoids all talk of predication (as distinct from that of copulation) of essences in both the glosses on the *Periermeneias* and *De differentiis topicis* and *TChr*[68]. While he does not talk of disjunction in these glosses, his comments about the distinction between conjunction and

[68] This would indicate that Abaelard composed the glosses on the *Periermeneias* and *De differentiis topicis* after completing *TSum*. The continuity in the evolution of his comments on identity and difference in his various glosses on Porphyry and in the *Theologia* makes it unlikely that he should return to discussion of *predicatio essentie* in *TSum* after avoiding the expression in glosses on the *Periermeneias*. However, the gloss on Porphyry '*Ingredientibus*' very likely precedes *TSum*, as its discussion of identity and difference does not depart from the argument of Porphyry, in the way that do the *Glosse super Porphyrium secundum vocales,* almost identical in this part to the comparable section of *TSum*. The *Glossule* revise the argument of these *Glosse secundum vocales,* while the discussion is taken further in *TChr*. Two other small features might help confirm the hypothesis that *TSum* was composed before the latter gloss. Abaelard refers in *TSum* III 63 (p. 90, 34-36) to an existing discussion of *translatio* — which corresponds to part of his gloss on the *Categories* (cf. *sup. Pred.* 121, 3-37; here he promises to discuss the subject further in glossing the *Periermeneias*, as in *sup. Per.* 327, 28-35; 336, 20-27; 338, 21-40; 478, 20-479, 40). He also promises in *TSum* II 6 (p. 30, 16-17) to deal further with providence and free will, a in *TSum* III 63 (p. 90, 34-36) to an existing discussion of *translatio* — which this section of the gloss (*sup. Per.* 426, 22-431, 12) Abaelard introduces a number of theological notions and references to patristic texts in a way which is not paralleled in any of his earlier writings on logic. While linguistic considerations dominated his analysis of the unity and trinity of God, one cannot rule out the possibility that some of his reflections in *TSum* may have stimulated further thought in his gloss on the *Periermeneias*.

predication provide a basis for the new ideas incorporated into *TChr*. In the *Grammatica* he re-analysed the meaning of predicaments and how they differed from each other — such as *album* and *albedo* — in the light of what he had written earlier about predication in a statement such as *Socrates est albus*.

The apparent refinement of these comments in the *Grammatica* echoes the evolution of his terminology about signification. The change from *vox* to *sermo* in the definition of a universal enabled him to emphasise that a *vox* was only a physical sound, the meaning of which depended on its context. Although he does not use *sermo* for *vox* in glossing the *Periermeneias* (as he does in *TChr* III 162) he denies that a *vox* signified in itself. Indefinite words had no intrinsic meaning, whereas in the *Dialectica* he had accepted that they had to have some meaning, albeit uncertain. Only in this gloss did he assert that *homo currens* and *homo currit* had an identical meaning, even though one was an imperfect construction, the other perfect. Similarly in his theory of predication he sought to distinguish the *vox* which was joined to a subject, from the predicate — that which was intended to be joined. The meaning of a phrase was to be judged by the understanding generated, not by its grammatical construction [69]. These are not simply alternative expressions of the same argument, revealing no significant change. Like the revisions made to discussion of identity and difference in the *Theologia*, the divergences between the *Dialectica* and the gloss on the *Periermeneias* reflect Abaelard's search for an explanation of language as a human construct, free from any notion that it was a set of word-signs each with a meaning determined by an external reality.

---

[69] *Sup. Per.* 373, 1-7: « Nos autem perfectionem orationis non iuxta perfectionem significationis pensamus, quod videlicet significatio huius perfecta est, illius imperfecta. Nam 'Socratem legere', que imperfecta est, idem penitus significat quod 'Socrates legit' et 'Socrates currens' eundem habet intellectum quem 'Socrates currit' et per se etiam dicta eandem animi conceptionem facit 'Socrates currit', non tamen perfecta dicitur, sicut et illa ». Cf. *Dial.* II 148, 17-149, 19. A small change to a reference to Priscian in *TSch* reflects a similar move away from the argument that a verb was necessary to the completion of a phrase. The text of *TChr* III 125 had been copied without change from *TSum* II 70: *Quod vero omnis hominum locutio ad creaturarum status maxime accommodata sit, ex ea precipue parte orationis apparet sine qua, teste Prisciano, nulla constat orationis perfectio, ex ea scilicet que dicitur 'verbum'.* The phrase *teste Prisciano, nulla constat* is rendered simply as *nulla dicitur constare* in *TSch* II 84 (1062 B), as if Abaelard no longer took the authority of Priscian quite so for granted.

What prompted Abaelard to write the *Grammatica?* In his gloss on the *De differentiis topicis* he devoted considerable attention to criticising the view of William of Champeaux and his followers that the grammatical sense of a phrase was different from its logical meaning. He argued that grammarians and dialecticians ultimately understood the same thing from a construction, but used different words to express the same opinion. The idea of composing a *Grammatica* may have been influenced in part by a desire to refute the opinion held by his former teacher. It is clear that Abaelard did not intend to base his work on traditional categories of grammar. He was concerned with questions of meaning and predication rather than with those of syntax. The *Grammatica* gave him an opportunity to develop ideas on the difference between predicaments further than he had in the first treatise, the *Liber partium*, of the *Dialectica.* He would incorporate many of these ideas into the first major revision of his treatise on the Trinity, the *Theologia Christiana*, as they had considerable implications for theology.

Un lecteur de Jérôme au XIIᵉ siècle : Pierre Abélard[*]

« Sicque me Francorum invidia ad Occidentem sicut Jheronimum Romanorum expulit ad Orientem[1] ». Pierre Abélard, dans son *Historia calamitatum* (écrite vers 1132-33) ne pouvait mieux démontrer qu'il se considérait comme un nouveau Jérôme au douzième siècle. On l'avait obligé à quitter l'oratoire du Paraclet qu'il avait construit au bord de l'Ardusson, près de Nogent-sur-Seine. Il avait passé cinq ans à en faire l'espace privilégié où lui et ses étudiants pouvaient continuer à étudier la philosophie sous l'égide du Saint-Esprit. Il était retourné en Bretagne en tant qu'abbé de Saint-Gildas, un monastère lointain dans une région non francophone. Les moines de Saint-Gildas ne s'intéressaient pas à sa vision de la vie monastique. L'expulsion en 1129 d'Héloïse et de ses sœurs du couvent d'Argenteuil lui donne l'idée de les inviter à reconstruire l'oratoire en tant que monastère reconnu par l'Église. Quand elles l'avaient sollicité de leur rendre visite, de mauvaises langues avaient dit qu'il recherchait toujours le plaisir charnel. La lecture de la lettre de Jérôme à Asella le soulagea : « Qui frequenter illam beati Jheronimi querimoniam mecum volvens qua ad Asellam de fictis amicis scribens, ait : « Nichil mihi obicitur nisi sexus meus, et hoc nunquam obiceretur nisi cum Iherosolimam Paula proficiscitur... Cum hanc, inquam, in tantum virum detractionis injuriam ad mentem reducerem, non modicam hinc consolationem carpebam...[2] » Abélard termine sa longue lettre de consolation en déclarant qu'il a été

[*] Je remercie vivement Pierre Lardet qui a eu l'obligeance de relire la version française de cette communication.

1. Abélard. *Historia calamitatum. Texte critique avec une introduction,* éd. J. Monfrin, Paris, 1978, p. 98. On citera les lettres d'Abélard et d'Héloïse selon les éditions de J.T. Muckle, *The Personal Letters between Abelard and Heloise* (= *Epist.* 2-5), dans *Mediaeval Studies,* 15, 1953, p. 47-94 et *The Letter of Heloise on the Religious Life and Abelard's First Reply* (= *Epist.* 6-7), *ibid.,* 17, 1955, p. 240-81, et de T.P. McLaughlin, *Abelard's Rule for Religious Women* (= *Epist.* 8), *ibid.,* 18, 1956, p. 241-92.

2. *Hist. cal.,* p. 101.

430

héritier de Jérôme dans la mesure où il a subi tant de critiques malveillantes. Il sait que son ami, inconnu de nous, est dans une mauvaise passe. Abélard conseille la lecture des lettres de Jérôme à Népotien, à Asella et à Héliodore à tous ceux qui s'imaginent être isolés du monde[3].

On a souvent remarqué qu'Abélard s'identifie à Jérôme, mais on a rarement observé ce fait en dehors de l'*Historia calamitatum*[4]. J'aimerais examiner l'image du savant docteur qui ressort de ses écrits destinés aux étudiants et de ses lettres et traités aux sœurs du Paraclet, pour mieux comprendre son récit autobiographique. Les deux hommes sont très différents. Jérôme est traducteur et exégète de l'Écriture sainte, Abélard maître en logique et en théologie spéculative. Jérôme fournit-il une clé essentielle pour comprendre le péripatéticien du Pallet, ou n'est-il qu'un nom célèbre qu'Abélard cite comme une figure de rhétorique ?

Abélard n'est pas le seul à adresser de tels éloges à ce docteur. Jérôme jouit d'un essor de popularité considérable en plusieurs milieux savants du XIIe siècle. Respecté en tant que traducteur de la Bible et exégète du sens littéral de ses passages les plus obscurs, il est qualifié d'*interpres* de l'Ecriture depuis six siècles[5]. Cependant Grégoire le Grand s'est établi très vite comme l'exégète magistral du sens allégorique et spirituel de l'Écriture. Jérôme n'a jamais accédé aux dignités ecclésiastiques d'Ambroise ou d'Augustin, encore moins de Grégoire. A la fin du onzième siècle et au début du douzième, des écrivains – ceux surtout qui appartiennent aux communautés réformatrices – s'intéressent à Jérôme avec un nouveau regard critique. Sa position intransigeante quant au rôle et à l'importance de la vie monastique aident beaucoup ceux qui veulent restaurer la vie religieuse en la fondant sur des principes plus sûrs. Guigues du Châtel (1083-1137), cinquième prieur de la Grande Chartreuse, commence une édition de ses lettres, en excluant celles dont l'authenticité est douteuse[6]. Nicolas

---

3. Ibid. p. 108 : « Que diligenter beatus attendens Jheronimus, cujus me precipue in contumeliis detractionum heredem conspicio, ad Nepotianum scribens ait : ' Si adhuc, inquit Apostolus, hominibus placerem... '. His itaque documentis atque exemplis animati, tanto securius ista toleremus quanto injuriosius accidunt ».

4. Cf. D.E. Luscombe, *Pierre Abélard et le monachisme*, dans *Pierre Abélard-Pierre le Vénérable : les courants philosophiques, littéraires et artistiques en Occident au milieu du XIIe siècle. Abbaye de Cluny, 2 au 9 juillet 1972*, Paris, 1976, p. 271-6 ; M.M. McLaughlin, *Peter Abelard and the dignity of women : Twelfth century « feminism » in theory and practice, ibid.*, p. 287-333 (surtout p. 308-11) ; E.R. Smits (à propos de l'*Epist.* 9), *Peter Abelard. Letters IX-XIV*, Groningen, 1983, p. 113-20 et 204 n. 11.

5. Cf. M.L.W. Laistner, *St Jerome in the Early Middle Ages*, dans *A Monument to St. Jerome*, éd. F.X. Murphy, New York, 1952, p. 235-56 ; P. Antin, *S. Jérôme dans l'hagiographie*, dans *Recueil sur saint Jérôme* (Collection Latomus 95), Bruxelles, 1968, p. 71-100 ; J. de Ghellinck, *Le mouvement théologique du XIIe siècle*, Bruges, 1948, p. 23 n. 2 and p. 514-7. E.F. Rice Jr. discute de l'image de Jérôme au Moyen Âge sans mentionner Abélard, *Saint Jerome in the Renaissance*, Baltimore-London, 1985, p. 23-48.

6. Guigues, *Ad Durbonenses fratres* [éd. Dom M. Laporte], *Lettres des premiers Chartreux*, Sources chrétiennes 88, Paris, 1962, p. 214-18. Voir aussi l'article de Dom Laporte dans le

Maniacutia (ou Maniacoria), moine cistercien de S. Anastasio, en Campanie, écrit deux traités sur la critique textuelle de la Bible et surtout des Psaumes avec un souci de l'*hebraica veritas* inspiré par la méthode exégétique de Jérôme. Nicolas fait la connaissance de Juifs pour l'aider dans son travail[7]. Plus important pour le destin de Jérôme en Occident, Nicolas écrit une nouvelle vie qui contribuera au quatorzième siècle à l'élévation iconographique de son héros au rang de cardinal de la curie.

Qui plus est, des centaines de copistes se mettent à transcrire les œuvres de Jérôme avec un enthousiasme qui se ne retrouve pas avant le xve siècle. Ses écrits polémiques, négligés aux siècles précédents par rapport à ses lettres et à ses commentaires, attirent plus d'attention[8]. De temps en temps un copiste ajoute un petit poème à son manuscrit pour exprimer la dévotion que lui inspire le saint docteur[9]. La passion du drame raconté dans la *Vita Malchi* crée une telle impression sur Réginald de Cantorbéry (c. 1030/50-1109 +) qu'il se met à écrire une nouvelle *Vie de Malchus* (et de sa femme) en hommage à son premier biographe[10]. Abélard, Nicolas Maniacutia, Guigues, Réginald et ces copistes anonymes se sont tous inspirés dans un certain sens des écrits de Jérôme. Pour apprécier comment Abélard se différencie des autres, il faut suivre le péripatéticien sur le chemin de sa découverte du docteur.

Un des premiers livres de Jérôme qu'il aurait étudié en détail fut le *Commentaire sur Ézéchiel*, pour rédiger ses propres gloses sur ce prophète vers 1113-14. Déçu

---

Dictionnaire de Spiritualité, t. 6, Paris, 1967, col. 1169-1176. Dans une étude inédite, il montre que le MS *Madrid, Bibl. Nacional 26* est très proche du recueil original de Guigues ; cf. P. Lardet dans l'introduction à son édition du *Contra Rufinum*, CCL 79, Turnhout, 1982, p. 57*, 72*, 104*-5*.

7. Sur Nicolas Maniacutia, voir V. PERI, *Notizia su Nicola Maniacutia, autore ecclesiastico del XII secolo*, dans *Aevum*, 36, 1962, p. 534-8 et *Nicola Maniacutia : un testimone della filologia romana del XII secolo*, *ibid.*, 41, 1967, p. 67-90. Sa *Vita Hieronymi* se trouve dans PL 22, 183-202.

8. P. Lardet observe que sur 198 MSS du *Contra Rufinum*, 7 % ont été copiés aux IX-XIe siècles, 20 % au XIIe, 16 % aux XIII-XIVe et 56 % au XVe siècles CCL 79, p. 193*-94*. Sur 1700 MSS connus des lettres de Jérôme, 25 % ont copiés au XIIe et 35 % au XVe siècles ; sur 58 MSS de sa traduction de Didyme, 14 % date des IXe-XIe siècles, 29 % du XIIe, 24 % des XIIIe-XIVe et 33 % du XVe siècle.

9. Le Ms *Paris, BN lat. 13350* de Corbie (s. XII) comporte ces vers (éd. L. Delisle, *Le cabinet des MSS de la Bibliothèque nationale*, t. 2, Paris, 1874, p. 116) :
Doctor amore tui celebris Hieronime librum
Fecit frater Iuo fieri, seruus tuus, istum.
Sub pedibus doctoris iners ego presbiter Iuo
Decubo qui meritis clarus coniungitur astris.

10. Reginald of Canterbury, *Vita sancti Malchi*, éd. Levi Robert LIND (Illinois studies in Language and Literature 26), Urbana, 1942. Voir aussi une notice anonyme tirée de cette édition (VI. 456-488, p. 149-150), *Éloge de saint Jérôme par Réginald de Cantorbéry*, dans *Revue du Moyen Âge latin*, 2, 1946, p. 317-18.

432

par Anselme de Laon, il déclare aux autres étudiants qu'il s'estime aussi capable de commenter l'Écriture, avec l'aide des Pères, que son maître. Ils lui demandent de gloser le prophète le plus obscur de la Bible. Son texte a disparu, mais, vu qu'il attend vingt ans pour écrire un deuxième commentaire sur l'Écriture, nous pouvons estimer qu'il n'a pas beaucoup aimé l'exégèse biblique comme genre littéraire. Dans la lettre-préface à l'*Expositio in Hexaemeron,* adressée à Héloïse, il avoue que Jérôme avait raison de mettre les jeunes en garde contre l'étude prématurée d'Ézéchiel[22]. Dans les années 1119-20, il préféra se mettre à l'analyse linguistique de la doctrine de l'unité et de la trinité de Dieu. Dans la version initiale de son traité à ce sujet (la *Theologia ' Summi boni '*), Jérôme ne joue aucun rôle important[12]. Abélard veut y montrer que les autres païens, surtout Platon et Aristote, ont compris certains aspects de la Trinité et qu'il peut lui-même utiliser leurs écrits pour comprendre la foi chrétienne. Le seul Père de l'Église qu'il connaît en profondeur est Augustin, surtout à travers son *De Trinitate.*

Sa connaissance des Pères s'est beaucoup élargie après que sa *Theologia ' Summi boni '* eut été jetée au feu au concile de Sens, en 1121. Au lieu de ne connaître qu'Augustin en détail, il commence a apprécier la grande diversité, voire les divergences parmi les opinions des Pères[13]. Il trouve beaucoup de textes dans des répertoires connus, tel le *Decretum* d'Yves de Chartres. Pourtant, il cite et commente un Père avec plus de profondeur que les autres. Jérôme devient l'autorité primordiale pour son sujet dans le nouveau deuxième livre de la *Theologia christiana,* où il justifie la lecture des auteurs païens. Abélard le cite longuement dans le prologue du *Sic et Non* pour justifier l'importance d'une évaluation critique des écrivains ecclésiastiques. La divergence entre l'esprit de Jérôme et celui d'Augustin, qu'il aime surtout à cause de ses *Retractationes,* est bien évidente.

Jérôme nous est présenté dans la *Theologia christiana* comme un savant, versé dans la philosophie antique et accusé par ses ennemis d'en avoir fait un usage excessif. Pour souligner qu'on peut effectivement tirer profit d'un livre qui n'était pas entièrement acceptable, Abélard cite à plusieurs reprises la lettre 70 à l'orateur Magnus[14]. Il renvoie aussi aux lettres 61 à Vigilance et 124 à Avitus, où Jérôme

---

11. *Hist. cal.,* p. 69 ; cf. *Expositio in Hexaemeron,* Praefatio (PL 178, 731B) où il fait allusion à Jérôme, *In Hiezechielem,* Prol. (CCL 75, 3-4). Sur la date de l'*Expositio,* voir Mews, *On dating the works of Peter Abelard,* dans *Archives d'histoire littéraire du Moyen Âge,* 52, 1985, p. 118-20.

12. Cf. *Peter Abaelards Theologia ' Summi boni ',* éd. H. Ostlender, BGPTMA 35. 2-3, 1939, p. 26.

13. L'étendue de ses lectures patristiques se dégage de l'index à l'édition de B.B. Boyer and R. McKeon, *Peter Abailard. Sic et Non,* London-Chicago, 1976-77, p. 647-663 et de l'Index scriptorum aux éditions de la *Theologia ' Summi boni '* (*TSum*) et de la *Theologia ' Scholarium '* (*TSch*) à paraître au CC Continuatio Mediaevalis. Ces éditions feront suite à celle de la *Theologia christiana* (*Tchr*) procurée par E.M. Buytaert. On citera *Tchr* et *TSch* par le livre et le paragraphe des éditions de Buytaert et de Mews.

14. *Tchr* I, 102, *TSch* I, 162 ; II, 1-11 ; *TSch* II, 1-11 ; *Tchr* CT II, 119a, *TSch* II, 21.

se défend contre l'accusation d'Origénisme. L'argument comme quoi un chrétien peut profiter de l'œuvre d'Origène est tout à fait traditionnel[15]. Cependant Abélard transforme une image reçue de Jérôme en s'appuyant sur la critique qu'on lui a fait de classicisme excessif.

L'image de Jérôme la mieux connue est celle du pénitent appelé au tribunal céleste. Yves de Chartres donne au récit de la lettre 22 une place importante dans sa discussion de l'étude des auteurs profanes[16]. Abélard met l'accent sur la position qu'a prise Jérôme beaucoup plus tard, en 396-7 dans la lettre 70, et non pas sur celle du cauchemar raconté dans la lettre à Eustochium[17]. De plus, il souligne la signification de la paraphrase de *Proverbes* 1, 6 que fait Jérôme dans la lettre 70, à propos de la nécessité de comprendre des énigmes « quae proprie dialecticorum et philosophorum sunt ». Ces six mots fournissent la justification principale de l'usage de la dialectique en théologie. Le génie de Jérôme fut de pouvoir distinguer ce qui est précieux de ce qui ne l'est pas, pour fabriquer une œuvre d'art — « quam in ornamento regio tamquam sapiens aurifaber valeat componere[18] ».

Augustin aurait pu servir aussi à justifier une telle approche, mais c'est à Jérôme qu'est donnée la place d'honneur dans la *Theologia christiana,* sans doute parce que Abélard le trouve meilleur polémiste. Ce n'est qu'à la fin de son deuxième livre, consacré à un éloge des philosophes, qu'il est question du sens du cauchemar de Jérôme, discuté dans une analyse plus longue des textes patristiques cités par Yves de Chartres[19]. Il veut y montrer que tous ces textes ne s'appliquent qu'à l'étude de ceux des poètes païens qui pouvaient distraire un chrétien par des histoires fabuleuses. Ils ne concernent pas l'étude des arts libéraux[20].

---

15. Cf. H. DE LUBAC, *Exégèse médiévale. Les quatre sens de l'Écriture,* Paris, 1959, t. I, p. 274-304.

16. Cf. Yves, *Decretum,* PL 161, citant l'*Ep.* 22, 29 (CSEL 54, 188-9). Sur l'histoire de son interprétation, voir P. ANTIN, *Autour du songe de S. Jérôme,* dans *Recueil sur saint Jérôme,* p. 71-100.

17. *Tchr* I, 102 and II, 2 (= *TSch* II, 2), citant l'*Ep.* 70, 2 (CSEL 54, p. 700-2). A cet endroit, les MSS de *Tchr* et de *TSch* fournissent un texte légèrement différent des MSS de Jérôme, selon l'édition de Hilberg, comme par exemple (CSEL 54, 701) : « Ductor Christiani exercitus et orator inuictus, pro Christo causam agens, etiam inscriptionem fortuitam *arte* (*arae* Hier.) torquet in argumentum fidei ». Ils omettent *saeculi* dans *Tchr* II, 3 (= *TSch* II, 3) dans leur texte de l'*Ep.* 70, 4 (CSEL 54, p. 707) à propos de quelques Pères grecs »... ut nescias quid in illis primum admirari debeas, eruditionem <saeculi> an scientiam scripturarum ». Abélard ne veut pas que Jérôme souligne trop l'opposition entre l'érudition et la connaissance des Écritures. Quand il cite l'*Ep.* 61, 1-2 (CSEL 54, p. 575-7) dans *Tchr* II, 4 (= *TSch* II, 4), il omet les passages contenant des critiques sévères d'Origène.

18. *Tchr* II, 5 (= *TSch* II, 5).

19. *Tchr* II, 121-124, citant Yves, *Decretum* IV, 121, 160-67 (PL 161, 311CD, 302C-303D).

20. *Tchr* II, 123.

Cependant, un problème se pose. Les censeurs d'Abélard pouvaient facilement utiliser contre lui la lettre 22. Son inquiétude apparaît dans la révision qu'il fait de son discussion dans la *Theologia christiana*. A travers deux manuscrits qui ne sont que des copies d'un brouillon, nous constatons qu'il a ajouté dans la marge de son manuscrit une interprétation nouvelle et plus détaillée du cauchemar[21]. Dans son texte corrigé, Abélard souligne que Dieu punira seulement ceux qui aiment l'éloquence au détriment de l'Ecriture et que, sans la grammaire, il serait impossible de pouvoir comprendre le texte sacré. Le centre du débat, c'est de savoir quelle lettre représente le mieux la position de Jérôme — la lettre à Eustochium ou la lettre à Magnus.

Abélard discute le sens de plusieurs lettres de Jérôme dans le prologue du *Sic et Non* pour expliquer l'attitude critique par rapport aux Pères de l'Église que doit prendre un chrétien intelligent[22]. Les *Retractationes* d'Augustin constituent la première source de réflexion (une forme abrégée de l'œuvre se figure en appendice au *Sic et Non*) parce que Augustin nous y montre la subjectivité de ses positions théologiques. Jérôme, qui ne manifeste jamais de tels doutes sur ses propres opinions, nous est présenté comme maître de la critique savante des opinions des autres. La position que prend Jérôme face à Origène est, selon Abélard, celle que devrait prendre un chrétien face à tout Père de l'Église, à savoir d'y rechercher ce qui s'y trouve de bien.

Une telle méthode critique ne pouvait plaire à tout le monde, et moins qu'à quiconque aux moines de Saint-Denis, où Abélard retourna après qu'ils l'eurent accusé de douter que l'Aréopagite fût leur saint patron, qu'il décida de se réfugier à Saint-Ayoul de Provins, en Champagne[23]. Là il trouva un endroit agréable, près de Nogent-sur-Seine, pour construire un oratoire, dédié d'abord à la Sainte Trinité, et ensuite au Paraclet « en remerciement de la consolation de l'Esprit-Saint ». Dans l'*Historia calamitatum*, l'éloge idéalisé que fait Jérôme dans le *Contra Iovinianum* de l'austérité de la vie menée par des philosophes de l'Antiquité lui fournit une bonne description de ce qu'il a voulu faire au Paraclet. Ce passage du *Contra Iovinianum* figure dans le deuxième livre de la *Theologia christiana*, écrite selon

21. *Tchr* CT II, 125-125b (= *TSch* II, 26-28) ; voir MEWS, *Peter Abelard's Theologia Christiana and Theologia ' Scholarium ' re-examined*, dans *Recherches de théologie ancienne et médiévale*, 52, 1985, p. 136.

22. *Sic et Non*, Prol., éd. Boyer-McKeon, p. 119 (cf. *Tchr* II, 4, 11) et p. 102-3, où Abélard cite les *Ep.* 61, 124, 29, 107, 129, 58.

23. Smits démontre que l'argument de l'*Epist.* 11 n'est pas en désaccord avec le récit de *Hist. cal.* (éd. Monfrin, p. 89-90), *Letters IX-XIV*, p. 137-53. E. Jeauneau doute de la sincérité d'Abélard quand il affirme n'avoir jamais douté que l'Aréopagite fût le patron de l'abbaye, mais ni l'*Epist.* 11 ni le récit autobiographique ne nous autorisent à tirer de telles conclusions, *Pierre Abélard à Saint-Denis*, dans *Abélard en son temps, Actes du colloque international organisé à l'occasion du 9ᵉ centenaire de la naissance de Pierre Abélard*, Paris, 1981, p. 161-73.

24. *Hist. cal.*, p. 93, citant le *Contra Iovianianum* II, 7-9 (PL 23, 297A-298A) à partir de *Tchr* II, 61-62 (mal identifié par Buytaert, CCCM 12, p. 156) ; *Hist. cal.*, p. 93-94, où il cite l'*Ep.* 125, 7 (CSEL 56, 125).

toute vraisemblance au Paraclet entre 1122 et 1126[24]. Dans sa lettre de consolation, Abélard dit aussi que lui et ses étudiants imitaient les fils des prophètes dont parle Jérôme dans sa lettre 125 à Rusticus et ailleurs. Chose curieuse, dans la *Theologia christiana* il n'invoque jamais l'exemple des fils des prophètes et, dans sa seule allusion à la lettre de Rusticus, il veut faire entendre – à tort – que Jérôme y fait l'éloge des philosophes païens[25]. Par contre, il fait mention de l'image des fils des prophètes dans ses sermons prêchés aux moines de Saint-Gildas ainsi que dans ses écrits pour les sœurs du Paraclet[26]. L'*Historia calamitatum* peut nous faire penser qu'Abélard est allé s'installer au Paraclet pour imiter les fils des prophètes et que ses étudiants vivaient comme des moines. En fait, ils ne suivaient pas de règle établie. Il est probable qu'ils n'avaient aucune idée à l'époque que l'on y construirait un monastère pour des femmes.

Quand Abélard cite Jérôme dans le deuxième livre de la *Theologia christiana,* il s'intéresse surtout aux exemples tirés de l'Antiquité. Il veut montrer dans ce livre que les philosophes, par leur vie et leur doctrine morale, nous offrent de meilleurs conseils pour la vie chrétienne que beaucoup de chrétiens et qu'il faut donc les respecter[27]. Abélard donne des preuves, tirées en grande partie de Jérôme, pour démontrer que les philosophes ont enseigné les valeurs de continence, d'abstinence et de fortitude ou magnanimité. De temps en temps, il cite Jérôme de telle façon qu'il détourne le sens original[28]. Du *Contra Iovianianum* il ne cite que des exemples païens pour dénigrer le mariage. Il cite in extenso le long extrait de Théophraste sur les ennuis liés au fait d'avoir femme et enfants[29]. Cet accent mis sur des exemples païens ne fait que renforcer l'image qu'il veut donner de Jérôme : celle d'un savant, fortement influencé par les valeurs de l'Antiquité[30]. Abélard ne

---

25. *Ep.* 125, 14-15 (CSEL 56, 132-4), résumé dans *Tchr* II, 67.

26. Sermon 33, éd. V. COUSIN, *Petri Abaelardi Opera,* t. 1, Paris, 1849, p. 569-70, 573, 581, où il cite les *Ep.* 58, 5 (éd. Cousin, p. 569-70 et 573) et *Ep.* 125, 7 (*éd. cit.,* p. 581) ; voir aussi son sermon 23 (éd. cit., p. 505), son *Epist.* 7 (éd. Muckle, p. 253), son *Epist.* 8 (éd. McLaughlin, p. 247-8), et son *Epist.* 12, contre la vie des chanoines (éd. Smits, p. 260, 262). Sur la date du sermon 33, voir MEWS, *On dating,* p. 124.

27. MEWS, *On dating,* p. 115-17.

28. Par exemple, on lit (*Tchr* II, 63) « Tales philosophiam Platonici sermonis imitantur... » au lieu de : « Tales Philo, Platonici sermonis imitator... » (*Ep.* 22, 35 ; CSEL 54, 200). L'omission d'un *non* (*Tchr* II, 26) détourne le sens de « Immortalem animam et post dissolutionem corporis subsistentem quod Pythagorus somniavit, Democritus <non> credidit, in consolationem damnationis suae Socrates disputavit in carcere ». (*Ep.* 60, 4 ; CSEL 54, 553). Voir aussi (*Tchr* II, 122) « Daemonum cibus est carmina poetarum, saecularis sapientiae <*sapientia* Hier.>, rhetoricorum pompa verborum ». Abélard veut que Jérôme condamne les poètes de la sagesse profane et non pas la sagesse profane en soi. Dans quelle mesure est-il tributaire de fautes contenues dans son manuscrit ? C'est une recherche qui reste à faire.

29. *Tchr* II, 99-100. Cf. Ch.B. SCHMITT, *Theophrastus in the Middle Ages,* dans *Viator,* 2, 1971, p. 259-63.

30. Ph. Delhaye fait cette observation à propos d'Abélard et de Jean de Salisbury, *Le dossier anti-matrimonial de l'Adversus Jovinianum et son influence sur quelques écrits latins du XII* *siècle,* dans *Mediaeval Studies,* 13, 1951, p. 65-86.

436

dit rien de la continence qui puisse étonner un auditoire monastique dont il a fait siennes les valeurs ascétiques. Ce qui est important dans son analyse, c'est qu'il suggère qu'on pouvait accéder à la vertu chrétienne par des voies naturelles plutôt que par l'infusion de la grâce dans une âme pécheresse. Les connaissances encyclopédiques de Jérôme ont fourni à Abélard les éléments de base pour élaborer ses propres idées sur la vie morale.

Les arguments qu'il retient du *Contra Iovinianum* touchent aux embarras de la vie mariée, et non pas à la nature peccamineuse de l'acte sexuel. On peut comprendre aisément son intérêt pour cet ouvrage de Jérôme, vu les circonstances de sa propre vie. Il est devenu moine ' plus par pudeur que par vocation religieuse '. L'oncle d'Héloïse l'avait fait émasculer peu de temps après leur mariage secret. Pourtant, il est arrivé, selon ce qu'il nous dit, à accepter son sort comme un juste châtiment et à en tirer profit[31]. Son seul regret, c'est de ne pas avoir écouté le conseil prophétique que lui a donné Héloïse. Le drame de son récit cache un problème textuel embarrassant. Abélard attribue à Héloïse beaucoup de citations du *Contra Iovinianum* qui paraissent être tirées du deuxième livre de la *Theologia christiana*[32]. Héloïse a-t-elle vraiment utilisé le *Contra Iovinianum* pour persuader son amant de ne pas l'épouser ? Dans sa lettre à Abélard, écrite tout de suite après avoir lu cette lettre de consolation adressée à un tiers, mais qu'un anonyme lui a apportée, elle souligne qu'elle n'a jamais voulu l'épouser et qu'elle ne l'aimait que pour lui-même. Elle cite le conseil d'Aspasia à la femme de Xénophon, cité par Eschine et par Cicéron, pour étayer sa position. Sa connaissance de la littérature classique ressort avec évidence de cette lettre[33]. Il est sûr qu'elle avait invoqué des arguments contre le mariage. L'accent mis sur la continence dans la *Theologia christiana* n'est que le fruit de l'expérience personnelle d'Abélard. Il savait très bien qu'il n'avait pas écouté le conseil du *Contra Iovinianum* et qu'Héloïse avait raison.

Quand Abélard commence à s'intéresser à Jérôme, ce n'est qu'à un aspect de sa personnalité, à savoir le savant persécuté à cause de son érudition, héritier des philosophes de l'Antiquité. On constate qu'il ne cite aucune lettre de Jérôme à une femme dans la *Theologia christiana*, à la seule exception de la lettre 22, dont on a déjà vu qu'il la considère comme moins importante que la lettre 70 à Magnus. Jérôme en tant que guide spirituel des femmes ne l'avait pas intéressé. Une des plaintes les plus dures d'Héloïse dans la lettre qu'elle lui envoie après avoir lu l'*Historia calamitatum* concerne le fait qu'Abélard ne lui a envoyé aucune lettre personnelle depuis qu'ils sont entrés dans la vie religieuse. Il est peu probable

---

31. *Hist. cal.*, p. 80-81 : « Occurrebat animo quanta modo gloria pollebam, quam facili et turpi casu hec humiliata, immo penitus extincta, quam justo Dei judicio in illa corporis mei portione plecterer in qua deliqueram ; ... In tam misera me contritione positum, confusio, fateor, pudoris potius quam devotio conversionis ad monastichorum latibula claustrorum compulit ».

32. *ibid.*, p. 76-78, citant le *Contra Iovinianum* I, 48 (PL 23, 278C-80A) selon *Tchr* II, 97, 101, 96-97 ; voir aussi *Tchr* II, 67 and II, 38.

33. *Epist.* 2 (éd. Muckle, p. 68).

qu'Abélard ait pensé à la possibilité qu'Héloïse et ses sœurs religieuses prennent possession du Paraclet avant qu'elles aient été expulsées du couvent d'Argenteuil en 1129. Même après cette invitation, il ne leur a rendu visite qu'après qu'elles l'ont accusé de négligence[34]. C'est à ce moment, nous dit-il, que la lettre (45) de Jérôme à Asella l'a soulagé, parce que Jérôme aussi se sentait persécuté du fait de ses relations avec les femmes. Dans l'*Historia calamitatum,* il ne s'intéresse pas à Jérôme en tant qu'il fut leur guide spirituel.

Sa remarque que l'*invidia* des Romains a expulsé Jérôme mérite un commentaire. Selon une biographie qu'il connaît, écrite au huitième ou au neuvième siècle, Jérôme avait quitté Rome à cause de l'influence des hérétiques dans la ville éternelle[35]. (Personne ne savait alors qu'il était parti à deux reprises pour l'Orient). Abélard tire son interprétation de la lettre 45 à Asella, tout en y introduisant une modification. Jérôme parle de l'*invidia* qui a poursuivi la sainteté d'Asella, de Paule et de Mélanie. Abélard nous donne à penser que les Romains ont dirigé leur *invidia* contre Jérôme à cause de son génie.

Dans la première lettre qu'elle lui envoie, Héloïse dit qu'elle éclata en sanglots en la lisant. Elle l'accuse de l'avoir délaissée. Elle veut savoir s'il est vrai qu'il ne l'a prise pour maîtresse que sous l'effet de la concupiscence charnelle et qu'il l'a abandonnée quand il n'a pas plus eu besoin d'elle, comme les gens le disaient. De plus, elle veut qu'il s'occupe davantage du Paraclet, sa propre fondation. Quand elle lui fait des reproches en citant l'exemple des Pères de l'Église qui ont tant écrit pour des femmes, on ne doute pas qu'elle pense à Jérôme, dont Abélard avait fait un tel éloge[36]. La lettre de réponse d'Abélard n'est qu'une exhortation invitant Héloïse à tirer son inspiration de l'Écriture sainte[37]. Il ne mentionne pas Jérôme. Puis Héloïse écrit une deuxième lettre pour dire qu'elle se souvient toujours du plaisir physique des années passées et qu'elle n'éprouve aucun sentiment de

---

34. *Hist. cal.,* p. 101 ; cf. *Epist.* 2 (éd. Muckle, p. 72) : « Dic unum, si vales, cur post conversionem nostram, quam tu solus facere decrevisti, in tantam tibi negligentiam atque oblivionem venerim ut nec colloquio presentis recreer nec absentis epistola consoler ; dic, inquam, si vales, aut ego quod sentio immo quod omnes suspicantur dicam. Concupiscentia te mihi potius quam amicitia sociavit, libidinis ardor potius quam amor. Ubi igitur quod desiderabas cessavit, quicquid propter hoc exhibebas pariter evanuit ».

35. *Vita Hier.* (« *Plerosque nimirum...* »), PL 22, 203. Ce texte (dont Mombritius édite la forme originale, *Sanctuarium seu vitae sanctorum,* t. 2, Paris, 1910, p. 31-36) comporte des interpolations de l'autre Vie connue à cette époque (« *Hieronymus noster...* ») qui attribue son départ à la méchanceté de ses ennemis (PL 22, 204 tiré de PL 22, 178). Abélard cite *Plerosque nimirum dans TSch* III, 38 et *Sic et Non* 35, 1. Sur ces Vies, voir A. VACCARI, *Le antiche vite di S. Girolamo,* dans *Scritti di erudizione e di filologia,* Rome, 1958, 2, p. 31-51 et RICE, *St Jerome in the Renaissance,* p. 23-28 and 209 n. 2-3.

36. Héloïse, *Epist.* 2 (éd. MUCKLE, p. 70) : « Quot autem et quantos tractatus in doctrina vel exhortatione seu etiam consolatione sanctarum feminarum sancti patres consummaverint, et quanta eos diligentia composuerint, tua melius excellentia quam nostra parvitas novit ».

37. *Epist.* 3 (éd. MUCKLE, p. 73-77).

remords parce que son intention a toujours été irréprochable. Pour terminer cette lettre où elle supplie qu'on ne lui demande pas de devenir plus vertueuse qu'elle ne peut l'être, elle cite (hors de son contexte) un passage de l'*Adversus Vigilantium* où Jérôme se montre très humain : « Fateor imbecillitatem meam ; nolo spe victoriae pugnare ne perdam aliquando victoriam. ... Quid necesse est certa dimittere, et incerta sectari[38] ? ».

La lettre 22 à Eustochium fournit à Abélard tous les éléments de sa réponse. Comme Héloïse lui avait fait remarquer en passant qu'il n'aurait pas dû mettre son nom à elle au début de sa salutation, il se justifie en disant qu'il s'est inspiré de la salutation *domina, sponsa domini* de Jérôme à Eustochium[39]. Suivant l'argumentation de la lettre 22, il s'engage dans un commentaire de quelques versets du *Cantique* (1 : 3-5 ; 3 : 1) pour souligner combien il est important de garder son âme seule et pure pour le Seigneur. Son exégèse ne se contente pas de répéter les idées de Jérôme. Il met l'accent sur des aspects littéraux et même sensuels du texte[40]. Cette deuxième réponse à Héloïse révèle une approche affective du texte biblique qui n'apparaît pas dans la *Theologia*. La lettre à Eustochium lui sert aussi à reprocher à Héloïse l'excès de modestie qu'elle manifestait en demandant qu'on n'attende pas trop d'elle. Il affirme que sa castration à lui n'a été qu'un châtiment mérité et profitable[41].

Après cette deuxième réponse, Héloïse ne fait plus état de ses sentiments personnels. Elle préfère critiquer le parti pris masculin de la Règle de S. Benoît, qu'elle oppose pour son intransigeance à celle de Jérôme[42]. Abélard répond d'abord par deux traités, une histoire des femmes religieuses et une règle pour le Paraclet. Dans l'*Historia calamitatum* il n'indique pas qu'il ait invité Héloïse au Paraclet avec l'intention d'écrire une règle particulière. Il n'a écrit celle-ci qu'à la demande d'Héloïse.

Dans le premier de ces deux traités, Abélard développe un thème mineur de la *Theologia*. Il avait indiqué dans cet ouvrage que Dieu s'est révélé aux femmes païennes (notamment à la Sibylle) aussi bien qu'aux hommes, mais il n'avait pas

---

38. Héloïse, *Epist.* 4 (éd. MUCKLE, p. 82), citant l'*Adversus Vigilantium* 16 (PL 23, 367B).

39. *Epist.* 5 (éd. MUCKLE, p. 83), citant l'*Ep.* 22, 2 (CSEL 54, 145).

40. *Epist.* 5 (p. 83-85) ; cf. JÉRÔME, *Ep.* 22, 1, 17, 19, 24-26, 41. Une remarque dans l'*Epist.* 5 (p. 85) ne se trouve pas chez Jérôme, mais témoigne d'un intérêt pour une explication littérale du texte : « Et frequenter accidit ut nigrarum caro feminarum quanto est in aspectu deformior, tanto sit in tactu suavior ; atque ideo earum voluptas secretis gaudiis quam publicis gratior sit et convenientior, et earum viri, ut illis oblectentur, magis eas in cubiculum introducunt quam ad publicum educunt ».

41. *Epist.* 5 (éd. MUCKLE, p. 89) : « Unde iustissime et clementissime, licet cum summa tui avunculi proditione, ut in multis crescerem, parte illa corporis mei sum imminutus in qua libidinis regnum erat et tota huius concupiscentiae causa consistebat ut iuste illud plecteretur membrum quod in nobis commiserat totum... ».

42. Héloïse, *Epist.* 6 (éd. MUCKLE, p. 242-3).

parlé des femmes de la Bible. Dans le premier traité, il réutilise les passages qui lui conviennent de la *Theologia christiana,* mais il met beaucoup plus l'accent sur les femmes de l'Ancien et du Nouveau Testament[43]. L'exemple de la Sibylle montre que la vie religieuse est enracinée dans l'Antiquité. Les dignités ecclésiastiques ne sont que la continuation à l'époque moderne de celles de la Synagogue et des cultes païens de Rome[44]. Une remarque de Jérôme sur l'interdiction évangélique d'appeler qui que ce soit *Père* lui sert à justifier qu'il faille utiliser *diaconissa* et non pas *abbatissa* pour désigner Héloïse[45]. Des trois docteurs de l'Église dont il dit qu'ils ont beaucoup écrit pour des femmes − Origène, Ambroise et Jérôme − on ne s'étonne pas que ce soit Jérôme qui reçoive la palme. Il cite le passage des *Retractationes* où Augustin explique qu'il n'a pas pu obtenir que Jérôme lui réponde à propos d'une question précise : « Regardez : un si grand homme (Augustin) attend et ne reçoit pas même quelques petits mots de lui (Jérôme). Nous connaissons l'ampleur de ses écrits pour des femmes, qui l'ont vénéré beaucoup plus que l'évêque[46] ». Cette comparaison montre bien la profondeur de sa sympathie pour son héros. Comme Jérôme, Abélard s'est trouvé guide spirituel d'une communauté de femmes. De plus, il savait que jamais il ne deviendrait évêque.

Dans le deuxième traité, à savoir la règle, Abélard explique à la fois les principes et les modalités quotidiennes de la vie religieuse pour les femmes qu'il veut voir mis en œuvre. Il reprend la division tripartite de la vertu en continence, abstinence et force, développée au deuxième livre de la *Theologia christiana,* avec une modification : le silence remplace la force[47]. On observe ici l'influence d'une idée chère à la règle de S Benoît[48]. Sans explorer la richesse des idées de la règle d'Abélard, on peut noter l'importance qu'il attache aux lettres de Jérôme[49]. Comme dans sa lettre précédente, il met l'accent sur la solitude et sur la pureté de l'âme. La doctrine spirituelle de Jérôme lui sert de base pour la sienne propre.

Son admiration pour ce docteur n'est pas aveugle. Tout en comprenant son insistance auprès d'Eustochium pour qu'elle ne prenne jamais de vin, il remarque que, selon Macrobe, les femmes sont moins sujettes que les hommes à s'enivrer

---

43. *Epist.* 7 (éd. MUCKLE, p. 271-2 et 276-7), citant *Tchr* I, 126-128 (= *TSch* I, 189-191) et II, 104, 106-106a.

44. *Epist.* 7 (éd. MUCKLE, p. 275-6).

45. *Epist.* 7 (éd. MUCKLE, p. 264) ; *Epist.* 8 (éd. McLaughlin, p. 252).

46. *Epist.* 7 (éd. MUCKLE, p. 279) ; citant les *Retractationes* II, 45 (CCL 57, 126-7).

47. *Tchr* II, 59-73 (abstinence), 74-86 (force d'âme), 87-108 (continence) ; cf. *Epist.* 8 (éd. McLaughlin, p. 243).

48. *Epist.* 8 (éd. McLaughlin, p. 245). Il cite aussi Augustin, Grégoire, les Pères du désert et l'Écriture pour souligner l'importance du silence.

49. *Epist.* 8 (éd. McLaughlin, p. 247, 249, 250, 251, 254, 255, 256, 262, 269, 271-2, 279, 280, 282, 289), citant les lettres 14 à Héliodore, 58 à Paulin, 125 à Rusticus, 52 à Népotien, 22 et 31 à Eustochium et 54 à Furia.

à cause des humeurs qui sortent de leur corps[50]. Donc il est absurde d'exiger que les femmes s'abstiennent de vin et de le permettre de temps en temps aux hommes. Seul l'excès de vin est mauvais. Par contre, Abélard accepte sans aucune hésitation tout ce que dit Jérôme de l'importance de l'étude. Il ne veut pas que les sœurs du Paraclet imitent ceux qui se soucient tellement du chant et de la bonne prononciation qu'ils ne comprennent plus rien de ce qu'ils lisent. Abélard cite Benoît ainsi que Jérôme pour souligner la nécessité de la lecture intelligente[51]. La manière dont il déforme une phrase bien connue de Jérôme est significative à cet égard : « *Ama scientiam litterarum et carnis vitia non amabis* ». Jérôme avait dit *Scripturarum* et non pas *litterarum*. Dans un troisième traité, la lettre 9 *De studio litterarum,* il a corrigé cette citation, mais l'interprétation qu'il en donne ressort très clairement de la conclusion de ce même traité : « Ce docteur éminent (Jérôme) vous exhorte par son écrit et par son exemple à vous mettre à l'étude des lettres, surtout pour que vous ne soyez pas obligées de faire appel aux hommes ni qu'un esprit attentif ne divague inutilement hors de son corps et, en abandonnant son époux, ne fornique avec le monde[52] ». Il ne voulait pas qu'un autre monastère prît la direction du Paraclet, risque encouru par toute nouvelle communauté à l'époque.

Dans la lettre 9, Abélard continue la discussion à propos de l'étude, commencée à la fin du traité précédent. Il encourage les sœurs à imiter les femmes qui ont entouré Jérôme. A la différence de ce qu'il avait fait dans la *Theologia christiana,* il cite longuement des lettres de Jérôme à des femmes, surtout les lettres 107 à Laeta sur l'instruction de la jeune Paula, 65 et 127 à Principia, les éloges de Blésilla adressé à Paula et de Paula, (lettres 39 et 108), la lettre 148 à Celancia (en fait de Pélage) et le *Contra Rufinum,* qu'il désigne du nom d'*Apologia ad Pammachium et Marcellam*[53]. Les passages choisis mettent l'accent sur l'importance de l'étude du Grec et de l'Hébreu, plutôt que sur l'étude de l'Écriture en elle-même. Il voulait que les sœurs imitent l'exemple de Paula et d'Eustochium. Si elles connaissaient bien le Grec et l'Hébreu, il ne serait plus nécessaire d'utiliser des traductions qui devaient forcément contenir beaucoup d'expressions ambiguës et douteuses[54].

Cet enthousiasme pour l'authenticité du texte scripturaire a amené Abélard (ou Héloïse) à substituer *supersubstantialem* à *quotidianum* dans le *Pater,* en arguant du fait que c'est le mot attribué au Seigneur par Matthieu (9 : 11). Seul Luc (11 : 3), évangéliste plus tardif, fait usage de *quotidianum.* Ce changement apporté à la prière la plus connue de l'Église, Abélard essaye de le justifier dans une homélie

---

50. *Epist.* 8 (éd. McLaughlin, p. 272), citant Macrobe, *Saturnalia* VII, 6, 16-17.

51. *Epist.* 8 (éd. McLaughlin, p. 288-9).

52. *Epist.* 8 (éd. McLaughin, p. 289) ; *Epist.* 9 (éd. Smits, p. 219, 237). Cf. Jérôme, *Ep.* 125, 11 (CSEL 56, 130).

53. Voir l'analyse détaillée de SMITS, *Letters IX-XIV,* p. 113-120.

54. *Epist.* 9 (éd. Smits, p. 235) : « Quas ad plenum si cognoscere studeamus, in ipso fonte magis quam in rivulis translacionum perquirende sunt, presertim cum earum diuerse translaciones ambiguitatem magis quam certitudinem lectori generent ».

et dans une lettre à Bernard de Clairvaux, qui avait émis des doutes sur l'utilité de cette réforme[55]. La méthode qu'Abélard applique à l'Écriture est celle qu'il conseille pour la lecture des Pères dans le prologue du *Sic et Non*. Cependant il ne s'est pas mis à l'exégèse de l'Écriture, si nous laissons de coté son ébauche sur *Ezéchiel*, avant qu'Héloïse lui eût demandé d'écrire un commentaire sur les premiers chapitres de la Genèse. Il fait suivre cette *Expositio* par son commentaire sur l'*Épitre aux Romains*[56].

Héloïse nous a laissé une œuvre littéraire moindre que celle d'Abélard, mais il est clair qu'elle a exercé une influence sur son mari. La lettre qui introduit quarante-deux *Problemata* qu'elle veut lui poser sur des questions d'exégèse et de morale (écrite vraisemblablement vers 1138-39) manifeste une fois de plus comment elle utilise l'exemple de Jérôme pour obtenir une réponse d'Abélard[57]. Ses questions témoignent d'un esprit critique qu'on retrouve rarement dans la littérature scolastique de l'époque. Elle demande si la réponse du Christ *Tu dixisti* est une *enunciatio veritatis* ; certaines contradictions dans l'Écriture lui posent des problèmes, souvent quand il s'agit des femmes ou du péché.

La dernière question cache beaucoup d'angoisse[58]. Héloïse demande s'il est possible de pécher en faisant une chose ordonnée par Dieu. Abélard répond à la question telle qu'il la comprend : est-ce qu'on pèche quand on fait l'amour, chose ordonnée par Dieu dans le mariage ? Sa réponse se fonde sur son interprétation de la doctrine d'Augustin dans le *De bono conjugali* et le *De nuptiis et concupiscentia*, que la copulation en elle-même est un *bonum nuptiale* et que la faute se trouve dans la motivation de celui qui fait l'amour. C'est une question qu'il examinera plus en détail dans son *Éthique*, sa dernière grande œuvre. Ici il présente une définition du péché nettement mieux formulée que dans ses écrits précédents. Dans le *Dialogue* entre un philosophe et un chrétien et dans son commentaire sur l'*Épitre aux Romains*, il avait dit en passant que le péché n'existe que dans la volonté mauvaise des gens, sans étudier le problème en profondeur. Dans l'*Éthique*, le péché n'est plus la volonté mauvaise, mais le consentement à cette volonté mauvaise. Pour parler plus clairement, désirer une femme n'est pas mauvais en soi, mais le consentement à la concupiscence est un péché[59].

55. Pour l'homélie authentique d'Abélard sur le *Pater*, voir Ch. S.F. BURNETT, The' *Expositio Orationis Dominicae*' « *Multorum legimus orationes* », dans *Revue bénédictine* 95, 1985, p. 60-72 ; cf. *Epist.* 10 (éd. Smits, p. 239-47).

56. MEWS. On dating, p. 119-20.

57. *Problemata Heloissae* (PL 178, 677-730) ; cf. P. DRONKE, *Heloise's Problemata and Letters* : *Some Questions of Form and Content*, dans *Petrus Abaelardus. Person, Werk und Wirkung*, éd. R. Thomas, Trier, 1980, p. 53-73.

58. *Probl.* 42 (PL 178, 723A) : <Héloïse :> « utrum aliquis in eo quod facit a Domino sibi concessum vel etiam iussum, peccare possit quaerimus ». <Abélard :> « Quod si, ut oportet, verum concedatur, quaestione gravi pulsamur, quomodo conjuges, vel in antiquo populo, vel in novo, carnalem concupiscentiam exercentes, in eo peccare dicantur, unde in posteros peccatum originale transfundunt ».

59. *Peter Abelard's Ethics*, éd. D. Luscombe, Oxford, 1971, p. 12-14 : « Non itaque

442

On n'est pas ici en contradiction complète avec l'enseignement de la *Theologia christiana*. Aux premières années du Paraclet, Abélard s'intéressait à la possibilité d'accéder à la vertu hors de l'Église. Dans l'*Éthique* ou *Scito teipsum*, il essaie de montrer que le péché ne s'identifie pas à la concupiscence et que l'Église ne joue qu'un rôle externe dans les rapports entre l'homme et Dieu. La doctrine du *Contra Iovinianum* ne lui sert plus. Il ne s'est jamais intéressé aux passages où Jérôme parle des tentations de la chair. Il n'y a qu'une seule occasion où il s'appuie sur son autorité dans l'*Éthique* : c'est pour justifier son interprétation de *Matthieu* 16 : 19, comme quoi le Christ n'a donné le pouvoir d'excommunication qu'aux apôtres et non pas à tous les évêques[60]. Encore une fois, Abélard sélectionne une idée de Jérôme qui sert à renforcer sa vision du monde et des rapports humains.

On trouve une démarche semblable chez Bérenger de Poitiers, auteur d'une *Apologia* dirigée contre Bernard de Clairvaux. Le langage au vitriol dont use Jérôme polémiste l'aide à trouver des images pour vilipender l'abbé cistercien. Il prend pour modèle l'*Apologia ad Pammachium et Marcellam* ou *Contra Rufinum*, texte transmis avec d'autres lettres de Jérôme à côté de l'*Apologia* de Bérenger dans deux manuscrits importants[61]. Cependant cette dernière *Apologia* n'est pas faite que de fiel. Le passage-clé est une citation d'une lettre d'Abélard à Héloïse écrite tout de suite après le concile de Sens où il affirme sa fidélité à la foi de l'Église. Cette lettre n'est connue qu'à travers le texte de Bérenger. Étant donné que l'*Apologia* et les autres lettres personnelles d'Abélard et d'Héloïse se trouvent ensemble dans le manuscrit le plus ancien de la correspondance, on se demande si Bérenger ne fut pas le secrétaire d'Abélard et le porteur de cette *Confessio fidei*, comme de l'*Historia calamitatum* et des autres lettres, au Paraclet[62]. Ce travail l'aurait familiarisé avec les lettres de Jérôme. Bérenger admet la possibilité que son maître se soit trompé sur quelques points, mais il souligne que, dans le passé, de grands docteurs de l'Église se sont trompés eux aussi sur des points de doctrine :

concupiscere mulierem sed concupiscentiae consentire peccatum est, nec uoluntas concubitus sed uoluntatis consensus dampnabilis est ».

60. *Ethica* (*éd. cit.*, p. 114 and n. 3), citant le *Comm. in Euang. Matth.* III (PL 26, 118AB).

61. *Apologia contra Bernardum*, éd. R.M. Thomson, *The Satirical Works of Berengar of Poitiers: An Edition with Introduction*, dans *Mediaeval Studies*, 42, 1980, p. 89-138 (surtout p. 111-30). L'éditeur signale des allusions aux lettres 60 (p. 114, 125), 147 (p. 115), 84 (p. 120, 122), au *Contra Rufinum* (p. 125), au *Contra Iovinianum* (p. 128, 129). Le *Contra Rufinum* se trouve à côté des œuvres de Bérenger dans les MSS *Oxford, Bodleian Add. C 271* et *Paris, Bibl. nat. lat. 1896* (tous les deux du xive siècle) correspondant au type g3, selon la classification de Lardet (CCL 79, p. 137*).

62. Les lettres d'Abélard et d'Héloïse se trouvent avec les œuvres de Bérenger dans les MSS *Paris, BN lat. 2923* (s. xiiiex avec annotations par Pétrarque), *Oxford, Bodleian Add. C 271*, et vraisemblablement dans le manuscrit utilisé par Jean de Meung pour sa traduction des lettres, y compris celle transmise par Bérenger, *Paris, BN fr. 920* (s. xiiiex). J'ai montré ailleurs que rien ne prouve que le recueil des lettres d'Abélard et d'Héloïse ait été rassemblé et copié par les religieuses du Paraclet, *La bibliothèque du Paraclet du XIIIe siècle à la Révolution*, dans *Studia Monastica*, 27, 1985, p. 31-67.

Hilaire de Poitiers qui a pensé que le Christ n'a jamais éprouvé la douleur, opinion contredite par Claudien Mamert ; Augustin qui a reconnu dans ses *Retractationes* avoir soutenu autrefois des opinions qu'il n'accepte plus ; Jérôme qui a affirmé contre Augustin que le *nuptiale bonum* n'était pas un bien en soi[63]. Quant à ce dernier, Bérenger observe qu'il avait scandalisé beaucoup de fidèles respectables, y compris le Sénateur Pammachius, et qu'ils lui ont écrit pour se plaindre de sa position intransigeante. Le disciple d'Abélard n'hésite pas à dire à propos de Jérôme : « inhumanius de nuptiis disputat[64] ».

Bérenger était tout jeune quand il a écrit ces pages, comme il l'expliquera plus tard dans sa vie. Il ne voulait que venir en aide à son maître, « praeceptor meus, dit-il, fidei buccina, legis armarium[65] ». On ne peut douter de la source de ces renseignements. Tous les textes patristiques, y compris ceux de Jérôme, que Bérenger cite ou auxquels il fait allusion dans cette section de l'*Apologia* se trouvent dans le *Sic et Non* et sont parfois commentés par Abélard dans son enseignement oral[66]. Son argumentation à propos du *bonum nuptiale* est, quoique exprimée sans grande finesse, celle d'Abélard dans sa réponse au dernier *Problema* d'Héloïse. L'allusion à Pammachius n'est pas tout à fait exacte, mais c'est une interprétation qu'on peut tirer de la lettre 48 de Jérôme, citée longuement dans le même chapitre du *Sic et Non*[67]. Mon hypothèse est que, dans cette *Apologia*, Bérenger expose l'opinion de son maître à propos de Jérôme, opinion qu'Abélard n'a jamais osé exprimer dans ses propres écrits, mais qui n'en était pas moins la sienne.

En fin de compte, Abélard, Héloïse et Bérenger s'intéressent tous à Jérôme davantage en tant que personnalité individuelle que comme autorité en matière d'exégèse ou comme guide spirituel. Pourtant il ne faut pas trop minimiser la contribution fournie par ses doctrines. Jérôme a procuré à Abélard beaucoup de renseignements sur l'Antiquité, surtout dans les années 1122-26 quand il écrivait au Paraclet sa *Theologia christiana*. Abélard s'est considéré comme le Jérôme du douzième siècle, persécuté par des rivaux jaloux de son génie. Sous l'influence d'Héloïse, qui invoque l'exemple de Jérôme pour demander qu'il s'occupe

---

63. *Apologia* (éd. Thomson, p. 128-30).

64. *Apologia* (*éd. cit.*, p. 129) : « Multos fideles uiros, inter quos et Pammachium senatorem, scandalizauit haec effera austeraque disputatio, doloremque suum scriptis super hoc epistolis eidem Hieronymo testati sunt ».

65. *Epistola Berengarii ad episcopum Mimatensem* (éd. Thomson, p. 135).

66. Il fait allusion au livre X du *De Trinitate* d'Hilaire de Poitiers, cité longuement dans le *Sic et Non* 80, 1-27 (éd. Boyer-McKeon) et au passage de Claudien cité dans *SN* 80, 50. Abélard censure la doctrine d'Hilaire dans les *Sententie magistri Petri Abelardi* (*Sententie Hermanni*) c. 25, ed. S. Buzzetti, Florence, 1983, p. 111-112 (PL 178, 1734CD). Les textes de Jérôme cités par Bérenger se trouvent dans *SN* 135, 3-5, 7. Sa citation (éd. Thomson, p. 130) de *Jac.* 3 : 2 est celle citée par Abélard (dans une citation des *Retractationes*) dans le prologue du *Sic et Non* (éd. Boyer-Mckeon, p. 100).

67. *Sic et Non* 135, 6, 13-18.

davantage de la communauté du Paraclet et d'elle-même, il se met à explorer d'autres aspects du savant docteur. L'importance qu'attache Jérôme à l'analyse textuelle et linguistique de l'Écriture et des langues scripturaires l'impressionne beaucoup, ainsi que sa doctrine spirituelle. Au fond l'exégèse de Jérôme l'intéresse moins que sa méthode exégétique. Il a toujours été grand moraliste, mais il est devenu moins intransigeant que Jérôme quand il s'agit du mariage et du péché. Abélard et Héloïse ne furent pas les seuls à s'intéresser à l'individu Jérôme, comme en témoignent Guigues le chartreux ou le cistercien Nicolas Maniacutia. Chacun tire de ses écrits des idées qui l'aident à comprendre sa propre situation. A sa manière, Jérôme a apporté une contribution non négligeable au dynamisme du douzième siècle[68].

---

68. Je n'ai pas pu tenir compte ici de la conférence d'Hubert Silvestre, prononcée devant l'Académie Royale de Belgique, ' L'idylle d'Abélard et Héloïse : la part du roman ', parue, dans le *Bulletin de la classe des lettres et des sciences morales et politiques*, 5ᵉ série, t. LXXI, 1985-5, p. 157-200, après la rédaction de cette communication. Son hypothèse est que Jean de Meung, ou quelqu'un de son milieu, a fabriqué l'*Historia calamitatum* et les lettres 2-8 d'Abélard et d'Héloïse au treizième siècle. Des contraintes d'espace m'empêchent d'expliquer ici pourquoi j'accepte l'authenticité de ces textes, travail que je ferai ailleurs.

X

Peter Abelard and the
Enigma of Dialogue

PETER ABELARD (1079–1142) IS OFTEN remembered as a victim of persecution. Punished by castration in 1117 following his affair with Heloise,
then accused of heresy at the Council of Soissons in 1121 and again by
Bernard of Clairvaux at the Council of Sens in 1140, Abelard has long been
considered a forerunner of the cause of toleration in the West. At one stage
in his career, he contemplated going to live in Muslim territory, where he
thought he would be made more welcome than in Christendom. Abelard
lived at a time of unusual interest by some Latin scholars in the non-Latin
world, even though strong forces were afoot to re-assert Latin orthodoxy
in Europe and the Middle East.[1] His *Dialogue of a Philosopher with a Jew and
a Christian* or *Collationes* has been seen by some as a plea for intellectual
toleration.[2] Is this too idealistic a perspective? Was he rejecting a contemporary trend toward exclusion of the outsider, or did he in fact participate
in that movement Anna Sapir Abulafia has identified as the Christianiza-
tion of reason in the twelfth century, by which Christian thinkers found
reasons for proving that Jews and pagans were blind to the truth?[3] In order
to assess Abelard's contribution to the idea and practice of religious toleration, we need to relate his *Dialogus* both to his other writings and to
those of his contemporaries, for whom dialogue was often a technique for
asserting the truth rather than for engaging in a listening exercise.

The Dialogue of a Philosopher with a Jew and a Christian

Abelard's *Dialogus* comprises two separate conversations, one of a philosopher with a Jew, the other of a philosopher with a Christian, introduced

by a prologue in which Abelard describes how he saw in a dream that he was asked by three individuals to adjudicate their debate about which path to take to supreme truth. When he asked their identity, they replied that they were pursuing the worship of one God "serving him variously in faith and way of life" (5–7; Payer, 19).[4] The philosopher explained that he had long pursued truth with philosophical reasoning, and that he had turned to moral philosophy, "which is the end of all disciplines and which I have judged to be tasted above all other things" (20–21; Payer, 20). He asked what both Jews and Christians taught about the supreme good and the supreme evil. Having found Jews foolish and Christians mad, he sought a rational conclusion to their debate. With no little self-confidence, Abelard had the philosopher praise his own skill and capacity both in philosophical and divine matters, demonstrated through "that wonderful work of the *Theologia* which envy could neither tolerate nor has been able to destroy, but which it has made more glorious by persecution" (50–52; Payer, 21–22). The prologue concludes with Abelard's recollection of an adage, in fact a remark of Augustine:

No teaching, as one of our own remembers, is so false that it does not contain some truth; I also consider that no disputation is so frivolous, that it does not provide some lesson. As the greatest of the wise said at the very beginning of his Proverbs [1:5], *by hearing a wise person will be wiser, an intelligent person will acquire the art of guidance*, and James the apostle [1:19], *Let every man be quick to listen, but slow to speak*. (68–78; Payer, 23; Payer's emphasis)[5]

Abelard was reminding his audience that the roots of toleration were to be found in the wisdom of Jewish and Christian tradition. The two dialogues which follow serve to instruct the reader in the underlying validity of Augustine's dictum. The discussion is not a report of an actual exchange between three parties but an extended argument about the foundations of ethics and the nature of good and evil.

Perhaps the biggest problem confronting any student of the *Dialogus* is lack of scholarly agreement about its date. This question relates to the broader issue of its interpretation. The traditional argument that Abelard wrote the *Dialogus* in his final years at Cluny (1140–42) derives from the claim that it is incomplete, and that therefore it must have been interrupted by his death. The second debate concludes with a lengthy dissertation by the Christian on the nature of the supreme good, but leaves space for further discussion:

Unless I am mistaken, I have said enough for the present to have shown these things, namely how the name of "good" is to be understood when it is taken simply for a good thing, or when it is applied to the occurrences of things, or to what are expressed by propositions. If there is anything left which you think should be questioned further because it related to inquiry into the supreme good, you are permitted to introduce it or hurry on to what remains. (3422–28; Payer, 169)[6]

While it is certainly true that in the surviving text of the *Dialogus* the Christian never delivers his response to the philosopher's exposition of how the supreme good was to be reached, there is no reason to assume that Abelard's death was to blame for the lack of a conclusion. Textual evidence suggests that it belongs to any time in the period 1125–33, perhaps before he had left the community of students that had gathered around his oratory dedicated to the Paraclete and certainly before he had prepared the *Theologia "Scholarium"* in the early 1130s.[7] At the end of the first conference, Abelard intervenes as a judge only to assert that he wishes to defer judgment, as he prefers to learn from arguments, so that he may become wiser by listening (1165–71; Payer, 71). The absence of adjudication is pedagogical technique. Abelard wants the reader to form his own judgment in the debate, exactly as he wanted the reader of the *Sic et Non* to evaluate for himself opposing views of the Church Fathers about a wide range of questions about Christian doctrine.[8]

The closing speech of the Christian introduces a certain element of finality to the *Dialogus*, even though no third party intervenes. In the first conference Abelard had set up the debate between the Jew and the philosopher, not to establish the superiority of one position over the other, but in order to elucidate the rationale for Jewish observance of the Law as well as the arguments from reason as to why it was not essential to submit to the obligations of the Law. In the second conference he investigated the relationship between the discipline of ethics, concerning how the supreme good was to be attained, and divinity, concerning the supreme good itself:

What you [the philosopher] are accustomed to call ethics, that is morals, we call divinity, giving it that name from what is aimed at being understood, namely God, while your name comes from those things through which it is reached, that is good moral behaviour, which you call virtues. (1265–69; Payer, 76)

Abelard allows the philosopher to present ethical teaching arrived at through natural reason before the discussion moves to a consideration of the supreme good, in which the Christian becomes the dominant voice. It is not clear whether he meant the Christian to present his own version of how the supreme good was to be attained. Having delivered his reflection from the standpoint of reason through the voice of the philosopher, Abelard uses the persona of the Christian to deliver his own reflection that, while we may call something good or evil because of some advantage or disadvantage to us, true goodness is an attribute of God alone, who allows all things to happen for a good reason, even if the cause is unknown to us. The fact that the final speech concludes in the same way as the *Historia calamitatum*, with the prayer "Thy will be done," suggests that Abelard never intended to take the *Dialogus* beyond this point.

The Tradition of Philosophical Dialogue

Although the idea of presenting separate but related dialogues of a philosopher with a Jew and then of a philosopher with a Christian had no immediate literary precedent, the genre of the philosophical dialogue as a means of developing one's ideas had been popularized in the late eleventh century by Anselm of Canterbury (1033–1109). Comparing Abelard's *Dialogus* with dialogues influenced by St. Anselm enables us to appreciate the extent of Abelard's originality. The format Anselm adopted in his early treatises, the *De veritate, De casu diaboli, De libertate arbitrio,* and *De grammatico* (composed c. 1080–85), was that of master and disciple, modeled on the early dialogues of Augustine.[9] Anselm had established the value of discussing issues "from reason alone," but he was not concerned with eliciting ideas from different points of view. The questioner in a dialogue simply served to bring out the inherent logic of Anselm's conclusion for an audience who shared the same assumptions about the pursuit of truth.[10]

Shortly before Anselm was enthroned as archbishop of Canterbury in September 1093, Gilbert Crispin, abbot of Westminster from 1085 to 1117 and a former pupil of Anselm, sent him a copy of a *Disputatio Iudei et Christiani*. Gilbert's dialogue came to enjoy great popularity in the twelfth century. The work is presented as the outcome of conversations Gilbert had with a Jew from Mainz, involved in building activity at Westminster.[11] It begins in a way that recalls Abelard's own *Dialogus*, with a description of how Gilbert was led to an inn where he came across two philosophers "of great fame, but following different paths," engaged in disputation on the worship of the one God. From the outset, Gilbert emphasized the spirit of tolerance in which the discussion was conducted: "As often as we got together we soon had a conversation in a friendly spirit about the Scriptures and our faith."[12] Gilbert had the Jew open the debate by invoking tolerance as an ideal: "Since Christians claim that you are learned in letters and ready with the faculty of speaking, I should like you to deal with me in a tolerant spirit."[13] The specific speeches Gilbert attributed to the Jew are too laden with careful argument and quotation to represent the actual words the Jew might have used. It is nonetheless significant that Gilbert should consciously distance himself from traditional anti-Jewish invective.

Gilbert wanted to formulate a convincing argument from reason by which he could justify the doctrine of the incarnation. Because of its sinful nature, mankind was unable to effect its own redemption. A God-man was thus logically necessary. Such ideas show strong similarities to those of St. Anselm, who came to England from Bec in September 1092.[14] It has a continuation in the *Disputatio cum gentili*, a dialogue between a Christian and a Gentile.[15] As Sapir Abulafia has observed, although Crispin may have introduced the figure of the Gentile to raise objections to Christian doctrine from reason alone (objections essentially similar to those of the Jew), he was unable to refrain from justifying his argument by reference to scripture.[16] Dialogue for Gilbert Crispin as for Anselm meant demonstration of the rightness of one point of view. The *Disputatio* concluded with the Gentile abandoning the discussion. His place was then taken by a disciple willing to learn, rather than argue about the truth of the doctrine of the Trinity. Gilbert drew his arguments from those of St. Anselm in his treatise against Roscelin, the nominalist theologian who became Abelard's teacher.[17]

A similar dialogue structure is employed in a little studied *Disputatio* between a Christian and a Gentile attributed to St. Anselm, not included within Schmitt's edition of the *Opera Omnia*.[18] It opens with a question from an imaginary Gentile: "I want to learn why the divine majesty humbled himself to beyond the sufferings of mortal nature, to accept the shame of the cross. I do not want this to be proved by the authority of your scriptures, in which I do not believe, but, if it has been done rationally, I want a reason for this event."[19] The Gentile's role is to extract from the Christian a rational argument why it should be that God became man in the way that he did, so ignominiously on the cross. The Christian argues that Christ's death was not shameful but rather a rational and fitting event: "Christ did what was fitting, nothing other than to say that he did what he ought. This.is the way of speaking about everything which God does. He does what he must, that is what is fitting for him, not because he is obliged by any debt demanded by anyone."[20] The final statement of the Gentile is an abject admission of the logic of the Christian's argument: "I admit that until now I have erred, and I acknowledge in heart and mouth that Christ is truly God and the author and healer of true salvation."[21] As in the closing section of Gilbert Crispin's disputation, the Gentile is then transformed into a "faithful disciple." In this case he questions his teacher about why God wanted to be honored by the sacraments and ceremonies which are read about in the Old Testament, and why they were replaced in the Christian church. This very Anselmian *Disputatio* concludes with an exhortation of the Master to the disciple to remain illumined by the light of Christ. Dialogue here was disputation to establish the truth of Christian doctrine against the error of the unbeliever.[22]

Although not developed with the same sophistication as in the *Cur Deus homo*, the underlying argument of this *Disputatio* is the same: given the sinfulness of man, unable to restore himself by his own efforts, the only person who could redeem mankind was someone who was sinless, in other words a man who was also God. The Christian tries to follow the instruction of the Gentile not to argue from the authority of the scriptures, but he finds it difficult to avoid falling into the occasional scriptural phrase. Twice he alludes to the formula "Unless you believe, you shall not understand" (Isaiah 7:9, as quoted by Augustine).[23] Like the dialogues of Gilbert Crispin, this *Disputatio* (a lost work of St. Anselm?) vindicates the rightness of one point of view. While Anselm had established a new point of departure for theological debate in insisting that all such enquiry had to be based on "reason alone," rather than on written authority which might not be acceptable to all parties, he never questioned fundamental Augustinian assumptions about the sinfulness of man and the priority of faith over understanding. Rational enquiry was confined by tight parameters. Anselm perceived Jews, pagans, indeed anyone suspected of being a nonbeliever (including dialecticians like Roscelin of Compiègne), as threatening the Christian community.[24] Rational argument did not necessarily make for greater tolerance.

Roscelin himself justified his search for a rational explanation of the Trinity on the ground that Jews and pagans (Muslims) both defended their faith, so Christians should do the same.[25] Shortly after disputing with St. Anselm in England in 1092, Roscelin obtained a canonry at the Angevin stronghold of Loches, where the young Peter Abelard happened to arrive at about the same time.[26] Studying in the Loire valley under a master who had acquired notoriety in monastic circles through controversy with St. Anselm, Abelard was exposed to very different attitudes from those promulgated by the abbot of Bec, now archbishop of Canterbury. From Roscelin, Abelard imbibed a sense of hostility toward intellectual persecution, even though he subsequently distanced himself from particular doctrines of his teacher on logic and theology.

At the time that the first Crusade was called in 1095, there was little consensus among educated Latin thinkers about the extent to which one could learn from non-Latin culture. There was more sympathy among some intellectuals for rational Arab wisdom than for Jewish tradition. Medical works had been translated from Arabic into Latin by Constantine the African, a monk of Monte Cassino.[27] Orderic Vitalis reports that in 1100 a Moorish doctor, versed in pagan medicine and philosophy, saved the life of the young prince Louis after an attempt to poison him, purportedly at the instigation of his step-mother, Queen Bertrada.[28] Adelard of Bath, who studied at Tours in 1107, was so enamored of Arab learning that he traveled East (certainly to Salerno, perhaps also further) to study under Arab masters, whom he praised for teaching "through the leadership of reason."[29] Works translated from Arabic by Adelard were known to Thierry of Chartres, from whom Abelard once tried to learn mathematics.[30] At the same time, Adelard's collaborator, Petrus Alfonsi, who brought many stories of Arab wisdom to the attention of the Latin West, composed inflammatory and very popular *Dialogi contra Iudaeos* between a Christian and a Jew, which used quotations from the Talmud to refute Jews with as much vigor as Gilbert Crispin.[31] Abelard's approach to exploring dialogue was rather different.

The Role of the Philospher in Abelard's Dialogus

The major difference between Abelard's *Dialogus* and the dialogues of Crispin and the Anselmian *Disputatio* lies in the prominence accorded the role of the philosopher. Rather than using the philosopher to elucidate the rightness of the Christian position, Abelard has him elicit truth from different points of view. By not placing the Jew and the Christian together in the same dialogue, Abelard replaced overt refutation with more subtle analysis. In the first conference, the Jew explains the reasons behind the ceremonies and observances of Jewish tradition, while the philosopher presents arguments against the necessity of following the precepts of the Law. The second conference permitted Abelard to explore the interconnection between the study of ethics, the prime concern of the philosopher, and that of divinity, the concern of the Christian. Abelard identified the insight each of the three figures could contribute, while explaining what he saw as the limitations of Judaism.

The method Abelard employed directly extends principles laid out in his preface to the *Sic et Non* ("Yes and No"). In that work, Abelard gathered together apparently contradictory statements from the Fathers of the Church about Christian doctrine, prefaced by advice on the methodology students should follow: "Since amidst a great profusion of words many sayings of the saints seem to be not only different from each other, but even mutually contradictory, it is not rash for judgment to be made about them, through whom the world itself will be judged."[32] Judgment must not be hasty. The student needed to be aware of being confused by unfamiliar forms of expression or of differing possible meanings of the same words. It was rash for someone to make a judgment about the meaning or understanding of another, given that hearts and thoughts were known to God alone. The preface to the *Sic et Non* was a plea for tolerance in debate about ecclesiastical tradition, argued above all from the authority of Augustine. The intelligent reader had to learn to sift out falsehood and error from the truth of what others had to say. Abelard complained that many pronouncements of the Fathers were delivered "more from opinion rather than from truth." Contradictions were to be resolved by appreciating the diversity of circumstance and intention in which apparently opposing statements were made. No one was to be convicted of being a liar who said something through ignorance rather than duplicity. Had not Augustine said, "Have charity, and do whatever you will"? Whoever spoke sincerely and not fraudulently was free from being guilty of falsehood.

The preface to the *Sic et Non* voiced a plea to move beyond rash judgment to considered reflection of the words used. The essence of wisdom lay in a spirit of enquiry: "The first key to wisdom is defined as persistent and frequent questioning. . . . By doubting we come to enquiry; by enquiry we perceive truth. As the Truth itself says, 'Seek and you shall find, knock and it will be opened to you' (Mt 7:7)."[33] Abelard invoked scripture to support a principle he had already formulated in his *Dialectica*. Questioning was a tool of dialectical inquiry, the science of investigating truth: "he who asks, expresses his own doubt, so that he may attain the certitude which he does not yet have."[34] He cited the example of Christ himself, who sat and asked questions of the elders in the Temple at twelve years of age, even though he was the embodiment of perfect wisdom.

In the *Dialogus* Abelard introduced his reader to a much wider range of views than those raised in the *Sic et Non*. His concern was with nothing less than supreme good and evil and how that supreme good was to be attained. The figure with whom he identified from the outset was the philosopher, who had devoted his life to investigating truth by philosophical reasoning and was now applying himself to moral philosophy, "the end of every discipline." He is interested not in the theory of toleration, but in rational dialogue as necessary for the pursuit of truth. The enemy was religious dogmatism.

The First Conference: The Philosopher and the Jew

The philosopher opens the first conference by observing that religious faith tends to be influenced more by upbringing than by blood or reason. It seemed absurd for believers to be so attached to one way of thinking that they considered all others as condemned by God, and refused to advance in asking questions about their faith. The Jew recognizes the truth of this observation, maintaining that it was all the more necessary for individuals as adults to follow the counsel "of reason rather than opinion" (174–83; Payer, 29). Abelard's presentation of the Jew as an intelligent, reflective commentator differed markedly from the stereotype in most Jewish-Christian dialogues. His sympathy for the position of the Jews in society is evident in a long, frequently quoted description of the practical problems they faced in society. He has the Jew make many perceptive remarks about the role of written Law. How else could any society be governed without a written Law (223–91; Payer, 31–33)? The philosopher sympathized with the Jew's plight, but asked whether the written Law imposed any greater advantage than the natural Law, observed by the patriarchs before the time of Abraham. The Jew's subsequent explanation of circumcision emphasized its social function as well as interior significance. It provided a way of keeping one people apart from the gentiles so that they would not be corrupted by association. Observance of the Law provided an opportunity for sanctification. The Jew rebutted the conventional criticism that observance of the Law conferred only material reward (738–97; Payer, 53–55). Its ultimate command was the perfect love of God and of neighbor. Abelard was raising the argument that the essence of the Jewish Law was the same as the natural law of the philosopher, the precept of perfect love. The Jew puts forward an ethical position, one with which Abelard sympathized: "For every virtue of the mind, the true love of God and of man is sufficient" (831–42; Payer, 57–58).

The philosopher's criticism relates not to this fundamental principle, identified as the core teaching shared by the two parties, but to the Jew's imposition of additional precepts. His argument turns on the narrowness of the Jewish Law, rather than the underlying ethical principle. God was also the God of the uncircumcised patriarchs, like Enoch and Noah, whose life was happier for not having a written Law. Why was it necessary to add additional precepts? The philosopher's critique of the Law resembles that of St. Paul in the Epistle to the Romans, but here it is made not from the standpoint of faith in Christ but from reason. His interpretation of scripture demonstrates the importance of a contrite heart rather than righteous actions. Ritual uncleanness cannot be identified with sin. What had a nocturnal emission of semen or menstruation to do with sinfulness? The philosopher's discussion of sin here is relatively simplistic. He makes the contrast between obvious sins, like murder and adultery, and ritual transgressions, but does not define sin itself except as the fruit of a perverse will. Sin was remitted simply by a contrite heart. Abelard's discussion of sin here has none of the subtlety of the *Scito teipsum* ("Know Thyself," or *Ethics*), written in the late 1130s. In that work Abelard argued that the will to sin was not itself sinful, only the deliberate consent to such a will.[35] When he composed the first conversation of the *Dialogus*, he was not concerned with the psychological and moral questions raised by Heloise in her letters to him, issues he was initially unwilling to confront in his first two letters to Heloise.

The Second Conference: The Philosopher and the Christian

Like so many of his educated contemporaries, Abelard was more favorably disposed to the arguments of the philosopher than to those of the Jew. This attitude was already evident in the second book of the *Theologia christiana*, added to his original treatise on the Trinity to provide further argument for reliance on pagan philosophers: "We seem not forced by any reason to despair about the salvation of such gentiles, instructed before the arrival of the Saviour not by any written Law; according to the Apostle [Rom 2:14–15], they did those things of the Law naturally; they were themselves the Law, showing the work of the Law written in their hearts, providing a witness for them in their own conscience."[36] Writing then in a flush of enthusiasm for the moral teaching of the ancient philosophers (which he contrasted with current monastic behavior), Abelard was not particularly interested in discussing the nature of sin. Rather, he wanted to demonstrate the validity of pagan philosophical insight for Christian reflection on the nature of the supreme good, which was God. The moral precepts of the Gospels he saw as no more than a reform of the natural law followed by the philosophers. He had also pursued this theme in his *Soliloquium*, an early internal dialogue in which he referred back to an "exhortation" (perhaps incorporated into the second book of the *Theologia christiana*) as proving that "philosophers are especially in fellowship with Christians not so much in name as in actual fact."[37] When preparing the *Theologia "Scholarium"* in the early 1130s, Abelard removed the lengthy ethical excursus incorporated into the second book of the *Theologia christiana*, perhaps because he had already given ethics separate treatment in the *Dialogus*.

The philosopher and the Christian agree on the relationship between ethics and divinity. Ethics concentrates on the path to the desired end, while divinity examines the supreme good itself, namely God. To the philosopher's request for a definition of "true ethics," the Christian replies that it should establish where the supreme good is and by what path it is to be reached (1280–82; Payer, 76). Other disciplines, like grammar and dialectic, lie far below the grand subject matter of the supreme good, even though they may prepare the way, introducing us to "the ladies-in-waiting," rather than the *domina* herself. Abelard uses the subsequent dialogue to advance a case for identifying Christianity as a truly rational religion, as well as to criticize those who consider that Christian faith precludes rational enquiry. Again these are not matters which are disputed by the Christian. The philosopher commends Christian preaching for its capacity to engage in rational debate, but insists that its teaching should not be accepted through faith alone.

The philosopher's criticism of those "who seek solace for their lack of skill" in the saying of Pope Gregory, "Faith has no merit for which human reason offers proof," closely echoes a theme Abelard reinforced in the revised introduction to the second book of the *Theologia "Scholarium."* This widely known saying of Gregory could easily be interpreted as asserting that the subject matter of faith was beyond rational discussion. In the original version of the treatise on the Trinity, it had been one of a number of quotations Abelard had used against Roscelin of Compiègne. By the time Abelard was writing the *Dialogus* and preparing the *Theologia "Scholarium,"* he had to defend his rational discussion of belief against those who were throwing the same argument against himself. He pointed out that if this saying of Gregory meant that there could be no rational inquiry into faith, there would logically be no place for the Christian to provide any kind of response or criticism relating to a matter of faith (1376–94; Payer, 81).[38]

The Christian in the *Dialogus* is fully in accord with the complaints of the philosopher about those who refuse to reason about their beliefs. Abelard is arguing for the cause of rational discussion. He uses the philosopher to put the argument he had raised in the prologue to the *Sic et Non* to criticize blind reliance on the judgments of others as authoritative, but in stronger terms: "In every philosophical disputation authority is thought to hold last place or no place at all to such an extent that it is shameful for those who trust in their own powers and scorn the refuge of another's wealth, to adduce arguments based on judgment of a matter [extrinsic judgment], namely on authority" (1413–17; Payer, 83). An argument based "on judgment of a matter" (*a rei judicio*) had been considered by Boethius to be weak because the orator had not constructed it for himself. Abelard insisted on applying to matters of faith the principle of questioning all authoritative statements. By demonstrating that this was common ground to the philosopher and the Christian, he was endeavoring to make his readers accept the rational necessity for such a principle, as he had argued in the second book of the *Theologia christiana*.

He then moved to presenting the philosopher's understanding of the virtues, followed by the Christian's commentary on the same subject. The philosopher interprets virtue as acquired through self-control: "a good will strengthened into habit can be called virtue" (1555–56; Payer, 90). This Aristotelian *habitus* theory of virtue as an acquired disposition was to become a significant theme in twelfth-century ethical thought.[39] The philosopher then presents the Stoic position that there can be no increase in beatitude without an increase in virtue, an assertion countered by the Christian locating supreme happiness not in this world but in the life to come. Whereas the philosopher sees virtues to be desired and vices avoided for their own sake, the teaching of Christ presents a better reason for pursuing virtue and avoiding vice. The philosopher suggests that there may simply be different names given to the goal of this beatitude: pleasure by Epicurus, the kingdom of heaven by Christ. Is not the intention of living justly the same for all people (1687–1720; Payer, 96–97)?

When the Christian accuses the philosopher of holding the idea that all good men are equally good and all the guilty equally guilty, following lengthy citation from Cicero's *De officiis*, the philosopher points to the teaching of Augustine that charity includes all the virtues under one name (1793–1823; Payer, 101–2). This prompts the Christian to argue that the presence of virtue in one individual does not mean that it is fully operative to the same degree as in another. The philosopher's teaching is not so much contradicted as clarified. A virtuous action to which one is obliged by precept is not the same as one (like virginity) not required by precept (1909–14, quoting 1 Cor 7:25; Payer, 105–6). No one who has virtue perishes, but not all are equal in virtue.

The philosopher's discussion of virtue in the *Dialogus* represents Abelard's first sustained treatment of the issue, certainly pre-dating that of the *Scito teipsum*. Virtue, he teaches, is an acquired habit of the mind, achieved through personal effort. His comment that chastity is not a virtue if no struggle is involved against concupiscence had particular relevance in Abelard's personal situation. The philosopher's exposition had none of the subtlety of the *Scito teipsum*, although some of its themes are hinted at. Some things are good and bad in themselves, like virtues and vices; others are indifferent, but are said to be good and bad by the intention by which they were done (1992–2030; Payer, 109–11). Although the framework for the philosopher's fourfold analysis of the virtues (prudence, justice, courage, and temperance) is based on a traditional source, Cicero's *De inventione*, there is considerable originality to the way he rearranges them. Abelard had the philosopher emphasize the role of justice (quoting examples given in the *Theologia christiana*) and the pre-eminence of the will in determining moral goodness.[40] Ciceronian themes are thus presented in an original way.

In the last section of the *Dialogus*, Abelard turned his attention back to the nature of the supreme good, the subject on which the Christian has the most to say. The discussion begins with his identification of what the philosopher believes about good and evil: that the supreme good is a future life of supreme happiness, the supreme evil that of perpetual punishment. Abelard uses both the philosopher and the Christian as mouthpieces for his argument. At stake is the thorniest issue in any providential view of the world: how can supreme evil be reconciled to supreme good? Abelard's resolution turns on careful distinction of the way in which words are used. To say that something is good is not the same as saying that it is a good thing. His distinction of the different ways *bonus* can be used is one he had made in his *Dialectica*.[41] A term's meaning is dependent on the usage to which it is put. Applied to the mystery of suffering, the philosopher observes that a punishment may be good because it is just, but this did not mean that we could say that it is a good thing. The punishment of man cannot be worse than the fault which makes a man evil (2324–50, 2437–46; Payer, 125, 128–29). The unhappiness of the wicked is self-inflicted. There may be great variety in beatitude, in proportion to each individual's mode of understanding. Once the philosopher accepts the argument that the supreme good or evil of man is that by which he becomes better or worse, the Christian moves to identifying the supreme good with the vision of God. Distinctions between substance and accident made by a philosopher apply only to the material realm, not to the heavenly (2557–2603; Payer, 133–35).

The Platonic aspect of this final section of the *Dialogus* has never attracted as much commentary as his logical or ethical writings, but it discloses the same sense of an ideal beyond language which pervades Abelard's thought. In the incomplete fifth book of the *Theologia christiana* Abelard had begun to sketch out his doctrine of God, argued from reason rather than from authority. The closing section of the *Dialogus* was similarly conceived as a natural theology, worked out from rational principles in dialogue with a philosopher. This was the goal to which the philosopher was moving in his ethical theory, although he had to turn to the Christian for a full picture of the goal. Only in this final section does Abelard introduce the notion of grace, not in the context of accomplishing virtue, but as the means through which God is present—as the sun fills the world with light (2744–57; Payer, 141).

The thrust of Abelard's final discussion was to reject any notion that Christian teaching about movement or place (like the bodily ascension of Christ into the heavens at the right side of the Father, or hell itself) had a physical meaning (2767–877; Payer, 142–47). Descriptions of hell in the Old and New Testaments cannot be taken literally, as they refer to the perpetual torment souls suffered in their consciences. If one followed "the common opinion of almost everyone" that the damned were placed in the same fire, how could there be any gradation in punishment? Suffering comes about not through any common substance but from the nature of those punished (3026–61; Payer, 153–54).

The discussion of the reward of the good and the punishment of the damned is followed by what the Christian admits is a most difficult task, the definition of good and evil. A good thing is something which does not have the effect of impeding the advantage of anything, something evil is the opposite (3153–56; Payer, 158). Good and evil cannot be used to refer to absolutes, as the same action can be good or evil, depending on the intention in the mind. There is properly no such thing as a good action, but an action done well, with a good intention. Judas' betrayal of Jesus was bad because of Judas' bad intention, while God's action of delivering up Jesus was good because it happened for a different reason. This led Abelard to argue that everything that happens is done for a rational reason, known to God, a theme with which he had concluded the *Theologia "Scholarium."* It might be good for an evil thing to exist, even though that evil could not be good (3220–70, 3381–82; Payer, 161–63, 167–68).

The Dialogus *and the Ideal of Toleration*

Modern notions of religious toleration should not be read back into the *Dialogus*. Abelard is never explicitly concerned in his writings with the right of alternative groups in society to hold dissenting views. Like St. Anselm and Gilbert Crispin, Abelard was laying out a rational framework for Christian doctrine. Nonetheless, there was a profound difference in perspective between Abelard's *Dialogus* and earlier disputations. Anselm and Gilbert Crispin never questioned traditional assumptions about the sinfulness of human nature. In the *Cur Deus homo* Boso had disagreed with the notion that the devil enjoyed any legitimate rights over mankind, but had never questioned the reality of this bondage. Abelard's initial assumption in the *Dialogus*, as in every version of the *Theologia*, was that human beings are not flawed by original sin. The ethical precepts of the Jewish Law are fundamentally the same as those of the natural law observed by the philosopher. Philosophical reflection on ethics is ultimately in harmony with Christian reflection on the supreme good.

Perhaps the most significant difference between Abelard's *Dialogus* on one hand and the disputations of Gilbert Crispin and St. Anselm (or attributed to him) on the other lies in their contrasting subject matter. From the time in the early 1090s that Roscelin emphasized the necessary distinction between God the Father and God the Son, both Anselm and Gilbert Crispin were preoccupied with proving the rightness of the doctrine of the incarnation, against rational doubt. Abelard was primarily concerned not with proving Jews wrong, but with understanding the supreme good and how that supreme good should be reached. In terms of existing dialogue literature, this was a novel perspective. By drawing attention to the common ground that was the goal of the philosopher, the Jew, and the Christian, Abelard avoided the customary arguments generated by the uniqueness of the Christian claim. Such inquiry provided a better starting point for discussion of ethical precepts. Abelard's theological investigations similarly centered around the supreme good and its three-fold attributes of power, wisdom, and benignity as glimpsed by gentile philosophers, rather than the doctrine of the incarnation in particular. He started to develop his ideas about pagan ethical philosophy at about the same time as he freed

X

himself from obligation to the abbot of St. Denis. In the *Dialogus* Abelard
was able to take those ethical reflections much further in the form of debates of a philosopher with a Jew and with a Christian. He wanted to show
that dialectical technique could become open-ended, in order to evaluate
the common ground of different religious traditions and challenge Christians to move away from rigidly confrontational attitudes.

While Abelard has the philosopher present a theory of ethics and the
Christian a vision of the supreme good as the focus of ethical discussion,
he does not have the Christian comment on the path to be taken to the
supreme good. The traditional explanation offered for this, that Abelard
must have died before he could complete the work, is difficult to reconcile with the evidence for an early date discussed above. Abelard may not
yet have fully worked out his own understanding of Christian ethics when
he wrote the *Dialogus*. Many of the issues about the Law and circumcision Abelard raised in the first conference are themes he discussed at much
more length in his commentary on St. Paul's Epistle to the Romans, written while he was working on the *Theologia "Scholarium."* In that commentary Abelard tackled the issues of sin and grace so conspicuously absent
from the *Dialogus*. In his account of the redemption in that commentary
on Paul, he expanded on the idea (introduced tentatively in the *Cur Deus
homo*) that the Devil enjoys no legitimate dominion over man. We are redeemed by the word and example of Christ, which prompts mankind to
the true love of God.[42] This theory of the redemption took for granted the
ethical principles laid out in the *Dialogus*.

In his position as abbot of St. Gildas from 1127 and as spiritual direc-
tor to the nuns of the Paraclete from 1129, Abelard was obliged to develop
his understanding of Christian doctrine. Certainly, by the 1130s, when he
had resumed teaching on the Mont Sainte-Geneviève, Abelard had developed his own distinctive interpretation of the redemptive action of Christ.
His lectures from the period are recorded in various collections of his *sententiae* about faith in God, the incarnation and redemption, the sacraments
and charity.[43] Abelard transformed the *Theologia christiana* into the *Theologia "Scholarium"* in the 1130s so as to place his discussion of the supreme
good within this wider framework. When he was writing his commentary
on Romans, he already had in mind ideas which he was reserving for his
Ethics or *Scito teipsum*. While the *Dialogus* has none of the Christological
reflection of the commentary on Romans or the psychological subtlety of
that later work, it anticipates themes about the priority of natural law and
the role of intention developed in these two later works.

The Enigma of Dialogue

Although it may be tempting to read Abelard's *Dialogus* as an early manifesto of religious toleration between a Jew, a philosopher, and a Christian, it is not the record of a discussion between historical individuals. Jolivet's suggestion that the picture Abelard has drawn there of the philosopher may have owed something to reports he had heard of a Muslim philosopher, Ibn Badadya (Avempace, d. 1138), cannot be sustained. Even if Abelard had thought of taking flight in Muslim territory in a moment of depression, too much should not be made of a passing allusion made by the Jew that the philosopher was of the seed of Ishmael. The philosopher is someone who has rejected the path of revelation, and considers the Jews "foolish" and the Christians "insane" (29; Payer, 21). He is an imaginary figure with whom Abelard identifies, as he strives to work out an ethical path to the supreme good, argued in relation to the role of the Jewish Law, the natural law of the philosopher, and Christian understanding of God as the supreme good. He was only imagining a situation of philosophical tolerance in order to debate the nature of truth and how it could be reached. The paradox of his position was that while he insisted there was a supreme truth to which all rational men were devoted, he was unwilling to come to a firm conclusion about what he thought.

A guiding thread in the *Dialogus*, as indeed through all Abelard's writing, is confidence in the power of rational discussion. He questions all attempts to impose belief by force: "Heretics are more to be coerced by reason than by power, since, according to the authority of the holy fathers, the faithful, for whom all things co-operate for the good (Rom 8:28), exercized by their disputations, are made more watchful and cautious."[44] In the *Historia calamitatum*, Abelard expressed only contempt for those who preached what they did not understand through their reason, a hostility to unreasoning belief that he developed further in his *Theologia "Scholarium."*[45] The very first question discussed in the *Sic et Non* is whether faith was to be supported by reason. Criticism leveled at his endeavor to understand Christian doctrine through examples and analogies from secular philosophy motivated him to find many patristic texts which showed that assertions qualified as "Christian tradition" were not as fixed as many Christians thought.

Abelard's confidence in the capacity of rational discussion to arrive at greater understanding of any subject, whether it be theology, ethics, or whatever, reflects a particular fascination with the process of dialogue. His reputation in dialectic turned not so much on the brilliance of his writing as on his ability to counter an argument in public disputation. This is the image Goswin remembered when he recounted to his biographer how he, the young Goswin, had dared to challenge the supreme master of dialectic at the public school of the abbey of Sainte-Geneviève (sometime around 1110). Goswin also recalled a conversation about the nature of honesty he had with the stubborn Abelard, when Abelard was incarcerated at the abbey of St. Medard after being found guilty of preaching heresy at the Council of Soissons (1121).[46]

Abelard tended to be remembered by his critics as a master of disputation who never grew beyond his early gifts in dialectic. Certainly his skill in argument made a negative impression on those who could not understand what he was saying. It is a mistake, however, to think that he saw dialectic as an end in itself. There was a Platonic idealism in his conviction that it was a tool in the service of truth. In his first major work of theology about God as a Trinity of persons, Abelard transferred ideas about the artificial nature of all language to theological concepts. No linguistic statement could ever define the totality of understanding, known ultimately only to God.

The *Dialogus* demonstrates how Abelard constructed his argument in the form of an ongoing dialogue. His philosophy of language militated against identifying any "final solution." The lack of a firm conclusion to this treatise is not an accident due to external circumstances beyond Abelard's control, but a characteristic of his thought. He observed in his *Theologia "Scholarium"* that he was not expounding the truth, but "the sense of our opinion."[47] More controversially, he defined faith as "the estimation of things not apparent to the senses," in accord with a theme he had developed in the *De intellectibus* ("On Understandings"), that an estimation (*existimatio*) of something was not the same as an understanding, which conferred certitude.[48] He did not deny the existence of truth, only our capacity to give it final definition.

The *Sic et Non* is like the *Dialogus* in being an invitation to thought rather than a finished work. Judgment on the questions under debate is left to the reader, rather than imposed by Abelard himself. The closest we can get to judgments delivered by Abelard on these questions are the various surviving collections of his *sententiae* recorded by students on matters of faith, the sacraments, and charity. The very fluid nature of these "sentences," each manuscript of which tends to be different from another, testifies to Abelard's unwillingness to deliver a final resolution of any question. The same lack of resolution applies to the *Theologia*, a treatise he kept on revising for over twenty years.[49]

The open-ended quality of Abelard's thought contrasts sharply with that of many of his contemporaries. Anselm of Laon and William of Champeaux were celebrated for delivering definitive "sentences" on a wide range of doctrinal questions being debated by students. They did not introduce into discussion of theology or ethics anything like the wide range of texts and ideas Abelard was willing to debate when dealing with these questions. Abelard was engaged in the same underlying program as St. Anselm and Gilbert Crispin, to lay out a rational framework vindicating the authority of Christian doctrine, but he was prepared to enter more into dialogue than into disputation with those who were not Christians. His sympathies were more with the idealized Gentile philosopher he constructed in his mind than with the rational Jew, whose arguments he still considered limited in nature.

Abelard's correspondence with Heloise can also be seen as a dialogue, albeit one in which Abelard was initially unwilling to engage. When Abelard wrote the *Historia calamitatum*, he was full of admiration for the ascetic virtue of pagan philosophers and claimed that he had contemplated living in a "pagan" society where there was greater toleration than in Christendom. The fact that it was addressed to a male friend struck Heloise as an alarming sign that there were severe constraints to his capacity to enter into dialogue with a woman with whom he had once had a sexual relationship. It is a measure of his personal evolution that, after Heloise had urged him to respond more fully to her requests, Abelard discussed in his *Scito teipsum* the psychology of sexual temptation and the difference between temptation and sin, issues never raised in the *Dialogus*. In that work, he was interested simply in the ideal of virtue, based on natural law. As in classical tradition, philosophical dialogue was a male affair. His analysis of ethics can be seen as providing discussion missing from the end of the *Dialogus*. Abelard now defined sin not as a wrong will as in the *Dialogus* and the commentary on Romans, but as consent to a wrong will in contempt of God. By the time he wrote the treatise he called "Know Yourself," Abelard had acquired a greater degree of self-knowledge.

Perhaps the most expressive articulation of Abelard's attitude to diversity occurs in his didactic poem, the *Carmen ad Astralabium*, addressed to his son. Given that Astralabe was born around 1117, the poem must belong to the final years of Abelard's life. The poem provides a moving summation of Abelard's wisdom, although it has never attracted the sort of critical attention devoted to his early writings on dialectic. In one passage, he raises the theme of the diversity of beliefs in a way that recalls the

opening of the *Dialogus*. The solution Abelard offers his son is to emphasize that only contempt for God, not ignorance, is truly sinful:

> The world is divided among so many sects
> that what may be the path of life is hardly clear.
> Because the world harbors so many conflicting dogmas,
> each makes his own, by way of his own background.
> In the end, no one dares rely on reason in these things,
> while he wants to live in some kind of peace with himself.
> Each person sins only by having contempt for God—
> only contempt can make this person guilty.
> One does not have contempt if one does not know what is to be done,
> unless not knowing is due to one's own fault.
> Sins abandon you more than you abandon them,
> if, when you cannot do more harm, you repent.
> There are those who so much delight in past sins
> that they never truly repent of them.
> Rather, the sweetness of that pleasure may be so great
> that no satisfaction for it has any weight.
> Because of this comes the frequent complaint of our Heloise,
> by which she often says to me what she says to herself:
> "If I cannot be saved without repenting
> of what I committed in the past, there is no hope for me.
> The joys of what we did are still so sweet
> that what pleased greatly gives help by being recalled."
> One who tells the truth does not strain in telling it:
> What is hard is first fabricating falsehood, then speaking.[50]

When Abelard wrote the *Dialogus*, he was not preoccupied at all with sin.
In the *Carmen*, he admits openly that it was Heloise who caused him to
be preoccupied with the issue. She had rebuked Abelard for looking at
her so much in terms of virtue that he had not recognized the reality of
her situation. Before he resumed contact with Heloise, Abelard had been
fascinated by the example of male pagan philosophers because their virtuous lives contrasted so sharply with the lives of Christian monks. Through
rational inquiry into Jewish and Christian tradition he thought that one
could arrive at an understanding of the truth sought by philosopher and
Christian alike. When he wrote the *Carmen* to Astralabe, he put more emphasis on practical wisdom and the search for inner peace. His image of
reason was still based on a male philosophical ideal, which subtly excluded
the anguished insight of Heloise.

Abelard touched most fully on the ethics of sexual relationships in his
Scito teipsum. As if responding to Heloise, he explained to his readers that

one could not sin through ignorance and that sin lay not in an evil will but in consent to an evil will in contempt of God. This definition provoked new controversy in 1140. Abelard's refutation of the idea that mankind was held in any legitimate bondage to the devil, an argument raised in St. Anselm's *Cur Deus homo*, struck Bernard as denying the reason Christ came to redeem man. He considered Abelard's thought dangerously open-ended. In his eyes, Abelard was "a monk without a rule, a prelate without responsibility, an abbot without discipline, who argues with boys and consorts with women."[51] Bernard's powerful rhetoric about the dangers of disputation illustrates well the fear such discussion generated. Ironically, Abelard had moved beyond the technique of disputation when exploring the common ground of philosophical, Jewish, and Christian perspectives on truth. Bernard did not appreciate that Abelard's version of disputation involved greater respect for alternative perspectives on the supreme good and how it was reached.

Not all Abelard's critics relied on such emotive language to express their criticism. Peter Lombard was a more assiduous critic who read the *Theologia "Scholarium"* with far more care than Bernard of Clairvaux and quoted many passages from the work with great accuracy.[52] Conscious of the need to provide teachings based on critical assessment of a wide range of disputed questions, he composed a vast treatise which provided firm answers to far more issues than Abelard had raised.[53] The Lombard was not afraid to question many of the arguments Abelard had put forward, such as the claim that divine truth had been perceived through reason by pagan philosophers.[54] The cautious judgments of Peter Lombard were more attuned to the needs of ecclesiastical authority in the second half of the twelfth century than Abelard's reflective self-questioning in the *Dialogus*. Certainly the Lombard's synthesis illustrates the powerful urge of a clerical class to systematize Christian doctrine in the twelfth century and thus impose a framework of orthodoxy in Latin Europe. Systematization was a response to much greater questioning in society. Abelard shared in this process by which Christian faith was identified as wholly consistent with reason, but he was critical of dogmatic attitudes toward those outside the Christian dispensation. In this sense he did defend values of religious toleration. Abelard's critics considered that he was questioning too much and wished to define a fixed conclusion to theological enquiry. In more ways than one, the problem with Abelard's dialogue was that it had no end.

Notes

1. Jacques Monfrin, ed., *Pierre Abélard: Historia calamitatum* (Paris: Vrin, 1959), 97–98; translated by Betty Radice, *The Letters of Abelard and Heloise* (Harmondsworth: Penguin, 1974), 94. The growing pressure toward establishing social and religious conformity in this period is analyzed by Robert Ian Moore, *The Formation of a Persecuting Society: Power and Deviance in Western Europe, 950–1250* (Oxford: Blackwell, 1987).

2. Rudolf Thomas, ed., *Petrus Abaelardus: Dialogus inter Philosophum, Judaeum et Christianum* (Stuttgart-Bad Canstatt: Friedrich Frommann Verlag, 1970); Pierre J. Payer, trans., *Peter Abelard: A Dialogue of a Philosopher with a Jew and a Christian* (Toronto: Pontifical Institute of Mediaeval Studies, 1979). A new edition and translation of the work is being prepared by Giovanni Orlandi and John Marenbon. Rheinwald's 1831 edition of the work was reprinted by Jacques-Paul Migne, Patrologia Latina [PL] 178: 1609–82. The rubric *Dialogus Petri Baiolardi* is added to one of two twelfth-century MSS of the work (Vienna MS, Oesterreichische Nationalbibliothek cvp 819), although the title *Collationes* is given in the Balliol College MS 296 (mid-fourteenth century). Abelard himself referred to the second discussion of the *Dialogus* as a *collatio* (see below, n.7). The term *Dialogus* will be maintained for consistency with earlier editions. It was the term used by a twelfth-century reader of the work, who composed an essay on the supreme good which follows it in the Vienna MS (see below, n.8). Aryeh Graboïs invokes the notion of "intellectual tolerance" when comparing it to a Jewish dialogue written in Spain at this time, "Un chapitre de tolérance intellectuelle dans la société occidentale au XIIe siècle: le «Dialogus» de Pierre Abélard et le «Kuzari» d'Yehuda Halévi," in René Louis and Jean Jolivet, eds., *Pierre Abélard-Pierre le Vénérable: Les courants philosophiques, littéraires et artistiques en Occident au milieu du XIIe siècle* (Paris: CNRS, 1975), 641–52; Graboïs defends his use of the notion of tolerance in conference discussion with Rudolf Thomas, recorded on p. 653.

3. *Christians and Jews in the Twelfth-Century Renaissance* (London: Routledge, 1995), 89–91, 124–25.

4. References to the *Dialogus* are to the line number of Thomas's edition and the page number of Payer's translation. While translations of the *Dialogus* are my own, I am frequently indebted to Payer's felicitous phraseology. Giovanni Orlandi pointed out that Thomas tends to follow readings of the Vienna MS, even though those are sometimes palpably inferior to those of the Balliol MS (consigned by Thomas to an apparatus), "Per una nuova edizione del Dialogus di Abelardo," *Rivista Critica di Storia della Filosofia* 34 (1979): 474–94. Three seventeenth-century transcriptions of the *Dialogus*, all based on the Balliol MS, have no independent value, but testify to a revival of interest in Abelard's ideas, even during the civil war; see my comments in the introduction to *Theologia "Scholarium" [TSch], Petri Abaelardi Opera Theologica III*, Corpus Christianorum Continuatio Mediaeualis [CCCM] 13 (Turnhout: Brepols, 1987), 258–61.

5. Augustine, *Libri duo quaestionum evangeliorum* 2.40, PL 35: 1354.

6. Rheinwald created the impression that the work broke off incomplete by

concluding his edition with a set of dots, not present in the original MS: *licet te subinferre vel ad reliqua festinare........* . Unaware that the text in the Balliol MS concludes at exactly the same point, Samuel Martin Deutsch considered that a faulty manuscript was to blame for the unfinished state of the work, *Peter Abälard: Ein kritischer Theologe des zwölften Jahrhunderts* (Leipzig: S. Hirzel, 1883), 451.

7. See my "On Dating the Works of Peter Abelard," *Archives d'Histoire Doctrinale et Littéraire du Moyen Age* 52 (1985): 73–134, especially 105–26. Abelard alludes to the last part of the second conference of the *Dialogus* in his *Expositio in Haemeron* (PL 178: 768A), which survives in three different recensions. Whereas Abelard refers nowhere in the *Dialogus* to texts unique to *TSch* (prepared in the 1130s), he does make specific allusion (1497–1503; Payer, 87) to the second book of his *Theologia christiana [Tchr]*, ed. Eligius M. Buytaert, CCCM 12 (Turnhout: Brepols, 1969), composed 1121–27. A little earlier (1458–77; Payer, 85–86), he cites two passages from Augustine about dialectic in exactly the same slightly inaccurate way as in the earlier recension of the *Tchr* II.117 [*R*, not *CT*], ed. Buytaert, CCCM 12: 184–85, not in the improved way characteristic of *TSch* II.19, ed. Buytaert-Mews, CCCM 13: 415 and in Letter 13 (critical of someone ignorant of dialectic), ed. Edmé Smits, *Peter Abelard: Letters IX–XIV* (Groningen: distributed by Bouma, 1983), 272, drafted in the early 1130s. In the earlier *Theologia "Summi boni" [TSum]* II.5, ed. Buytaert-Mews, CCCM 13: 116, Abelard's misquotation had been even more inaccurate.

8. In one of the two twelfth-century manuscripts of the *Dialogus*, the work has been copied alongside the *Sic et Non*; in the Vienna MS it is followed by a reflection of a teacher to a student on the nature of the supreme good, responding to questions raised in the *Dialogus*, ed. Edward A. Synan, "The Exortacio Against Peter Abelard's *Dialogus inter Philosophum, Iudaeum et Christianum*," in J. Reginald O'Donnell, ed., *Essays in Honor of Anton Charles Pegis* (Toronto: PIMS, 1974), 176–92.

9. Franciscus Salesius Schmitt, ed., *Sancti Anselmi Opera*, 6 vols. (Edinburgh: Thomas Nelson, 1946–61), 1: 146–276.

10. Anna Sapir Abulafia makes this point in an excellent article, "St. Anselm and Those Outside the Church," in David Loades and Katherine Walsh, eds., *Faith and Identity: Christian Political Experience*, Studies in Church History, Subsidia VI (Oxford: Blackwell, 1990), 11–37.

11. Edited by Anna Sapir Abulafia and Gillian R. Evans, *The Works of Gilbert Crispin Abbot of Westminster*, Auctores Britannici Medii Aevi (London: British Academy, 1986), 8–53; see also her studies: "The 'ars disputandi' of Gilbert Crispin, Abbot of Westminster (1085–1117)," in C. M. Cappon, ed., *Ad fontes: Opstellen aangeboden aan Professor Dr. C. van de Kieft* (Amsterdam: Verloren, 1984), 139–52; "An attempt by Gilbert Crispin, abbot of Westminster, at rational argument in the Jewish-Christian debate," *Studia Monastica* 26 (1984): 55–74; *Christians and Jews*, 77–81.

12. *Disputatio* 4, *Works of Gilbert Crispin*, ed. Abulafia and Evans, 9.

13. *Disputatio* 4, *Works of Gilbert Crispin*, ed. Abulafia and Evans, 10.

14. Richard W. Southern suggested that Gilbert both profited from Anselm's company in 1092/93 and prompted Anselm to think further about that subject, "St.

Anselm and Gilbert Crispin, Abbot of Westminster," *Mediaeval and Renaissance Studies* 3 (1954): 78–115.

15. The work, which survives in only a single manuscript, was first edited by Clement C. J. Webb, "Gilbert Crispin, Abbot of Westminster: Dispute of a Christian with a Heathen Touching the Faith of Christ," *Mediaeval and Renaissance Studies* 3 (1954): 55–77; *Works of Gilbert Crispin*, ed. Abulafia and Evans, 61–87.

16. Anna Sapir Abulafia, "Jewish-Christian Disputations and the Twelfth-Century Renaissance," *Journal of Medieval History* 15 (1989): 105–25.

17. I have edited a hitherto unnoticed draft of this treatise, dating from Anselm's first months in England in 1092, in "St. Anselm and Roscelin: Some New Texts and Their Implications. I. The *De incarnatione uerbi* and the *Disputatio inter christianum et gentilem*," *Archives d'Histoire Doctrinale et Littéraire du Moyen Age* 58 (1991): 55–97.

18. It occurs within a larger corpus of Anselmian texts than the corpus preserved at Bec or Canterbury, which includes a hitherto unpublished draft of part of the *De incarnatione Verbi*, a judgment about marriage, and copies of secret letters of Pope Pascal II to Henry I, quoted by Eadmer but not preserved in most MSS of the letters of Anselm. I have provided a provisional transcription in "St. Anselm and Roscelin: Some New Texts and Their Implications," 86–98, from British Library MS, Royal 5.E.xiv (s. xiii) and argue that this dossier was compiled separately from the more official collection of Anselm's writing compiled at Christ Church, Canterbury. The *Disputatio* is incomplete in the London MS, as in a sizable number of related fourteenth-century manuscripts, mostly from the West country. A complete version survives in three twelfth-century MSS: Hereford Cathedral MS O.I.xii; Berlin, Staatsbibliothek Preussische Kulturbesitz theol. lat. fol. 276 (from Maria Laach); and Cambridge, Cambridge University Library Gg.V.34 (written at the abbey of St Werburgh, Chester, whose community was visited by Anselm in 1092–93); see Colin Gale, *Delivered to the Devil? St. Anselm and His Circle on the Consequences of the Fall* (Cambridge University, Faculty of History, 1993), 33–37.

19. Ed. Mews, 86: "Maiestas divina cur ad dolores mortalis nature insuper et usque ad opprobria crucis se humiliauit, uellem addiscere. Quod quidem ex auctoritate uestrarum scripturarum nolo [mistakenly printed as *uolo*] michi probari, cui non credo, sed si rationabiliter factum est, huius rei rationem quero."

20. Ed. Mews, 95: "Quod dicitur: fecit quod decuit, nichil aliud est dicere quam fecit quod debuit. Secundum hanc formam loquendi dicitur de omnibus que facit Deus. Facit quod debet, id est quid eum decet, non quia obligatus sit ullo debito ab aliquo exigendo."

21. Ed. Mews, 95: "Fateor me hoc usque errasse, et Christum uerum Deum et uere salutis auctorem et reparatorem corde et ore contestor."

22. Sapir Abulafia identifies its author as Pseudo-Anselm in "Christians Disputing Disbelief: St. Anselm, Gilbert Crispin, and Pseudo-Anselm," in Bernard Lewis and Friedrich Niewöhner, eds., *Religionsgespräche im Mittelalter*, Wolfenbütteler Mittelalter-Studien IV (Wiesbaden: Harrassowitz, 1992), 131–48 and *Christians and Jews*, 85–87, 104–5, 156 n.4. Its relationship to other Anselmian writings needs further study. The absence of any explicit refutation of the legitimacy of the

devil's power over man, comparable to Boso's argument, argues against the idea that the *Disputatio* is based on a complete version of the *Cur Deus homo*. The Gentile does not articulate Boso's explicit rejection of the rights of the devil, although he does say that the devil does not "deserve" to have power over man (*Disputatio*, ed. Mews, 86). Part of the *Disputatio* (ed. Mews, 90) explicitly addresses the question raised by Roscelin, why the incarnation should not have involved all three persons, not an issue raised in the *Cur deus homo*.

23. Ed. Mews, 90: "Si credere uolueris quod impossibile tibi uidetur, ipso Christo adiuuante in ueritate esse comprobabis. Scriptum est enim: *Nisi credideritis non intellegitis*. . . . Hoc est quod iam dixi, et nunc iterum dico: *Nisi credideritis, non intelligitis*." Cf. *Cur Deus homo*, Commendatio operis, ed. Schmitt 2: 40 (alluding to Augustine, *Sermo* 91, PL 38: 571). It was also cited in a Commentary on the Apostle's Creed attributed to Augustine, but in fact by Rufinus, *Commentarius in Symbolum Apostolorum* 4, ed. Manlius Simonetti, CCSL 20 (Turnhout: Brepols, 1961), 136. This is not a phrase cited by Gilbert Crispin, according to the scriptural concordance provided by Abulafia and Evans.

24. This is the implication of an analogy he once provided for his monks: the Jews and pagans lived in the Devil's territory outside a city in which Christians lived, who could only seek refuge within the keep of the city's castle, where the monks lived; *De humanis moribus per similitudines* 75–76, ed. Richard W. Southern and Franciscus Salesius Schmitt, *Memorials of St. Anselm*, Auctores Britannici Medii Aevi 1 (Oxford: Oxford University Press, 1969), 66–67, commented on by Abulafia, "St. Anselm and Those Outside the Church" (n.10 above).

25. Reported by St. Anselm, *Epistola de incarnatione verbi* 2, ed. Schmitt, 2: 10.

26. Joseph Reiners, ed., *Der Nominalismus in der Frühscholastik. Ein Beitrag zur Geschichte der Universalienfrage im Mittelalter. Nebst einer neuen Textausgabe des Briefes Roscelins an Abaelard*, Beiträge zur Geschichte der Philosophie des Mittelalters [BGPM] 8.5 (Münster, 1910), 63.

27. The most recent survey of Constantine's writing and influence has been edited by Charles Burnett and Danielle Jacquart, *Constantine the African and 'Aku ibn al-'abbas ak-magusi: The Pantegni and Related Texts* (Leiden: Brill, 1994).

28. Orderic Vitalis, *Ecclesiastical History* xi.9, ed. and trans. Marjorie Chibnall (Oxford: Oxford University Press, 1969), 6: 50–52.

29. *Quaestiones naturales*, ed. Martin Müller, BGPM 31 (1934): 11: ". . . a magistris Arabicis ratione duce didici." See Marie-Thérèse d'Alverny, "Translations and Translators," in Giles Constable and Robert L. Benson, eds., *Renaissance and Renewal in the Twelfth Century* (Oxford: Clarendon Press, 1982), 421–62, esp. 440–43 and Jean Jolivet, "The Arabic Inheritance," in Peter Dronke, ed., *A History of Twelfth-Century Western Philosophy* (Cambridge: Cambridge University Press, 1988), 113–48.

30. Charles Burnett summarizes information about these and other translations of the period in his chapter "Scientific Speculations" in Dronke, ed., *History of Twelfth-Century Western Philosophy*, 151–76; see also the studies in Burnett, ed., *Adelard of Bath: An English Scientist and Arabist of the Early Twelfth Century*, Warburg Institute Studies and Texts 14 (London: Warburg Institute, 1987). Abelard's

attempt to learn from Thierry is related in a humorous anecdote, which I discuss in "In Search of a Name and Its Significance: A Twelfth-Century Anecdote About Thierry and Peter Abaelard," *Traditio* 44 (1988): 175–200.

31. J. V. Tolan, *Text as Tool: Petrus Alfonsi and His Medieval Readers* identifies sixty-three manuscripts of the *Dialogi* (compared to thirty-four for Crispin's *Disputatio*). Abelard's *Dialogus* by contrast survives in only three medieval manuscripts.

32. Blanche Boyer and Richard McKeon, eds., *Peter Abailard: Sic et Non* (Chicago-London: University of Chicago Press, 1976–77), 89.

33. *Sic et Non*, Pref., ed. Boyer-McKeon, 103: "Haec quippe prima sapientiae clavis definitur assidua scilicet seu frequens interrogatio. . . . Dubitando quippe ad inquisitionem venimus; inquirendo veritatem percipimus. Iuxta quod et Veritas ipsa *Quaerite* inquit *et invenite, pulsate et aperietur vobis*."

34. Lambert Marie De Rijk, ed., *Petrus Abaelardus: Dialectica*, 2d ed. (Assen: Van Gorcum, 1970), 153: "Qui autem querit, dubitationem suam exprimit, ut certitudinem quam nondum habet, consequatur."

35. David E. Luscombe, ed., *Peter Abelard's Ethics* (Oxford: Clarendon Press, 1971), 14.

36. *Tchr* II.19, ed. Buytaert, CCCM 12: 141.

37. Charles Burnett, ed., "Peter Abelard «Soliloquium»," *Studi Medievali* 3ª ser. 25.2 (1984): 889 (859–94): "Quam quidem exhortationem quisquis legerit, videbit philosophos non tam nomine quam re ipsa Christianis maxime sociatos."

38. *TSch* II.46–47, ed. Buytaert-Mews, CCCM 13: 431.

39. Among the isolated comments of Aristotle on virtue available prior to the translation of the *Ethics*, see *Categories* 8b25, ed. Lorenzo Minio-Paluello, *Aristoteles Latinus* (Bruges-Paris: Desclée, De Brouwer, 1961), 63, as well as the remark of Boethius, *De divisione* (PL 64: 885B): "Virtue is an excellent habit of the mind." Abelard's role in the development of these ideas has been emphasised by Cary J. Nederman in numerous studies, notably "Nature, Ethics, and the Doctrine of 'Habitus': Aristotelian Moral Psychology in the Twelfth Century," *Traditio* 45 (1989–90): 87–110. Marcia Colish observes that Anselm of Laon employed the traditional definition, while Abelard developed it in a more Aristotelian sense, *Peter Lombard*, 2 vols. (Leiden: Brill, 1994), 476–77.

40. John Marenbon, "Abelard's Ethical Theory: Two Definitions from the *Collationes*," in Haijo Jan Westra, ed., *From Athens to Chartres: Neoplatonism and Medieval Thought, Essays in Honour of Édouard Jeauneau* (Leiden: Brill, 1992), 301–15.

41. *Dialectica*, ed. De Rijk, 116.

42. *Commentaria in Epistolam ad Romanos*, ed. Eligius Marie Buytaert, CCCM 11 (Turnhout: Brepols, 1969), 113–18.

43. The most important of these sentence collections have been edited, very imperfectly, by Sandro Buzzetti, *Sententie magistri Petri Abelardi (Sententie Hermanni)* (Florence: La Nuova Italia Editrice, 1983). I present my arguments for rejecting Ostlender's hypothesis that these sentences were written by a certain Hermannus in "The *Sententiae* of Peter Abelard," *Recherches de Théologie Ancienne et Médiévale* 53 (1986): 130–84, summarized in the introduction to the edition of the *Theologia "Scholarium*," CCCM 13: 221–26. In *Peter Lombard*, 51 n.43, Marcia Col-

ish accepts Ostlender's hypothesis, without presenting any substantive proof for her statement that opinions in these *Sententiae* differ in some respects from teachings of Abelard. She refers back to David Luscombe's *The School of Peter Abelard* (Cambridge: Cambridge University Press, 1969), without appreciating the historiography of this debate or realizing that Luscombe has himself since acknowledged that the *Sententiae* "represents the teaching given by Abelard to students," in "The School of Peter Abelard Revisited," *Vivarium* 30 (1992): 128 (127–38). Her reference in that footnote to my comments in CCCM 13 needs to be completed with reference to my fuller discussion on 221–26. Ostlender's hypothesis that the sentence collections had been compiled by other individuals than Abelard had been questioned by Artur Landgraf in relation to the *Sententiae Parisienses* in the introduction to *Ecrits théologiques de l'école d'Abélard* (Louvain: Spicilegium Sacrum Lovaniense, 1934). Colish cites the *Sententiae Parisienses* as the work of a disciple "who rushed to his support" (*Peter Lombard*, 295), even though Landgraf explicitly defends the idea that it is a record of Abelard's lectures in its introduction.

44. *Tchr CT* IV.74-b, ed. Buytaert, CCCM 12: 299, transferred into *TSch* II.41, ed. Buytaert-Mews, CCCM 13: 427.

45. *Historia calamitatum*, ed. Monfrin, ll. 699–701; cf. *TSch* II, 1–61, ed. Buytaert-Mews, CCCM 13: 406–38.

46. *Vita Goswini*, ed. Richard Gibbons (Douai, 1620), reprinted in *Recueil des historiens des Gaules et de la France*, vol. 14 (Paris, 1877), 442–48.

47. *TSch* Pref. 5, ed. Buytaert-Mews, CCCM 13: 314.

48. *De intellectibus* 24–27, ed. Patrick Morin, *Des intellections* (Paris: Vrin, 1994), 42–44.

49. Colish observes that "he was one of those academics constitutionally incapable of finishing anything he started," *Peter Lombard*, 48, a claim that does a manifest injustice to the works which are complete (the treatises on logic, the epistolary treatises, the liturgical writing, the commentary on Romans, the *Theologia* "'Summi boni,'" etc.).

50. This translation follows the edition of the passage by José M. A. Rubingh-Bosscher, *Peter Abelard: Carmen ad Astralabium* ll. 363–84 (Groningen: privately published, 1987), 127. Dronke edits and translates this passage (following a MS which reads *cultus* for *mundus* in l.363) in *Abelard and Heloise in Medieval Testimonies*, 14–15, 43, reprinted in *Intellectuals and Poets in Medieval Europe*, Storia e Letteratura 183 (Rome: Edizioni di Storia e Letteratura, 1992), 257, 279–80. Rubingh-Bosscher, *Carmen*, 97–102, puts forward strong arguments for accepting the attribution to Abelard given in a number of MSS of the poem. This passage occurs in Recension I, represented by four manuscripts, ranging in date from the early to the late thirteenth century.

51. Bernard, *Ep.* 332 to Cardinal G., ed. Jean Leclercq, *Sancti Bernardi Opera*, vol. 8 (Rome: Editiones Cistercienses, 1977), 271: "Disputantem cum pueris, conversantem cum mulierculis."

52. I have been able to document the remarkable accuracy with which Peter Lombard cites passages from the *Theologia "Scholarium"* in the introduction to my edition, CCCM 13: 264–67, bearing out the truth of the comment of John of Cornwall that Lombard was always reading Abelard's *Theologia* and drew ideas from

Abelard, Nikolaus Häring, "The Eulogium ad Alexandrum Papam tertium of John of Cornwall," *Mediaeval Studies* 13 (1951): 265. There is a strong possibility that one manuscript of the *Theologia* was used to list books belonging to Peter Lombard, one which also happens to contain a thirteenth-century copy of John of Cornwall's *Eulogium* (CCCM 13: 244–45).

53. For a comparison of the attitude of Peter Lombard and Robert of Melun to Peter Abelard, see my study "Orality, Literacy and Authority in the Twelfth-Century Schools," *Exemplaria* 2 (1990): 475–500. On the urge to systematization in scholasticism, see Richard W. Southern, *Scholastic Humanism and the Unification of Europe* (Oxford: Blackwell, 1995), 1: 6–13.

54. Colish observes that Lombard expresses in this respect the orthodox consensus of his time, *Peter Lombard*, 259.

ADDENDA ET CORRIGENDA

I The Development of the *Theologia*
I 194 n.8 BGPMA XXI.1–3 (1919–27) 51 [not 57].

II A Neglected Gloss on the *'Isagoge'*
For discussion and edition of part of the *Glossae secundum vocales*, see John Marenbon, 'Abelard, *ens* and unity,' *Topoi* 11 (1992): 149–58.
II 39 n.20 and n.21 should be inverted.
II 46 I have subsequently argued (VII 74–5) Abelard's earliest glosses are the 'literal glosses,' edited by Mario Dal Pra, not the *Introductiones parvulorum*, referred to by Abelard in his *Dialectica*, but no longer extant.

IV The Lists of Heresies
While here I followed the assumption that the council of Sens was held on the octave of Pentecost 1140 [2 June], I am now persuaded that although William of St Thierry wrote to Bernard in Lent 1140, the council was more likely held on the octave of Pentecost 1141 [25 May], *The Lost Love Letters of Heloise and Abelard. Perceptions of Dialogue in Twelfth-Century France* (New York: St Martin's Press, 1999), pp. 37, 174, 303 n. 22. The controversy between Bernard and Abelard thus developed during the period 1140/1141. Bernard's preaching in Paris took place in November 1140, rather than 1139. For new editions of Abelard's confessions of faith, see C. S. F. Burnett, 'Peter Abelard, *Confessio fidei 'Universis'*: A Critical Edition of Abelard's Reply to Accusations of Heresy', *Mediaeval Studies* 48 (1986): 111–38 and '"Confessio fidei ad Heloisam"– Abelard's Last Letter to Heloise? A Discussion and Critical Edition of the Latin and Medieval French Versions', *Mittellateinisches Jahrbuch* 21 (1986): 147–55.

V Peter Abelard's *Theologia Christiana* and *Theologia 'Scholarium'* re-examined
V 114: What I here claim was a single tract (*Est una et perfecta unitas... explicit: et in homine deus*) is in fact a set of four treatises, as Buytaert correctly observed. I provide a more detailed discussion of the first treatise, *Est una*, in 'St Anselm and Roscelin: Some New Texts and their Implications II. An Essay on the Trinity and Intellectual Debate 1080–1120', *Archives d'histoire doctrinale et littéraire du moyen âge* 65 (1998): 39–90.
V 127, 150 On the excerpt of the *Sic et Non* in the Turin manuscript, see J. S. Barrow, 'Tractatus Magistri Petri Abaielardi de Sacramento Altaris,' *Traditio* 40 (1984): 328–36.
V 138 line 21: read 'work being written' [instead of 'work written']

VI The *Sententie* of Peter Abelard
A new critical edition of the *Sententie Petri Abaelardi*, edited by D.E. Luscombe, is forthcoming in the series Corpus Christianorum Continuatio Mediaeualis.

VII On Dating the Works of Peter Abelard
VII 75 Paris, BN lat. 13368 is not our only copy of early glosses of Peter Abelard. Related, but shorter glosses on Porphyry's *Isagoge*, Aristotle's *Periermeneias* and Boethius's *De topicis differentiis* in Munich, Clm 14779, may also be those of Abelard. The Porphyry glosses in this manuscript are edited by Iwakuma Y., who then argued that they might be by Roscelin, in 'Vocales, or early nominalists,' *Traditio* 47 (1992): 74–102. J. Marenbon convincingly argues that they represent the teaching of Abelard himself, 'Glosses and commentaries on the *Categories* and *De interpretatione* before Abelard,' in J. Fried, ed., *Dialektik und Rhetorik im früheren und hohen Mittelalter* (Munich, 1996), pp. 21–49 and *The philosophy of Peter Abelard*, pp. 38–9.
VII 75 Iwakuma Y. has edited two versions of the *Introductiones* of William of Champeaux, 'Introductiones dialecticae secundum Wilgelmum and secundum G. Paganellum,' in: *Université de Copenhague. Cahiers de l'Institut du Moyen-Age Grec et Latin* 63 (1993): 45–114.
VII 96 John Marenbon has argued that Abelard's reference in the *Dialectica* to an accusation that it was not licit for a Christian to discuss matters not relating to faith, is more likely to have been written before 1117, *The philosophy of Peter Abelard*, pp. 41–42. While the early part of the treatise may date to c. 1112/13, I am disinclined to date its completion to much before 1117. In this preface to tract four, Abelard defends dialectic as necessariy to explain the divine Trinity, foreshadowing the concerns of the *Theologia 'Summi boni'*. Marenbon also makes a valid point (p. 43) that in the *Dialectica* Abelard's critique of identifying the world soul with the Holy Spirit is less sophisticated than in the *Theologia 'Summi boni.'* This digression does reinforce the idea, however, that he is thinking about theological issues while completing the *Dialectica*. The frequency of references to 'our teacher' in the early sections, suggests that Abelard may have commenced the *Dialectica* c. 1112/13, but not finished it until c. 1117.
VII 105, 132 On the date of the council of Sens, see my notes to article IV above.
VII 115 On the *Soliloquium*, see C. S. F. Burnett, 'Peter Abelard, "Soliloquium". A Critical Edition', *Studi Medievali* 3a Ser. 25 (1984): 857–94.

X Peter Abelard and the Enigma of Dialogue
X A new edition and translation of the *Dialogus* or *Collationes*, prepared by John Marenbon and Giovanni Orlandi, is *Abelard's Collationes* (Oxford, 2001). I follow their suggestion (pp. xxvii–xxxii) that it was probably written 1127–32. This essay was written without knowledge of a paper by Peter von Moos, 'Les *collationes* d'Abélard et la 'question juive' au XIIe siècle', *Journal des Savants* (July–Dec 1999): 449–89, or Julie A. Allen, 'On the Dating of Abelard's *Dialogus*: A Reply to Mews', *Vivarium* 36 (1998): 135–54.

INDEX OF PERSONS AND PLACES

INDEX OF MANUSCRIPTS CITED